I0129611

THE NEW HAMPSHIRE GENEALOGICAL RECORD

An Illustrated Quarterly Magazine

DEVOTED TO GENEALOGY, HISTORY AND BIOGRAPHY

OFFICIAL ORGAN OF THE NEW HAMPSHIRE GENEALOGICAL SOCIETY

The publication of an exact transcript of the
Genealogical Records of New Hampshire
is the special province of the magazine

VOLUME 7: January 1910 – April 1910
and
COMBINED INDEX TO ALL VOLUMES

Edited by
Charles W. Tibbetts

HERITAGE BOOKS
2025

HERITAGE BOOKS

AN IMPRINT OF HERITAGE BOOKS, INC.

Books, CDs, and more—Worldwide

For our listing of thousands of titles see our website
at
www.HeritageBooks.com

A Facsimile Reprint
Published 2025 by
HERITAGE BOOKS, INC.
Publishing Division
5810 Ruatan Street
Berwyn Heights, MD 20740

Originally published by
Dover, N.H.
Charles W. Tibbetts, Editor and Publisher.
1910

Published in Cooperation with
The New Hampshire Historical Society
Which Provided the New Master Index
in this volume.

— Publisher's Notice —
In reprints such as this, it is often not possible to remove
blemishes from the original. We feel the contents of this
book warrant its reissue despite these blemishes and
hope you will agree and read it with pleasure.

International Standard Book Number
Paperbound: 978-1-55613-156-1

CONTENTS OF VOLUME VII.

January, 1910 - April, 1910

Book Notices	92
Donations	48, 96
First Congregational Church Records, Concord, N.H.	
Marriages	17, 65
First Congregational Church Records, Rochester, N.H.	
Admissions	89
Baptisms	27, 85
In Memoriam	
Col. Henry Oakes Kent	35
Dr. Henry Rust Parker	81
George Frederick Evans	33
Newmarket Town Records	
Births, Marriages, and Deaths	37, 55
North Church Records, Portsmouth, N.H.	
Baptisms by Rev. Joseph Buckminster	11, 73
Notice	84
Origins of the name Pinkham	46
Queries	47, 94
Richard Hussey and His Descendants	1
Thomas Downes, Dover, N.H., and His Descendants	49
Wants	10

COL. HENRY OAKES KENT.
See page 35.

THE NEW HAMPSHIRE GENEALOGICAL RECORD.

VOL. VII.   DOVER, N. H., JANUARY, 1910.   No. 1.

RICHARD HUSSEY AND HIS DESCENDANTS.

THIRD GENERATION.

[Continued from Vol. VI, page 103.]

10. RICHARD[3] HUSSEY* (*Richard*,[2] *Richard*[1]), born in Dover, N. H., August 12, 1722, married before 1745, Phebe, daughter of Benjamin Varney, of Somersworth, N. H. (Ham's *Dover, N. H. Marriages.*) He is described in deeds as a "husbandman." August 31, 1765, he deeded to Moses Roberts, of Dover, his homestead farm in Dover, the same deeded him by his father, for £500. (*N. H. Prov. Deeds, 96: 207.*) In this deed he is described as of Dover, but he soon afterwards moved to Lebanon, Me., whither his brother Reuben, and perhaps his mother, had preceeded him. August 31, 1768, Richard Hussey, of Lebanon, in the County of York and State of Massachusetts, conveyed to Ebenezer Clements, for £15 15s, "the Pew in Dover first Parish meeting house Number four." (*N. H. Prov. Deeds, 94: 398.*) May 20, 1776, he was chosen one of the Committee of Safety. (*Diary of Rev. Isaac Hasey.*) The diary also contains the following entries: "1777, Feb. 3. Richard Hussey's wife died last night." "1786, Aug. 7. Rich[d] Hussey died." "Aug. 9. Sac. Lec: Rich[d] Hussey from y[e] meeting house." Mr. George W. Chamberlain says:—"The meeting house then stood at South Lebanon about one-half mile north of Richard Hussey's home."

A correspondent assigns to Richard and Phebe Hussey the

*Reference numbers have been placed before the names carried forward.—ED.

following children, but adds "of these and their descendants I am considerably in doubt."

Children:

28. i. BENJAMIN.[4]
     ii. HANNAH,[4] m. in Lebanon, Me. Angust 3, 1769, James Door.
     iii. PATIENCE,[4] m. in Lebanon, April 16, 1775, Joseph Door.
29. iv. ROBERT.[4]

11. REUBEN[3] HUSSEY (*Richard*,[2] *Richard*[1]), was born in Dover, N. H., and moved to Lebanon, Me. He married Anna Young of Madbury, N. H. She died "of y[e] Measles" March 5, 1784. (*Hasey's Diary*.) He was living September 18, 1788, as Hasey mentions a deed from him to "Zac. Hussey" of that date.

His children, probably all born in Lebanon, were:

30. i. JOHN,[4] b. 1753.
     ii. REUBEN,[4] m. July 26, 1786, Experience Yeaton. A correspondent says:—"Moved to Shapleigh, Me. about 1788 with his brother John. and later moved to Winslow, Me., where he was living in 1800. I have lost track of him since that time."
31. iii RICHARD,[4] b. Feb. 14, 1759.
     iv. ELIZABETH,[4] m. Jacob Buzzell.
     v. ANNA,[4] m. Jan. 12, 1777, Ebenezer Pierce, Jr., of Lebanon.
     vi. SARAH,[4] m. a Rowe.
32. vii. ZACHARIAH.[4]

12. ROBERT[3] HUSSEY (*Job*,[2] *Richard*[1]), married in 1757, Mercy Hanson, widow of John Hanson, and daughter of William Horne. He died in Somersworth, N. H., in 1797. His will, dated February 9, 1791, proved January 30, 1797, mentions wife Mercy, sons Job and Benjamin, and daughters Betty Austin and Rachel Randel. The two sons were executors. The widow appears to have soon married a Tibbetts, as there is a deed, dated Sept. 23, 1797, from Job to Benjamin Hussey of "20 acres of land out of the lands that was set out to Mercy Tebbetts our Mother for her thirds out of the estate of Robert Hussey late of Somersworth, deceased."

Children:

     i. ELIZABETH,[4] b. April 26, 1758; m. an Austin.
     ii. JOB,[4] b. May 31, 1760; m. in Somersworth, N. H., Nov. 12, 1789, Elizabeth Downes of Rochester.
33. iii. BENJAMIN,[4] b. July 10, 1762.
     iv. RACHEL,[4] b. Dec. 8, 1764; m. in Somersworth, Dec. 21, 1784, Daniel Randel of Somersworth.

13. JOHN[3] HUSSEY (*Job*,[2] *Richard*[1]), moved from Somersworth, N. H., to Damariscotta, afterwards Newcastle, Me., as early as 1753, as is evidenced by a deed, dated July 5, 1753, in which "John Hussey of Damariscotta so called in the County of York" joins with Robert Hussey and others in

quitclaiming their interest in the estate of Joseph Tibbetts. Damariscotta was a general name applied to the locality before the incorporation of Newcastle in 1753. It was not used as the name of a town until 1847. July 14, 1756, Job Hussey of Somersworth, "in Consideration of the Natural affection which I have & Do Bear unto my Son John Hussey of New Castle in the County of York," conveys to him two tracts of land in Rochester, N. H., comprising about one hundred acres, with his interest in undivided lands. (*N. H. Prov. Deeds, 50: 398.*) May 29, 1759, "John Hussey of New Castle . . . . . Gentleman" conveys the same to Ebenezer Horn of Dover. (*N. H. Prov. Deeds, 65: 57.*)

Cushman's "History of Ancient Sheepscot and Newcastle" says that John Hussey came from Scituate, Mass. I have lately inquired among John's descendants for the origin of this statement, and am informed that it sprang from a vague notion that he was connected in some way with a Robert Hussey who was enrolled in Duxbury, Mass., in 1643, and therefore must have come from that vicinity.

John Hussey of Newcastle married Jane Rollins, born 1736. She was the fifth child of John Rollins of Exeter, N. H., from which place he removed to East Bradford, now Groveland, Mass., and thence with most of his family to Damariscotta, Maine, in 1736, where he died in 1776. (*Rawlins or Rollins Genealogy.*) John Hussey was living September 16, 1795, as is shown by his acknowledgment of a deed on that date. His wife Jenny joins in the deed, but does not sign.

The children of John and Jane (Rollins) Hussey were:

i. SARAH,[4] m. Thomas Chapman of Nobleboro, int. pub. Sept. 15, 1778. "She and her husband both died in one day and were buried in the same grave."

ii. MARGERY,[4] m. Joseph Weeks of Jefferson, int. pub. July 23, 1781.

iii. SUSANNAH,[4] m. Benjamin Barstow, int. pub. May 7, 1782.

iv. ELIZABETH,[4] m. Sept. 5, 1786, Nathaniel Rollins of Newcastle.

v. JOHN,[4] m. March 14, 1792, Patience Rollins; resided in Jefferson, Me., and in Ohio.

vi. MARTHA,[4] twin; m. Joseph Chapman, Jr., of Nobleboro, int. pub. July 25, 1793. Called Polly in town records.

vii. LYDIA,[4] twin; m. August 25, 1795, John Glidden, of Newcastle.

34. viii. JOB,[4] b. March 8, 1770.

ix. JANE,[4] m. Isaac Teague, of Nobleboro, int. pub. Oct. 25, 1794.

x MARY,[4] m. John Teague, of Newcastle, int. pub. Oct. 15, 1793. Called Polly in town records.

    xi. BENJAMIN,[4] m. Mrs. Sarah Rigby, of Newcastle, int. pub.
           April 29, 1809.
    xii. DEBORAH,[4] m. Nov. 11, 1802, John Fowler, of Newcastle.
    xiii. ISAAC,[4] d. aged 2 yrs.
    xiv. ELEANOR,[4] b. June 13, 1787; m. Joseph Teague, of New-
           castle in 1808 or 1809.

14. MARY[3] HUSSEY (*Job*,[2] *Richard*[1]), married near 1754,
Ebenezer Varney; he died March 13, 1802; she died August
17, 1819.

Their children born in Rochester, N. H.:

    i. CALEB[4] VARNEY, b. Aug. 18, 1756; m. in Dover, N. H.,
        Dec. 11, 1782, Huldah[4] Hussey, dau. of Paul[3] (William,[2]
        Richard[1]). He d. June 6, 1828; she d. March 26, 1837.
        They had six children, born in Rochester:
          i. William[5] Varney, b. Dec. 21, 1783; m. Anna Varney.
          ii. Job[5] Varney, b. Aug. 3, 1786; d. Dec. 31, 1825, unm.
          iii. Paul[5] Varney, b. Dec. 29, 1788; moved to Wolfboro.
          iv. Mary[5] Varney, b. Oct. 30, 1791; m. Moses Hanson.
          v. John Hanson[5] Varney, b. Aug. 31, 1794.
          vi. Elizabeth[5] Varney, b. Mar. 2, 1799; m. James Austin.
    ii. BENJAMIN[4] VARNEY, b. Jan. 9, 1759; disowned by Friends
        Society April 20, 1782; d. March 19, 1826.
    iii. EBENEZER[4] VARNEY, b. Feb. 18, 1761; disowned March,
        1791.
    iv. ELIZABETH[4] VARNEY, b. Nov. 29, 1765; disowned Sept.,
        1791.

15. JANE[3] HUSSEY (*Joseph*,[2] *Richard*[1]), married about
1745, Joshua, son of Stephen and Mary (Young) Otis, born
about 1720. He died in Barrington, N. H., 1810; she died
in Barrington, 1790.

Children:

    i. NICHOLAS[4] OTIS, b. March 29, 1746; m. Esther, dau. of
        Nathaniel Berry of Barrington.
    ii. MICAJAH[4] OTIS, b. May 21, 1747; m. 1769, Sarah, dau. of
        Joshua Foss of Barrington, formerly of Rye, b. Dec. 30,
        1748, d. Jan. 20, 1827. A Free Will Baptist preacher in
        Barrington; d. May 20, 1821.
    iii. ELIJAH[4] OTIS, b. June 10, 1749; m. July 19, 1771, Dorothy,
        dau. of Jethro Locke; she d. in Rochester, N. H., 1824;
        he d. in Durham, N. H., Apr. 8, 1838.
    iv. MARY[4] OTIS, m. Elder Winthrop Young and moved to
        Canterbury, N. H.; he d. Jan. 8, 1833; she d. Apr. 11,
        1849, a. 98. It would appear that Mary and Sarah were
        twins.
    v. SARAH[4] OTIS, b. May 18, 1751; m. John B. Parshley and
        settled in Barnstead, N. H.; he d. Apr. 3, 1829, a. 82; she
        d. July 6, 1825.
    vi. STEPHEN[4] OTIS, b. June 24, 1753; m. Nov. 30, 1786, Han-
        nah, dau. of Solomon Emerson of Madbury; d. in Bar-
        rington, Dec. 4, 1835; she d. in Maine, Aug. 24, 1848, a.
        82.
    vii. PAUL[4] OTIS, b. Mar. 4, 1755; m. Elizabeth Parshley; d. in
        Gilmanton, N. H., July 17, 1848; she d. Nov. 8, 1837, a. 84.
    viii. JOSHUA[4] OTIS, b. Mar. 30, 1764; m. Jan. 15, 1788, Lydia
        Meader; he d. in Parishville, N. Y., Mar. 4, 1834.

ix. JANE[4] OTIS, m. July 9, 1777, Moses Meader, Jr., of Durham, N. H.; moved to Alton.
x. REBECCA[4] OTIS, m. a Wilkinson.

16. DANIEL[3] HUSSEY (Joseph,[2] Richard[1]), born 4, 9 mo., 1738; married Bethiah daughter of Nathaniel and Content (Gaskill) Varney; he died March 19, 1785; she married 2d, in Dover, N. H., March 21, 1789, Jacob Tabor of Vassalboro, Maine. Children:

35. i. JOSEPH,[4] b. Sept. 3, 1765.
ii. SARAH,[4] b. Nov. 13, 1766.
iii. JOHN,[4] b. Sept. 13, 1768.
iv. LYDIA,[4] b. Aug. 10, 1771.
v. PATIENCE,[4] b. June 4, 1774.
vi. HANNAH,[4] b. Nov. 15, 1776.
vii. CONTENT,[4] b. May 22, 1780.
viii. HULDAH,[4] b. May 22, 1780.
ix. Daniel,[4] b. Sept. 2, 1783.

17. ELIZABETH[3] HUSSEY (Joseph,[2] Richard[1]), born 20, 10 mo., 1740; married in Dover, N. H., November 30, 1763, Joseph, son of Joseph and Sarah (Huckins) Tibbetts, of Rochester, N. H., born October 30, 1741, died November 5, 1823; she died January 24, 1819. Children:

i. HANNAH[4] TIBBETTS, b. Aug. 2, 1765; m. Apr. 2, 1797, Paul Libby.
ii. SAMUEL[4] TIBBETTS, b. Nov. 10, 1767; m. Nov. 2, 1797, Dorothy Wentworth.
iii. ABIGAIL[4] TIBBETTS, b. Nov. 10, 1767; m. 1st, Peter Hanson, 2d, Aaron Downs; d. in Brooklyn, N. Y., Jan. 16, 1850.
iv. ENOCH[4] TIBBETTS, b. Apr. 11, 1772; d. about 1783.
v. SARAH[4] TIBBETTS, b. Feb. 15, 1776; m. James Hubbard; d. Mar. 4, 1846.
vi. ELIZABETH[4] TIBBETTS, b. Feb. 24, 1778; m. Abner Clements, of Somersworth, N. H.

18. SAMUEL[3] HUSSEY (Joseph,[2] Richard[1]) born 12, 10 mo., 1742; married in Dover, N. H., May 3, 1769, Mercy, daughter of Joseph and Elizabeth (Hanson) Evans; he died April 17, 1814; she died in Somersworth, January 25, 1828. Children:

i. PETER,[4] b. Oct. 29, 1769; m. Lydia ..... He administered on his father's estate. His deeds of real estate in Somersworth run from Sept. 5, 1794, to Mar. 21, 1835. In this last deed he is described as of Dover, in all the others as of Somersworth. His wife Lydia joins in 1816 and 1829. I should be glad to receive further information concerning him.
ii. ELIZABETH,[4] b. Mar. 1, 1771; m. in Dover, Feb. 3, 1808, Timothy[3] Hussey (William,[2] Richard[1]); d. Jan. 25, 1828.
iii. MARY,[4] b. Sept. 26, 1772; m. in Dover, Dec. 25, 1793, Samuel, son of Timothy and Abigail (Hussey) Varney, of Berwick, Me., b. Feb. 16, 1767.

6   RICHARD HUSSEY AND HIS DESCENDANTS.

  iv. SUSANNAH,[4] b. June 3, 1774; m. a Clements of Dover.
  v. SAMUEL,[4] b. Feb. 17, 1776.
36. vi. ABIGAIL,[4] b. Sept. 3, 1779.
  vii. MERCY,[4] b. Oct. 19, 1783; d. 1846. She lived in the family
   of her sister Abigail, the mother of John Greenleaf
   Whittier, from the time of the poet's earliest recollec-
   tion until her death. She was the "Aunt" commemora-
   ted in "Snowbound":—
     "The sweetest woman ever Fate
     Perverse denied a household mate."
   Whittier's biographer, Mr. Pickard, says of her:–"With
   less of dignity and 'presence' than her sister, she had a
   singular sweetness of disposition, and loving, helpful
   ways. Her gentle ministrations at the bedside of the
   sick and suffering gave a peculiar significance to the
   name her parents bestowed on this Quaker, 'sister of
   mercy'."
  viii. RUTH,[4] m. Ezekiel Jones of Amesbury.
  ix. ANNA,[4] m. in Dover, Nov. 1, 1820, Paul[5] Hussey (Elijah,[4]
   Paul,[3] William,[2] Richard[1]).

 19. PHEBE[3] HUSSEY (*Joseph,*[2] *Richard*[1]), born 12, 11
mo., 1744; married in Dover, January 14, 1765, Moses, son
of Benjamin and Sarah (Pinkham) Austin, born in Somersworth 13, 4 mo., 1734.
   Their children born in Rochester:
  i. SARAH[4] AUSTIN, b. July 9, 1765; m. in Dover, Dec. 7, 1786,
   Obadiah, son of Joseph and Sarah (Greenleaf) Whittier,
   of Haverhill, Mass., who was b. Sept. 2, 1758, and d. in
   Dover, N. H., July 28, 1814.
  ii. MARY[4] AUSTIN, b. Jan. 31, 1772; m. in Rochester, Oct. 2,
   1806, Daniel, son of Zephaniah and Ruth Breed of Weare,
   N. H.
  iii. ELIZABETH[4] AUSTIN, b. Jan. 31, 1772; m. in Rochester,
   Sept. 17, 1801, Jonathan, son of Joseph and Anna Cartland of Lee, N. H.
  iv. ANNA[4] AUSTIN, b. Feb. 4, 1775; m. in Rochester, July 8,
   1813, Israel, son of Ebenezer and Abigail Peaslee of
   Weare, N. H.

 20. SUSANNAH[3] HUSSEY (*Joseph,*[2] *Richard*[1]), born 28,
1 mo., 1750; married in Dover, January 22, 1772, John, son
of Israel and Mary (Johnson) Hodgdon of Kensington, N.
H., born in Dover, April 22, 1745, died January 15, 1821.
She died December 6, 1841. Births of children are from the
Hodsdon or Hodgdon Genealogy, which contains an extended
sketch of John Hodgdon.
       Children:
  i. MOSES[4] HODGDON, b. in Weare, N. H., Aug. 22, 1775.
  ii. ABIGAIL[4] HODGDON, b. in Weare, Aug. 7, 1778; m. 1799,
   Daniel Breed.

 21. HANNAH[3] HUSSEY (*Joseph,*[2] *Richard*[1]), born 1, 3 mo.,
1753; married in Dover, October 27, 1773; (see *Friends Records*; Tate says October, 25). Jedediah, son of Hatevil and
Sarah Hall of Falmouth, Maine, born in Dover, June 21,

1748; she died December 21, 1814, and he married 2d, Elizabeth Clough; he died November 20, 1824.

Children:

i. PETER[4] HALL, b. June 1, 1774; m. Anna Hunnewell.
ii. JOEL[4] HALL, b. Dec. 15, 1775; m. Sarah Houston.
iii. ELIZABETH[4] HALL, m. Moses Goddard.
iv. AARON[4] HALL, d. at sea, a. 35.
v. MERCY[4] HALL, m. Peter Morrill.
vi. MOSES[4] HALL, b. June 15, 1784; m. Sarah Thompson.
vii. ABIGAIL[4] HALL, m. John Rogers.
viii. DAVID SANDS[4] HALL, m. Lydia Hanson.
ix. JONATHAN[4] HALL, b. Sept. 5, 1791; m. Mary Smith.
x. ANNA[4] HALL, m. Moses Hawkes.
xi. DORCAS[4] HALL, died young.

22. PAUL[3] HUSSEY (*William*,[2] *Richard*[1]), born 1730; married early as 1760, Mary, daughter of Joseph and Peniel (Bean) Hall. Joseph Hall and Peniel Bean were married December 19, 1731. Mary was their second child, and was baptized May 23, 1736. Joseph Hall, born March 26, 1706, died November 14, 1762, was the son of Ralph Hall and Mary Chesley, his 2d wife, whom he married May 26, 1701, and the grandson of John Hall, who was born in England about 1617, and first appears, with his wife Elizabeth, on the church records of Charlestown, Mass., at the baptism of their son John, in 1645. He removed to Dover, N. H., in 1648 or 1649, and was deacon of the first church in Dover as early as 1655. (See Rev. David B. Hall's *"Halls of New England."* The name of the husband of Mary Hall is erroneously given as *"Hessey"* in this work.)

Paul Hussey died November 22, 1796; his wife died in 1813.

The following is from the files of the Probate Court of Strafford County, N. H.

"We the subscribers the widow and eldest son of Paul Hussey late of Dover, husbandman, deceased intestate, hereby certify that we decline taking upon ourselves the administration of his estate and pray that the Judge of Probate would appoint Elijah Hussey, the second son of the deceased, administrator on his estate.   Mary Hussey
July 2d 1798.   Micajah Hussey
                                                     Daniel Hussey"

Elijah was appointed administrator July 21, 1798.

The children of Paul and Mary (Hall) Hussey were:

37. i. DANIEL,[4] b. Sept. 22, 1760.
38. ii. HULDAH.[4]
39. iii. ELIJAH,[4] b. Mar. 18, 1765.
40. iv. MICAJAH,[4] b. 1767.

23. WILLIAM[3] HUSSEY (*William*,[2] *Richard*[1]), born 2, 7 mo., 1739, married 1st, in Dover, N. H., January 6, 1768, Phebe, daughter of John and Phebe (Austin) Hanson, born

18, 4 mo., 1744, died July 16, 1792; he married 2d, in Berwick, Maine, September 24, 1795, Sarah, daughter of Isaac, late of Somersworth, and Sarah Hanson, and widow of Batchelor Hussey of Berwick, to whom she was married in Berwick, December 12, 1768. William Hussey died June 3, 1821.

His children, born in Berwick, Maine, were:

41. i. JAMES,[4] b. Nov. 14, 1768.
 ii. JOHN,[4] b. Mar. 8, 1771.
 iii. HANNAH,[4] b. Mar. 13, 1773; m. Nov. 3, 1791, Christopher, son of John and Elizabeth Cole of Sanford, Me.
 iv. SARAH,[4] b. Aug. 21, 1774.
 v. WILLIAM,[4] b. Sept. 21, 1776.
 vi. PAUL,[4] b. May 26, 1779.
 vii. AHIJAH,[4] b. July 7, 1781.
 viii. MARY,[4] b. Mar. 13, 1783.
 ix. ELIZABETH.[4]

24. MARY[3] HUSSEY (William,[2] Richard[1]), married October 2, 1765, Ebenezer, son of William and Abigail (Varney) Frye of Kittery, Maine, born 30, 6 mo., 1734, his 2d wife. His 1st wife, whom he married November 4, 1760, was Mary, daughter of Joshua and Elizabeth Buffum of Berwick, born 1742, died 1764.

The children of Ebenezer and Mary (Hussey) Frye, born in Kittery, Maine, were:

 i. JOHN[4] FRYE, b. May 4, 1767; m. Nov. 1, 1797, Martha, dau. of Mussey and Elizabeth Gould, of Dover.
 ii. OBADIAH[4] FRYE, b. Aug. 8, 1771.

25. ABIGAIL[3] HUSSEY (William,[2] Richard[1]), born 15, 7 mo., 1744; married January 4, 1764, Timothy, son of Samuel and Mary Varney of Dover, born 1, 7 mo., 1742, died September 30, 1808.

Their children were:

 i. HANNAH[4] VARNEY, b. Feb. 14, 1765; m. Jan. 4, 1787, Samuel, son of Joshua and Elizabeth Buffum of Berwick, Me.
 ii. SAMUEL[4] VARNEY, b. in Dover, N. H., Feb. 16, 1767; m. Dec, 25, 1795, Mary[4] Hussey, dau. of Samuel,[3] (Joseph,[2] Richard[1]) and Mercy Hussey, of Somersworth.
 iii. HULDAH[4] VARNEY, b. in Dover, Apr. 1, 1769; m. 1st, Jan. 24, 1788, Benaiah, son of Moses and Peace Purinton, of Berwick, Me., 2d, May 29, 1800, Thomas, son of Jonathan and Elizabeth Varney, of Wells, Me.
 iv. MERCY[4] VARNEY, b. in Dover, Mar. 8, 1771; m. Dec. 30, 1790, Amos, son of Joseph and Mary Hill, of Berwick.
 v. MARY[4] VARNEY, b. in Berwick, Me., June 28, 1775; m. Jan. 2, 1794, Ezekiel, son of Jonathan and Elizabeth Varney, of Wells, Me.
 vi. TIMOTHY[4] VARNEY, b. in Berwick, Feb. 11, 1781.
 vii. ABIGAIL[4] VARNEY, b. in Berwick, May 30, 1785, d. Aug. 3, 1786.

26. TIMOTHY[3] HUSSEY (William,[2] Richard[1]) born 1748;

married 1st, in Falmouth, Maine, November 24, 1782, Sybil, daughter of Paul and Eleanor Thompson, of Scarboro, Me., who died in Dover, N. H., December 28, 1806; he married 2d, February 3, 1808, Elizabeth[4] Hussey (*Samuel*,[3] *Joseph*,[2] *Richard*[1]), born March 1, 1771; he died February 21, 1824; she died January 25, 1828.

"The sixth falls, of Cochecho Falls, are called Hussey's falls and upper Eel Weir Falls. The name of Hussey's Falls was derived from Timothy Hussey and his nephew Elijah, who once owned this water privilege and the adjoining land. No mention is made of any mill here. Timothy Hussey and Elizabeth, Dec. 11, 1821, conveyed to Isaac Wendell, for the Dover Cotton Factory, one acre of land 'at a place called Eelware falls', together with the falls. This was on the easterly side of the river. Elijah Hussey and Jane, that same day, conveyed to said Wendell one acre on the west side of the falls, including all the water privilege adjoining said lot."—(Landmarks in Ancient Dover, p. 47.)

Elizabeth Hussey was appointed administratrix of the estate of her husband Timothy, March 29, 1824. There was a partition of his real estate, June 8, 1830, to Thomas Snell in right of his wife Mary and to Hannah Hussey.

Children of Timothy and Elizabeth (Hussey) Hussey were:

i.   HANNAH,[4] b. Oct. 16, 1808; m. Joseph Whitney, and had children:
   i.   Laurentia Amorette[5] Whitney, b. Aug. 15, 1833; m. Abraham Bachelder, of Loudon, N. H.
   ii. Eliza Ann[5] Whitney, b. Sept. 18, 1838; m. Joseph Porter Bachelder, of Loudon, N. H.
   iii. Amanda[5] Whitney.
   iv. William[5] Whitney.
   v.   George[5] Whitney.
   vi. Frank[5] Whitney.

ii. MARY ELIZABETH,[4] b. Dec. 22, 1809; m. March 3, 1830, Thomas, son of John and Elizabeth (Caldwell) Snell, of Madbury, N. H., b. in Lee, N. H., May 14, 1798; he d. in Dover, May 5, 1859. Their children were:
   i.   Timothy Hussey[5] Snell, b. Oct. 19, 1830; m. 1st, Mary Ann Foss, 2d, ... Foss, sister of first wife.
   ii. Alfred William[5] Snell, died young.
   iii. Elizabeth[5] Snell, died young.
   iv. Three, who d. in infancy.
   v.   Lydia Jane[5] Snell, b. April 26, 1841; m. in Somersworth, Nov. 21, 1871, Charles Moses[6] Hussey (Moses B.,[5] Elijah,[4] Paul,[3] William,[2] Richard.[1])

27. STEPHEN[3] HUSSEY (*William*,[2] *Richard*[1]), born 21, 1 mo., 1750; married in Dover, October 5, 1774, Priscilla, daughter of Stephen and Mary (Austin) Hanson, born August 7, 1756; he died in Berwick, Me., 1828.

Children, born in Berwick, were:

i.   LYDIA,[4] b. Dec. 30, 1775. Disowned.
ii. MARY,[4] b. Feb. 11, 1778; d. Dec., 1786.
iii. HANNAH,[4] b. Oct. 14, 1780.

42. iv.   STEPHEN,[4] b. Mar. 29, 1783.
      v.   HANSON,[4] b. May 8, 1785.
43. vi.   TIMOTHY,[4] b. May 13, 1787.
     vii.   MERCY,[4] b. July 3, 1789.
     viii. MARY.[4]
      ix.   MIRIAM.[4]
       x.   SYBIL,[4] b. July 3, 1796; d. June 22, 1815.
      xi.   ELIJAH.[4]

(To be continued.)

HENRY SEWALL WEBSTER,

Gardiner, Maine.

CORRECTION.

The words Peter Bell, in the *New Hampshire Genealogical Record*, Vol. V, p. 41, last line, should read Peter Ball.—ED.

WANTS.

Once more we come to the question of wants of the library of the New Hampshire Genealogical Society. The last time we published a special call, it was for directories. We are still short of directories of Nashua and Keene, and have but a few of Manchester. From a genealogical point of view directories are of great importance, and we wish to secure a copy of every directory ever published in, or pertaining to, New Hampshire or any of its counties, cities and towns.

Town histories are another class of books of which the library has but few, and it aims to have a copy of every history in New Hampshire and would like histories of every town and city in New England. Genealogies are always welcome donations, the more the better.

Another class of donations, which we especially welcome is original private manuscript diaries and journals of different individuals; these, though of a private nature, almost always contain records which, in the future, will be of vast importance and interest to the families related, and even to the public in general. How much the public is indebted to Pike's Journal; to Tate's and Atkinson's Records and other private records and diaries, for their valuable historical references. Will those persons interested in the library make a continuous effort to secure the desired books and manuscripts.

C. W. TIBBETTS, Librarian.

NORTH CHURCH RECORDS, PORTSMOUTH, N. H.

BAPTISMS BY REV. JOSEPH BUCKMINSTER.

[There are two records of baptisms; we have followed the one in the handwriting of Rev. Mr. Buckminster and given in brackets any additional information contained in the other record.]

[Continued from Vol. VI, page 80.]

1779 Decemb^r 19 Charles Cutter Son of Jacob Treadwell & wife [Anne]

  19 Nehemiah Son of W^o Elizabeth Rowell [Posthumus son of Nehemiah Rowell]

  26 Benjn Son of Neil McIntier and wife [Mary] Dr Haven

  26 Olive D^r of John Pitman & Lucy his wife   Dr Haven

1780 January 2 Caroline D^r of Woodbury Langdon & wife [Sarah]

  9 Peggy D^r of [Capt.] Wm Brewster & Ruth his wife (N. C. R., I: 221.)

  16 Samuel Son of Benjamin Slade and wife

  Phebe D^r of Tim^y Ham & wife

  23 Susannah D^r of [Capt] Robert Parker & wife   Mr Mautimora?

  Sam^{ll} Son of Tobias Walker & wife   Mr Mautimora?

 Feby 13 Joseph Sherburne Son of Sam^{ll} Hill & Mary his wife

  28 Elizabeth Daugh^r of Ezek^l Pitman & Sarah his wife   Dr Haven

  28 Lydia Daugh^r of Richard & Esther Jackson   Dr Haven

 March 5th Thomas and James Sons of James Hart and Mary his wife

  5 John Son of Sam^{ll} Ham tertius [of Samuel Ham Tert^s Son of John Ham]

 12 Margaret Daugh^r of Enoch and Margaret Meloon

  26 Joseph Son of Sam^{ll} Sherburne & wife [Plains] Dr Haven

12   NORTH CHURCH RECORDS.

1780   April 2ⁿᵈ   John Son of Richᵈ and Hannah Billings
    9   Elizabeth Moore Dʳ of Mark Seavey and wife
June 4   John Son of Benjamin Crocket & wife
   25   Thomas Son of Nathˡ Peverly & wife [Anne]
   25   Clement March Son of Henry and Margaret Nut-
       ter   Mʳ Thayer   [son of Henry and Margery Nut-
       ter]
July 23   Wᵐ Son of Seth and Temperance Walker
Augᵗ 13   Anna Dʳ of Jnᵒ & Abigail Reed   Mʳ Spring
       [of John & Anna Reed]
Septʳ 17   Henry Son of Jnᵒ Junʳ & Abigail Salter
Octoʳ 15   Jnᵒ Son of Edward Park and [Jerusha] his
       wife   Mʳ Belknap
Novʳ 13   Sarah Daughʳ of Stephen Chase & his wife
       Mʳ Mautimora?
   19   Nehemiah Son of Nathˡ Pitman & wife [Mary]
Decʳ 3   Moses Son of Aaron Hodgdon & wife
   10   Enoch Greenleaf Son of Jnᵒ Parrott & wife [Mar-
       tha]   Mʳ McClintock
   17   Jacob Freeman Son of Newport & Violet his wife
   24   Margaret Meloon Dʳ of Ebenʳ Light & Hannah
       his wife
1781   Janʸ 21   Ephraim Son of Ephraim Dennet & wife
       Mʳ Mautimora?
   28   John Son of Woodbury Langdon & wife [Sarah]
   28   Mary Bateman Dʳ of Wᵐ Martin & wife [Priscilla]
March yᵉ 4   Anna Dʳ of Jeremiah and Susanna Dennet
   11   John Son of Elisha Hill and wife [Elizabeth]
   11   Joseph Son of Jacob Walden and wife [Abigail]
April 1   Samuel Son of Michael Whidden and Mary his
       wife
       Robert Stokle Son of Doeg & wife [of George &
       Mary Doeg]
       William Sewall Son of Winthrop Bennet and wife
   15   Betsey Dʳ of James Hill and Eunice his wife
   22   Charles Son of Neil McIntier and wife [Mary]
   22   Elizabeth Dʳ of Aaron Hodgdon & wife
July 8   Elizabeth Dʳ of Mark Nelson & wife   Dʳ Langdon
   29   Sarah Dʳ of Danˡ Hart & wife   Mʳ Spring
                    (N. C. R., I: 222.)
August 12   Alexander Son of Tobias Warner & wife
   19   Polly Dʳ of Henry Sherburne & wife   Mʳ McClin-
       tock

1781 August 19 Abigail D^r of John Mendum & wife [Susanna] M^r McClintock

Sepr 23 Danl Son of Jacob Treadwell and Ann his wife Mr Mansfield

Octo^r 14 Saml Ham Son of Elihu Langly & Sarah his wife

14 Ann D^r of John Mendum & wife [Susanna]

21 Fanny D^r of Ezekiel Pitman & wife [Sarah] Mr Stevens

Decr 30 Jeremiah Son of Prince, Negro Servant of Genl Whipple, and wife [Dinah]

1782 Jany 13 George Gains Son of Peter Man and wife [Elizabeth]

20 Patty D^r of Benj^a Miller and wife [of Benjamin Miller son of Moses Miller]

Feby 17 John Son of Benja^n Slade and wife

17 Theodore Son of Jno Pitman and wife [Lucy]

24 Mark Son of Tobias Walker and wife Dr Haven

24 Saml Son of [Capt] Robert Parker and wife Dr Haven

April 14 Anna Phips D^r of Mark Seavey

May 19 Wm Pierce Son of Peter Pierce private baptism

20 Nathl Son of Nathaniel Dennett private baptism

June 9 Deborah Walker and Martha Brackett [Twins] D^{rs} of Jno Parrott & wife [Martha]

23 Elizabeth D^r of John Reed and wife [Anna] Mr Stevens

July 14 ———— Son of Mastin in Covenant at Greenland [Thomas Meed, Son of Lemuel & ———— Marston]

Augt 4th Jane Caverly an adult owned ye covenant and was baptized [Jane Caverly Daughter of Nathl Caverly Dec^d]

10th Robert Son of Samuel and Jane Wallas

25 Wm Son of Timo^y Ham and wife

Novr 3 Wm Leonard Son of Capt Elijah Hall and Elizabeth his wife

3 Dorothy D^r of Capt Jno Salter and Jane his wife

17 Daniel Son of Ric^d Jackson and wife [Esther]

24 Thomas Son of Capt Thomas Dalling and Eliz^a his wife Mr Spring

Decem^r 15 Polly Libbey D^r of Enoch Meloon & wife

22 Sarah Ann D^r of Thomas Penhallow and Hannah his wife

14

1783 Jany 19   Betsey Briard D^r of Seth Walker
      19   Stephen Son of Winthrop Bennet and wife
Feby 12   Nicolas Son of Nicolas Pickering baptized at
          his house the day his wife was buried
      16   Wm Son of Saml Hill & wife [Mary]   Mr Stevens
March ye 1   Sarah D^r of Wm Gardner private baptism
       9   Daniel Son of Nathl Pitman [son of Nathaniel &
          Mary Pitman]
      23   James Son of Eph^m Dennet
                              (N. C. R., I: 223.)
      30   James Son of James Hill and wife [Eunice]
      30   Polly D^r of Benj^a Woodbury and wife [Mary]
April ye 13   Mark Son [of] Jeremy and Susannah Den-
          net   Mr Mautimora?
May ye 4   Harriet D^r of Woodbury and Sarah Langdon
      25   Matthew Clarke Son of Tobias Warner & wife
          Mr Stevens
June 22   Daniel Son of Elisha Hill & wife [Elizabeth]
      29   Sukey D^r of Charles Roberts [& Mary Roberts]
July 28   Jno Son of Capt Jno Tuckerman & wife [Eliza-
          beth]
Augt 17   Charles Son of Henry Nutter and wife [Mar-
          gery]
      24   Katharine D^r of Neil McIntyer and wife [Mary]
      31   Anna D^r of Edward Parks and wife [Jerusha]
          Mr Noble
Sepr 7   Stephen Huse Son of Joseph Walker and wife
      27   William Son of D^e Hart & wife, private baptism
      28   Zebulon and Richard Sons Mr Wiggins young Lads
          M^r M
Novr 3   Danl Son of Nahum Ward and wife [Margery]
          Mr Stevens
       3   Hannah D^r of Ezekiel Pitman and wife [Sarah]
          Mr Stevens
Decem^r 14   Olive Dr Ichabod Hill and wife
1784 Jany 25   Thomas Wibird Son of Thos Penhallow
          [& Hannah Penhallow]   Dr Haven
Feby 22   Ebenezer Son of Joshua Pike Junr
March 28   Sukey D^r of Jno Pitman and wife [Lucy]
          Dr Haven
April 9   John Heath Son of Dr John Goddard and wife
       9   Sarah Ann D^r of Tobias Walker and wife
      11   Nancy D^r of Aaron Hodgdon   Mr Stevens

1784 April 23 Elizabeth Bennet an adult private baptism dangerously ill

May 25 Mark Son of Barnet Akerman & Sarah his wife

2 Mary Jane baptized on yᵉ behalf of Sʳ Parrot [child of Ebenʳ Bracket on acco. of Martha Parrot wife of Capᵗ John Parrot]

30 Joseph Stevens Son of [Rev.] Joseph Buckminster & Sarah his wife

June 13 John Son of John and Jane Delphin

July 4 Elizabeth Dʳ of John Salter and Jane his wife

18 Josiah Son of George Gains & wife

18 Betsey Briard Dʳ of Seth Walker & wife

18 Betsey Dʳ of Sarah Talpey Wᵒ [Betsey, Girl, Daughter of Sarah Talpey widow]

August 8 Elizabeth Hart an Adult [Elizabeth Hart wife of Edward Hart]

August 22 Mary yᵉ Dʳ of Mary Hooper single woman [Mary, child of Mary Hooper Daughter of John Hooper]

25 Augustus Son of Wᵒ Mayo private baptism [Augustus Son of ——— Mayo widow of Augustus Mayo Decᵈ]

(N. C. R., I: 224.)

Septemʳ 5 George Son of Edward B. Loud [& Sarah Loud]

13 Susannah Clark adult private baptism

19 Joseph Son of Benjᵃ Miller and wife

26 Elizabeth Dʳ of Elijah and Elizabeth Hall his wife

26 Wᵐ and George Sons of Wᵐ Fernald and wife

Octoʳ 24 Betsey Dʳ of William Martin [& Priscilla Martin]

31 Winthrop Son of Winthrop Bennet & wife

Novʳ 28 Joshua Son of Woodbury Langdon & wife [Sarah] Dʳ Haven

Dec 5 Martha Dʳ of Thoˢ Harvey [& Hannah Harvey]

[Dec 12 Betsey daughter of John & Elizabeth Tuckerman]

19 Prince Negro adult [Late Servᵗ of General Whipple]

19 Esther Dʳ of Prince & wife [Dinah]

1785 Janʸ 2 Lydia Dʳ of Ezekiel Pitman & wife [Sarah]

2 Polly Dʳ of Jnᵒ Gooch and wife

9 Peggy Dʳ of Enoch Meloon

1785   Jany 29   Sarah D^r of Capt Cullum & wife private
          baptism
       Feby 13   Son of James Hill [Jeremiah child of James &
          Eunice Hill]
          20   Theodore Son of Nathaniel Pitman [& Mary Pit-
          man]
          27   Joseph Son of Neil McIntire [& Mary McIntire]
          Dr Haven
       April 4   Samuel Haynes Son of Eli Sumner in Coven^t at
          Milton
          10   Hall Jackson Son of Saml Ham [of Samuel Ham
          son of William Ham]
       May 1   Jane D^r of Tim^y Ham and wife
       June 5   John March Son of Mark Seavy and wife
          5   John Plummer Son of Jeremiah and Susannah Den-
          net
       July 3   Mary Ann D^r of George Freeze & Ann Wig-
          gin
          24   Samuel Son of Edward Park & wife [Jerusha]
       Augt 21   Polly D^r of Ichabod Hill & wife
       Sepr 25   Theodora D^r of Danl Hart and wife
       Octr 9   George Son of Benj^a Jackson baptized on ye ac-
          count of ye wife of Natha^l Jackson
          16   George Son of Edward Loud & wife [Sarah]
          30   Dolly D^r of Henry Sherburne and wife
          30   Nancy Wilson D^r of Joshua Pike [Junr] & wife
       Novr 20   Betsey Coffin D^r of Lemuel Mastin & wife
          27   Henry Son of John & Susannah Goddard   D^r
          Haven
       Decem^r 25   Sarah D^r of George Gains and wife
1786   March 12   Benjamin Tappan Son of Jno Chase and
          wife
          D^o   William Son of Wm Coffin & wife
          19   Theodore Son of Stephen Chase & wife   Mr Mau-
          timora?
       April ye 9   Elizabeth D^r of Nahum Ward and wife [of
          Nahum & Margery Ward]
          30   William Son of Ezekiel Pitman & wife
                              (N. C. R., I: 225.)
       May ye 7   Nathaniel Son of John Tuckerman & wife
          [Elizabeth Tuckerman]
          14   Susannah D^r of Prince Whipple & wife [Dinah]
          Negroes

FIRST CONGREGATIONAL CHURCH RECORDS, CONCORD, N. H.

1730—1905.

MARRIAGES BY REV. ASA McFARLAND, D. D.

[Continued from Vol. VI, page 170.]

1818. Jany 1. Morril Farnum of Rumford, District of Maine & Sarah Virgin of Concord were married.

Jany 27. Asaph Evans & Eliza Green both of Concord were married.

Feb. 8th Richard Bradley & Elizabeth Ayer* were married.

Feb. 23. Nathaniel Evans of Bow and Harriet Wiggin of Concord were married.

Feby 26. Abel Baker & Lydia Hazeltine both of Concord were married.

March 31. James Hoit & Nancy Abbot both of Concord were married.

April 8th Nathaniel Parker & Betsy Underhill both of Concord were married.

May 16. Herman Price & Hannah Coffin both of Concord were married.

May 31. Nathan Kelly & Mary Abbot both of Concord were married.

June 1st Moses L. Sargent of Pittsfield & Sarah Thorndike of Concord were married.

June 2. Asa Hardy, Ju^r & Judith Colby both of Concord were married.

July 16. John Knowlton & Experience Hardy both of Concord were married.

July 28. Samuel Seavey & Nancy Stephens both of Concord were married.

August 16. Isaac Porter of Pembroke & Mary Kent of Concord were married.

Sept. 3^d John P. Rand & Sarah Burleigh both of Concord were married.

*Concord City Records read, both of Concord.—ED.

1818.   Septr 7th Phinehas Stephens & Betsey Hutchins both of Concord were married.

Sept. 10.   Elliot Chickering of Danvers, Commonwealth of Massachusetts & Ruth Wilson of Concord were married.

Sept. 19.   Robert Davis, Jr. & Almira B. Dearborn both of Concord were married.

Sept. 29.   Samuel F. B. Morse of Charlestown, Commonwealth of Massachusetts & Lucretia P. Walker of Concord were married.

Octr 8.   Dr. Thomas Chadbourne & Clarissa D. Green both of Concord were married.

Octr 29.   Joseph Carter West & Mary Abbot both of Concord were married.

Decr 24.   Benjamin Wheeler & Hannah Clement both of Concord were married.

1819.   April 6.   Josiah Leonard of Allenstown and Sally Currier of Bow were married.

April 15.   Jacob Flanders & Huldah Abbot both of Concord were married.

April 26.   Benjamin Bickford & Sarah Blaisdell both of Pembroke* were married.

July 5.   Benjamin Hoit and Hannah Eastman both of Concord were married.

August 5th Abraham Sanborn, Ju^r & Mary K. Rogers† both of Concord were married.

October 5th Philip Watson & Mary W. Russell both of Concord were married.

Novr 28.   William Fisk, Esqr of Amherst and Hannah Walker of Concord were married.

Novr 30.   William Lynn and Elizabeth Ann Pillsbury both of Concord were married.

Decr 2.   Abiel C. Carter & Patty Farnum both of Concord were married.

1820.   Jany 13th Henry Martin, 3^d and Sarah Flanders both of Concord were married.

Jany 19.   Andrew Buswell & Zelphia Dimond both of Concord were married.

D^o 20.   Calvin Abbot of Barnard, State of Vermont and Polly Burnham Abbot of Concord were married.

D^o 24.   Leavit C. Virgin of Rumford, District of Maine and Hannah Osgood of Concord were married.

*City Records read, both of Concord.   †City Records read, Mary H. Rogers.—ED.

1820. Jany 27. Hon. James H. Bingham of Alstead and
Charlotte M. Kent of Concord were married.

Feby 28. Pelatiah B. Kemp of Groton & Dolly Dimond
of Concord were married.

Feby 29. Nathaniel Carter of Concord and Elizabeth Robertson of Bow were married.

March 6. William Abbot and Dorcas Carter both of Concord were married.

March 21. Josiah Hardy & Margaret Colby both of Concord were married.

March 28. Jeremiah Wheeler, Ju^r and Sarah Whidden
both of Concord were married.

April 4. Eleazer Davis and Hannah Dow both of Concord were married.

April 20. George Hutchins and Sarah R. Tucker both of
Concord were married.

August 8. George J. Eastman and Judith Elliot both of
Concord were married.

Sept. 14. John H. Sinclair & Dorothy Paige both of
Haverhill were married.

October 12. Josiah K. Locke & Lydia Philbrick both of
Concord were married.

October 15. Amos Abbot, 3^d & Sally Gould Foster both
of Concord were married.

Decr 12. John Stewart Bowers* of Fryeburg, State of
Maine and Ann Ayer Bradley of Concord were married.

Decr 27. John True, Esqr of Hampstead & Anne Parker
of Concord were married.

Decr 29. Moses Colby of Hopkinton & Else Abbot of
Concord were married.

1821. Jany 30. William Gault and Harriet Stickney both
of Concord were married.

Feby 6th Levi Brigham of Boston, Commonwealth of
Massachusetts and Nancy Hazen Ayer of Concord were
married.

Feb. 15. Jeremiah Arlin and Nancy Chandler both of
Concord were married.

Feb. 25. Stephen Hall and Charlotte Bradley both of
Concord were married.

April 25. John Nevins of Groton and Mary Elliot of
Pembroke were married.

*City Records give the name as, Barrows.—ED.

1821. April 26.   David Noyes of Enfield and Polly Carter of Concord were married.

May 30.   Samuel P. Newman of Brunswick, Maine & Caroline Kent of Concord were married.

D° 31ˢᵗ   Carter Buswell of Hopkinton & Mary Abbot of Concord were married.

June 14.   Jere Abbot and Rebecca Chandler both of Concord were married.

Sept. 16.   Levi Brigham of Jaffrey and Ann L. Bronsdon of Concord were married.

Octʳ 2ᵈ   Nathaniel W. Appleton of Portsmouth & Mary C. Green of Concord were married.

Octʳ 22ᵈ   John Clement and Lucinda Elliot both of Boscawen were married.

Novʳ 29.   John Berry of Loudon & Sophronia Tenny of Concord were married.

D°   Rufus Kimball of Bradford, Massachusetts & Lucinda Rodgers of Concord were married.

1822. Janʸ 20.   Stephen Lang, Juʳ and Sally W. Waldron both of Concord were married.

May 23.   Luke Baker of Bow and Ann Carter of Concord were married.

June 23.   Henry Lovejoy and Sarah L. Thorn both of Concord were married.

July 9.   Richard Herbert, 3ᵈ and Nancy Kendall both of Concord were married.

D° 11.   Ivory Hall and Pamelia L. Clement both of Concord were married.

Sept. 27.   Amos Stephens and Susan F. Eastman both of Concord were married.

Octʳ 29.   Jeremiah Pecker and Mary Lang both of Concord were married.

November 24.   James Stephens and Ismenia Washer both of Concord were married.

December 3ᵈ   Henry Todd and Sarah Russ both of Concord were married.

D° 12.   Francis W. Rogers of Bow and Miriam C. Garvin of Concord were married.

D° 30.   Jonathan Runnels, Juʳ and Mary Dimond* both of Deering were married.

1823. Janʸ 7ᵗʰ   Andrew Willey of Hopkinton and Betsey Carter of Concord were married.

*City Records read, both of Concord.—ED.

1823. Jany 20th   John K. Wilson and Hulda P. Emery both of Pembroke were married.

Feby 5.   Joseph Calef Morse of Boscawen and Nancy Bricket Abbot of Concord were married.

Feby 13.   St. Luke Morse of Rumford, Maine and Judith Wheeler of Concord were married.

March 20.   Jedediah Hoit, Ju^r and Betsey Dow both of Concord were married.

April 15th   James Lougee of Boscawen & Phebe Carter of Concord were married.

May 11th   John Buzzel and Betsey Hill both of Northwood were married.

Sept. 2^d   Samuel Elliot and Martha Green both of Bow were married.

D^o 21.   Jeremiah Martin and Nancy Brown both of Concord were married.

D^o 22^d*   Rev. Charles Walker of Rutland, State of Vermont and Lucretia Ambrose of Concord were married.

Nov. 5.   Peter Elkins and Harriett Hall both of Concord were married.

11th   Dr. Thomas Brown of Deerfield and Mary Moor of Concord were married.

18th   Aaron Carter and Eliza Hazeltine both of Concord were married.

D^o 27th   Abiel Walker and Mary Thorndike both of Concord were married.

Decr 25th   Colⁿ Robert Ambrose and Jane Johnson Hutchins both of Concord were married.

1824. Jany 27.   William B. Willey and Mahala Dearborn both of Northwood were married.

D^o 28.   Joshua Grant, Ju^r of Salem, Massachusetts and Nancy Tuttle of this Town were married.

March 29.   Charles Wells of Amherst and Mary G. Wiggin of Concord were married.

April 14.   Revd John Woods of Newport and Achsah Baker of this town were married.

July 6.   Hazen Walker of Berwick, State of Maine and Eliza R. Kimball of this town were married.

July 9.†   John Little of Boscawen and Miriam Lovejoy of this town were married.

July 22^d   John Clement and Hannah Hammond both of Bow were married.

*City Records read, Sept. 23.   †City Records read, July 6.—ED.

1824. August 3ᵈ Jesse Durgin & Clarissa Baker both of Concord were married.

October 5ᵗʰ Aaron Abbot and Nancy Badger both of Concord were married.

Novʳ 11. David Stephens* and Hannah Brown of Concord were married.

D° Jesse Morgan of Bow and Mary Seavy of Concord were married.

D° 17ᵗʰ John H. Durgin of Sandbornton & Lucretia K. Brown of Concord were married.

D° 18. Peter Griffin and Hannah Allen both of Concord were married.

Decʳ 30ᵗʰ John Miller and Sarah Bailey Emery both of Concord were married.

1825. Janʸ 11. Solomon Payne of Canterbury, State of Connecticut and Sarah Baker of this town were married.

MARRIAGES BY REV. NATHANIEL BOUTON, D. D.

1825. April 12. James Straw to Sarah Shute, both of this town.

13. Walter French of Hopkinton to Senith Herrick of Concord.

May 24. Solomon Arlin of Barrington to Ruth Baldwin of Concord.

June 16. Ezra Ballard to Mary Flanders, both of this town.

Aug. 2. Ezekiel Webster, Esq. of Boscawen to Miss Achsah Pollard of this town.

14. William Dame of Portsmouth to Abigail Fife of Pembroke.

14. Joseph Lougee of Loudon to Pamelia Kimball of Concord.

Nov. 1. Henry E. Moore of Plymouth to Susan D. Farnum of this town.

10. John P. Sargent of Gloucester, Mass. to Charlotte G. Arlin of Concord.

Dec. 8. Henry Martin to Polly Abbot, both of Concord.

15. Isaac Dow, Jun. to Nancy Austin, both of Concord.

27. Moses Davis to Esther Martin, both of Concord.

28. William Yeaton of Pittsfield to Sally B. Locke of Deerfield.

*City Records read, of Loudon.—ED.

1826. Jan. 24. Thomas Choate of Hopkinton to Harriet Swan of Concord.

26. William M. Virgin to Lavinia Tyler, both of Concord.

Feb. 14. William Pickering to Susan B. Walker, both of Concord.

16. Samuel Clifford, Jun. of Loudon to Mary B. Kimball of Concord.

20. David Benson to Laura Kimball, both of Pembroke.

April 24. Joseph W. Carey of Danvers, Mass. to Abigail Fife of Concord.

May 11. George Wilkins to Nancy Shute both of Concord.

15. Augustine C. Pierce, Danville, Vt. to Sarah R. Carter of Concord.

16. Benjamin Bordman of Ossipee to Ann Stickney of Concord.

June 29. Isaiah S. Robinson, of Concord to Abigail Colby of Warner.

Sept. 12. John D. Abbot to Elizabeth Bartlett both of Concord.

Nov. 30. Benjamin Morril, Jr. to Eleanor Simpson, both of Concord.

Dec. 5. John Shute to Hannah K. Flanders, both of Concord.

12. Abira Fisk to Eunice B. Abbot, both of Concord.

Dec. 19. Elisha Turner of Harvard, Mass. to Caroline G. Giles of Concord.

25. Joshua Emery of Loudon to Eliza Eastman of Concord.

25. Jacob A. Potter of Concord to Sophronia Moore of Loudon.

26. Reuben Goodwin to Betsey Webber, both of Concord.

28. Chandler Lovejoy, Jun. to Fanny H. Virgin both of Concord.

1827. Feb. 6. Nehemiah Putnam of Rumford, Me. to Hannah Whidden of Concord.

D° 18. Tappan W. Noyes to Sally D. French, both of Warner.*

22. Isaac F. Williams to Mary Ayer, both of Concord.

*Concord City Records read, both of Concord.—ED.

1827. Feb. 24. Samuel T. French to Sarah F. Blake, both
of Dover.
April 11. Eben S. Towle to Esther W. Emery, both of
Concord.
June 13. Samuel Runnels, Jr. to Anna Abbot, both of
Concord.
July 23. Philip Eastman of North Yarmouth, Me. to
Mary Ambrose of Concord.
August 27. Walter Berry of Loudon to Sarah F. Potter
of Concord.
Nov. 28. Satchel Clark to Priscilla Stevens, both of Concord.
Dec. 12. Simon Carter to Elizabeth Abbot, both of Con-
cord.
13. Charles Abbot to Sarah Carter, both of Concord.
25. James Prescott to Mary E. Cunningham, both of
Portsmouth.
26. Joseph S. Abbot to Esther Farnum, both of Concord.
1828. Jan. 29. Philip Ferrin to Dolly W. Smith, both of
Concord.
31. David McIntire of Dixfield, Me. to Phebe Fisk of
Concord.
Feb. 10. Levi Morse to Ann Potter, both of Loudon.
15. Nathan H. Cate to Abigail T. Worth, both of Concord.
25. Hiram Eastman to Mary Kimball, both of Concord.
March 6. James Moulton, Jr. to Rebecca A. Chandler,
both of this town.
19. William Green of Plymouth to Harriet Kimball
of Concord.
27. Thomas Rowell to Bridget W. Farnum, both of
Concord.
April 28. David Morrison to Abigail Stevens, both of
Concord.
May 29. Andrew Seavey to Betsey Fisk, both of Con-
cord.
June 1. Luther Roby to Mary Ann Kimball, both of
Concord.
Sept. 1. Enos Shattuck of Plymouth to Rebecca Shute of
Concord.
29. Joseph Brown of Canterbury to Hannah W. Cleas-
by of Concord.

1828. Oct. 9. Rufus G. Lewis to Sally Smith, both of New Hampton.

Dec. 14. Jefferson Pettengill to Mary Ann Quimby, both of Concord.

21. Cyrus Kimball of Boston, Mass. to Charlotte G. Kimball, of Concord.

24. Aaron A. Palmer, of Hopkinton to Sarah George of Concord.

25. David Symonds to Nancy P. Flanders, both of Concord.

D° Hammond Buswell to Martha Conner, both of Concord.

1829. Jan. 22. Josiah Chandler of Grafton to Mehitable Merrill of Concord.

Feb. 16. Andrew Moody of Rumford, Me. to Ruth W. Wheeler of Concord.

17. Ephraim F. Sweat to Susan Philbrick, both of Concord.

March 25. Guy Roach to Eliza Ann Nichols, both of Hooksett.

April 16. Samuel Uran to Clarissa Chase, both of Concord.

29. John C. Ordway of Concord to Louisa W. Bohonon of Salisbury.

29. Leonard Russell of Bow to Sarah Hall of Concord.

June 8. William G. Webster of Rochester to Susan Ambrose of Concord.

11. Hial Proctor to Louis Haynes, both of Dunstable.

11. John Emerson to Mary A. Stevens, both of Concord.

25. Daniel Arlin, Jun. to Mrs. Jane Ferrin, both of Concord.

July 6. John Estabrook to Emeline Abbot, both of Concord.

21. George Mills to Abigail Sargent, both of Concord.

Oct. 27. Elijah Colby to Susan Eastman, both of Concord.

Nov. 4. Oliver L. Sanborn to Mary Sherburne, both of Concord.

26. John Carter, Jr. to Margaret Dow, both of Concord.

Dec. 24. Jeremiah Chandler to Fidelia E. Chase, both of Concord.

1829. Dec. 31. Dudley S. Palmer to Esther Wilkins, both of Concord.

1830. Jan. 14. Carleton G. Ward to Betsey Brown, both of Concord.

Feb. 9. Smith Lawrence of Meredith to Miranda Wilson of New Boston.

March 11. Charles Cross of Canterbury to Rebecca M. Hoyt, of Concord.

April 16. Charles H. Crandall, of North Brookfield, Mass. to Elsy Chase of Concord.

25. Horatio Hill to Clarissa W. Emery, both of Concord.

29. Nathaniel C. Elliot to Sophia Austin, both of Concord.

May 11. Spencer Beatley of Boston, Mass. to Mary B. Porter of Concord.

25. Mark Tarbox of Stoddard to Susan Abbot of Concord.

June 10. Henry Moulton, Jr. to Maria Page, both of Hooksett.

July 12. Rev. Moses G. Thomas to Mary Jane Kent, both of Concord.

14. Seth Eastman to Sarah Coffin, both of Concord.

Aug. 24. James Powell to Parna B. Sargeant, both of Concord.

31. Thomas J. Elliot to Julia A. Frost, both of Boscawen.

Sept. 17. Simeon C. Gleason of Mexico, Me. to Lydia Osgood of Concord.

22. Francis W. Tucker of Canton, Mass. to Prudence Hoit of Concord.

Oct. 17. Stephen Mascall, Jr. of Bevely, Mass. to Mary K. Stevens of Loudon.

Nov. 17. John Hanniford, Jr. of Northfield to Nancy Flanders of Concord.

25. Moses Clement, Jr. of Salisbury to Cynthia Wilkins of Concord.

25. Joseph Graham to Lucinda Lovering, both of Concord.

Dec. 21. Alfred C. Abbot to Sarah B. Knowles, both of Concord.

1831. Jany 17. Seth Judkins of Bow to Phebe Abbot of Concord.

FIRST CONGREGATIONAL CHURCH RECORDS, ROCHESTER, N. H.

BAPTISMS BY REV. JOSEPH HAVEN.

[Continued from Vol. VI, page 176.]

1792 May 9th Edmund, Son of Sam¹ Furber   Thomas, Son of Ezekiel Ricker   Nabby, Daughter of Ephraim Kimball.   Polly, Daughter of Sam¹ Furber.

June 3d Ebenezer, Son of John Musset Place

June 10th Mercy, Daughter of Ichabod Wentworth.

July 8th Abigail, Daughter to Joseph Page

July 22d Lydia White, Daughter to Dan¹ Wingate Junʳ

July 29th Mary, Daughter of John Raynel

August 5th Ruthy, Daughter to Joseph Haven

Septʳ 30th Olly, Daughter of Enoch Burnham

Novʳ 4th Isaac, Son of Thoˢ Pinkham.   Susa, Daughter of Benj. Forst.

Novʳ 11th James, Son of John Richards Junʳ   Sarah, Abigail & Elizabeth Daughters of John Richards Junʳ

Decʳ 9th Benjamin, Son of Benj. Page

1793 Febʳ 28th Baptized at the House of Capt James Adams his Children; the Sons named, 1st Benjamin, 2d Amos, 3d Augustus, 4th James, 5th Jesse, the Daughter named Elizabeth

April 25th Baptized a Daughter of Ichabod Hill by the Name of Betsy.

June 22d Baptized Amos, Son to Dan¹ Wingate   Baptized Abigail, Daughter to Wᵐ Leighton

July 7th Baptized, Walter Briant, Son to Hatevil Knight

July 14th Baptized, Rebecca, Daughter to James Wentworth   Baptd Mary McDuffe, Daughter to David Corson

Septʳ 22d Baptized Jenny Daughter to Joseph Tucker

Septʳ 29th Baptized, Mercy Daughter to Eleazer Ham

1793 Nancy, Daughter of Joseph Clark

Novʳ 12th John, Son to Sam¹ Jenness   Mercy, Daughter to Sam¹ Hayes

Decʳ 29th Joseph Hilliard, Son of Joshua Lane

28   ROCHESTER BAPTISMS.

1794   April 10th   Benjamin, Son of Benj. Scates   Olly, Daughter of Joseph Hoit

June 4th   Lydia, Daughter of Nath¹ Heard   James, Son of Nath¹ Heard

June 8th   Nehemiah, Son of Ephraim Kimball

July 26th   Joshua, Son of Edmond Wingate

August 31st   Benjamin, son of Benj. Page   Noah, son of Joseph Haven

Septr 14th   Debby, Daughter to James Chesley

Septr 28th   Martha, Daughter to Ichabod Wentworth

Octr 7th   An infant, daughter to Abner Hodgdon

Octr 19th   Enoch, Son of Enoch Burnham   Nathaniel, Son of Eleazer Hodgdon

Novr 24th   William, Son of Ezekiel Ricker

Decr 14th   Joshua Paine, son of Joseph Clark

1795   May 10th   Lydia, Daughter of Dummer Farnum

June 11th   Joseph Willard, son of Dr James How

July 12th   William, John, Sons of Dan¹ Calf   Susanna, Daughter of Dan¹ Calf.

July 19th   Mary Dole, Daughter of Hatevil Knight

July 20th   Thomas Furbur Junr by his own desire

August 23d   Sarah, daughter of Joseph Page, baptized by Mr Thurston

August 28th   Hannah Twombly, (aged 29 years) upon her confession of Faith in Christ

Septr 13th   Daniel Gardener, Son of Dan¹ Wingate

Octr 22d   Anna, Daughter of Levi Dearborn Esqr

Novr 29th   Edward Bell, son of Edward Cole

Decr 3d   Phineas, son to Ezekiel Ricker   William, Son to Sam¹ Jennes

Decr 17th   Phebe Heard, daughter of Joshua Rollins

1796   Febr 7th   Jacob Main, upon his confession of faith in Christ

May 18th   Patience Seavey, Daughter of Sam¹ Doust Forst

May 28th   John, son of Wm Leighton.

June 22d   Ichabod Hayes, Son to Wm Wentworth   Mehetabel, Daughter of Dudley Burnham

June 30th   Samuel & Peter, Sons to David Wallingford Anna, Daughter to Elijah Horn. Abigail, Daughter to David Wallingford

Septr 4th   William Messer, upon his confession of Faith in Christ. Nathaniel, Son of the above Wm Messer

1796 Octr 9th Joshua, Son of Joshua Lane ⎫ by the Rev^d
William, Son of Benj. Furbur ⎭ Mr Gray
1797 Feb^r 23^d John, Son of Ephraim Kimball Sarah,
Daughter of Saml Jennes
May 14th Martha Burleigh, Daughter of Joseph Clark,
by the Revd Benj. Balch, of Barrington
June 12th John Carter, Grandson to Dodavi Garland
Sally, Grandaughter to Dodavi Garland, this child with
John Carter adopted by Said Garland
July 30th Sally Nowell, and Nancy, Daughters of Benj.
Evens
Septr 10th Richard, Son of John Musset Place Sarah
Fisher, Daughter of Joseph Haven
Septr 28th Nathaniel Horn, Son of Nathl Heard Hannah,
Daughter of Nathl Heard
Octr 22^d Jonathan, Son of Eleazer Ham, (by Mr Hilliard)
1798 Feb^r 16th Luke, Son of Saml Furbur
June 17th John Wingate, Son of Richard Furbur Junr
(by Mr Thomson)
June 24. Lois, Daughter of Silas Dame, by Mr Balch of
Barrington.
Septr 16th Elizabeth, Daughter of Wm Conner, by Rev^d
Robert Gray.
1799 Feb^r 20th Mark Huntress, upon his making his confession of Faith Liberty, Daughter of Abner Hodgdon
Elizabeth Emersom, Daughter of Mark Huntress Dolly
Daughter of Mark Huntress Henrietta, Daughter of
Mark Huntress Joseph Peterson, Son of Mark Huntress John, Son of Mark Huntress Joshua, Son of
Stephen Brewster Rosietta, Daughter of Stephen Brewster Eliza, Daughter of Stephen Brewster
July 7th Rufus King, Son of Benj. Evans Wealthy,
Daughter of Benj. Page
1800 Feb^r 17th Benjamin Heard, Son of Joshua Rollins
Joshua Nutter, Son of Joshua Rollins
April 13th Phebe Heard ⎫ twin Daughters of Joshua Rollins
Hannah Heard ⎭ lins
April 27th Rachel, Daughter of Elijah Horn
May 12th Stephen Twombly, upon a Sick bed, upon his
confession of his Faith in Christ & the Christian Religion.
May 17th John Smith Bryant, Son of Hatevil Knight.

1800   June 19th   Stephen, Son of Stephen Twombly   Anna & Betty Daughters of Stephen Twombly

Octr 12th   James, Son of Eleazer Ham

Octr 26th   John Place, Son of Benj. Evans.

Novr 30th   Jabez, Son of Caleb Dame   Anna, Daughter of Caleb Dame

1801   Septr 27th   Solomon Perkins, & at the Same time received him into full Communion with ye Chh

Octr 18th   John Musset, Son of John Musset Place

Novr 1st   Elizabeth Furbur, Daughter of Stephen Place

1802   Jan^r 5th   Rachel, Daughter of Widow Alice Horn.

Feb^r 24th   Thomas Downs, Son of Moses Downs.

July 11th   Joseph, Son of Benj. Page.

July 18th   Elizabeth, Daughter of Capt Saml Furbur Eleanor Cooper, Daughter of Ephraim Kimbal

August 19th   Reuben Hanniford & his Wife, Sarah   Levi Dearborn, Son of Reuben Hanniford   John Prentice, Son of Saml Adams   John Brewster, Son of Thomas Chesley

Octr 17th   Peter, Son of Widow Alice Horn; (By Mr Piper)   Elizabeth Downing, Daughter of Widow Alice Horn by Mr Piper

Octr 24th   Meribah Emery, Daughter of Caleb Dame

1803   Feb^r 14th   Elizabeth Lewis Prentis, Daughter of Moses L. Neal

Feb^r 20th   Thomas, & Vincent, Sons of Thomas Pinkham Rebecca, Daughter of Thomas Pinkham

March 14th   John, Son of John Brewster Junr

July 7th   Moses Leavitt; John Prentis & Samuel Adams, all Sons of Moses L. Neal.

Octr 2^d   Baptized—Mary, Daughter of Nathl Upham

Octr 23^d   Polly, daughter of Silas Dame

1804   March 14th   Betty, Daughter of John Brewster Junr

May 13th   Nancy, a Negress, called Nancy Patterson, by her desire, & upon her confession of faith in the Christian religion, or doctrines of the Gospel.

June 10th   Joseph Lemmon, Son of Moses L. Neal Esqr Susanna, Daughter of Stephen Place. Elizabeth Dennett, Daughter of Thos Chesley.

June 17th   Samuel, Son of Samuel Adams, (of Durham)

Septr 16th   Alfred, Son of Nathl Upham

1805   Jany 18th   Sally, daughter of John M. Place.

May 24th   Anne Hilton, daughter of Reuben Hanniford

1805   July 24th   Mary, Wife of Ichabod Corson, upon her bed, being almost exhausted with consumption

Sept[r] 8th   Abigail Roberts, daughter of Edmond Wingate

Sept[r] 22[d]   Joseph, Son of Silas Dame

Sept[r] 29th   Sally, & John, a daughter & Son of Stephen Brewster

1806   May 25th   Charles, Son of Stephen Place

June 8th   James Armstrong, Son of Moses L. Neal

July 6th   George, Son of John Haven

Sept[r] 28th   Son of Joseph Clark Esq[r] by the Name of Simon

Oct[r] 19th   James, Son of Thomas Chesley.

Dec[r] 15th   Baptized the widow Anne Clark upon her confession of her faith in Christ & his gospel; She being Sick & in danger; but appearing to be under due concern for her Spiritual interest. Her age 72 Years

1807   May 31st   Baptized Timothy, Son of Nath[l] Upham

August 30th   Baptized Elizabeth, daughter of Benj. Page

1808   Oct[r] 9th   Rev[d] Isaac Smith baptized James Horn, Son of Stephen Place

1809   Jan[r] 19th   Baptized the widow Hannah Rogers of Rochester, on a Sick bed, upon her confession of her faith in Jesus Christ & hopes of glory thro' him.

Jan[r] 28th   Baptized Comfort Trickey upon a sick bed, upon her confession of faith in Christ Jesus and hopes of Salvation thro' him

August 13th   Baptized James Willard, Son of John Haven

August 20th   Baptized Sarah Ann, Daughter of Josepl Clark Esq[r] baptized Joseph Badger, Son of Nath[l] Upham Esq[r]

Oct[r] 8th   Elijah, & Daniel Wentworth, Sons of Elijah Horn of Milton

1810   April 22[d]   Baptized Cornelia, Daughter of Oliver Crosby Esq[r] of Dover, & at Dover.

August 19th   Baptized, Lois, daughter of John Richards, by her own desire

Oct[r] 4th   Baptized of the Children of Ens[n] Nath[l] Hayes, at a Lecture; Nabby, Wife of Thomas Downs Jun[r] Sons, Ezra, & Zenus; Daughters, besides Nabby, above recorded, Sabra, Hannah, & Lucinda.

Oct[r] 7th   John, Son to John Haven

1811   April 5th   Mary Elizabeth, Daughter of Joseph Hanson of Durham

1811   June 9th   Judith Almira, Daughter of Nathl Upham
       Esqr
       August 22^d   Lucy Elvira, Daughter of Joseph Clark Esqr
       Septr 29th   Anna, Wife to Paul Downs
       Octr 13th   Hannah & Jonas Children of Paul Downs
       James, Son of Thos Downs Junr
1812   Jan^r 22^d   Ephraim Hammet upon a bed of Sickness
       & danger, upon his declaring his repentance & faith in
       Jesus Christ, & trust in his merits for eternal Life
       March 10th   Baptized Thomas Plumer, 72 Years of age,
       he being much out of health; upon his professing his
       faith in Jesus Christ, his repentance, & resolution to
       lead a pious & holy life So long as he lives.
       Novr 2^d   Baptized Noah Horn of Farmington, upon his
       professing his Faith in Jesus Christ, & his gospel &
       resolution to lead a Cristian & holy life.
       Decr 3^d   Easter, Abigail, Rebecca, and Mary, Daughters
       of Noah Horn   Baptized Jonathan, Son of Noah Horn,
       with the above Daughters of Said Horn   Baptized
       Mary Ann, & Tryphena Berry, Daughters of Lieu^t
       James Pickering Junr of Rochester
1813   July 4th   Baptized John Burnham, Son of Joseph
       Hanson, of Durham.   Baptized Mary Wingate, Daugh-
       ter of Pierce P. Furbur of Farmington.
       July 14th   Baptized Deborah, Wife of Wm Palmer Esqr
       of Milton upon a Sick bed.
       August 25th   Baptized Joanna, Wife of Thomas Davis,
       when She was Sick, of Farmington.
       August 26th   Baptized Mary Esther, Charles William,
       Jeremiah Hall, & Sarah Tebbets, Children of Jeremiah
       H. Woodman
1814   June 19th   Baptized Molly Perkins, Daughter of
       Paul Downs
1815   Jan^r 22^d   Samuel Augustus, Son of John Parker
       Hale Esqr
       May 12th   Henry, Son of John P. Hale Esqr
       Sep^t 4th   Baptized Theodore Chase, Son of Jeremiah H.
       Woodman
       June 11th   Baptized Nathaniel Hayes, Son of Thos
       Downs
1816   Feb^r 18th   Baptized Ruth Cogswell, Daughter of
       Nathl Upham Esqr
       June 23^d   Baptized Ely, Son of Paul Downs

GEORGE FREDERICK EVANS.

IN MEMORIAM.

[The following memorial addresses were delivered by Hon. Joseph Burbeen Walker, of Concord, N. H., September 2, 1909 at the Annual Court of the Society of Colonial Wars in the State of New Hampshire and are published at the request of the said society.]

Two valued members of the Society of Colonial Wars in the State of New Hampshire passed from earthly life during the last year:—George Frederick Evans, of Portland, Me., on the 10th day of January, 1908, and Henry Oakes Kent, of Lancaster, on the 21st of March, 1909.

GEORGE FREDERICK EVANS.

George Frederick Evans, son of Elias and Mary (Pierce) Evans, was born in Concord on the 11th day of March, 1845. He was educated in the public schools of his native city and graduated from its High School in 1862, as the Salutatorian of his class.

He soon afterwards entered the office of Col. J. M. Macomb, of the United States Army Corps of Engineers, at Portsmouth, where, for the next four years, he devoted his attention to the study and practice of civil engineering, with the exception of a brief service as timekeeper in the machine shops of the Northern Railroad, at Concord.

In 1867, he went west, where he gave himself to professional work. From this, he was diverted, in 1881, by appointments to the offices of Secretary and Treasurer of the Louisville, Evansville and St. Louis Railroad. Three years later he was made manager of its operating and traffic departments. All these positions were, at this time, owing to the condition of the road, of unusual importance, demanding great ability on the part of the incumbent and accompanied with large responsibility. In 1885, he was also made its Receiver and General Manager by Judge Gresham of the United States Circuit Court. By his exertions, and to his high credit, as well as to the satisfaction of its stockholders, he succeeded in relieving this important thoroughfare from its embarrassments and in making it self-sustaining. Later, in 1892, his attachment to New England seems to have led

to his return thereto. Here he served for a time as Assistant
General Manager of the Boston and Maine Railroad and as
Superintendant of its Southern Division.

The railroads in Maine, as elsewhere, originally consisted
of independent lines, constructed generally by local enterprise to meet local wants. They were built with little reference to each other, or to afford, by combined efforts, general
accommodations to large sections. Their operations were
largely governed by limited considerations, at times in sharp
competition with one another, and not unfrequently with little, if any, pecuniary profit to their stockholders.

To improve this undesirable condition, a combination of
neighboring lines was proposed. It was begun in 1862, by the
consolidation of the Androscoggin and Kennebec and the Penobscot and Kennebec corporations, into one general system,
since greatly enlarged and now known as The Maine Central
Railroad. In 1896, this consisted of four separate lines owned
by this railroad, and of nine leased lines; the thirteen having
an aggregate length of a little over eight hundred miles.

Upon the retirement of Mr. Payson Tucker, in 1896, from
the position of General Manager of this important system, a
successor, competent to the discharge of its arduous, compli-
cated and at times delicate duties, was sought with no little
anxiety. To persons conversant with the high reputation
as an organizer and manager of such property which Mr.
Evans had brought with him from the west, it seems natural
that early attention should have been focused upon him;
that he should have been appointed General Manager of the
System, and elected, a little later, one of its Vice-Presidents.

In this action, the Directors of the Maine Central Railroad
system made no mistake. In addition to high integrity,
courage, reliable judgment and kindliness of interest in the
welfare of all with whom he had to deal, he posessed a rare
faculty of clearly comprehending and remedying the intri-
cate and adverse conditions so often experienced in the reor-
ganization of extensive systems of railway transportation.
By the patient exercise of these qualities for a continuous
period of a dozen years, he gained and held the confidence
of his superior officers, the respect of the public and the
loyalty of the large corps of employees who co-operated with
him in making his administration a success.

On the 10th of January, 1908, Vice-President and General
Manager Evans was at Vanceboro, Maine, having just com-

pleted a careful inspection of several sections of his road. While reading a paper which he held in his hand, quick as a lightning flash he fell upon the floor in instant death. The report of his unanticipated demise caused a painful shock to thousands who had known him personally or by reputation. As the car which bore his lifeless body to his home in Portland proceeded on its way, it was given mournful welcome at each successive station by companies of employees and citizens, who manifested by low tones and sad looks their high regard, and a deep sense of their loss, of a valued friend and fellow citizen.

A little later, on the day of his obsequies, the whole Maine Central System by a general impulse gave mute expression of its sorrow for the loss of its chief executive officer. Precisely at eleven o'clock, A. M., and for a limited time thereafter, the revolution of every wheel in all its machine shops was arrested; every office connected with it was closed and every engine and car, wherever at that time it chanced to be,—in village, open country or densest forest—stood still, all the way from the Piscataqua to the St. Croix and from the head waters of the Penobscot and the Kennebec to the Atlantic shore; while, during the same period, the several financial institutions of Portland with which he was connected manifested a like regard by a suspension of their usual business.

Although the earthly activities of Vice-President and General Manager Evans have ceased, his achievements still live, in accordance with the Divine law, whereby "God buries his workmen but carries on their work."

COL. HENRY OAKES KENT.

Col. Henry Oakes Kent was of the seventh generation in descent from Thomas Kent, who came to this country and settled at Gloucester, Mass., at some time prior to 1643. His father was Richard P. Kent, who came to Lancester in 1825, where he served for a time as a clerk in a store of Royal Joslyn and subsequently became one of the town's most enterprising and influential citizens. Of his three sons, the subject of this sketch was the oldest and was born in Lancaster on the 3rd day of February, 1834. He received his preliminary education in the schools of his native town and went thence to Norwich, Vt. (now Northfield) University, at which he graduated in 1854. Soon after returning to

Lancaster, he became a student of law in the office of the
Hon. Jacob Benton and, upon completing the required course
of study, was admitted to the bar in 1858.

Here, in his native town, Col. Kent established his home
and set up his household gods. Possessing a taste for
journalism, he soon became the editor and publisher of the
Coos Republican, a position which he held for the succeeding
twelve years. This brought him into close touch with the
various interests of the town. To the promotion of these he
contributed liberally of his time and sympathy. In 1861
and 1862 he served as moderator of the town meetings.
For a time, he was clerk of the Lancaster Fire Engine Company, and, from 1869 to 1871, was a fire warden. He was
also, for a time, treasurer of the Lancaster Bridge Company
and of the Coos Agricultural Society. In 1884 he was made
chairman of the committe in charge of the Soldier's Park.
He was prominent in Masonry, and in 1898 was chosen a
warden of St. Paul's Episcopal Church. In larger measure,
however, than to any of these, his attention was given to the
responsible duties attaching to the Presidency of the Lancaster Savings Bank and of the Lancaster Trust Company.

But multifarious as were these home duties he found time
to render important service to the State. He was Assistant
Clerk of the House of Representatives in 1855 and 1856;
Clerk, from 1857 to 1859; and in 1862, 1868, 1869, and
1883, was a Representative of his town in that body. He
was twice the Democratic Candidate for Governor and several
times for Member of Congress from his district.

All through the Civil War, Col. Kent was an active friend
of the Union cause, and was commissioned Colonel of the
17th New Hampshire Regiment. He later became a Liberal
Republican and supported Horace Greely for President in
1872. Still later, he joined the Democratic party and served
as United States Naval Officer, at Boston, from 1885 to 1890.

He was also interested in American history and was a
valued member of the Sons of the American Revolution, of
the Society of the Cincinnati and of the Society of Colonial
Wars in the State of New Hampshire, being Governor of the
latter from 1894 to 1900.

Col. Kent possessed an attractive personality and a wide
knowledge of mankind and of affairs. His business life was
of continuous activity for half a century. He died on the
21st of March, 1909, at the mature age of seventy-five years.

NEWMARKET TOWN RECORDS.

BIRTHS, MARRIAGES AND DEATHS.

[Continued from Vol. VI, page 160.]

Rockingham ss. Newmarket, N. H. March 19th 1829.
This certifies that on this 19th day of March A. D. 1829
Mr. William A. Shackford and Miss Entwinett C. Lanveat
both of Newmarket aforesaid were duly joined in the ordinance of Marriage as the law directs.

By me Samuel Kelley, V. D. M.

A copy, James Coleman, Town Clerk.

(N. T. R., II: 501.)

Died in Newmarket February 24, 1850 Phebe A. Blair wife
of William Blair aged 26 years and 9 mos.

(N. T. R., II: 514.)

Marriages Solemnized by Revd David Sanford.

1828. August 10th Mr. Ebenezer Meserve to Miss Olive
Jane Pickering Both of Newmarket.

April 17. Mr. John Marsh to Miss Abigail Thomas both
of Durham.

Octo. 5. Mr. Daniel Jewell to Miss Clarissa Cox Both of
this town.

Novr 9. Capt Nathaniel E. Burley to Miss Mary Ann
Hilton Both of Newmarket.

Decr 9. Mr. James G. Page to Miss Maria Davis both of
this town.

Decr 16. Mr. Alexander Whipple to Miss Dorothy Shepard of this town.

25. Capt. James Pickering to Mrs. Elizabeth Flanders
of this Town.

1829. Jany 18. Mr. Dana Ballard of Somersworth Great
Falls to Miss Mary Ann Tarlton of Newmarket.

Marriages Solemnized by David Murray, Esq.

Mr. Ebenezer H. Hanscomb and Miss Deborah G. York
both of Newmarket were married together this day before me

David Murray, Justice of the Peace.

Newmarket March 13th 1830.

A true copy attest, D. Murray, Ju^s Peace.

(N. T. R., II: 515.)

Married in Newmarket Mr. Joseph Smith of Salem, Mass. to Miss Sarah Colcord of Newmarket. Newmarket August 22ᵈ 1830. By me   Willᵐ Rowland.
Attest,   James Coleman, Town Clerk.
Newmarket, N. H. August 27ᵗʰ 1832.
Married in this town Mr. John Johnson to Miss Mary S. Fernald both of Dover N. H. by E. W. Stickney, minister in the Methodist E. Church at Lamprey River.
A true copy, attest,   James Coleman, Town Clerk.
(N. T. R., II: 516.)
Newmarket Sept. 10ᵗʰ 1829.
State of New Hampshire, County of Rockingham.
To whom it may concern this certifies that on this 10ᵗʰ day of Septʳ 1829 Mr. Henry Baker & Miss Susan Murrey both of Newmarket were duly Joined in marriage by me as the law directs.
Samuel Kelley, V. D. M.
Town of Newmarket. Rockingham ss. State of New Hampshire. To whom it may concern that on this 18ᵗʰ day of January, A. D. 1830, Mʳ John Folsom, Esq. of Raymond and Miss Sally Pillsbury of Newmarket both of the County & State aforesaid were Joined in the ordinance of marriage as the law directs. By me   Samuel Kelley, V. D. M.
Janʸ 18ᵗʰ 1830.
A copy, attest,   James Coleman, Town Clerk.
The marriage of Mr. George P. Kelley of Stratham and Miss Martha Speed of Newmarket was Solemnized Oct. 7ᵗʰ 1832 in Newmarket, N. H. by   E. W. Stickney.
Attest, a copy,   James Coleman, Town Clerk.
(N. T. R., II: 517.)
Marriages of J. Brodhead.
Married Doct. Enoch Faulkner of Hamilton, Mass. to Miss Mary Louisa Lord of Newmarket in September 1812.
Doct. Daniel Cook of Waterville, Me. to Miss Clarissa Watson of Newmarket, January 1813.
Mr. David Godfrey to Miss Sally Pinder both of Exeter in June 1815.
Mr. Peter Hersey to Miss Mahala Wood both of Newmarket on March 4ᵗʰ 1816.
Mr. Moody Smith to Miss Charlotte Durgin both of Newmarket April 11, 1816.
Mr. Warren Smith to Miss Susannah Chapman both of Newmarket July 21, 1816.

Mr. Thomas Pendergrass to Miss Charlotte Smart both of Newmarket April 6, 1816.

Tho⁸ Pendergast & Charlotte Smart Ap¹ 6, 1817.

Mr. Ebenezer Flanders to Miss Nancy Pinder both of Sandown, May 10, 1817.

Mr. Stephen Nudd to Miss Elizabeth Wiggin, both of Durham Sept. 20, 1817.

Mr. James Burley 3ᵈ to Miss Martha Watson both of Newmarket Dec. 21, 1817.

Mr. James Weston of Bloomfield, Me. to Miss Betsey S. Smith of Newmarket March 3ᵈ 1818.

Mr. Phineas Willey of Durham to Miss Welthen Sias of Newmarket, March 25, 1818.

Mr. George Ayres of Barnstead to Miss Phenney Brackett of Newmarket, Sep. 29, 1818.

(N. T. R., II: 518.)

Mr. Moody Smith to Miss Sally P. Smith both of Newmarket, Dec. 15, 1818.

Mr. Benjamin Watson of Northwood to Miss Rebecca Chapman of Lee, Dec. 31, 1818.

Mr. Nathan Preston of Newmarket to Miss Eliza Downing of Durham, March 19, 1819.

Mr. John Ayre 3ᵈ of Greenland to Miss Lydia Brackett of Newmarket, March 31, 1819.

Mr. Joseph R. Doe to Miss Sarah Gains both of Newmarket, April 15, 1819.

Abner P. Stinson Esqʳ to Mrs. Olive R. Neil both of Newmarket, July 21, 1819.

Mr. Thomas Dodge of Portland, Me. to Miss Betsy Smith of Newmarket, October 21, 1819.

Mr. John Edgerly of Durham to Miss Mary Langley of Newmarket, Nov. 6, 1819.

Mr. Nathan Smith of East Kingston to Miss Martha H. Pillsbury of South Hampton, November 14, 1819.

Mr. John Marsh to Miss Betsy Osgood both of Exeter, Nov-28, 1819.

Mr. Edmund Pillsbury to Miss Eliza D. Barnard both of South Hampton, December 2ᵈ 1819.

Mr. Thomas Chapman of Greenland to Miss Almira Robinson of Newmarket, February 1, 1820.

Hon. William Plumer Jr. of Epping to Miss Margaret F. Mead of Newmarket, Sept. 19, 1820.

(N. T. R., II: 519.)

Mr. John C. Fowler of Newmarket to Miss Mary Nutter of Newington, April 2, [torn]

Capt Robert Clark to Mrs. Hannah Fowler both of Newmarket April 4, 1822.

Henry Wiggin Esq. to Miss Olive Smith both of Newmarket, Nov. 18, 1820.

Mr. James Thurston to Miss Deborah Cha[se torn] both of Epping, April 5, 1822.

Mr. Johnathan Davis of Brentwood to Miss Mary S. Tetherly of Newmarket, April 27, 1822.

Mr. Thomas B. Hall to Miss Mehitable Bennett both of Newmarket, March 12, 1821.

Mr. Jeremiah Sanborn to Miss Mehitable Wiggin both of Epping, Sept. 20, 1822.

Mr. John Kelley of Exeter to Miss Mary Ann Henderson of Durham, December 4, 1822.

Mr. Temple Paul to Miss Susan W. Burleigh both of Newmarket, Dec. 8, 182[2 torn]

Mr. Nathan B. Wiggin of Boston to Miss Deborah Wentworth of Newmarket, January 8, 1823.

Mr. Nathan Smith to Miss Sally Kenniston both of Epping, Jan. 3ᵈ 1823.

Mr. Noah Thompson of Lee to Miss Susan Kelsey of Nottingham, Jan. 13, 1823.

Mr. George Robinson of Greenland to Miss Betsy Watson of Newmarket [date cut off in trimming book]

(N. T. R., II: 520.)

Mr. Henry Gilman to Mrs. Mahala Hersey both of Newmarket, April 16, 1823.

Revᵈ Samuel Norris of Barre, Vermont to Miss Elizabeth H. Brodhead of Newmarket, August 30, 1823.

Mr. Thomas I. Clark to Miss Priscilla C. Lang both of Stratham, Oct. 12, 1823.

Doct. George W. Gale to Miss Ruth Wood both of Newmarket, Nov. 12, 1823.

Mr. Theodore Hilton to Miss Polly Butler both of Deerfield, Nov. 19, 1823.

Mr. Johnathan Fogg Jr. to Miss Nancy D. Pike both of Epping, Dec. 7, 1823.

Mr. Hall J. Jenness to Miss Marcy H. Tarlton both of Newmarket, Feb. 24, 1824.

Mr. Asa Sandborn of Brookfield to Miss Judith Burley of Newmarket Feb. 24, 1824.

Mr. Thomas Caswell of Barrington, Miss Betsy S. Burleigh of Newmarket, Aug. 1st 1824.

Mr. Hamden Williams of Exeter to Miss Mary G. Smith of Newmarket, Nov. 18, 1824.

Mr. Chase Gilman to Miss Eliza Lawrence both of Epping, Dec. — 1824.

Mr. Hale Stevens of Newmarket to Miss Sally T. Tilton of Exeter Oct. -— 1824.

Mr. Winthrop H. Clerage to Miss Lydia Fullington both of Portsmouth, March — 1825.

(N. T. R., II: 521.)

Births.

Asa Neal.*

Jacob Burley born November 17th 1783.

Lois Burley born July 26th 1798.

Ages of their children:

Jasper H. Burley born April 5th 1812.

Frederic P. Burley born December 25th 1813.

Mary C. Burley born June 7th 1817.

Reuben M. Burley born January 8th 1822.

Abner P. Stinson was born in Bowdoinham, State of Maine May 11, 1794.

Olive R. Neil his wife was born in Newmarket January 1, 1788.

Married July 23, 1819.

Their children:

Harriet Fink & Clarissa Meak Stinson—Twins was born August 29, 1820.

Hannah Coleman Stinson was born Sept. 3^{d} 1821.

Children of David & Nancy Chapman:

Olive H. Chapman born Novr 27th 1807.

John M. Chapman born Septr 6th 1809.

Warren Chapman born July 24th 1812.

Daniel Chapman born August 11th 1814.

Newmarket Novr 14, 1831.

James Coleman, Town Clerk.

Mary Annah Day born September 20th 1829 Daughter of Ephraim & Annah Day.

Newmarket Jan. 20th 1832.

James Coleman, Town Clerk.

Children of Jason & Sarah A. Sawyer.

Sarah Ann Sawyer Sept. 26, 1826.

*Vital Records in Vol. III are not paged.—ED.

Jason Sawyer Nov. 23, 1827.
Moody Kimball Stacy was born July 11 1825.
Sarah Ann Stacy was born April 4th 1827.
Catharine Spofford Stacy was born August 4th 1829.
  Children of Timothy and Sarah Stacy.
  A true copy,   James Coleman, Town Clerk.
      The age of Josiah Burleigh and Family:
Josiah Burleigh senior born May 23^d A. D. 1759, wife Ditto
  1766.
1st Josiah Burley Junr born May 26, A. D. 1792.
2^d Susannah Burleigh born February 3^d A. D. 1794.
3^d Mark Burleigh born August 23rd A. D. 1796.
4th Clarissa Burleigh born July 26th A. D. 1798.
5th Deborah Burleigh born August 29th A. D. 1800.
6th Betsey Burleigh born August 25th A. D. 1802.
7th Jonathan Burleigh born October 9th A. D. 1804.
8th Jeremiah Burleigh born April 19th A. D. 1807.
9th Lavina Burleigh born August 25th 1809.
  A true copy   James Coleman, Town Clerk.
George W. Burleigh was born December 21st 1834 son of
  Peter & Sally Burleigh. Newmarket April 7th 1834.
  Recorded   James Coleman, Town Clerk.
Hyram S. Chapman son of Ebenezer L. & Mary A. Chapman
  born June 30th 1834.
              Newmarket March 22^d 1836.
  A true copy   James Coleman, Town Clerk.
Charles Henry Tetherly son on (of) William and Margaret
  Tetherly born May 30th 1834.
              Newmarket March 24, 1836.
  A true copy   James Coleman, Town Clerk.
George Alfred Walker son of George R. & Ann E. Walker
  born October 1st 1836.
              Newmarket November 25th 1836.
  A true copy   James Coleman, Town Clerk.
      Marriages———By whom Solemnized.
James Brown, Mary Foot—Rev. Thomas Cheswell
Jason Sawyer, Sarah Newhall—Rev. Mr. Lowell, Boston,
  Mass. January 1825.
Jason Sawyer Born at Brinton, Mass. Oct. 1803.
Sarah Newhall, Boston, Born Sept. 21, 1799.
David French of Stratham & Susan Burley of Newmarket
  N. H. were joined in marriage Dec. 13, 1830.
                          O. Tinker.

A true copy   James Coleman, Town Clerk.
Newmarket Sept 22, 1831. John S. Meserve & Ann Hill
were joined in marriage this day.
                                        O. Tinker.
A true copy   James Coleman, Town Clerk.
Nov. 25th 1831. Jeduthen Bruce of Lynn, Mass. & Susan
Hilton of this town, were joined in marriage this day.
                                        O. Tinker.
A true copy   James Coleman, Town Clerk.
Newmarket Decr 26, 1831.   Ebenezer E. Demeret of Mad-
bury & Sophia Young of this town were joined in mar-
riage this day.
                                        O. Tinker.
A true copy   James Coleman, Town Clerk.
Newmarket, Feb. 14, 1832.   Mark Brewster of Somersworth
& Harriet Coonn of this town were this day joined in
marriage.
                                        O. Tinker.
A true copy   James Coleman, Town Clerk.
Newmarket, July 4th 1832.   Ephraim Day & Mariah Weth-
erby of this town were joined in marriage this day.
                                        O. Tinker.
A true copy,   James Coleman, Town Clerk.
Newmarket, July 30th 1832.   James W. Smith & Mehitable
Smart, both of this town, were this day joined in marriage.
                                        O. Tinker.
A true copy,   James Coleman, Town Clerk.
Newmarket, Aug. 26, 1832.   Lemuel Perkins & Maria B.
Young, the former of Strafford & the latter of this town
were this day joined in marriage.
                                        O. Tinker.
A true copy,   James Coleman, Town Clerk.
Mr. George P. Kelly of Stratham to Miss Martha Speed of
Newmarket, Oct. 7th 1833, Rev. Ezekiel W. Stickney.
Mr. Joseph D. Pinder to Miss Hannah Ham, both of New-
market, Nov. 15th 1832, Rev. Ezekiel W. Stickney.
Mr. Christopher Rymes to Miss Louisa Bean, both of New-
market, Nov. 27th 1832, Rev. Ezekiel W. Stickney.
Mr. Stephen Jones to Miss Mary Holt, both of Durham, Decr
11th 1833, Rev. Ezekiel W. Stickney.
Mr. Samuel C. Carlton to Miss Eliza Goodwin, both of New-
market, Jany 7th 1833, Rev. Ezekiel W Stickney.
This may certify that on the 26th ult I joined in marriage

44   NEWMARKET TOWN RECORDS.

Mr. Smith Chapman & Miss Harriet Furnal both of this
town.   Daniel P. Cilley.
Newmarket March 5ᵗʰ 1833.
A true copy,   James Coleman, Town Clerk.
This may certify that on Thursday eve, March the 7ᵗʰ solem-
nized in marriage Mr. William W. Smith, of Lynn, Mass.
and Miss Lavinia A. Sanborn of this place, also Mr.
Joseph H. Smith, and Miss Sarah B. Lamprey, both of
this place.
                               Daniel P. Cilley.
A true copy,   James Coleman, Town Clerk.
Newmarket March 19ᵗʰ 1833.
This certifies that on Sat. eve, March 1ˢᵗ I joined in mar-
riage, Mr. Asa Caverly to Miss Sally Pinkham of New-
market.   Daniel P. Cilley.
A copy,   James Coleman, Town Clerk.
This may certify that on this the 31ˢᵗ day of March A. D.
1833, I Solemnized marriage between Ezekiel Wentworth
and Shuah Carter both of Exeter, they producing their
legal certificate to me.
                  Benjamin B. Tuttle, Justice Peace.
A true copy,   James Coleman, Town Clerk.
This certifies that on April 10, 1833, I joined in marriage
Alexander Ewin and Ann M. Brodhead.
                               John Brodhead.
A true copy,   James Coleman, Town Clerk.
I certify that Mr. Samuel S. Pickering of Durham and Miss
Ann E. Brackett of Greenland were joined in marriage by
me in this town, on the 14ᵗʰ of April, 1833.
               E. Mason, Preacher of the Gospel.
Newmarket, April 16ᵗʰ 1833.
A true copy,   James Coleman, Town Clerk.
This may certify that Mr. John Speed and Miss Sarah Tuck
of this town were agreeably joined in marriage by me, on
the 21ˢᵗ of April, 1833.
               E. Mason, Preacher of the Gospel.
Newmarket, May 10ᵗʰ 1833.
This may certify that on the eleventh day of March, in the
year of our Lord one thousand eight hundred and thirty-
four, John Burley & Sally Perkins both of Newmarket,
were joined in marriage by me.
               Benjamin Loverin, Justice of Peace.
Attest,   James Coleman, Town Clerk.

Newmarket Sept. 9th 1832. Joel Laney and Sarah Weymouth both of this town, were this day joined in marriage.

O. Tinker.

A true copy, James Coleman, Town Clerk.

Jany 14th 1833. William C. Page & Dorcas Felker, were
this day joined in marriage. O. Tinker.

A true copy, James Coleman, Town Clerk.

Newmarket, Jany 22^d 1833. Thomas Leach of Lowell,
Mass. & Sarah Ann Wiggin of this town, were this day
joined in marriage.

O. Tinker.

A true copy, James Coleman, Town Clerk.

Newmarket, Feb. 9th 1833. Thomas Haywood of Portsmouth & Abigail Berry of this town, were this day joined in
marriage.

O. Tinker.

A true copy, James Coleman, Town Clerk.

Newmarket, Feby 28th 1833. Ebenezer Joy of South Berwick, Me. & Mehitable M. Doe of this town were this day
joined in marriage.

O. Tinker.

A true copy, James Coleman, Town Clerk.

Newmarket, April 11th 1833. Jacob Johnson and Betsey
Farnsworth, both of this town were this day joined in
marriage.

O. Tinker.

Newmarket, July 24th 1833. This certifies that Mr. Benjamin Mathes & Miss Abigail Smart, both of Newmarket,
were joined in marriage by me on the 28th inst.

Ossemus Tinker.

A true copy, James Coleman, Town Clerk.

Mr. Coleman, Dear Sir, please record the following marriages.

Dec. 11th 1832. Mr. Stephen Jones, to Mrs. Mary Hall,
both of Durham.

June 22^d 1833. Mr. Alfred Pinkham to Miss Harriet
Burnham, both of Newmarket. By E. W. Stickney.

A true copy, James Coleman, Town Clerk.

Newmarket, Aug. 16th 1833. This certifies that on the
fifteenth of this month, I joined in marriage the following
persons, viz: William B. Glidden of Tuftonboro to Drusilla
B. Pendexter of Dover. John Brodhead.

A true copy, James Coleman, Town Clerk.

THE ORIGIN OF THE NAME PINKHAM.

While it has been said that "the sources from which names are derived and the circumstances which dictated their taking are so numerous as to be beyond all knowledge" yet the origin of a great many have been discovered as the result of careful study and prolonged research.

A number of theories have been advanced relative to the origin of the "Pinkham" name, for the most part these theories are of a superficial nature being based on its modern orthography.

Probably the most striking fact about the name is that its orthography and phonetics are at variance which suggests that the name has not come down to us in its original form.

The early records of Dover, N. H. contain the following variants of the name: (a) Pinckum, (b) Pinckhame, (c) Pincham, (d) Pinkom.

The fact that the name was apparently pronounced like Pinkum or Pinkom by the Dover ancestor and his contemporaries and that "c" or "k" or both were used without discrimination suggested the probability of Pinkum, Pincum, Pinkom, or Pincom being the original form.

Investigation, along the lines suggested, developed the fact that the name "Pincomb" is mentioned by several authorities; one of these states that it was derived from articles of dress; another, the Herald's Visitations of Devonshire shows conclusively the evolution of the name from "Pyncombe" in 1485 to "Pincomb" in 1620, and mentions the following variants of the "Pyncombe" name:—(e) Pincombe, (f) Pincomb, (g) Purcomb, (h) Bincomb.

It will be noted that variants (a) and (d) very closely resemble variant (f) and that the first syllable of variant (c) in conjunction with the last syllable of variant (d) forms "Pincom" which is identical with variant (f) except that the silent "b" is absent.

A careful study of the orthographic and phonetic principles involved, will it is believed, lead to no other conclusion than that "Pyncombe" is the ancient form of the "Pinkham" name.

Variant forms of family names are common, since in those

early days, it was not unusual that a man should write his name in three or four ways, due possibly in some degree to the prevailing lack of education, but in a greater degree to the fact that the orthography of the English language was as yet variable and unsettled.

Writers have classified surnames variously according to their origin as local, official, occupative, baptismal and sobriquet, and the "Pyncombe" name would come under the class entitled "local" as the name was undoubtedly derived from "Pyne" the ancient form of "pine" and "combe" which is "that unwatered portion of a valley which forms its continuation beyond and above the most elevated spring which enters into it," or as another authority has it "a valley or amphitheatre like spot in a hill side," or still another "a cell or hollow in a hill side."

It is said to be typical of the manner in which such surnames first came into use, that if, for instance the given name of the first "Pyncombe" was John, his neighbors would speak of him as "John at the pyne combe," having reference to his hill side home among the pines, soon this would be shortened to John Pyncombe, then as his descendants became scattered they would lose sight of the origin of the name and while retaining the phonetic principle, variant spellings would become common.

FRANK L. PINKHAM,
438 Franklin Street, Wilkinsburg, Penn.

QUERIES.

104. CRAM.—Wanted, the names of the parents of the following persons:

Of Phebe Ann Cram, who married Thomas P. Rich, September 6, 1851, in Haverhill, Mass.

Of Mary J. Cram, who married Henry L. Morrill, August 24, 1854.

Of Lovina Cram, of Derry, N. H., who married Benjamin L. Chase, December 1, 1860. He was born January 3, 1821.

Of Ephraim Cram, who married Ella Copeland, May 31, 1873.

Of Henry Cram, who married Eulthena Kimball, of Walpole, N. H., February 7, 1826.   John G. Cram,
105 Charles Street, Boston, Mass.

105. EPSOM CHURCH RECORDS.—I would be grateful for any information of the Epsom, N. H., Church Records for the years, 1784 to 1813, during the pastorate of Rev. Ebenezer Hasletine. His successor Rev. Jonathan Curtis, evidently had access to them in 1823, as in a pamphlet written at that time he gave the number of admissions, baptisms and deaths.

John M. Moses,
Northwood Ridge, N. H.

106. JONES.—Ellis Jones was born in Hawke, N. H., June 6, 1794, daughter of Jonathan Jones; wanted, the maiden name of her mother.

Wanted, the names of the father and mother of Jonathan Jones, who was living in Hawke, N. H., in 1794.

(Mrs.) Helen M. Barker,
Lawrence, Mass.

DONATIONS.

During the last three months the New Hampshire Genealogical Society has received the following donations in books and pamphlets, for which I am directed to present the grateful thanks of the society.

Donors.	Residence.	Number.
Hon. Arthur G. Whittemore,	Dover,	23
Charles S. Cartland, Esq.,	"	3
Mrs. Hannah C. Tibbetts,	"	6
Fred E. Quimby, Esq.,	"	4
Mr. Charles H. Foss,	"	2
Cambridge Historical Society,	Cambridge, Mass.,	1
Library of Congress,	Washington, D. C.,	2
Frank L. Pinkham, Esq.,	Wilkinsburg, Penn.,	4
John S. Sargent, Esq.,	Chicago, Ill.,	1
University of California,	Berkeley, California,	4
Historical and Philosophical Society of Ohio,	Cincinnati, Ohio,	2

Total, books and pamphlets,	52
Number of previous donations,	8,376

Total, since incorporation of society,	8,428

CHARLES W. TIBBETTS, Librarian.

DR. HENRY RUST PARKER.

(See page 81.)

THE NEW HAMPSHIRE GENEALOGICAL RECORD.

Vol. VII.   Dover, N. H., April, 1910.   No. 2.

THOMAS DOWNES OF DOVER, N. H., AND HIS DESCENDANTS.

By WILLIAM E. D. DOWNES, Ph. D.

[Continued from Vol. VI, page 150.]

17. AARON[5] DOWNES (*Gershom,*[4] *Gershom,*[3] *Thomas,*[2] *Thomas*[1]), of Rochester, N. H., married 1st, Susanna Hammock June 22, 1755, who was baptized September 16, 1767; married 2d, widow Margaret Willey at Dover, N. H., April 11, 1776. The census of 1790 shows two males over and two males under 16, and one female in his family.

18. MOSES,[5] (*Gershom,*[4] *Gershom,*[3] *Thomas,*[2] *Thomas*[1]), of Rochester, husbandman, married 1st, ———; married 2d, October 14, 1779 Elizabeth Trickey; married 3d, September 5, 1792 Mercy Robinson.

Children:

42. i.   JOHN.[6]
43. ii. MOSES.[6]
44. iii. AARON.[6]
45. iv. PAUL.[6]
     v.   SUSANNAH.[6]
     vi. ELIZABETH.[6]
     vii. HANNAH.[6] All the above children were baptized Feb. 4, 1777.
     viii. MARY,[6] bapt. as Molly May 26, 1783; d. Sept. — 1828, aged 44 yrs.; gravestone on Teneriffe; m. William Foss who d. March 27, 1846, aet. 63 yrs. They had children:
          i.   Samuel,[7] m. Eliza Warren.
          ii. Judith,[7] m. Ivory Hanscom.
          iii. Harriet,[7] m. Owen Roberts.
          iv. Eri,[7] d. Oct. — 1828, aet. 5 yrs. 10 mos.
46. ix. THOMAS,[6] bapt. Feb. 24, 1802.

19. GERSHOM,[5] (*Gershom,*[4] *Gershom,*[3] *Thomas,*[2] *Thomas*[1]), of Rochester; married Lydia Tripe or Traip. Census of 1790 shows two males over 16, one under 16 and two females

in the family. A deed dated in 1770 shows wife Lydia and mentions land willed by grandfather Gershom.

Children, 8:

47. i. THOMAS.[6]
48. ii. AARON.[6]

19[a] JAMES,[5] (*Gershom*,[4] *Gershom*,[3] *Thomas*,[2] *Thomas*[1]), of Rochester and Farmington, laborer; married Patience ————. His widow had dowry assigned April 10, 1810. Will of Patience dated June 29, 1821, proved March 25, 1822, names children and grandson James, Jr.

Children:

49. i. JOHN.[6]
50. ii. JAMES.[6]

20. THOMAS,[5] (*Thomas*,[4] *Gershom*,[3] *Thomas*,[2] *Thomas*[1]), of Berwick, Maine, yeoman; selectman for several years; Thomas Downes died January 5, 1815, "who lived in celibacy all his days". Will December 14, 1814, proved March 1815, mentions nephew Thomas Tebbetts and niece Lovicy Tebbetts, and leaves property to Jere. Nock, Rev. Joseph Hilliard, and Ichabod Wentworth.

21. JOSHUA,[5] (*Thomas*,[4] *Gershom*,[3] *Thomas*,[2] *Thomas*[1]), of Berwick, Maine. He was a minute man in 1775; a lieutenant in Capt. Hamilton's company in 1780. He married May 5, 1768 Hannah Nock of Berwick. Census of 1790 shows three males over, two males under 16 and three females in the family.

24. PHINEAS,[5] (*John*,[4] *Gershom*,[3] *Thomas*,[2] *Thomas*[1]), of Hollis, Maine; married December 19, 1771 at Biddeford Mary Dyer. His will December 5, 1811, proved May 10 ,1821 mentions wife Molly, granddaughter Molly Haley, oldest daughter wife of James Haley of Cornish, youngest daughter Olive wife of Abraham Peavey of Phillipsburd. Phineas is on list of soldiers at Little Falls, 1778.

Children:

i. MOLLY,[6] bapt. June 20, 1773 at 1st. Cong. Church, Biddeford, married James Haley of Cornish. Child:
  i. Molly, single in 1811.
ii. OLIVE,[6] m. July 4, 1802, at Buxton, Abraham Peavey of Phillipsburd.

25. REUBEN,[5] (*John*,[4] *Gershom*,[3] *Thomas*,[2] *Thomas*[1]), of Lyman (Coxhall), Maine, yeoman; married July 21, 1774 Hannah Roberts.

Children:

    i.   MOLLY,[6] born Nov. 11, 1774.
51. ii.   JOHN,[6] b. Sept. 10, 1776.
52. iii.   LOVE.[6]
53. iv.   EBENEZER,[6] bapt. No. Par. Chh., Berwick, July 23, 1790.
54. v.   REUBEN,[6] bapt. July 23, 1790.
55. vi.   JACOB,[6] bapt. July 23, 1790.
56. vii. JEDEDIAH.[6]
    viii. MARGARET.[6]
    ix.   HANNAH.[6]

26. GERSHOM,[5] (*John*,[4] *Gershom*,[3] *Thomas*,[2] *Thomas*[1]), of Coxhall, Maine in 1793, yeoman; married Ruth ——

28. POMFRET,[5] (*Richard*,[4] *Gershom*,[3] *Thomas*,[2] *Thomas*[1]), of Lyman, Maine, yeoman; married March 21, 1776 Ruth Meader of Dover, N. H. In list of soldiers at Massabesic, Capt. John Smith's company August 20, 1778. Wife Ruth administered October 31, 1814. Ruth's estate admimistered by Nathan Douglas May 8, 1826.

Children:

57. i.   ISAAC,[6] a joiner, d. 1825; his only property one sixth of reversion of wid. Ruth's dower.
58. ii.   JOSEPH.[6]
59. iii.   JAMES.[6]
   iv.   NANCY.[6]
   v.   MARY,[6] m. Dominicus Neal of Kittery; published April 26, 1806, at K.
   vi.   REBECCA,[6] m. John Hooper, before 1814.

34. PHINEAS,[5] (*Samuel*,[4] *William*,[3] *Thomas*,[2] *Thomas*[1]), of Somersworth, N. H. Estate administered by Moses R. Downs January 20, 1835.

35. JONATHAN,[5] (*Samuel*,[4] *William*,[3] *Thomas*,[2] *Thomas*[1]), of Somersworth, N. H., died May 31, 1835; married April 9, 1795 at Lebanon, Maine, Abigail daughter of Moses and Sobriety (Knox) Ricker, born December 19, 1767, died February 3, 1848.

Children:

60. i.   SAMUEL,[6] b. Aug. 26, 1796.
   ii.   SOPHIA R.,[6] b. July 19, 1798.
61. iii.   MOSES R.,[6] b. June 16, 1802; will Sept. 17, 1858, proved Nov. 1, same year, mentions sister Abigail A. Smith wife of George Smith and sister Sophia R. Downs.
   iv.   JUDITH,[6] b. Sept. 20, 1805; d. May 22, 1864; m. Jacob Whitehouse.
   v.   ABIGAIL ANN,[6] b. Oct. 16, 1810; m. Nov. —, 1829 George J. Smith of Somersworth.
       Children:
       i. Mary Jane.[7]
       ii. Judith.[7]

36. JEDEDIAH,[5] (*William*,[4] *William*,[3] *Thomas*,[2] *Thomas*[1]), of Berwick and Lebanon, Maine; married May 1, 1771 at Berwick, Mary Lord (or May 2 by No. Par. Church record).

A minute man 1775. Census of 1790 shows two males above, one male under 16, and three females in the family.

Child:

62. i. WILLIAM.[6]

37. AARON,[5] (*William*,[4] *William*,[3] *Thomas*,[2] *Thomas*[1]), of Berwick, Maine; married 1st, June 30, 1782 Hannah daughter of Benjamin Nock; married 2d, November 12, 1829 Abigail (Tibbetts) Hanson widow of Peter Hanson. Aaron served in Col. Francis's regiment at Dorchester Heights, November 4, 1776. Estate of widow Abigail administered by Ichabod Goodwin October 6, 1851.

Children:

         i.   SALLY,[6] b. Dec. 25, 1785.
63.   ii.   EDMUND,[6] b. Dec. 10, 1789.
64.   iii.   AARON,[6] b. May 9, 1793.
        iv.   BENJAMIN,[6] b. Aug. 15, 1796, d. at Barnstead, N. H., unmarried Feb. —, 1891.
65.   v.   WILLIAM,[6] b. Nov. 14, 1799.
        vi.   LYDIA,[6] b. Feb. 5, 1803, unmarried.
        vii.   HANNAH,[6] b. Nov. 5, 1805, d. Dec. —, 1861, unmarried.

38. MOSES,[5] (*William*,[4] *William*,[3] *Thomas*,[2] *Thomas*[1]), of Berwick, Maine, yeoman; married Abigail daughter of Nathaniel Nock. His estate was administered by his brother Aaron October 29, 1810. Census of 1790 shows one male above 16 and one female in the family.

Children: (somewhat uncertain except where descendants are mentioned).

66.   i.   OLIVER.[6]
67.   ii.   MOSES.[6]
68.   iii. LEWIS,[6] b. July 11, 1800.
69.   iv.   CHARLES,[6] d. unmarried.
70.   v.   NATHANIEL.[6]
71.   vi.   HIRAM.[6]
        vii. SABRA.[6]

39. WILLIAM,[5] (*William*,[4] *William*,[3] *Thomas*,[2] *Thomas*[1]), of Berwick, Maine; married November 30, 1774 Mercy Nock who married 2d, March 26, 1781 Nathan Lord 3, Son of Ebenezer and Martha (Emery) Lord. "William Downs's son William, of Berwick was killed by a log at Lebanon, Saturday January 31, 1778." (Tate's Diary).

Child:

72. i. LEVI.[6]

40. DANIEL,[5] (*Daniel*,[4] *William*,[3] *Thomas*,[2] *Thomas*[1]), of Berwick, and Lebanon, Maine; married July 10, 1788 Tamson daughter of Jonathan Ricker. He died in 1831-2.

Children:

73. i.   ISAAC.[6]
74. ii. EPHRAIM,[6] b. Oct. 12, 1789.

75. iii. DANIEL,[6] b. in 1791.
    iv. LUCY,[6] b. 1793; m. at Boston, Dec. 7, 1826, William son of
        William and Mary (Stanley) Emery, b. March 29, 1799,
        d. May 8, 1864.
76. v. REUBEN,[6] b. 1795.
    vi. PHEBE,[6] b. June 17, 1797; d. at Roxbury, Mass., March 13,
        1885; m. Ephraim Daniels. Child:
        i. George Snow, b. July 26, 1837 at Roxbury.
    vii. JUDITH,[6] b. May 15, 1799; d. Nov. 16, 1898 at Lebanon,
        Me.; m. May 21, 1827 at Lebanon, (May 29, 1826 by fam-
        ily Bible) Jesse Ricker. Children:
        i. Edmund,[7] b. June 28, 1827, d. July 29, 1849.
        ii. Lucy Ann,[7] b. Oct. 4, 1828, m. Daniel W. Lord.
        iii. Daniel Downes,[7] b. Feb. 6, 1831, d. April 1, 1865 at
            war.
        iv. Tamson Downes,[7] b. Aug. 26, 1832, m. 1. Augustus
            W. Burrill, m. 2. ——— Taber.
        v. Elizabeth Jane,[7] b. June 22, 1835, m. James Murray.
        vi. Clarinda,[7] b. April 16, 1838.
        vii. Sarah F.,[7] b. Dec. 25, 1842, d. Nov. 7, 1847.
    viii. TAMSON,[6] b. 1801, d. 1819 unmar.
77. ix. MARK,[6] b. 1803.

41. STEPHEN,[5] (Daniel,[4] William,[3] Thomas,[2] Thomas[1]),
of Lebanon, Maine, died April 1, 1811; married November
10, 1796 Betsey Jones who was born July 28, 1776, died
July 21, 1858. His widow married 2d, January 24, 1815
Andrew Carr who died October 19, 1817, by whom she had
two children: i. Andrew,[6] born March 10, 1818, died September 12, 1822; ii. Clarissa W.,[6] born June 18, 1816, died
May 11, 1841, married John B. Caverly of Lowell. Betsey
married 3d, June 22, 1826 James Twombly of Milton, N. H.
Stephen's will March 20, 1812 names wife and children.

Children:

i. BETSEY,[6] b. June 8, 1797, d. Jan. 1, 1822, m. May 29, 1817
    John Lord 3, and had children·
    i. Stephen Downes.[7]
    ii. James,[7] whose descendants live at Kennebunk.
ii. ANN,[6] b. Aug. 24, 1799, d. Aug., 1889; m. Jan. 1, 1824 Eben
    Legro; m. 2, John Lord (widower of her two sisters).
78. iii. JOHN JONES,[6] b. Jan. 15, 1802.
    iv. DORCAS D.,[6] b. March 7, 1804 (twin), m. Sept. 16, 1836 at
        Somersworth Moody Haskell of Burlington, Vt., and
        had children: i. Clara W.[7] ii. Delia.[7]
    v. POLLY,[6] b. March 7, 1804 (twin), d. Jan. 6, 1857, m. John
        Lord, Jr. (widower of her sister Betsey) published at
        Lebanon, May 15, 1825, and had children:
        i. John Calvin,[7] of Lebanon.
        ii. Moody,[7] d. unmar.
        iii. Robert,[7] d. unmar.
        iv. Stephen Downes,[7] of Lebanon.
79. vi. FREDERICK GATES,[6] b. May 28, 1806.
    vii. STEPHEN,[6] b. Sept. 6, 1808, d. April 13, 1816.
    viii. MEHALY,[6] b. June 1, 1810, d. April 15, 1811.

42. JOHN,[6] (Moses,[5] Gershom,[4] Gershom,[3] Thomas,[2] Thom-

54 THOMAS DOWNES

as[1]), of Milton, N. H., husbandman, died February 1823; married December 3, 1792 at Rochester, Sarah daughter of John and Charity (Wentworth) Door of Lebanon. His will February 4, proved February 18, 1823 names children.

Children:

    i.   HANNAH,[7] m. Thomas Warren.
    ii. NANCY,[7] m. Moses Stevens.
    iii. DOLLY,[7] d. unmarried.
    iv. SUSAN,[7] m. Benjamin Farnham of Lebanon, Me., published April 15, 1820 at L.
80. v. MOSES.[7]
    vi. SALLY,[7] m. Daniel Hill of Lebanon, published Feb. 8, 1823 at L., and had children: i. John.[8] ii. Warren,[8] m. Betsey Rankins. iii. Sarah,[8] m. Charles Ricker. iv. Hannah,[8] m. Simon Door.
    vii. BETSEY,[7] b. July 15, 1805, d. April 16, 1859; m. 1825, Mark Hunking, son of Nathaniel and Betsey (Connel) Hart, b. Strafford, N. H., Aug. 25, 1807, d. Jan. 2, 1872. Children:
      i. Lydia Ann,[8] b. June 2, 1826.
      ii. John Francis,[8] b. Jan. 4, 1829.
      iii. Mary Jane,[8] b. Sept. 14, 1831.
      iv. Sarah Elizabeth,[8] b. Oct. 28, 1833.
      v. Mark,[8] b. Sept. 14, 1835.
      vi. Daniel Quimby,[8] b. Jan. 4, 1838.
      vii. Sophia Elizabeth,[8] b. July 31, 1841.
      viii. Sarah Abigail,[8] b. March 21, 1842.
      ix. Hannah Susan,[8] b. Sept. 25, 1843.
      x. Albert Nathaniel,[8] b. May —, 1847.
81. viii. STEPHEN,[7] b. Sept. 12, 1808.
82. ix. JAMES DOOR,[7] b. 1815.
    x. SOPHIA,[7] m. Daniel Quimby, no issue.

43. MOSES,[6] (*Moses,*[5] *Gershom,*[4] *Gershom,*[3] *Thomas,*[2] *Thomas*[1]), of Milton, N. H., died November, 1822; married April 5, 1788 at Rochester, Sarah Tripe or (Traip). His will November 1, proved November 29, 1822 names wife and children.

Children:

83. i. WILLIAM,[7] b. March 18, 1788.
    ii. HANNAH,[7] d. at Wolfboro, N. H., June 1, 1863; m. 1, Nov. 3, 1811 John son of Samuel and Sarah (Stone) Wentworth, b. 1790, d. in Prov. Quebec, Sept. 1823. Children: i. Stephen.[8] ii. Mary.[8] iii. Lucy.[8] iv. John.[8] She m. 2, about 1834, Daniel Thompson of Lebanon, by whom she had no issue.
    iii. PEGGY.[7]
84. iv. JAMES.[7]
    v. POLLY,[7] m. Stephen Main and had children: i. William.[8] ii. Lucinda.[8] iii. Irene.[8] iv. Warren W.[8]
    vi. MARIA,[7] m. James Noah Varney of Milton and had children: i. Sarah.[8] ii. Abigail.[8] iii. John Orrin.[8]
    vii. SOPHIA,[7] b. 1807, d. unmar. May 21, 1883, aged 76 yrs.
    viii. SARAH T.,[7] b. Oct.—, 1810, d. April 26, 1881; m. Augustus Jenkins of Milton, d. Jan. 6, 1864. Children: i. Augustus F.[8] ii. George.[8] iii. Charles.[8] iv. Sarah F[8].
    ix. CYNTHIA,[7] d. unmar.
    x. JOHN H.,[7] d. young.

NEWMARKET TOWN RECORDS.

BIRTHS, MARRIAGES AND DEATHS.

[Continued from Vol. VII, page 45.]

Mr. Timothy S. French of Stratham to Miss Mary J. Chapman of Newmarket, Sept. 5, 1833. (N. B.) at which time an infant child born of the bride, was presented to the bridegroom, and owned by him as his heir.

Also, Mr. Moses F. Kimball of Newmarket to Miss Cassandra Merrill of Tuftonboro, Sept. 29th 1833.

Mr. Joseph Bodge of Portsmouth and Miss Sarah Jane Burley of Newmarket Feb. 26th 1834.

Mr. Albert Foster to Miss Lucy B. Chapman Apr. 10, 1834.

The above were joined in marriage by E. W. Stickney. Newmarket June 10th 1835.

James Coleman, Town Clerk.

This certifies that on the 2d Instant, I joined in marriage Mr. Issacher W. Smith to Miss Martha A. Fifield both of Newmarket.

Daniel P. Cilley.

Newmarket Sept. 15, 1834.

A true copy,   attest   James Coleman, Town Clerk.

Married in Newmarket, Decr 11th 1834, Mr. George Jenness to Miss Mary A. H. Corson, both of Newmarket.

Newmarket, Jany 3d 1835.

Daniel P. Cilley.

A true copy, Att.,   James Coleman, Town Clerk.

This certifies that Mr. Calvin Garland of North Hampton and Miss Elizabeth Speed of Newmarket were legally joined in wedlock by the Subscriber, Jany 4th 1835.

William J. Kidder.

Newmarket, January 20th 1835.

A true copy,   James Coleman, Town Clerk.

L. River Jany 23, 1835.

To the Town Clerk.

This may Certify that on the 22d of this month, I married

Mr. Thomas Langley to Miss Charity H. Allard, all of L.
River, at Lamprey River.

Yours, Daniel P. Cilley.

Newmarket Jany 30th 1835.

A copy,   James Coleman, Town Clerk.

This certifies that marriage was legally Solemnized by me
between Mr. Thomas Delmer of Durham and Miss Polly
Perkins of Newmarket, Sept. 12th 1834.

Constantine Blodgett, Minister of the G.

A true copy,   James Coleman, Town Clerk.

This may certify that I legally solemnized marriage between Mr. Samuel B. Clark and Miss Elizabeth Clough both
of Barnstead, Oct. 15th 1834, Newmarket.

Constantine Blodgett, Minister of the Gospel.

A true copy,   James Coleman, Town Clerk.

This may Certify that I solemnized marriage between Mr.
Ezekiel Clark of Barnstead, N. H. and Miss Hannah Littlefield, of Wells, Me. Oct. 15th 1834, Newmarket.

Constantine Blodgett, Minister of the Gospel.

A true copy,   James Coleman, Town Clerk.

This may certify that marriage between Mr. Jeremiah
Moulton of Exeter and Miss Jane P. Watson of Nottingham, was duly solemnized by me, Decr 16, 1834, Newmarket.

Constantine Blodgett, Pastor.

A true copy,   James Coleman, Town Clerk.

This certifies that I Solemnized marriage between Mr.
Joseph Floyd and Miss Eliza Smith, both of Newmarket,
Jany 15th 1835.   Constantine Blodgett, Pastor.

A true copy,   James Coleman, Town Clerk.

This certifies that I Solemnized marriage between Simon
P. Green and Miss Sarah Smith, both of Newmarket, Feb^y
1st 1835.

Constantine Blodgett, Pastor.

A true copy,   James Coleman, Town Clerk.

This certifies that I Solemnized marriage between Mr.
Lyman Morse and Miss Mary P. Smith, both of Newmarket,
Feby 9th 1835.

Constantine Blodgett, Pastor.

A true copy,   James Coleman, Town Clerk.

Asa Neal was born in Newmarket, March 29, 1786.

Rebeka Gale was born in Gilmanton, Mar. 24, 1786.

Married Feb. 28th 1811.

Their Children:

Samuel Neal Born in Newmarket, March 11th 1812.
Daniel Neal Born Oct. 25, 1813.   Died August 19, 1815.
Henry Neal Born Dec. 23, 1815.
Veline Neal Do May 14, 1818.
Asa Neal Jr Do June 10, 1821.
Abigail Neal Do January 6, 1824.
Jonathan Burley was Born October 9th 1804.
Sarah C. Neal was Born September 28th 1807.
      Jonathan Burley was married to Sarah C. Neal, December 28th 1831.
Ann Augusta Burley was born November 14th 1832.
Harrison Gray Burley was born December 9th 1834.
                    Lamprey River June 25th 1835.
This certifies that marriage was legally Solemnized this day between Mr. Daniel Wiggin and Miss Elizabeth Jane Hastings, both of Newmarket.
                        Constantine Blodgett, Pastor.
A true copy,   James Coleman, Town Clerk.
                    Lamprey River June 25th 1835.
This certifies that marriage was Solemnized by me this day between Mr. George O. Davis and Miss Joannah Gerrish both of Newmarket.
                        Constantine Blodgett, Pastor.
A true copy,   Newmarket July 2d 1835.
                        James Coleman, Town Clerk.
Joshua Brackett Treadwell born October 17, 1840 son of Wm H. H. and Martha Treadwell.
Benjamin Franklin Treadwell born June 7, 1842 son of Wm H. H. & Martha Treadwell.
Martha Jane Brackett Treadwell born Aug. 24, 1843 Daughter of Wm H. H. & Martha Treadwell.
John D. Shackford Died April 30, 1844, aged 49.
George Ellridge Churchill Died May 21, 1844, Aged 5 yrs.
Judith Prescott Died April 25, 1844, Aged 91 yrs.
Hannah Sandborn Died May 20, 1844, Aged 52 yrs.
Bradbury F. Jewell Died December 23, 1843, Aged 8 months.
Bradbury Jewell Died April 30, 1844, Aged 37 yrs.
John Marden Died — 1844, Aged —
Thomas Brown Died June 22, 1844, Aged 84 yrs.   Revolutionary Pensioner.
Mary Ellen Harris Died August 4, 1844, aged 1 day.
Cyrus B. Hoitt Died August 8, 1844, aged 1 yr. 15 days, son of W. K. A. & Sarah Hoitt.

Olivera Jane Swain born Feb. 20, 1839, Daughter of Elijah C. & Susan C. Swain.

Mr. Henry Shattuck & Miss Libicy J. Banfield Married August 4, 1844 by Rev. H. N. Taplin.

Mr. James G. Bennett Died Sept. 11, 1844, aged 67.

Mr. George Harrison Smith Died Aug. 26, 1844, aged 21 yrs.

Mehitable C. B. Bunker wife of John Bunker Died September 21, 1844, Aged 27 years.

Olivera Jane Swain Died Oct. 23, 1844, Aged 5 [and] 8/12 years Burned to Death Daughter of Elijah C. & Susan C. Swain.

(N. T. R., V: 1.)

Mr. Ezekiel Sandborn of Epping and Miss Clara J. Lock of this Town, Married Nov. 3, 1844, by Rev. Horatio N. Taplin.

Widow Lydia Lucy died Nov. 23, 1844, Aged 66 years.

Lorindia C. Chapman Born Sept. 16, 1844, Daughter of John F. & Lydia Chapman.

Mr. Samuel Mathes and Miss Abigail Willey both of this Town were married March 31, 1844, By Rev. Samuel Kelley.

Mr. William F. Chapman and Miss Fanny J. Basset both of this Town were married April 27, A. D. 1844, By Rev. Samuel Kelley.

Mr. Eben Tuttle of Dover and Miss Henrietta Tuttle of Newmarket were married June 20, A. D. 1844, By Rev. Samuel Kelley.

Mr. Elijah Harris and Miss Mary Ellen Davis both of Newmarket were married June 23, A. D. 1844, By Rev. Samuel Kelley.

Mr. John O. Langley and Miss Sophia H. Tuttle both of Newmarket were married Sept. 4, 1844, By Rev. Samuel Kelley.

Mr. Elijah Harriss and Miss Sarah A. Chapman both of Newmarket were married October 13, A. D. 1844, By Rev. Samuel Kelley.

Mr. William Thompson of Durham, N. H. and Miss Mary Jane Chapman of Newmarket were married Jany 1, 1845, By Rev. Samuel Kelley.

Mr. David S. Glidden of Lee, N. H. and Miss Charlotte M. Dearborn of Lowell, Mass. were married Feb. 10, 1845, By Rev. Sam. Kelley.

Mr. John Hains & Miss Mary Neal both of this town were married April 7, 1844, By Rev. Elias Hutchins.

(N. T. R., V: 2.)

Mr. Charles Smart and Miss Mary Burleigh both of Newmarket were married April 10, 1844, By Rev. Elias Hutchins.

Mr. Paul Gerrish and Miss Mary Jane Winslow both of Newmarket were married April 21, 1844, By Rev. Elias Hutchins.

Mr. Jonathan S. French and Miss Mary Ann Gilman both of Newmarket were married Feb. 9, 1845.

Mr. John W. Durgin and Miss Roxanna B. York both of Lee were married March 6, 1845, By Rev. Elias Hutchins.

Peter Burleigh Died March 11, 1845, Aged 48 years.

Timothy M. Joy Died March 2, 1845, Aged 9 months Son of Ebenezer & Mehitable M. Joy.

Harriet Eastman Died February -— 1845, Aged 20 years formerly of Conway, N. H.

Mr. Joshua W. Neal and Miss Frances R. Colcord both of this Town were married April 30, 1843, By Rev. E. W. Tucker.

Mr. Chase Wiggin of Exeter & Miss Lydia Ann Neal of Newmarket were married June 13, 1844, By Rev. E. W. Tucker.

Mr. Epps Choate of Boston, Mass. & Miss Ann B. Kennard of Newmarket were married Jany 14, 1845, By Rev. E. W. Tucker.

Mr. Samuel Willis and Miss Lucretia Sinclair both of Exeter, were married April 20, 1845, By Rev. Horatio N. Taplin.

Miss Harriet Morrill of Northwood, N. H. Died April 30, —————— aged 16 years. (N. T. R., V: 3.)

Mrs. Helen St. John Grant, wife of Gilbert A. Grant Esqr and Daughter of Hon. Asa Aikins of West Port, Essex County, N. Y. Died April 16, 1845, Aged 26 years.

Helen St. John Grant, born Oct. 9, 1844, at West Port, New York, Daughter of Gilbert A. and Helen St. John Grant of this Town.

Mr. Charles O. Cumming of Manchester and Miss Abbey W. Lock of this Town were married May 15, 1845, By Rev. Horatio N. Taplin.

Mr. Enoch Bunker Died June 1, 1845, Aged about 70 yrs.

Mr. Sally Smith wife of Capt. Ebenezer Smith Died January 6, 1845, Aged 64 years.

Charles Franklin Brackett Died ———— Aged ———— son of Martha & John Brackett.

Mr. William O'Brine, Irishman Drowned near the Factorie March — 1845, Aged ————

Mary Jane Chapman born October 24, 1825.

Sarah Augusta Chapman born June 11, 1827.

Charles Henry Chapman born Sept. 1, 1829.

Alonzo Y. Chapman born March 10, 1832.

Susan Matilda Marshall Chapman born Oct. 25, 1834.

Albert Foster Chapman born May 1, 1836.

Ann Martha Chapman born August 6, 1838.

Emily Melissa Chapman born Oct. 24, 1840.

Helen Mar Chapman Born May 6, 1842.

Edwin Burtin Chapman Born Jany. 5, 1844.

Children of Jeremiah Y. & Martha Ann Chapman.

Frances Jane Trickey Died June 27, 1845, Aged 74 y. 3 mo. 3 days, Daught. of Henry & Aveline Trickey.

(N. T. R., V: 4.)

Orrin Murray born October 17, 1837.

Henry Hanson Murray born January 18, 1841.

Charles Fabyan Murray born August 5, 1845, Children of Timothy & Mary H. Murray.

Elizabeth Ann Meader born March 24, 1843 Daughter of William & Hannah E. Meader.

Lycurgus E. Gilman Died July 10, 1845, Aged 30 yrs.

Lydia L. Davis wife of Capt. Samuel C. Davis Died July 8, 1845, Aged 52 years.

Nancy Roberts of Mount Vernon, Me. Died July 10, 1845, Aged 17 yrs & 6 Days.

Mrs. Sarah Neal Died July 1, 1845, Aged 86 yrs.

Mrs. Anna Watson Died July 14, 1845, Aged 84 yrs.

Rosswell Hutchins Dearborn son of George W. & Martha Dearborn Died July 24, 1845, Aged 2 years 10 months & 11 Days.

Mr. Edmund Shute and Mary Brock both of Durham were Married August 28, 1845, By Rev. Horatio N. Taplin.

Mr. Andrew Hall Jr. and Mrs. Sally Howard both of this Town were Married Sept. 7, 1845, By Rev. Horatio N. Taplin.

Mr. Nathaniel F. Kimball and Miss. Lydia H. Lock both of this Town were married October 2d 1845, By Rev. Horatio N. Taplin.

Miss Susan N. Speed Died Nov. 5, 1845, Aged 20 years.

(N. T. R., V: 5.)

State of New Hampshire, Rockingham ss.
On the twenty-third day of October in the year eighteen
hund[red] and forty-five at Newmarket in said County
came John Bradford of said Newmarket and Nancy G.
Chomet of Durham in the County of Strafford and State
aforesaid and were lawfully joined in marriage Before me,
James M. Chapman, Justice of the Peace.
A true copy of record,
   Attest,   James M. Chapman, Justice of the Peace.
A true copy,
   Attest,   Timothy Murray, Town Clerk.
Record of a Marriage.
State of New Hampshire, Rockingham ss.
On the twentieth day of November in the year eighteen
hundred and forty-five at Newmarket in said County
came James M. Chapman and Martha Mallard both of
said Newmarket and were lawfully joined in marriage
Before me
         George W. Kittredge, Justice of the Peace.
A true copy of Record,
   Attest,   George W. Kittredge, Justice of the Peace.
A true copy,
   Attest,   Timothy Murray, Town Clerk.
George H. Hyde Born May 3, 1845 son of Lorenzo D. &
   Mary L. Hyde.
Mrs. Sarah Swaine wife of Reuben Swaine Died Feb. 2,
   1846, Aged 56 years.
John C. Brown son of Elizabeth Brown Died Feb. 8, 1846,
   age 3 y. 11 mo.
                    (N. T. R., V: 6.)
Mr. William Speed Died Oct. 6, 1845, Aged 69 years.
Miss Mary O. Lock Daughter of Simeon & Clarissa Lock
   Died Oct. 20, 1845, Aged 17 yrs. 5 mo.
Otis A. Bazin Died Jany. 14, 1846, Aged 3 years & 7 mo.
Horace G. Bazin Died Jany. 18, 1846, aged 7 months.
Mr. Daniel W. Bazin Died Jany. 24, 1846, Aged 34 years.
Elizabeth Ann Wiggin Born March 20, 1846 Daughter of
   Wingate & Ann D. Wiggin.
State of New Hampshire, Rockingham Co. ss.
Be it remembered that at Newmarket in State & Co. afore-
said on this 17th day of July A. D. 1845 Mr. Nathaniel B.
Crummet of Newmarket, State & Co. aforesaid & Miss

Susan M. Decature of Newmarket, State & Co. aforesaid
were duly joined in Marriage.

By L. D. Burrows, Minister of the Gospel.

A true copy,   attest,   L. D. Burrows.

State of New Hampshire, Rockingham Co. ss.

Be it remembered that at Newmarket, State & Co. aforesaid
on the 17ᵗʰ day of Sept. A. D. 1845 Mr. Lycurgus N.
Smith of Durham, State of N. H. Strafford Co. & Miss
Priscilla Aldrich of Durham, N. H. Strafford Co. were
duly joined in Marriage by me,

L. D. Burrows, Minister of the Gospel.

A true copy, Attest,

L. D. Burrows.

State of New Hampshire, Rockingham Co. ss.

Be it remembered that at Newmarket, State of N. H. & Co.
aforesaid on this 5ᵗʰ day Feb. A. D. 1846 Mr. Sylvester
F. Doe & Miss Martha J. Spofford both of Newmarket,
State & Co. aforesaid were duly joined in Marriage by me,

L. D. Burrows, Minister of Gospel.

A True copy, Attest,

L. D. Burrows.

(N. T. R., V: 7.)

State of New Hampshire, Rockingham Co. ss.

Be it remembered that at Newmarket in State aforesaid on
the 24ᵗʰ day of February A. D. 1846 Mr. Newhill A.
Rundlet & Miss Harriet N. Smith both of Newmarket,
State & Co. aforesaid were duly joined in marriage by me,

L. D. Burrows, Minister of the Gospel.

A true copy, Attest,

L. D. Burrows.

Mr. Eliphalet Currier, Esq. of Portsmouth and Miss Sophronia Safford of Exeter were Married April 29, 1845, By

Rev. Stephen S. N. Greely.

Mr. Robert Jewell and Miss Mary Ann Marshall both of
Newmarket were married June 26, 1845, By

Rev. Stephen S. N. Greely.

Mr. William P. Hanson and Miss Olivia A. Rollins both of
Exeter were Married July 27, 1845, By

Rev. Stephen S. N. Greely.

Mr. George F. Nelson and Miss Mehitable S. Pendergast
both of Newmarket were married Jany. 27, 1846, By

Rev. Stephen S. N. Greely.

(N. T. R., V: 8.)

Mr. Charles Lane born November 27th 1796.

Hannah French born Feb'ry 3d 1802; they were married Sept. 24th 1821.

Children of Charles and Hannah Lane:

Olivia E. Lane born Novemr 14th 1825.

John Wm Lane born Sept. 27th 1827.

Mary Elizabeth Lane born April 28th 1830.

Ann Lucy Lane born Sept. 1st 1834.

Charles E. Lane born Dec. 27th 1837.

Married by Rev. Preston Rand at South Newmarket July 4th 1846, Mr. Levi Walbridge of Boston to Miss Isabel C. Lovering of South Newmarket.

Aug. 30th 1846. Mr. Thomas Hanford to Miss Evelyn K. Lord both of Newmarket.

I hereby certify that on the thirty-first day of August 1846 I solemnized the Marriage of Mr. George O. Paul of Newmarket to Harriett R. Osgood of Dover.

Attest   Homer Burrows,
            Minister of the Gospel.

This certifies that after a legal notification Mr. John N. Howard of Newmarket, N. H. and Miss Nancy Smith of Epping, N. H. were on 20th day of July 1846 duly joined in marriage by me

            Charles N. Smith.

Mr. Samuel S. Huckins and Miss Lucy M. Chapman were married August 29, 1845 by Rev. Israel Chesley both of Newmarket, N. H.

            (N. T. R., V: 9.)

This certifies that after a legal notification Mr. Josiah Smith Jun. and Miss Susan Wiggin both of Newmarket, N. H. were duly joined in marriage by me

            Chas. N. Smith, Minister of the Gospel.

State of New Hampshire, Rockingham ss.

At Newmarket, Aug. 27th 1846. Mr. Oren Head and Miss Lydia A. Briant both of Exeter, County and State aforesaid were duly joined in marriage by me

            O. C. Baker,
            Minister of the Gospel.

Alanson C. Haines, born June 12, 1843 at Newmarket, N. H. Dr. William Folsom attended. Copyed from day book of Dr. Wm Folsom and entered on this book Nov. 9, 1905.

            Matthew T. Kennedy, Town Clerk.
            (N. T. R., V: 10.)

The following marriages were solemnized before me in the year ending March 18, 1845.

June 1st 1845. Marriage was solemnized between Mr. James Stilson of Dover, N. H. and Miss Vranna D. Chapman of this town.

Nov. 6, 1845. Between R. G. W. English of Springfield, Mass. and Miss Nancy P. Wiggin of Durham, N. H.

Jany. 19, 1846. Between Mr. Jacob C. Harvey and Miss Sabrina H. Goodrich both of Nottingham, N. H.

D. Sidney Frost,
Pastor of the F. Baptist Church.

Newmarket, March 1847. Marriage has been solemnized by me at the times and between the persons the year ending March 1847 as follows.

April 5, 1846. Timothy Chapman to Esther W. Foss both of this town.

May 12, 1846. James Thompson to Susan A. Priest both of Nottingham, N. H.

May 31, 1846. Mark Kinison to Asenath S. Caswell both of this town.

June 7, 1846. Marquis McDuffee of Great Falls, N. H. to Dorothy E. Wiggin of this town.

Sept. 1, 1846. John N. Durrell of Durham, N. H. to Clara M. Jewell of this town.

Sept. 1, 1846. Ira H. Jenness of Tamworth, N. H. to Eliza A. Quint of this town.

October 4, 1846. Joseph P. Ham to Eunice Wilson both of this town.

Nov. 8, 1846. David Brackett of this town to Elizabeth B. Francis of Durham, N. H.

(N. T. R., V: 11.)

Nov. 26, 1846. Levi Towle of Epping, N. H. to Caroline Bartlett of this town.

February 4, 1847. Thomas N. Rundlet to Abby S. Andrews both of this town.

March 3, 1847. Ezekiel Hayes to Susan Foss both of Strafford, N. H.

March 7, 1847. Levi W. Sewall of Epping, N. H. to Lydia A. Jones of this town.

March 14, 1847. Samuel Edgerly of Durham, N. H. to Abigail J. Pinkham of this town.

Attest   D. Sidney Frost,
Pastor of the F. Baptist Church of this town.

FIRST CONGREGATIONAL CHURCH
RECORDS, CONCORD, N. H.
1730—1905.

MARRIAGES BY REV. NATHANIEL BOUTON, D. D.

[Continued from Vol. VII, page 26.]

1831. Feb. 20. Ira Abbot to Hannah A. Capen both of Concord.

April 18. Rev. William Claggett, Wendell, Mass. to Sarah K. Morrill of Concord.

24. James Pettingill to Hannah Ryan both of Concord.

June 21. Asaph Evans to (widow) Almira B. Davis, both of Concord.

July 30. William A. W. Neal to Comfort Moore, both of Concord.

Sept. 14. Joseph Manahan to Ellen D. Montgomery, both of Concord.

Oct. 25. Henry M. Moore to Lydia Baker, both of Concord.

Dec. 22. Maximilian J. Webber of Hopkinton to Clarissa S. Sweat of Concord.

1832. Jan. 5. Dea. Nathaniel Ambrose to Miss Martha Eastman, both of Concord.

Feb. 28.* James Buswell to Miss Judith Davis, both of Concord.

March 20. Samuel D. Baker of Bow to Miss Eliza A. Glover of Concord.

April 5. Hazen Runnels to Miss Sarah B. Fiske, both of Concord.

25. William M. Haskell of Boston, to Miss Emily Virgin of Concord.

May 6. Winthrop B. Norton, Esq. of Oxford, Me. to Mrs.† Sally Symonds of Concord.

15. Lieut. Lewis Heath to Miss Sarah W. Edwards, both of Bristol.

*Concord City Records read, Feb. 25.
†City Records read, Miss.—ED.

1832. May 22. Alvah Kimball to Miss Lydia Marden, both of Dunstable.

23. Robert E. Pecker to Miss Esther J. Lang, both of Concord.

June 29. George Willson of Detroit (Mich. Ter.) to Miss Arabelle M Farrand of Concord.

Sept. 2. Alexander Albee of Littleton, to Mrs. Dolly Chandler of Concord.

17. John W. Moore to Miss Emily J. Eastman, both of Concord.

18. Gardner Tenney to Miss Lydia H. Seavey both of Concord.

Oct. 11. George C. Aiken of Andover, Mass. to Miss Eliza W. Baker of Concord.

11. Benjamin F. Adams of Sutton, to Miss Nancy N. White of Bow.

17. Asa Wilkins of Wiscasset, Me. to Miss Frances M. White of Concord.

Nov. 6. Peter Lovejoy to Miss Sophia Smith, both of Concord.

21. Adams Foster of Canterbury to Miss Sarah* B. Eastman of Concord.

Dec. 25. Thomas C. Capen to Miss Mary Corliss, both of Concord.

1833. Jan. 30. James Bartlett to Miss Catharine Seavey, both of Concord.

Feb. 28. James C. Whittemore to Miss Elizabeth K. Hoit, both of Concord.

March 26. Thomas Noyes of Dorchester to Mrs. Hannah Jackson, of Concord.

April 25. Moses Smith to Miss Laura L. Clark, both of Concord.

June 3. Ebenezer Eastman, Jun. to Miss Ruth Hoit, both of Concord.

4. Robert Hall to Miss Lucinda S. Capen, both of Concord.

26. Theodore Stevens to Miss Eunice Haines, both of Concord.

July 15. John Eaton to Miss Judith Johnson, both of Concord.

18. William W. Estabrook to Miss Mary Ann H. Damon, both of Concord.

*Concord Marriages read, Susan; Publishments read, Sarah.—ED.

1833. Aug. 25. Samuel L. Baker of Medford, Mass. to Miss Eliza A. Proctor of Concord.

Sept. 12. Samuel Neal of Boston, Mass. to Miss Sarah A. Virgin* of Concord.

30. Rev. Warren Nichols of Loudon to Miss Ann M. Morril of Concord.

Oct. 7. Charles Mills to Miss Mary Brown, both of Concord.

8. Simon Virgin of Rumford, Me. to Miss Abigail Blackburn of Concord.

Dec. 3. Zara Cutler Esq. of Conway to Miss Judith Coffin of Concord.

24. Michael Blake to Miss Ruth Anne Knowles, both of Concord.

1834. Jan. 14. Joseph Greenough, Boston, Mass. to Miss Eliza J. Kelly of Hopkinton.

22. Shadrach Seavey to Miss Belinda Herbert, both of Concord.

30. Dana Woodman of New Hampton to Miss Jane Wilson of New Boston.

Feb. 2. Anthony Hatch of Medford, Mass. to Miss Mary W. Currier of Concord.

13. Ethan Hoit of Hopkinton to Miss Emily Scales of Concord.

26. Washington Williams of Dover to Miss Charlotte Ayer of Concord.

March 1. John Hanson, Jun. to Miss Elsey Arlin, both of Boscawen.

April 14. Rev. Samuel Utley, Middleborough, Mass. to Miss Mary Jane Eastman of Concord.

15. Mr. Cyrus Dustin to Miss Ednah P. Fisk, both of Hopkinton.

22. Mr. John Fox to Miss Clarissa E. Kimball, both of Concord.

22.† Samuel Lane of Medford, Mass. to Miss Fanny Tufts of Concord.

May 19. Charles T. Mixer of Saco, Me. to Miss Eliza Jane Morrill of Concord.

29. Elias C. Horner of Concord, to Miss Eliza Brown of Peeling.

*Concord City Marriages read, Sarah S. Virgin; Publishments read, Sarah A. Virgin.

†City Records read, April 25.—ED.

1834. June 23.   Amasa Walker of Boston, Mass. to Miss Hannah Ambrose of Concord.

Aug. 20.   James M. Tarleton of Montgomery, Alabama to Miss Sarah W. Fisk of Concord.

Sept. 18.   Thomas Butters to Miss Sarah Dunckley, both of Concord.

22.   Thomas Graham of Quincy, Mass. to Miss Jane M. Stevens of Concord.

Oct. 5.   Moses Ordway to Miss Sarah M. Chase, both of Concord.

9.   William Pecker to Miss Susan D. Chandler, both of Concord.

14.   Samuel C. Cockran to Miss Elizabeth Dearborn, both of Concord.

Oct. 27.   William F. Goodell to Miss Sarah Hall, both of Concord.

Oct. 27.   Joseph Ropes, Jr. Salem, Mass. to Miss Zurviah Tuttle of Concord.

Nov. 27.   Anson W. Brown of Loudon to Miss Alvira W. Potter of Concord.

Dec. 11.   Joel S. Morrill to Miss Mary Ann Eastman, both of Concord.

23.   Charles Gibson of New York to Miss Mary Frances Stickney of Concord.

1835. Jan. 13.   William Moore, Jun. of Chester to Miss Judith Abbot of Concord.

20.   Robert Thompson to Miss Susan Bartlett, both of Warner.

Feb. 5.   John A. Richardson of Durham to Mrs. Frances J. Murdock of Concord.

March 4.   Asa F. Bradley to Miss Rachel T. Hoit both of Concord.

17.   Charles Chase, Esq. to Miss Mary Evans, both of Hopkinton.

19.   Isaiah Farnum to Miss Clarissa Mooney, both of Concord.

31.   Daniel Harvey of Nottingham to Miss Sarah Ewer of Concord.

May 26.   Charles W. Underhill to Miss Susan E. Kimball, both of Concord.

July 2.   Jonathan A. Virgin of Macon, Ga. to Miss Judith S. Goodwin of Concord.

1835. July 9. Joseph L. Jackson to Miss Cynthia M. Shute both of Concord.

Aug. 17. Thomas F. Wells to Miss Lucy H. Currier, both of Goffstown.

25. William K. Holt of Loudon to Miss Eliza T. Virgin of Concord.

Sept. 17. James Davis to Miss Melinda Cleasby both of Concord.

Oct. 21. Cyrus Tucker of Loudon to Miss Fanny Jane Hoit of Concord.

29. Caleb Parker to Miss Abigail D. Virgin, both of Concord.

Nov. 11. Asa Fifield of Loudon to Miss Sophia Hoyt of Concord.

17. John A. Bell of Hooksett to Miss Sarah Blake of Lowell, Mass.

25. Adam C. Holt to Miss Hannah R. Emery, both of Lowell, Mass.

26. Daniel J. Dinsmoor of Meredith to Miss Caroline Stark of Goffstown.

26. Benjamin S. Bohonon of Lowell, Mass. to Miss Maria L. Capen of Concord.

1836. April 19. Mr. Samuel W. Phelps of Cincinnati, Ohio to Miss Harriet E. Drake of Concord.

May 3. Asaph Evans Jun. of Montgomery, Ala. to Miss Clarissa N. Fisk of Concord.

5. Joseph Greenough to Miss Lydia L. Stanwood, both of Hopkinton.

19. Moses Greeley of Salisbury to Miss Sarah Bridges of Andover, Mass.

24. Isaac K. Palmer of Chicago, Ill. to Miss Almira Clement of Concord.

June 9. Alanson Mitchell to Miss Catherine G. Mills, both of Lowell, Mass.

Oct. 20. William Jennisson Esq. of Worcester, Mass. to Mrs. Mary C. Walker of Concord.

Nov. 16. Thomas F. Farrington to Hannah L. Dodge, both of Concord.

Dec. 6. Amos Bean to Miss Phebe A. Potter both of Concord.

22. Isaac Emery Jun. to Miss Eliza L. Eastman, both of Concord.

1837. March 26. John H. Maynard to Miss Jane K. Kimball, both of Concord.

May 3. Charles Libbey to Miss Ruhamar Tandy, both of Concord.

July 11. Abram R. Libbey to Miss Jane E. Hildreth, both of Pembroke.

Aug. 8. Ivory Hall to Miss Sarah Dow, both of Concord.

Oct. 18. Robert Saunders of Ossipee to Miss Abigail B. Locke of Concord.

Dec. 3. Willard Saunders to Miss Rosanna E. Capen, both of Concord.

1838. Jan. 25. Philip Eastman of Fryeburg, Me. to Miss Martha Lovejoy of Concord.

March 6. Gilbert McMillan Esq. of Conway to Miss Susan K. McFarland of Concord.

April 2. William H. Hardy to Miss Priscilla M. Morgan, both of Hopkinton.

26. George W. Moody to Miss Mary Gale, both of Concord.

June 5. Albert G. Capen of Lowell, Mass. to Miss Mary Hall of Concord.

12. Rev. Edward Buxton of Boscawen to Miss Elizabeth McFarland of Concord.

Nov. 3. Joseph B. Crummett of Bedford, Mass. to Miss Louisa Fifield of Lowell, Mass.

4. Benjn G. Davis of Boston to Miss Phebe A. Farnum of Concord.

Dec. 20. Smith Rowe to Miss Caroline Sanborn, both of Andover.

1839. Jan. 1. Nathaniel Rolfe Jun. to Miss Mary Jane Moody, both of Concord.

March 11. Calvin Smart to Miss Susan Piper, both of Concord.

April 9. Henry S. G. French, of Boscawen to Miss Sarah C. Allison of Concord.

May 10. Thomas S. Hyatt of Albany, N. Y. to Miss Nancy Eastman of Concord.

July 25. Thomas B. Sargeant of Concord to Mrs. Lavina W. Puffer of Saco, Me.

Sept. 19. George N. Guthrie of Putnum, O. to Miss Sarah A. McFarland of Concord.

1840. March 9. Samuel Marden 3d of Epsom to Miss Deborah H. Silver of Concord.

1840. April 7. Joseph B. Marston of Gilmanton, to Miss
Olive Maria Ladd of Loudon.

April 23. Mark Marden of Epsom to Miss Ruth Jane
Silver of Concord.

Aug. 10. John G. Meader to Mrs. Lydia S. Tasker,
both of Barnstead.

Sept. 3. William B. Heard to Miss Nancy Blake both of
Concord.

14. John C. Hagar of Manchester to Miss Sophronia
T. Tufts of Concord.

24. Charles H. Clough to Miss Mary C. Lang both of
Concord.

Nov. 3. Harrison Simons of Weare to Miss Lydia Ann
Foster of Concord.

11. Edward L. Staniels of Boston to Miss Ruth B.
Eastman of Concord.

18. Franklin Evans to Miss Sarah E. Davis, both of
Concord.

Rev. Jubilee Wellman of Westminster, Vt. to Miss
Hannah B. Kelly, Concord.

Dec. 3. John Brown to Miss Clara A. Shute, both of
Concord.

15. Timothy W. Emery to Miss Comfort Potter, both
of Concord.

17. Hazen K. Farnum to Narcissa Favor, both of Concord.

1841. Feb. 4. Gilman Morrill of Concord to Miss Martha
Jane Elliot of Bow.

April 28. Richard H. Jones to Miss Anna J. Varney,
both of Gilmanton.

Sept. 21. William Kelsea to Miss Sarah D. Abbot, both
of Concord.

Oct. 26. Chauncey C. Bartlett to Miss Sarah C. Boise,
both of Concord.

Nov. 25. Thomas Puffer, Jr. to Miss Dorcas C. Chandler,
both of Concord.

Dec. 28. David Pettengill to Miss Martha Sargeant, both
of Concord.

Lorenzo S. Pettengill to Miss Rosette Jane Merrill,
both of Concord.

1842. Jan. 26. Stephen H. Parker of Andover, Mass. to
Miss Ann M. Abbot of Concord.

1842. Feb. 23. Hezekiah Bacon of Newton, Mass. to Mrs. Elizabeth C. George of Concord.

March 5. Henry Thornton of Albany, N. Y. to Miss Margaret Hancock of Concord.

April 19. Hazen Runnels to Miss Sarah E. Corliss, both of Concord.

April 19. Albert Gilchrist of Andover to Miss Abigail S. Corliss, of Concord.

May 3. Jonathan Towle of Andover, Mass. to Miss Almira Emery of Loudon.

Aug. 2. Abial R. Crosby of Montgomery, Ala. to Miss Judith Chandler of Concord.

Sept. 4. Lewis Devon to Miss Margaret LaBonta, both of Concord.

Oct. 17. Harry J. Gilbert of Savannah, Ga. to Miss Priscilla H. Morril of Concord.

20. Joseph Tilden, Jun. of Hanover to Miss Mary E. Virgin of Concord.

1843. Feb. 15. William Thayer of Manchester to Miss Sarah A. Allison of Concord.

May 2. William T. Emery to Miss Jennette Elliott, both of Concord.

Sept. 20. Windsor Fairbanks to Miss Eliza H. Brown, both of Concord.

Oct. 5. Jonathan S. Hazeltine of Springfield to Miss Esther B. Webster of Hooksett.

Nov. 14. John Briggs of Boston to Miss Mary E. West, of Concord.

Nov. 14. Lyman A. Walker to Miss Lucy Ann Pratt, both of Concord.

28. John C. Gage of Boscawen to Miss Elizabeth S. Sargeant of Canterbury.

Dec. 5. Cyrus H.* Dow to Miss Deborah S. Charles, both of Canterbury.

23. Plummer Ordway to Miss Dolly F. Elliot, both of Concord.

1844. Jan. 10. Orre Hand of Albany, Vt. to Miss Eliza McCoy of Bow, N. H.

July 3. John A. Burnham of Manchester to Harriet W. Davidson of Concord.

Aug. 1. William P. Dolloff of New Hampton to Miss Maria L. Sanborn of Canterbury.

*Concord City Records read, Cyrus K.—ED.

NORTH CHURCH RECORDS, PORTSMOUTH, N. H.

BAPTISMS BY REV. JOSEPH BUCKMINSTER.

[There are two records of baptisms; we have followed the one in the handwriting of Rev. Mr. Buckminster and given in brackets any additional information contained in the other record.]

[Continued from Vol. VII, page 16.]

1786　May 15　Ann Wendell D^r of Samuel Penhallow Junr and wife baptized on the behalf of Sister Ann Penhallow Grandmother in law to whom the child was committed by the Mother on her death bed with a desire that she would have it baptized and admitted as her own. Private baptism for particular reasons. [Ann Wendell child of Samuel Penhallow Junr & Hannah Penhallow]

21　Charlotte D^r of John and Susannah Mendum

June 4　Walter Son of Woodbury & Sarah Langdon

25　James Son of Elijah Hall & wife [of Capt. Elijah Hall & Elizabeth Hall]

July 2　Elizabeth D^r of Tobias Walker & wife

23　Margaret D^r of William Fernald & wife

30　Jeremiah S^n of Winthrop Bennet & wife

Augt 6　Nancy D^r of Seth Walker & wife

Septem^r 3　George Son of Elisha Hill and wife [of Elisha & Elizabeth Hill]

3　Samuel Son of Thomas Harvey & wife [of Thomas & Hannah Harvey]

Septem^r 28　Margery Clark an adult wife of Joseph Clarke baptized in private dangerously ill

Octr 8　Joseph Clark an adult baptized and received into covenant

Joseph & William Sons of Joseph & Margery Clark

15　Lucy Maria D^r of [Rev.] Joseph and Sarah Buckminster

21　Mehitable D^r of James Hill & wife [of James & Eunice Hill]

Decem^r 10　Stephen Parsons Son of John Jones Junr & wife

1786   Decem^r 17   Barnet Son of Barnet Akerman & wife
[of Barnet & Sarah Akerman]
1787   Feby 4   Wm Frost Son of [Capt] John Salter & [Jane]
his wife
    11   Olive D^r of Enoch Meloon & wife [of Enoch &
Mary Meloon]
    25   Charles Son of Aaron Hodgdon
March 18   Elisha Callender, Thomas, John, Joseph Buck-
minster, Charles Cutter, William Callender Sons of
Edward & Elizabeth Hart baptized on their mothers
account and in ye house for private reasons
Elizabeth D^r of Edward & Elizabeth Hart baptized
by Dr. Haven some months before
April ye 1st   Sophia D^r of Aaron Hill & Hannah his wife
    29   Abigail Libbey D^r of Joshua Pike Junr & wife   D^r
Haven
May 20   Polly Plaisted D^r of Saml Hill & wife [of Sam-
uel & Mary Hill]
June 3   John Son of Wm Parker & Mary his wife
Ditto   John Son of Thomas Moses & Elizabeth his wife
July 8   Samuel Son of Dr John Goddard & Susannah his
wife
(N. C. R., I: 226.)
July ye 8   John Son of John Gooch & wife
July 8   Rebecca D^r of Kittery & Margaret free negros
private B.
    11   Joseph Son of Mr Hight, Newington private bap-
tism at ye funeral of his Father
July 22   Katharine Whipple D^r of Woodbury & Sarah
Langdon
Augt 5   James Boyd Son of Edward [Brown] Loud &
wife [Sarah]
Sep^t 30   John Son of Capt John Mendum & wife [Susan-
na]
Octr 7   William Langdon Son of George Gains & wife
1788   March ye 16   Supply Son of Timo^y Ham & wife
April ye 27   Robert Son of Prince Whipple & wife [Di-
nah] blacks
[May 4   Maria child of Tobias &   Walker]
June 13   Adee Weeks an adult baptized on her death bed
July ye 6   Katharine D^r of Jeremiah and Susanna Den-
net
    20   John Son of [Capt] John Salter and Jane his wife

1788 August 10 Harriet D^r of Aaron & Hannah Hill
Wm Son of Wm Currier & wife [Hannah] Maria D^r
of Wm Seavy & wife [Martha] Dr Haven
  24 George Massy Son of James Hill & wife [Eunice]
  D^o Mary Griffis D^r of William Fernald & wife
Sepr 7 Cuff Negro man Late Servant of Joseph Whipple
  7 Daniel Son of Cuff and wife Blacks
  28 George Son of Daniel Hart & wife
  28 Sally D^r of Lemuel Mastin & wife
Octo^r 5 Walter Son of Woodbury & Sarah Langdon
Novr 2 Sarah D^r of Edward & Elizabeth Hart
Novr 9 Nancy Willson D^r of Joshua Pike & wife D^r
Stevens
  16 George Son of Henry Parcher & wife
  30 John Son of John Jones & wife Mr Macclintock
Decr 7 Nancy D^r of George Gains & wife
  14 Walter Son of Barnet & Sarah Akerman
1789 March ye 28 Elizabeth D^r of [Rev.] Joseph & Sarah
Buckminster
May ye 17 Mary Ann D^r of Nahum Ward & wife [Margery]
  17 Nancy Lang D^r of Thos Harvey & wife [Hannah]
June 7 Mary & W^m D^r & Son of Thos Moses deceased
presented by y^r Mother in Law his relict [of Thomas & Lydia Moses Deceas^d]
July ye 5 William & Jane Boyd twins Son & D^r of John
& Jane Goddard
  D^o Elizabeth D^r of Mary March Relict of Nathaniel
Augt 2 John Son of John March & Sarah his wife
  30 Lucy D^r of Enoch Meloon & wife [Mary]
  30 Hannah D^r of Aaron Hodgdon & wife Mr Gray
Sepr 20 Jane Grand D^r of Sr Martha Harvey presented
by her
Octr 4 Mary D^r of Cuff Whipple & wife Blacks [of
Cuffy Late servant of Joseph Whipple Esq]
  11 Robert Son of [Robert] Orum & Abigail his wife
(N. C. R., I: 227.)
Decem^r 6 Jeremiah Son of Prince Whipple & wife
[Dinah] Black
[Mary Hobart wife of Saml Hobart made a Profession
of Religion]
  13 Jane Stevens D^r of Capt Hobart & wife [child of
Samuel & Mary Hobart]

1789   Decem^r 13   Samuel Son of D^o

    20   Lucy Maria D^r of Seth Walker & wife

1790   Feby 7   Henry Son of Mrs Sarah Orn formerly Mrs Moore

    14   Olive D^r of Tobias Walker & wife

    14   James Son of Capt [Aaron] Wingate & Ruth his wife

March 21   Nancy D^r of James Hill & wife [Eunice]

    28   Samuel Son of [Capt] Wm Parker & Mary his wife

April 4   Hannah Man D^r of Edward Brown Loud & Sarah his wife

    16   George Washington Son of John Tuckerman & wife [Eliz^a]   private baptism

    18   Thomas Quincy Son of Aaron Hill & Hannah his wife

May 2   Aaron Son of Aaron Wingate and Ruth his wife

    30   Joshua Son of Joshua Pike & wife

June 20   James Son of James Orne & wife

    27   Charlotte D^r of Wm Currier & wife [Hannah]

July 4   Maria Jane D^r of [Capt] John Salter & Jane his wife

    Caroline D^r of [Capt] Elijah Hall & Elizabeth his wife

    Henry Son of Henry Parcher & wife

July 18   Hall Jackson & Richard, twins, Sons of [Capt] Richard & Sarah Tibbits

    [22   John child of Edward Damorel & Elizabeth]

Aug^s 22   Anna Maria D^r of [Capt] George Long & Mercy his wife

Octo^r 3   Harriet D^r of John Goddard & Jane his wife

    17   John Wingate Son of John W. Chase & wife [Nabby]

Novr 7   Joseph Son of Ezekiel Pitman & wife

Novr 7   Jeremiah Son of Jeremiah Dennet & wife [Susanna]

1791   Jany 23   Henry Seaward Son of Nathl Pitman & wife [Mary]

    30   Joseph Son of John Jones & wife

Feby 13   Rebecca an adult wife of Cuff Whipple   Blacks

March 6   John Son of John Abbot & wife [Sarah]

March 13   Maria D^r of John Melcher & wife   Mr Porter

May 1   John Son of Capt Hobart & wife [of Samuel & Mary Hobart]

1791 June 12 Sarah D^r of Barnet & Sarah Akerman
      Lucy D^r of Enoch & Mary Meloon
    26 Saml Son of George Gains & wife
    Henry Son of Tim^y Ham & wife
  July 3 Nabby D^r of Saml Neal & wife
    Peggy D^r of Cuff Whipple & wife Blacks
    31 Saml Son of John Gooch & wife
  Augt 7 Nathl Son of Nathl Folsom & wife [Olive]
  Sepr 4 Hannah D^r of Thos Harvey & wife [Hannah]
    11 Mercy Collins D^r of George & Mercy Long
             (N. C. R., I: 228.)
  Octo^r 2 Fanny D^r of James Hill & wife [Eunice]
    Sarah D^r of John March & wife
  Novr 6 William Son of [Col.] Aaron Hill & wife
    Lydia D^r of John & Lydia Bowles
  Nov 6 Mercy, a serv^t girl in Deacon Penhallows family
    baptized on their account [Mercy, child of Thos &
    Sarah Thurbur]
  Novr 13 Joshua Son of John Abbot & wife [Sarah]
    27 Elizabeth D^r of Prince Whipple & wife [Dinah]
    blacks
1792 Jany 1 Eliza D^r of Orne & wife [Sarah] baptized by Mr Noble
  Feby 5 Katherine D^r of Wm Seavy & wife
    12 John Son of John Penhallow Junr & wife [Sarah]
    [26 Peter Man child of Edward B. Loud & Sarah Loud]
  April 22 Benj^a Son of [Capt] John Salter & wife [Jane]
    Sally D^r of Capt Tibbits & wife
  May 31 Eliezer Son of Nahum Ward & wife
  June 3 Temperance D^r of Seth Walker & wife
  July 1 Anna Maria D^r of Amm R. Hall & wife
    12 Theodore Jackson Son of Nathl Currier & Lydia his wife private baptism
    15 Saml Son of John Tuckerman & wife [Elizabeth]
    15 John Son of Mastin [John Caverly child of Lemuel & Marston] Mr Jackson
  Augt 12 Wm Hale Son of [Robert] Orum & Abigail his wife
    19 John Son of Benj^a Clark & wife
  Sepr 7 Sarah D^r of Elijah Hall & Elizabeth his wife private baptism
  D^o Eliza D^r of Wm Currier & wife private baptism

1792 Sep[r] 9   Samuel, Sally Twin child[n] of Sam[l] Neal & Sally his wife
  16   Mary Ann D[r] of Edward Melcher
  23   George Son of George & Mercy Lang
  30   John Son of Cap[t] Hobart & Mary his wife [Samuel & Mary Hobart]
  30   Amos Son of Sam[l] Tappan & Aurelia his wife
 Octo[r] 8   Hannah Odiorne an Adult [wife of Thomas Odiorne]
 Nov 4   Aaron Son of Aaron Hodgdon & wife
  4   John Mycall Son of John Pillow & wife
 Decem[r] 2   Susannah Mendum D[r] of W[m] Currier & wife
  2   Abigail D[r] of M[r] [Thomas] Odiorne & Hannah his wife
  23   Joseph Son of Enoch Meloon & wife [Mary]
       (N. C. R., I: 229.)
1793 Feb[y] 3   Lucy Maria D[r] of John & Mary Goddard
  20   Samuel Peverly Son of Sam[l] Lear   private baptism
 March 10   Caleb Son of Caleb Currier
  17   W[m] Eustis Son of Henry S[herburne] Langdon & Nancy his wife
 April 6   Jeremiah Son of Joshua Pike & wife   private baptism
  7   Theodore Son of James Hill & wife [Eunice]
 [May 4 ˙ Mary wife of Benj G. Carter]
  11   Charles Son of Cap[t] [Aaron] Wingate & wife [Ruth]
  19   Nathan[l] Jackson Son of John March & wife
 June 9   Anna Walker D[r] of Nathan[l] Ham & wife
  9   Joseph Osburne Son of Cap[t] Brown & wife [of Joseph & Elizabeth Brawne]
  [30   Hannah child of Barnet & Sarah Akerman]
 July 14   John Son of Cuff Whipple & wife   blacks
  21   Katharine D[r] of Henry Parcher & wife   M[r] Litchfield
 Aug[t] 4   Mary Ann D[r] of [Cap[t]] Elijah Hall & wife [Elizabeth]
  11   Olive Hunt D[r] of Nat[l] Folsom & Olive his wife
 Sep[t] 8   Harriett D[r] of [Col.] Eliphalet Ladd & Abigail his wife
  8   Nabby D[r] of John Bowles & Lydia his wife
  22   Nabby Maria D[r] of John Jones & wife
 Dec[r] 15   Henry Son of John Abbot & wife [Sarah]

1793 Decr 22 Josiah Gilman Son of Josiah Folsom & wife
   22 Polly D^r of D°
   29 Betsey D^r of John Gooch & wife
1794 Jany 5 Hannah D^r of Prince Whipple & wife
    [Dinah]
   12 Sarah D^r of   Orne & wife [Sarah]
Feby 16 Sarah Ann D^r of John Salter and Jane his wife
March 16 Sarah Wentworth D^r of John Penhallow Junr
   & Sarah his wife
June 8 William Son of Benj^a Clark & wife
  29 Frances Emory D^r of Henry S. Langdon & Nancy
   his wife
  29 Mary Barnes D^r of Wm Furber & wife
  29 Hannah Dame D^r of Mr Lindsey deceased presented by her Aunt Hannah Dame to whose care she
   is committed
July 13 Candace an adult wife of Pomp. Spring
  27 Mary Jackson D^r of [Nathaniel] Currier & Lydia
   his wife
Augt 3 Joshua Henshaw Son of A. R. Hall & wife
   [Ammi R. Hall]
  14 John Son of Joseph Man & Elizabeth his wife
Sep^t 14 Samuel Son of Seth Walker & wife
   Henry Son of James Hill & wife [Eunice]
   W^m & Nathan^l twins Sons of Edward Brown Loud
   & wife [Sarah]
         (N. C. R., I: 230.)
Sep^t 16 Saml Son of George & Mercy Lang private
  18 Hannah D^r of Thos Odiorne & Hannah his wife
Nov 2 Richard Fitzgerald an adult
   Martha D^r of George Gains & wife
   Nancy D^r of Wm Dame and wife
   Elizabeth Bumberry D^r of D°
   Mary Yeaton D^r of Richard Fitzgerald & wife [Abi-
   gail]
   Thos Son of Wm Currier & wife
Nov 9 Anna D^r of Wm Lary & wife [Martha]
   Wm Son of John Pillow & wife
  [29 Charles child of Nabby Chase widow of John
   Chase]
Decem^r 28 Stacy Kenistone an adult
  D° Betsey D^r of Stacy Kenistone & wife
1795 Jany 11 Wm Dixon an adult

1795   Jany 11   Sarah Ann D^r of Nathan^l Folsom & wife
[Olive]
Sukey Ham D^r of Edw Melcher & wife
[Feby 15   Elizabeth Sewall child of John & Mary Goddard]
[Katharine child of John &   March
March 8   Olive Dr of Capt Brown [of Joseph & Elizabeth Brawn]
22   Ephraim Son of Nathl Ham & wife
April 5   Harriet Chase D^r of Capt Tibbets & wife
Mary Ann D^r of Wm Pitman & wife
12   Joshua Byron Son of Elijah & Elizabeth Hall
Eliza Ann D^r of John and Elizabeth Maulintock
19   Emily D^r of Joseph Akerman Junr & wife
Supply Jackson Son of Joseph Akerman Junr & wife
May 3   George Walker an adult
Eliza D^r of George Walker & Elizabeth his wife
10   Elizabeth D^r of Joshua Pike & wife
Rocksby Harris D^r of Edward John Peirce & wife
17   Frances D^r of [Rev.] Joseph Buckminster & Mary his wife
June 14   Mary D^r of Saml Neal & wife
July 5   Henry Sherburne Son of Henry S. Langdon & wife
Septem^r 6   Katharine Rosseter D^r of Elisha Whidden & wife
20   John Collins Son of George Lang & Marsy his wife   (N. C. R., I: 231.)
Octr 4   Theodore Pickering son of Theodore Furber & wife
18   Polly Marden an adult owned the Cov^t & was baptized
William son of Wm Marden & Polly his wife
Hannah D^r of D^o D^o
Polly Wendell D^r of D^o D^o
18   John Wingate son of Prince Whipple & wife
[Dinah]   Blacks
Novr 22   Harriet D^r of James Rundlet & wife
Decem^r 6   Benjamin son of James Orn & wife [Sarah]
1796   Jany 10   Arthur son of Nathl Folsom & Olive his wife
Feby 14   John son of Wm Currier & wife [Hannah]
William son of John Abbot & wife [Sarah]

IN MEMORIAM.

Dr. HENRY RUST PARKER.

Dr. HENRY RUST PARKER, First Vice-President of the New Hampshire Genealogical Society, died at his home in Dover, on the twenty-ninth day of December, 1909, after a brief illness of pneumonia, aged 73 years, 6 months and 5 days.

Were it permitted us, in mortal guise, to penetrate "the blind cave of eternal night" and glance adown futurity's misty reaches, is it not probable that, enchanted with the supernal grandeur of the scene, we would hail with glad acclaim, the dawn of that sempiternal day whose effulgent glory reaches to the sable borderland of death? In the bright aurora of that dawning shall we not meet again the friends who have gone before? While no voice has ever reached us from beyond the sunset's bourn, yet the heart is bouyed with loving faith that communion will be again restored "when the mists have cleared away."

The possibilities of moral and material achievement were conspicuously evidenced in the life-work of our departed friend and colleague.

Orphaned at the age of twelve, he was the architect, in large measure, of that ethical superstructure which won and held the admiration of his friends and acquaintances of later years, whose towering pinnacles gleamed in crystal brightness high above the mists of ordinary ambition and desire. From the bench of the artisan he rapidly ascended, by dint of painstaking study and self-training, to the position of instructor of others, teaching for some time in the academy at Wolfborough, N. H., his native town.

Supplementing his academic training by a course in the Dartmouth Medical School, he received the degree of "M. D.," making his initial appearance as a practicing physician in the place of his nativity.

In the year 1881 Dr. Parker moved to Dover, N. H., where he continued an uninterrupted residence until his death.

Endowed with a studious and analytical mind, Dr. Parker

became not only eminently successful in the practice of his profession, but refreshed and broadened his essentially wide range of human experience by frequent incursions into the realms of science and of letters. Although singularly free from the ordinary errors and foibles of life, he was, nevertheless, eminently human in all his relations with his fellow-men. Tenacious of purpose, yet free from dogmatism; assertive, yet unofficious; dignified, yet never austere, he won and held the entire confidence and respect of all who came within the radius of his vigorous personality, by the exercise of those excellent qualities which form the basis of earnest, honest, conscientious manhood.

On the seventh day of January, 1891, Dr. Parker was formerly inaugurated Mayor of his adopted city. He enjoyed the distinction of being the first Democrat, after more than two score years of uninterrupted Republican supremacy, to wield the gavel as Dover's Chief Executive, having been elected to that high office by a substantial majority in one of the most memorable political contests in the city's history. He was re-elected in the campaign of 1891, serving two full terms as the official head of Dover's municipal government.

Dr. Parker served as president of the board of Examining Surgeons for Strafford County, an office under the jurisdiction of the Department of Pensions, during the administrations of President Cleveland; he was a member of the Dover Medical Society, Strafford County Medical Society and the New Hampshire Medical Society, and also one of the consulting physicians and surgeons on the staff of the Wentworth Hospital. He sought relaxation and diversion from the exacting demands of professional life by uniting with kindred spirits in philanthropic and charitable movements, as well as in the fellowship and cheering amenities of fraternal association. He was a member of Moses Paul Lodge, A. F. & A. M., Belknap Chapter, Royal Arch Masons, St. Paul Commandery, Knights Templar, and A. and A. Scottish Rite.

He was one of the incorporators of the New Hampshire Genealogical Society and a faithful servitor upon its directory. He was also connected with the Northam Colonists, the Society of Colonial Wars of New Hampshire and the Sons of the American Revolution. He was a member of St. Thomas Episcopal church, and evidenced a deep interest in its spiritual and material advancement.

Dr. Parker was united in marriage on the twenty-seventh day of May, 1866, with Miss Ella M. Thompson of Wolfborough, and by this union there were three children: Nathalie S., who married George B. Harper, of Montreal, Canada; Alberta T., wife of Harry P. Henderson, of Dover, N. H.; and Henry R. Parker, Jr., who died December 27, 1894, aged 19 years.

"With silent obsequy and funeral train" all that was mortal of our lamented friend was laid at rest in the family lot at Pine Hill Cemetery, on the dawning day of the new year, Saturday, January 1, 1910, business of all kinds being suspended throughout the city during the hour of service.

The following is the genealogical line of Dr. Parker:

WILLIAM[1] PARKER, born in England about 1662; married February 26, 1703, Lady Zerviah Stanley, daughter of the Earl of Derby, and took up his residence in Portsmouth, N. H., soon thereafter.

HON. WILLIAM[2] PARKER, of Portsmouth, born in 1704; died April 29, 1781, aged 77 years. He was admitted to the bar in 1732; served as clerk of the commission appointed to settle the boundary line between New Hampshire and Massachusetts in 1737; was appointed Register of Probate by Governor Belcher; afterwards became Judge of Admiralty; served in the General Assembly from 1765 to 1774, and held the position of Judge of the Superior Court from August, 1771, until the office was vacated by reason of the Revolution. He married Elizabeth Grafton about 1726.

MATTHEW STANLEY GIBSON[3] PARKER, born in 1747; died in 1787; removed to Wolfborough; married Anna Rust, daughter of Col. Henry and Ann (Harvey) Rust. She was born November 4, 1751, and died at Wolfborough June 17, 1786.

HENRY RUST[4] PARKER, born February 6, 1778; died September 18, 1848; married Hannah, daughter of Henry and Hannah (Horne) Rust. She was born December 21, 1784.

JOHN TAPPAN[5] PARKER, born September 5, 1804; died September 25, 1848; married Sally L. Seavey.

DR. HENRY RUST[6] PARKER, born in Wolfborough, N. H., January 24, 1836; married May 27, 1866, Ella M., daughter of Moses and Hannah Marble (Rust) Thompson; died December 29, 1909.

FRED E. QUIMBY,
Necrologist, New Hampshire Genealogical Society.

NOTICE.

Until within a few days the editor has been away nearly all of the time since the January number of this magazine was issued, hence the delay in issuing this number. Under the present arrangement when the editor is away there is no one to carry on or look after the magazine for the New Hampshire Genealogical Society. When the society was organized it was thought best to have a genealogical magazine, but the society did not have the money to assume the financial responsibility of such an enterprise. The editor came forward as a make-shift for the time being and assumed the cost and labor of the undertaking. Seven years have passed since that agreement was made but the arrangement cannot continue indefinitly. The editor has other important interests demanding attention as well as other genealogical and historical work of great importance that must be attended too. This volume will be published in full as opportunity permits, but with the next volume we feel that a new arrangement should be made. Our readers should have no fear that the magazine will be discontinued for we confidently believe that some way will be found for continuing the work. The editor would willingly be one of four to assume the expense of publication. Perhaps the society could furnish a part, and there ought to be others who would take hold, enough to make up whatever deficiency there might be, if any. The editor contemplates an extended genealogical and historical trip to England, after this matter is arranged. He has, with the exception of a large power press, one of the largest and best printing outfits in Dover which was purchased expressly for the magazine and can be used for the same in the future. As financial agent for the N. H. Genealogical Society he would like to receive a personal letter from each member or friend of the society expressing their wishes and what they are willing to do in regard to the permanent continuance of the magazine. He invites correspondence in regard to the matter. New Hampshire furnishes a large field for genealogical and historical research and the "Record" should be enlarged and placed on a permanent basis. We believe such will be the final outcome of the situation.

FIRST CONGREGATIONAL CHURCH RECORDS, ROCHESTER, N. H.

BAPTISMS BY REV. JOSEPH HAVEN.

[Continued from Vol. VII, page 32.]

1816 Octr 27th Baptized in Kensington, N. H. the Son of a Widow Woman, by the name of Benjamin Cram

1817 June 8th Baptized Sarah Jane, Daughter of Jeremiah H. Woodman Esqr

1818 May 24th Francis William, Son of Nathl Upham Esqr Baptized by Revd Asa Piper of Wakefield

July 5. Rev. Isaac Jones Baptized a child of Jeremiah H. Woodman Esqr by the name of Harriet Crosby.

August 28th Elizabeth, Wife of Eli Sumner, Susanna, & Martha Thomas, Eli, and Charles children of Moses Brown

Novr 1st Elizabeth Tripte, Daughter of Thos Downs Junr

1819 March 30th Tamma, Wife of Wm Hurd upon her confession of Faith in Christ Jesus (upon a Sick bed)

May 9th Ann Elizabeth, Daughter of John Haven

July 4th Baptized Lydia, Wife of Jonas C. March Esqr

Novr 21st Baptized Albert, Son of Nathl Upham Esqr

1820 June 11th Baptized Maria Barker, Daughter of J. H. Woodman Esqr

1821 Decr 2^d Baptized Charlotte Cheever, Daughter of J. H. Woodman Esqr

1822 March 3^d Baptized Sarah, Wife of Trustrum Hard upon a Sick Bed, upon her confession of repentance of her Sins, her faith in Jesus Christ as her only Saviour, & resolution, thro' divine grace, to pay a ready & cheerful obedience to his gospel

July 21st Baptized Benjamin Corson, before his being received into the Church

July 28th Baptized Benajah, Son of Benajah Ricker

1823 June 15th Baptized Lois, Wife of Tobias Twombly before being received into the Church.

Record of Baptisms since the ordination of Thomas C. Upham July 16, 1823.

1823. August 3ᵈ Mr. Buzzel, by name of John Burnham.
August 3ᵈ Widow Adams, by name of Elizabeth.
  N. B. Both of the above joined the Church at time of being baptized.
August 10. Abigail, wife of Sam'l Chamberlain, baptized by Mr. Haven.
August 12. Moses, Mary, Enoch, Lydia and Sarah children of Samuel and Abigail Chamberlain.
  N. B. The above mentioned children were baptized at request & in name of their mother, who was upon her dying bed, upon their first giving their assent to the confession of Faith, & expressing their willingness that the Baptism should be performed.
September 14. Jones, Mary, Chestnut Hills.
September 14. Wingate, Elizabeth, Salmon Falls.
  N. B. These two were baptized by Mr. Haven & were admitted into the church at the time of Baptism.
October 26. Hayes, Mary, Back Road.
October 26. Shorey, Mary, Norway Plain.
October 26. Hurd, William,   do.
1824. January 4. Sam'l Allen, Hannah Varney & Mary Ela.
April 4. Olive Hussey, Sophia Stackpole, Mary Bell Brown, Amos Main, Susan Buzzell, all admitted at this time, members in full Communion with the Church.
May 15. Aaron Patten, (infant child of Sally & Shadrach Wingate.)
May 21. Margaret Elizabeth Neal & Robert Neal, children of Elizabeth & Joshua Brewster.
June 6. Sophia, Charlotte & Emily Ann, children of Wᵐ and Tammy Hurd.
May 23. Mary McDuffee, on the New Durham road.
July 4. Alice Furber, daughter of Alice & Wᵐ Furber.
July 4. Clarissa Kimball of Chestnut Hills.
July 4. Lucinda Garland, wife of Hiram G., Maine Road.
July 4. Peter Folsom, Norway Plain.
September 5. Betsy Horne, wife of Jonathan H., Maine Road.
September 5. Eliza Goodhue of Brookfield.
September 5. Lucy Hurd of Norway Plain.
September 5. Elizabeth G. Wallingford, daughter of Jacob W.
October 3. Samuel, infant child of Jeremiah H. Woodman Esq.

1824. Nov. 7. Dorothy Allen, Salmon Fall Road.
Nov. 7. Betsy Cross, Formerly of Wolfborough.
Nov. 7. Mary Jane Jones, wife of Oliver J., Gonick.
1825. Jan. 16. Stephen Jackson, Maine Road.
Jan. 16. Rosanna Stackpole, wife of Samuel S.
Jan. 16. Nancy Wentworth.
May 29. Joseph Corson, Salmon Fall.
May 29. Polly Clark, Salmon Fall.
May 29, 1825. Ended the ministry of Rev. T. C. Upham, he having accepted a Professorship at Bowd. College.
[Baptisms by Rev. Isaac Willey.]
1827. April 22. Baptized by Mr. Willey, George Freeman his son.
June 20. Caroline March, Sarah Ann March, Caroline Knight, Sarah Bartlett.
1828. June 8th Ann Pinkham.
1829. May 3d Delia Jane, daughter of Matthew Merriam; Daniel Needham, son of Isaac Willey; Hannah Elizabeth, daughter of Shadrach Wingate.
1830. —— Sarah Flint, daughter of I. Willey. Mary, daughter of Mr. James Towner.
1831. May 8. Mrs. Eliza Barker, Miss Emily March, Miss Melinda Kimball.
July — Mrs. Pickering.
Sept. 4th Mrs. Hurd, wife of Nathaniel Hurd. Mr. Javis McDuffee.
Nov. 6. Miss Caroline Augusta Chase, Miss Susan Wentworth, Mrs. Joseph Hurd.
1832. May 6th Temperance Lock & Charles Henderson.
July 8th Louisa Browne, Louis Hayes, Abel Spaulding.
August 26. Mary Ann Bell, daughter of James Bell, Esq. at Exeter.
Isaac Willey, Son of Rev. I. Willey.
1833. Jan. 6. Sarah Jane Varney.
July 7. John Roberts & Nancy Rogers.
1834. April 30. Sarah Tebbetts, Martha Jane Roberts, Elias Cornelius Willey, Sarah Olivia Spaulding, John, Ruth Abigail & James Roberts, David Alexander & Mary Upham Barker.
July 7. Mrs. Hale, Miss Rebecca Rogers.
Sept. 7. Mrs. Browne & Mary Tibbetts.
Record of Baptisms since the ordination of Francis V. Pike, February 20, 1839.

1839. August 4. Mrs. Sophia Hubbard on admission to church

Sept. 29. Mrs. Charlotte Flagg on admission to chh.

1840. June 16. William Twombly on admission to the church.

July 5. Jona Tasker Seavey on admission to the church.
Sam¹ Stackpole on admission to the church.
Mrs. Sarah Allen on admission to the church.
Mrs. Chloe Twichell on admission to the church.
Hannah Hayes on admission to the church.
Lucy Allen on admission to the church.
Elizabeth Pinkham Rodgers on admission to the church.
Clarissa Roberts on admission to the church.
Mary W. Horne on admission to the church.
Julia Celeste, infant of Wᵐ & Chloe Twichell.

Aug. 23. Richard Kimball, on admission to the church.
Mrs. Margaret Jane Kimball on admission to the church.
Isabella Graham, infant of R. & M. J. Kimball.
Ellen, infant of Charles & Mary Henderson.

Dec. 30. Francis Holmes, infant of Rev. F. V. & C. R. Pike. The Baptism took place at the time of the mothers funeral.

1841. July 4. Frances Farnum Pray, on admission to the church.
Mary Allen on admission to the church.

1843. Jan. 1. Mrs. Abigail Seavey on admission to the church.

29. Benjamin Hayes on admission to the church.
Aaron Flagg on admission to the church.
Mrs. Nancy Henderson on admission to the church.

Record of Baptisms during the ministry of Rev. J[ohn] E. Farwell commencing April 1843.

1843. July 9. Edwin Folsom Hurd, admitted to the church.
Abra C. Hayes, admitted to the church.

Nov. 5. Isaac Bickford by immersion admitted to the church.
Mary Sophia Bickford by immersion admitted to the church.
Mary Hayes by immersion admitted to the church.

1844. July 7. Mary Louisa child of Chs. & Mary Henderson.

1847. March 7. Mrs. Caroline Turner, (rec^d to the chh.)
Sarah West Pray, (rec^d to the chh.)
Oct. 7. Edward Sherman Farwell.
Charles William Henderson.
1849. July 2. Sarah Hayes on admission to the chh.
Eliza Jane Hayes on admission to the church.
Mary Frances Crawford on admission to the chh.
1850. April 28. Rose Ann Lavender, child of Robert Lavender. (Irish)
June 16. Benjamin Thaxter, child of J. E. Farwell.
July 7. Sarah, child of Charles & Mary Henderson.
Dec. 7. William Cumston & George Russell, children of James M. & Eliza Fessenden.
1851. May 4. Miss Sarah Folsom Hurd on admission to chh.
July 6. Miss Sarah Chase Tebbetts on admission.
Sept. 7. James, child of Robert Lavender.
1852. July 4. Samuel Parris, Son of J. E. & E. S. Farwell.
Record of Baptisms during ministry of Rev. Geo. Spaulding.
1853. Jan. 2. Mary Joanna Hayes united with the church.
2. Theodore Norton Son of Geo. & E. A. Spaulding.
March 6. Anna S. Barker admitted to the church.
Festus Allan Crawford.
Oct. 14. ――― Lavender daughter of Robert.

ADMISSIONS TO CHURCH,
ROCHESTER, N. H.

1737. Sep. 18. Joseph Walker, Elizabeth Ham wife of Eleazer Ham & Mary ye wife of John MacFee were admitted into Full Communion with this chh.
Oct. 9. Richard Wentworth & Joseph Richards Tertius were admitted into full communion with this Church.
Oct. 16. Stephen Berry & John Jennes were Received into full communion with this chh. by a dismission from ye chh. at Rye.
At a church meeting Nov^r — 1737 Stephen Berry & Joseph Walker were chosen deacons for this church by a vote of ye chh.
Feb. 26. Admitted into full communion with y^s chh. by a dismission from ye chh at Rye Anna Berry.

1737/8. Feb. 26.   Admitted into full communion with y^s chh Sarah Richards ye wife of Joseph Richards Tertius & Phebe Dam.

1738.   April 30.   Robert Knight Junr & his wife Elizabeth & Abigail Walker ye wife of Joseph Walker & Jane Hard were admitted into full communion with this chh.

June 25.   William & Mark Jenness were admitted into full communion with this chh.

July 2.   ———— ye wife of William Jenness was admitted into full communion with this chh.

Aug. —.   Jane ye wife of Ebenezer Plaice was admitted to full communion with this chh.

Feb. 25.   Rebecca ye wife of Joseph H[u]rd & Jane ye wife of John Wentworth were admitted into full com^n with y^s chh.

1739.   May 13.   Robert Knight aged above 70 was admitted into full communion with this chh.

June 10.   Esther ye wife of Jonathan Cops & Anne ye wife of Ichabod Horn were admitted into full communion with y^s chh.

July 15.   Abigail ye wife of Mark Jennes was admitted into full communion with this church.

July 22.   Sarah ye wife of Henry Allard was admitted into full communion with this chh.

Aug. 12.   Hannah ye wife of John Blagdon was admitted into full communion with this church.

Aug. 26.   Sarah Bickford ye wife of John Bickford was admitted into full communion with this chh.

1740.   Oct. 12.   Henry Allard was admitted into full communion with this church.

1741.   Aug. 2.   Sampson Babb of Barrington was admitted into full communion with this chh.

Sep. 27.   John Wentworth, Samuel Whitehouse & Experience ye wife of Samuel Whitehouse were admitted into full communion with this chh.

Dec. 6.   Thomas Drew was admitted into full communion with this chh.

Jan. 7.   Gershom Downs & his wife Margaret & Mary Chamberlain were admitted into full communion with this chh.

Feb. 14.   Edward Tebbetts & his wife Mary, James Buzzell & his wife Rachel, Joseph Richards Junr, Thomas

Hamock & Abigail Tebbetts were admitted into full communion with this chh.

1741/2. Feb. 12. William Chamberlain made a Satisfaction to this chh. for what was offensive to them heretofore in his Behavior & was by a vote of ye chh. admitted to occasional communion with this chh.

Feb. 12. At a chh. meeting Held in ye Meeting House in Rochester s^d meeting being seasonably notified.

Voted by this church that if any member of y^s chh. do Raise or spread a false & Evil Report of any of the communicants of this chh or of their neighbors it shall be deemed matter of scandal & offence & y^t upon its Being made known to ye Revd Pastor of y^s church such offender or offenders shall be & are by this vote of y^s chh from time to time suspended from ye communion of y^s chh until that Publick satisfaction be given to this chh by ye Person or Persons so offending.

May 23. Lucy ye wife of John Jennes was admitted into full communion with this chh. Jno Blagdon was admitted into full communion with this chh.

Oct. 3. John Trickey & Rebecca his wife were admitted into full communion with this chh.

1743. Jany 9. Samuel Drown & his wife were admitted into full communion with this chh.

Hannah ye wife of Joseph Edgerly was admitted into full communion with this chh.

Hannah ye wife of Clement Dearing was admitted into full communion with this church. Abigail Allen was admitted into full communion with this chh.

Judith ye wife of Deac. Berry was admitted into full communion with this chh.

1744. May 11. Mary Chamberlain came before y^s chh & made satisfaction for her withdrawing from ye communion thereof for sometime past, & she was restored to ye communion again by a vote of ye chh.

May 13. Admitted into full communion with y^s chh Margaret Cate of Barrington.

1745. May — Lieut Wm Chamberlain desired forgiveness of ye chh in a church meeting for all offences Past y^t He had given y^m & ye chh by a great majority voted him forgiveness upon the satisfaction he gave y^m & y^t He should have ye liberty of sitting down at ye Ld^s Table with y^m as an occasional communicant.

BOOK NOTICES.

THE BREWSTER GENEALOGY—1566—1907. *By Emma C. Brewster Jones, Cincinnati, Ohio.* Printed by the Grafton Press, New York, 1909. Cloth, 8vo., 2 Vols., pp. lxxviii and 1415. 52 Illustrations.

The Brewster Genealogy contains a record of the descendants of William Brewster of the "Mayflower," Ruling Elder of the Pilgrim Church which founded Plymouth Colony in 1620. Elder William Brewster was born in the latter part of 1566 or early in 1567, probably at Scrooby, Nottinghamshire, England. He was the son of William and Prudence Brewster of Scrooby. His father died in 1590 and for many years had been receiver of Scrooby and bailiff of the manor house of that place; also had held the office of "Post," which office had previously been held by his father, the grandfather of Elder William. December 3, 1580 at the early age of fourteen, Elder William matriculated at Peterhouse, one of the colleges forming the University of Cambridge, England, but does not appear to have remained long enough to receive his degrees. He was next appointed assistant clerk to William Davison, Secretary of State to Queen Elizabeth and accompanied that gentleman on his embassy to the Netherlands in August 1585 and served him at court until his downfall in 1587. Elder William then returned to the manor house at Scrooby and three years later was administrator on his father's estate. He was soon appointed "Post" which office he continued to hold until September 30, 1607.

At an early age he became a convert to the doctrine of John Robinson, the founder of Congregationalism, and after his return to Scrooby his residence, the manor house, became the place of worship for the members of the new church in that vicinity. At length the government began to enforce the strict laws against the new religion, when in 1607 Elder William and the other members determined to flee to Holland. He, with others, was arrested at Boston, England, and detained there for a month. He finally reached Leyden, the rendezvous of the new church. Here for twelve years he resided, during which time he was engaged in teaching school

and in the printing business. Finally it became necessary
to secure a new home for the growing church and it was de-
cided that a part of the members should emigrate to America
and Elder William was chosen Ruling Elder to head the
party. A big mistake was made in sending out the colony
on the eve of the approaching winter, which cost the lives of
half the company, but in spite of the cold, inclement weather
and scant provisions, through the foresight and indomitable
courage of Elder William the colony succeeded. He died
at Plymouth, Mass., April 16, 1644.

The work contains a record of more than twenty thousand of his descendants. It is well written, concise, clear,
and its general arrangement is excellent. It is a great credit
to the writer, and she can well be proud of her life's work,
for a work like this takes and represents the greater part of
one's life. It has a complete index of names. Reference
authorities are given for the first seven generations, which is
a very nice feature and not usually found in genealogies.
We have long thought that all genealogies should give their
reference authorities. The time will come when every genealogy will be tested, time and again, by the future generations and if it can be easily verified it will stand the test, if
not then it will not be long in finding its way into the waste
basket and some other work better written for reference will
take its place.

Price of the work is $15.00 net, per set. Address,
EMMA C. BREWSTER JONES,
Norwood, Cincinnati, Ohio.

THE URANN FAMILY OF NEW ENGLAND, INCLUDING THE
DESCENDANTS OF MARGARET (URANN) GAMMELL. *By*
Charles Collyer Whittier. Boston, Mass. Press of David
Clapp & Son. Boston, 1910. Paper, 8vo. pp. 59.

The above is a sketch of the descendants of William Urann
or Urin who was of the Isles of Shoals as early as 1653. He
was a fisherman and had a grant of land located between
goodman Jackson and William Cotton with convenient land-
ing 12 September, 1653. He died at the Isles of Shoals, and
the inventory of his estate was filed July, 1664, amounting
to £433. 12. 8. The genealogy is arranged on the plan of
the genealogies published in the "New England Historical
and Genealogical Register" which has become the standard
system now in use by most genealogists in this country.
The work shows much research and care in the collecting of

data and compilation of the same. It contains a complete index of names. A limited number of copies of the work have been printed; price is seventy-five cents per copy. Address, Charles Collyer Whittier, 374 Blue Hill Avenue, Roxbury, Mass.

QUERIES.

107. LAMSON.—In the Strafford County Deeds, I find that, "Samuel Harris of Sandwich, Taylor, for 50 pounds, paid by Joseph Lamson, of Exeter, Gentleman, conveyed land in Sandwich, 100 acres, being lot number 24 in the 6th range, drawn in the original right of James Thurston; deed dated 8 June, 1793." Identification of this Joseph Lamson is desired; also when and to whom did he transfer the same.

YOUNG.—COLLY.—CALBY.—CALLY.—Ancestry of David Young and Phebe Calby (or Colly) of Machias, Maine is desired; they had a daughter Phebe, born in Machias, July 7, 1769, who married Thomas Eaton, at Amesbury, Mass., Nov. 14, 1793.

HICKS.—Ancestry of Joseph Hicks (Hix) of Dover and Durham, N. H., is wanted; also when and where he was born. Was he connected with the Portsmouth or Kittery Hicks family?

FURLONG.—Patrick Furlong, one of the early settlers of Limerick, Maine, married twice, the first wife died before 1799. Her name and parentage is desired or anything relating to her.

Albert H. Lamson,
Elkins, N. H.

108. CRAM.—The surname of Abigail ——— who married Jonathan Cram of Brimfield or Holland, Mass., is wanted. Their children were born in Holland; in 1785 he settled in Lancaster, N. H., where several of his children were married.

Henry and Ardella Cram, son and daughter of Simon and Clarissa (Straw) Cram were born in Lancaster, N. H., wish to know who they married and where they settled.

John G. Cram,
105 Charles Street, Boston, Mass.

109. FOSTER.—I would like to know the maiden name of "Hannah" wife of James[5] (James,[4] Joseph,[3] Jacob,[2] Reginald[1]) Foster. He was born August 30, 1749, son of James[4]

and Sarah (Hart) Foster of Ipswich; He was a Revolutionary Soldier and lived in Temple, N. H. The first child of James and Hannah Foster was born in 1770.

Susan A. Smith,
Kingston, Mass.

ANSWER TO QUERY.

31. MORSE.—The Rev. John Morse had letters of dismissal and recommendation from the church at Wells, Me., and was ordained at Blackberry Hill, Berwick, Me., 30 April, 1755. He died in November, 1764; his daughter Mehitable married Vincent, son of Vincent and Lois (Pinkham) Torr, 30 March, 1783. Vincent was a soldier of the Revolutionary army, 1775-77; he joined the West Society, Baptist, of Newfields, 2 March, 1784; bought pew No. 47 in 1791, and was active in parish affairs 1791-8-9. His Tax was abated 13 March, 1804, on account of a sick son; he died 11 May, 1829. Mehitable was the earliest member on the church roll, now extant, 1814. She died 9 February, 1821.

Children:

John Morse Torr, born 25 September, 1783; died 4 September, 1806.

Sarah, born 17 March, 1785; married 29 November, 1804 Ebenezer Doe of Durham: died 26 January, 1846. She was enrolled on Newmarket church records 1814.

Lois, born 13 September, 1786; died 13 October, 1795.

Susanna, born 29 February, 1788; married late in life and settled in the northern part of the State.

Vincent, born 19 March, 1790; married 1st, Deborah Jacobs: married 2d, Susan Spinney 3 May, 1825 by Rev. John Osborne.

Sophia, born 6 October, 1791; married John Putney of Lowell, Mass.

Mehitable, born 25 November, 1793; married August, 1822, William L. Fobes, who died at sea August 1, 1824. She married 2d, John S. Meserve of Newmarket, of Rollinsford after 1850.

Charlotte, born 3 December, 1795; married Amos Chamberlain of Lebanon, Maine.

Nancy, born 25 January, 1798; married 27 May, 1819 Joshua Doe of Durham, by Rev. John Osborne.

George Jerry Torr, born 12 December, 1799; married 1st, Nancy Whittemore of Great Falls; married 2ᵈ, Anna Young of Wakefield.

Eliza, born 30 January, 1801; married 1st, Henry Allen; 2nd, Rev. Byron Morse of Haverhill, Mass.; 3rd, ———– Merrill. She died 10 February, 1881.

Vincent Torr, 3rd, was a privateersman in 1812; also was at Fort Constitution with Paul Chapman, Joseph R. Doe, and Arthur Branscomb of Newmarket.

W. S. MESERVE,
Durham, N. H.

DONATIONS.

During the last three months the New Hampshire Genealogical Society has received the following donations in books and pamphlets, for which I am directed to present the grateful thanks of the society.

Donors.	Residence.	Number.
Hon. Arthur G. Whittemore,	Dover,	2
Mrs. Hannah C. Tibbetts,	"	2
Dover Public Library,	"	65
Mrs. Anna M. C. Riley,	Claremont,	1
Henry S. Webster, A. M.,	Gardiner, Me.,	1
Henry E. Woods, A. M.,	Boston, Mass.,	1
Mr. C. N. Quimby,	" "	1
Charles C. Whittier, Esq.,	" "	1
Mrs. Mary B. Morse,	Haverhill, "	2
Also 8 Manuscripts.		
Mrs. Louie Brown Ingalls,	Hyde Park, "	11
Mr. Harold Clarke Durrell,	Cambridge, "	2
Mrs. A. C. Hall,	Stamford, Conn.,	2
Smithsonian Institution,	Washington, D. C.,	1
University of California,	Berkeley, California,	3
Historical and Philosophical Society of Ohio,	Cincinnati, Ohio,	3

Total, books and pamphlets,   98
Number of previous donations,   8,428

Total, since incorporation of society,   8,526
CHARLES W. TIBBETTS, Librarian.

CUMULATIVE INDEX

----, Lydia 7:5
ABBOT-ABBOTT, Aaron 3:22-
3:72:7:22 Abigail 5:40-6:162
Alfred C. 7:26 Alice M. 5:85
Amos 3rd 7:19 Ann M. 7:71
Anna 6:53-7:24 Anne 5:140
Asenath 6:108 Benjamin
6:110,111 Calvin 7:18 Charles
7:24 Charles B. 5:85 Chloe
6:163 Deborah 6:50,104 Dorcas
6:50 Elizabeth 3:120,131,-
6:105-7:24 Els(i)e 7:19
Emeline 7:25 Esther 6:106
Eunice B. 7:23 Fanny 6:167
Hannah 6:58,108,168 Henry
2:176-6:105-7:78 Huldah 7:18
Ira 7:65 Jacob 6:105 Jane
4:180 Jere 7:20 Job 6:161 John
2:168,183-3:91,174,-6:106,
-7:76-78,80 John D. 7:23
Joseph 1:22,-5:140 Joseph S.
7:24 Joshua 6:162,-7:77 Judith
7:68 Levi 6:54,58,169 Lydia
3:91,-6:104,165,-7:5 Mary
6:111,-7:17,18,20 Minerva A.
5:85 Miss 5:2 Moses 6:167
Mrs. 5:140 Nancy 7:17 Nancy
Bricket 7:21 Nathaniel 2:185
Pamelia 6:169 Peter 3:131
Peter H. 6:168 Phebe
6:55,108,-7:26 Polly 7:22
Polly Burnham 7:18 Rachel
6:165 Rebecca 6:107 Reuben
1:181,-6:51,168 Rhoda
6:52,164 Richard 1:10 Rose
6:170 Ruth 6:7,8,105 Ruth N.
6:110 Samuel 4:119,-6:52
Sarah 6:50,107,110,168,-7:76-
78,80 Sarah D. 7:71 Susan 7:26
Susanna 6:55 Theophilus 3:24
Thomas 6:106 Timothy

ABBOT-ABBOTT (continued)
6:165,166 Walter 1:9,10,22,-
2:24-27 William 7:19,80 Zerviah 6:162
ABRAMS, William 3:167
ACCABY, Thomas 1:12
ACKLIN, Richard 5:41
ADAMS, Abel 1:13 Abigail
4:64,106,108,110,154,158,
-5:74,77,-6:1 Alexander 6:1
Amos 7:27 Amy 3:56 Ann 6:1
Anna 5:183 Anne 6:4 Augustus
7:27 Avis 6:1,3 Benjamin
2:176,-3:109,4:63,64,106-108,
110,112,152,155,156,158,
-5:53,74, 77,80,-7:27 Benjamin F. 7:66 Caleb G. 5:169
Charles 1:178 Deborah 5:136
Dudley G. 4:147 Ebenezer
3:2,9,64,-4:60,105,110,
-5:77-79 Eleanor 3:4 Elizabeth
2:175,-3:9,60,63,64,109,
4:106,153,-5:77,79,130,134,
136,139,183,186,-6:3,134,
-7:27,86 Elizabeth L. 1:102
Esther 2:168 Ezekiel G. 3:7,-
4:61,-5:75 George H. 1:102,-
5:48,192,-6:192 Hannah
2:167,-3:63,-6:1 Henry
2:167,-3:169 Hugh 1:180,-
6:1-5 James 4:64,-7:27 Jane
6:1 Jesse 7:27 Joanna
4:64,105,107,110,111,153,
154,156,158 Joanna G. 5:79
John 2:176,-3:21,55,71-
73,125,-4:50,111,-5:139,
-6:1,3-5,155 John H. 5:139
John Prentice 7:30 Joseph
2:122,167,-3:3,6,9,57,60,
63,64,109,-4:61-64,105,107,
110,111,153,154,156,158,

ADAMS (continued)
-5:44,77,79,80,-6:3 Josiah
6:5,64,133-136,139,151,153
Katherine 6:1 Lois 4:110 Lydia
5:78 Margaret 3:52 Mary
3:50,56,-4:112,-5:51,75,80,
134,-6:1,5 Mary N. 6:134 Matthew 6:1 Meriel 3:1 Mr. 5:90
Mrs. 4:62 Nancy 6:5,134
Nathan W. 4:108,152 Nathaniel
2:160,161,-4:158,-5:130,132,
134,136,139,183,186,-6:134
Phebe 1:180,-6:4,5 Peter
3:20,73 Rebecca 1:180,-
6:4,5,134 Ruth W. 3:9,-4:110
Samuel 1:102,180,-3:10,-
4:110,-6:1,3-5,134,-7:30 Sarah
6:5,134 Solomon 6:33 Sophia
6:38,134 Susanna 1:180,-6:1-3
Thomas 4:57,-5:77 Widow
7:86 William 4:110,-5:75,186
Winborn 6:3,5 Winthrop 5:120
AIKIN(S), Asa 7:59 George C.
7:66 Helen St. John 7:59
AISTEN, Reuben 6:136
AKERMAN, Amy 6:45 Anna 6:79
Barnett 5:38,88,-7:15,74,75,
77,78 Benjamin 2:159,-
4:56,98,-5:88,91,-6:77
Elizabeth 4:51,56,-5:183
Emily 7:80 George 5:138 Han-
nah 4:104,-7:78 John 2:186,-
5:183 Joseph 5:183,188,-
6:42,45,77,79 Joseph Jr. 7:80
Josiah 5:136,138,183,187
Katharine 5:187 Mark 7:15
Mary 4:56 Mr. 4:100,-5:86
Mrs. 3:175,-5:138,183,187,
188,-6:42,45,79 Phebe
4:101,-5:86 Rachel 5:118
Samuel 6:42 Sarah 4:56,103,-
7:15,74,75,77,78 Supply Jack-
son 7:80 Walter 2:161,-7:75
AKERS, Johanna 3:41
ALAIN, Louis 3:69,76
ALBEE, Alexander 7:66
ALCOCK, Benjamin 1:19,-4:104
Captain 3:55 Dorothy 3:52
Elizabeth 3:50,56,-4:52 Ensign
3:104 Joanna 4:101 Job 2:102,
-3:50,52,173,-4:49 Joseph
1:19,-2:173,-4:101 Keturah

ALCOCK (continued)
1:19,-4:101 Mary 5:38 Mrs.
3:175 Samuel 3:152,-4:52
ALDREDGE, Mr. 2:37
ALDRICH, Phebe 6:164 Philadel-
phia 6:170 Priscilla 7:62
ALEXANDER, David 7:87 Henry
4:104 Jemima 4:101 John
4:103,-5:43 Joseph 3:174
Samuel 3:129 Thomas 4:101
ALLABEN, Frank 2:188
ALLARD, Aaron 6:120 Bethena
6:66 Charity H. 7:56 David
6:70 Elizabeth 3:156 Grace
4:13 Henry 2:171,-3:112,156,
-6:67,147,-7:90 Job 6:70
Joseph 6:73 Lydia 6:75 Sarah
3:112,-7:90 Shadrach 3:156
William 6:36
ALLEN, Abigail 1:111,-4:150,
-5:59,-7:91 Ann 1:52,-4:12
Anna 5:58 Anne 2:76,125,-4:39
Aza 5:58 Bathsheba 4:43 Benjamin 2:76 Bozoun 6:3 Charles
1:10,13,-3:50,173,174 Content
4:43,-5:58,-6:81 Daniel 3:174,
-4:39,-5:59 Desire 4:43 Dorcas
1:116,-4:44,-5:60 Dorothy
5:52,-6:39,-7:87 Edmund 4:43
Eleanor 6:115 Elijah 1:61,120,
123,-4:39,70 Elisha 5:49,-
6:116 Elizabeth 1:52,57,120,
123,140,-2:145,-4:11,41,43,
70,-5:124,-6:3 Ephraim
4:39,-5:58 Ezekiel 4:43 Francis 1:52,53,56,57,64,-2:76,
-4:44 Francis A. 4:188 George
W. 4:188 Hannah 1:51-53,
56,-2:124,-5:58,117,-7:22 Hervey 4:186 Ichabod 6:113 Jacob
2:76,-4:11,39 James 3:27,74,
82,-4:147,-6:162 Jedediah
1:65,116,121,-4:44 Jerusha
4:43 John 2:184,-3:81,84,-
4:150 Jonathan 4:39 Joseph
6:75 Joshua 4:148 Judah 3:5
Lavinia 5:58 Leah 4:11 Lucy
7:88 Lydia 1:56,64,-4:38,44,
124,-5:32,58 Mandland 4:101
Martha 4:146 Mary 1:53,57,64,
-2:75,149,- 4:11,43,181,-7:88
Mercy 4:151 Miss 4:146

ALLEN (continued)
Moses B. 5:58 Mrs. 3:50,56,
175 Nathan 6:75,113,115,116
Nathaniel 3:72 Rachel 4:10
Ruth 4:43,44 Sabina 5:58
Samuel 1:140,-3:104,-4:147,
183,-5:1,-7:86 Sarah 1:64,116,
121,123,-4:43,44,70,159,-5:17-
2,174,-7:88 Thomas 5:41 William 3:98,-5:151 Zaccheus
3:36
ALLEY, Content 5:32 Mary 5:55
ALLISON, Mrs. 3:103 Sarah A.
7:72 Sarah C. 7:70
ALLS, Elizabeth 6:167 Mary
4:189
ALLT, John 1:178
ALMERY or Almerry, Bar-
tholomew 3:53 George 3:53,-
4:102,-5:42 Hannah 3:51,53,
54,56,-5:39 Martha 4:100 Mary
3:52,-4:101,103 Mr. 4:100 Mrs.
3:175 Robert 3:53,54,173,-
4:100,101,-5:43
ALMY, Charles 5:36
AMAZEEN, Abigail 2:37 Christopher 1:21,22 Elizabeth
2:35,37 Ephraim 2:35 Henry
2:37 Jane 2:36 John 1:11
Lucretia 2:37 Sarah 2:36
AMBLAR, John 4:12 Mrs. 3:146
AMBROSE, Abigail 6:53 Hannah
7:68 Henry 2:82 Lucretia 7:21
Mary 7:24 Nathaniel 6:51,-7:65
Robert 6:52,164,-7:21 Samuel
2:82 Stephen 6:104 Susan 7:25
AMES, Abel 6:56 Anna A. 5:85
Daniel 2:142 Israel 5:58 Jacob
6:137 Joseph 5:40 Katherine
4:134 Mary 4:89 Rhoda 6:138
Robertson 6:162 Samuel 2:142
Sarah 6:62,138 Sophia 5:58
ANCE, Caroline 6:166
ANCESTRY, George 6:48,96,192
ANDERSON, Elizabeth 2:36 Jane
5:46 Mr. 4:1 William 2:183
William S. 2:187,-3:70
ANDREWS, Abby S. 7:64 Edward
4:13 Jane 5:46 Jediah 6:145
Thomas 6:145
ANDRUS, Sarah 2:45

ANGIER, Calvin 1:101 Charles
1:101 Jefferson 1:102 John
1:101,102,106 Joseph 1:106
Luther 1:101 Rebecca 1:102
Sarah 6:10 Sophia 1:101
APPLEBEE, Elizabeth 4:79 Wil-
liam 1:155
APPLETON, Col. 3:148 Hannah
4:182 Mary 3:168 Nathaniel W.
7:20
ARCHER, Mary 1:46
ARCHIBALD, David 5:131
Elizabeth 5:134 John 5:90 Mrs.
5:134,140 Robert 5:90,131,134,
140 Sarah 5:140
ARLIN, Charlotte G. 7:22 Daniel
Jr. 7:25 Elsie 7:67 George 6:54
Jeremiah 7:19 Mary 6:169
Priscilla 6:168 Solomon 7:22
ARNOLD, Aza 6:90,184 Elizabeth
6:90 James 5:167 Samuel A.
6:90
ASH, Abigail 5:54 John 3:147
Judith 4:146 Kezia 5:54
ATKINS, Abigail J. 5:185 Edward
5:185,188 Joseph 1:10 Love
5:185,188
ATKINSON, John 3:88 Joseph
1:13,-5:110 Mary 3:54,-5:42
Reuben 5:110 Sergeant 3:147
Theodore 1:22
ATWOOD, Lowell 4:180 Moses
4:174
AUDERWAY, Sarah B. 4:130
AUSTIN, Aaron 6:54 Abigail 4:159
Andrew 1:118,123-125,128,162,
-2:124,-4:69,70,-5:31,-6:18,55
Ann 1:52,-2:75 Anna 1:125,
168,170,-2:124,-5:64,-7:6
Anne 1:53,57,-2:74,146,
-4:40,70,121,124,159 Benjamin
1:53,60,64,-2:75,147,148,
-4:68,-7:6 Betty 7:2 Catherine
1:54,56,57,60,63,113,169,
-4:67,-5:32,64,-6:81 Cato 4:31
Daniel 2:148,162 David S. 5:64
Deborah 6:112 Ebenezer 2:147
Elijah 1:63,126,169,-2:124,
-4:121,122,-6:40 Elizabeth
1:61,162,168,-4:68,70,122,
124,-5:64,-6:20,82,-7:6

3

AUSTIN (continued)
Francis 2:82,190 Hannah
1:126,169,-4:122 Isabelle 2:82
Isaac 6:39 James 1:171,
-2:124,-4:69,-5:62,64,
-6:89,-7:4 Jemima 2:82 John
1:123,-4:66,69 Jonathan L.
5:167 Joseph 1:177,-2:75,123
Keziah 2:82,-4:122 Lydia
4:121,-6:18,150 Mary 1:56,118,
123-125,128, 162,165,168,170,
171,174,-2:124,146,148,-4:39,
70,124,-6:20,54,-7:6,9 Mary E.
6:89 Matthew 3:102 Mehitable
3:165 Mercy 1:123,-4:70,
-5:172 Miss 6:81 Moses 1:64,
119,162,165,168,-2:148,-3:33,
-4:124,-7:6 Nancy 7:22
Nathaniel 1:51,54,56,57,60,
63,113,117,118,168,170,171,
174,-2:74,123,124,-4:40,41,67,
69,-5:64,-6:89,150 Nicholas
1:57,-2:75,124,148,-4:40,70
Paul 2:23,-4:159,-5:5 Peter
2:148 Phebe 1:54,119,126,162,
165,168,-3:31,-4:122,-5:175,
-7:7 Priscilla 2:124,-4:67
Rebecca 1:56,162,-2:124,
-4:38,70 Rose 2:74,76,123,
125,-4:43 Samuel 1:52,-2:75,
146,-4:159 Sarah 1:51,54,60,
63,64,113,117,119,128,174,
-2:74,123,124,148,-3:32,
-4:70,121,123,124,-5:64,124,
-7:6 Solomon 2:146,-4:159
Sophia 7:26 Stephen 2:146,
-4:159 Thomas 1:51-53,
-2:74,123,148,-3:148 William
4:159
AVERY, Abigail 3:184 Anna
2:49,120 Benjamin 5:67 Chase
2:120 Daniel 2:49,-4:116 David
5:67 Elizabeth 2:53,-5:67 Hannah 2:49 Jeremiah 2:53 John
2:49,53 Joseph 5:67 Joshua
2:16,49 Lydia 4:75 Mary 2:49
Nathan 2:120 Nathaniel 2:120
Rebecca 5:67 Samuel 2:49,
-5:67 Sarah 2:53 Thomas
1:9,13,-3:174,-4:11
AYER, AYERS, Abia 4:52 Abigail
4:98,-5:40,131,132 Abraham

AYER, AYERS (continued)
4:101,-5:38 Alice 1:16,
-5:88,133,134,136 Amy 3:50,
52,53,56 Charlotte 7:67 Daniel
4:175 Dependence 3:7,66,73
Edward 1:16,-2:102,173,
-3:174,-4:14,15,17,19,-5:135,
140,185,-6:44 Eliza 6:108
Elizabeth 1:18,-4:58,101,
-5:89,91,135,137,185,-7:17
Franklin D. 6:15,16 George
5:41,87,88,90,91,133,135,
-6:154,-7:39 Hannah 2:18,
-3:61,63,-5:41,-6:44 Honor
5:131 Hopley 4:54 James
3:7,66,73 John 4:52,100,
-5:44,45,76,89,91,129,
131,132,137,139,140,-6:154
John 3rd 7:39 Jonathan
2:161,-5:38,86,88,131,133,
134,136 Joseph 5:79 Mark
3:5,53,174 Mary 3:17,56,106,
-4:16,17,19,52,54,98,103,112,
-5:39,41,43,91,134,-7:23
Mehitable 3:63,-4:19 Miss
5:44 Mrs. 3:175,-5:135,
137,139,140,-6:44 Nancy
Hazen 7:19 Nathaniel 3:50,
52,53,55,174,175,-5:131,134
Perkins 3:17,-5:90,-6:170
Phebe 4:52 Rebecca 2:170,
-3:64 Richard H. 2:133,-6:111
Ruth 4:16,98,-5:134,135
Samuel 2:175,-4:103 Sarah
1:18,-3:53,-4:98,-5:77,133,
135,139 Stephen 3:8,-5:77
Susan 6:167 Susanna 2:176,
-4:53,103,-5:43,129 Tem-
perance 5:79 Temperance P.
5:78 Thomas 3:53,61,63,
-4:98,112,-5:42,87,-6:153
Timothy 4:136 William 4:54,
98,-5:74
BABB, Benjamin 4:149,-6:65
Dorothy 3:112,-6:67 Elizabeth
3:56,-6:70 Isaiah 4:56 John
6:65 Joshua 2:168,-5:184 Mary
2:169,-5:146,6:66 Moses 4:150
Mrs. 5:184 Peter 3:174 Philip
5:184 Richard 6:65,73 Sampson
3:112,174,-5:117,-6:69,-7:90
Sarah 3:112,-6:66 Solomon

4

BABB (continued)
6:36 Susanna 4:118 Thomas
4:147 William 2:171,-6:69
BABCOCK, A. Emerson 1:108 A.
J. 1:108 Charles H. 1:108 Edward 1:108 Isaiah 1:108 James
1:108 Stephen 1:107,108
BABSON, Joseph 4:76
BACHELDER (see Batchelder)
BACKER, Mrs. 3:175
BACON, Abigail 2:189 Ebenezer
2:189 Hezekiah 7:72
BADGER, Anna 3:91 Benjamin
3:169 Eleanor 4:77 Giles 6:141
Hannah 6:3,135 Hannah C. 4:93
James 4:93 John C. 4:94,96,
-5:48,-6:141,144 John E. 4:93
Joseph 4:93,-6:139 Leander
4:93 Lydia 5:43 Mary 3:91,
-5:20 Nancy 4:93,-7:22
Nathaniel E. 4:93 Samuel
4:93,-6:61,143 Sarah 4:179,
-6:143 Stephen 4:93 Thomas
4:93 Warren 4:93 William
4:93,179,186
BADSON, John 3:100
BAGGS, Philip 1:22
BAGLEY, Enoch 4:176 Jerusha
3:129 Jonathan 3:89 Mary 3:89
Merah 5:104 Nancy 4:174 Or-
lando 5:104 Phineas 3:89 Ruth
3:171 Sarah 4:180 William
3:129
BAIKIE, Anna 4:3 Barbara 4:3
Elspeth 4:3 James 4:3
Katherine 4:3 Marjorie 4:3
BAILEY, Abijah 6:169 Benjamin
6:165 Isaac 2:32 John 6:53,163
Mary A. 2:32 Moses 2:32
Samuel 5:163 Susanna 6:110
Thomas 2:163,-6:109
BAINBRIDGE, Capt. 4:6
BAIRD, Charles 6:38
BAKER, Abel 6:170,-7:17 Abigail
2:37 Achsah 7:21 Alexander
6:172 Benjamin 4:168,-5:167,
-6:111 Bethulia 4:51,-5:40
Charity 6:147 Charles 6:74,
113,147 Clarissa 7:22 Daniel
5:16,50 Deborah 5:180 Dorothy
5:181 Eliza W. 7:66 Elizabeth
6:109,140 Henry 7:38 John

BAKER (continued)
1:179,-6:172 Levi 5:181 Love
6:113,147 Luke 7:20 Lydia
7:65 Marshall 6:161 Mary
5:180, -6:107 Mary A. 5:59
Moses 5:180 Philip 6:111 Ruth
5:71,181 Samuel D. 7:65
Samuel L. 7:67 Sarah 5:16,
-7:22 Sarah J. 5:101 Seth 6:62
Tamson 5:146 Thomas 6:51,
114,147 William 5:181
BALCH, Benjamin 4:31,-7:29
Deborah 5:118 Israel 4:31 Mr.
7:29 Thomas 4:31
BALDEN, Thomas 4:15
BALDWIN, Ruth 3:159,-7:22
Thomas 3:159,-6:163
BALFOUR, Barbara 4:3 George
4:3 James 4:1 Marjorie 4:3
BALL, Ebenezer 6:164 John 2:163
Mrs. 3:175 Peter 3:173,185
Reuben 3:114 Sarah 4:52,-5:42
BALLARD, Abigail 1:101 Dana
7:37 Dorothy 5:44 Elizabeth
1:101,-6:57 Ezra 7:22 John
3:174 Joshua 1:101 Lydia
1:101 Mary 1:101 Phebe 6:57
Sarah 1:99,101 Timothy 1:99
BALLENDEN, Margaret 4:3
BAMFORD (see Banford),
Elizabeth 4:46 Ruth 4:76
BAMPTON, Ambrose 1:57,114,
-4:40 Anna 4:140 Hannah
1:57,-4:40 John 1:57,-4:40
Mary 1:114,-4:40,-5:32
Nathaniel 4:40 Rebecca 1:114
BANCROFT, Lieutenant 3:80
BANFIELD, Abigail 4:53 Chris-
topher 3:149 Elizabeth 4:84
George 5:40 Hugh 2:169 John
1:12,-3:173 Libicy J. 7:58
Mrs. 3:56,175 Samuel 2:104
BANFORD (see Bamford), Robert
5:45
BANGS, Caroline 6:84 Charles E.
6:84 Chipman 4:31 Cyrus
1:170,-5:172,-6:83 Cyrus K.
6:84 Edward S. 6:84 Elizabeth
1:170,-6:84 Ellen 6:84 James
1:170 Maria 6:84 Mary 6:84
Sarah 6:84 Walter 6:84 Walter
S. 6:84 William J. 6:84

5

BANKS, Charles E. 2:191 General
6:130 James 4:177
BARBER, Deborah 4:131
Elizabeth 5:159 Esther 6:29
Hannah 5:110 John 4:148
Joseph 4:148 Katherine 4:169
Lydia 5:153 McDaniel 3:120
Nancy 4:136 Robert
3:91,147,-5:110,153,159,-6:29
Sarah 6:137
BARD, Martha 3:91 William 3:89
BARKER, Abigail 2:119 Ann
3:123,124 Anna 2:119,174,
-3:123 Anna S. 7:89 Benjamin
2:50,-6:36 Charles 3:123 David
6:33,117 David T. 6:10
Deborah 4:90 Ebenezer 2:49
Eliphalet 3:181 Eliza 7:87
Elizabeth 2:49,6:117,170
Enoch 5:40 Ephraim 2:50 Ezra
2:49,119 George 6:38 Helen M.
6:47 John 2:49-6:117 Jonathan
2:164,-6:139 Josiah 2:50 Levi
2:119 Louisa A. 5:152 Mar-
garet 3:126 Martha 2:49,50,
119,-3:123,-6:10 Mary 3:123,
-6:117,169 Mary A. 5:37 Mary
L. 4:24 Mary Upham 7:87
Nathan 2:50,-3:123,124
Nathaniel 2:50 Noah 2:49,50,
-3:124 Sarah 3:124,-4:88
Sophia 3:123 Susanna 2:49,
-4:86 Thomas 4:31 William
6:10
BARLOW, Levi 5:169
BARNARD, Alice 3:132 Eliza D.
6:154,-7:39 John 2:132,
-3:37,129,-6:10 Joseph 6:170
Lucretia G. 6:58 Matthew 2:76
Sarah 3:136
BARNES, Abraham 5:41 Elizabeth
4:13,-5:41 Henry 3:82,104 John
5:90 Mary 5:90 Mr 5:90
BARNEWELL, Widow 3:176
BARRETT, Hannah 3:86
BARRY, John 2:179,180 Thomas
F. 2:139
BARSHAM, John 1:12 Mrs. 3:51
BARSTOW, Benjamin 7:3 Emily
A. 5:18 Hannah 5:18 Hannah B.
5:20 Joshua 4:174 Margaret
4:173 Mary J. 5:18

BARTEN, Mark 6:105
BARTER, Elizabeth 5:135 Henry
5:133 John 2:186,-6:137 Mary
4:177 Nancy 4:125 Pelatiah
2:186 Sarah 5:135
BARTLETT, Abigail 3:115,-5:18
Abram 3:173,176 Alexander
5:102 Amelia 5:90 Caroline
7:64 Chauncey C. 7:71 Daniel
W. 4:183 David 4:174 Dorcas
3:8 Dorothy 3:168 Dr. 6:31
Ebenezer 4:174 Elizabeth
5:111,-7:23 Ezra 3:169 Gilman
5:20 Hannah 5:42,158 Harriet
4:183 J. 6:60 James 4:80,
-5:20,-7:66 John 3:41,173,175,
-4:91,132,176,178,-5:21,110,1-
11,158,-6:27,60 Jonathan 4:80
Joseph 3:90,-4:132 Josiah
2:95,-3:87,-4:21,117 Levi
4:176,-6:168 Luella J. 5:19
Martha 4:187 Mary 2:95,
-3:87,89,131,-5:17,110,-6:31
Matthias 4:175 Miriam 3:131
Moses 3:130 Mr. 6:31 Mrs.
3:175,176 Nancy 3:113
Nathaniel 6:27,60 Nehemiah
4:132 Peter 3:120 Priscilla
4:173 Rhoda 3:133 Rhoda E.
1:173 Richard 3:118,6:139
Samuel 4:173 Samuel C. 6:12
Sarah 3:130,167,171,4:21,131,
-6:5,-7:87 Stephen 3:87 Susan
7:68 Thomas 4:78,-5:90 William 4:79 Zipporah 3:170
BARTO, Abraham 1:22
BARTON, Edward 1:5,9,10,-
2:23,61 Mr. 1:3
BASS, Clara F. 5:142 Gillam
(William?) 1:110 Joseph 5:163
Moses B. 1:110
BASSETT, Abigail 2:30 Daniel
1:166,176,-2:30,-5:128,-6:25,
82 Fanny J. 7:58 Gulielma M.
6:91 Hannah 1:16,-5:128,-6:19
Hannah B. 6:24,127 John
1:161,166,176,5:128 Lydia
5:128 Rebecca 5:128 Ruth
1:161,166,176,-5:128 Sarah
5:128 Susanna 6:25 Thomas
5:19 Ursula 6:82 Ursula C.
6:179

6

BATCHELDER, A. S. 4:96
Abigail 2:67,105,-4:115,-5:19
Abraham 4:187,-7:9 Alexander
1:6,9,-2:23,62 Amos 3:168
Anna 2:66 Benjamin 2:71,111,
-3:90,132 Benjamin P. 3:178
Charles H. 3:186 Daniel 2:68,
133 Deborah 2:69,84,86,88,90,
105,107,110,111,133 Ebenezer
2:45,69,71,130 Elijah 5:107
Elisha 4:180,-6:28,31
Elizabeth 2:69,71,130,133,
-3:169,-6:32 Ephraim 4:91 Esther 2:90 Francis 5:107 Gideon
4:186 Huldah 3:136 Jane 2:107
John 2:66,-4:130 Joseph 2:36
Joseph Porter 7:9 Josiah
2:67,69,71,130,133,-3:38,39,
-6:28 Mary 2:48,67,-3:38,
132,135,-4:89 Mr. 6:47 Mrs.
6:28 Nahum J. 1:30 Nathan
2:44,69,70,-3:38,136,-4:90,176
Nathaniel 2:46,70,84,86,88,90,
105,107,110,111,-3:38,114,
-5:182,-6:160 Page 4:125
Phineas 2:44,48,68,69,130,133,
-3:39 Richard 2:71 Ruth 2:88
Samuel 4:85,131,-5:36 Sarah
6:31 Smith 6:162 Stephen
2:48,110,-6:32
BATHORICK, Abel 4:32
BATS, Mary 1:92
BATSON, Elizabeth 2:35,36 Mary
2:35 Nathaniel 2:35,37 Samuel
2:35 Stephen 2:36
BAWE, Deborah 2:168
BAXTER, Eunice 2:127 John 2:19
Rebecca 2:19 Richard 2:184,
-3:70,74
BAZEN or Bazin, Daniel W. 7:61
Horace G. 7:61 Margaret 4:175
Mr. 5:189 Mrs. 5:189 Otis A.
7:61 Susanna 5:189 Victor
3:67,175
BEACH, Polly 2:93
BEAL, Ebenezer 4:31 Hannah
6:139 Nicholas 2:183
BEAN, Abigail 1:166,175,-3:91,
-5:125,159,-6:18 Abigail S.
4:176 Abraham 5:125 Alice
2:48,70 Amos 7:69 Anna
3:40,-5:125,154 Anna A. 6:18

BEAN (continued)
Bathsheba 5:154 Benjamin
1:163,-2:68,-3:43,-5:125,
-6:127,184 Catherine 3:41,
-5:107 Chandler 3:182
Coleman 2:46,132 Cornelius
3:90,-5:106 Curtis 3:91 Cyrus
B. 6:82 Daniel 2:43,48,
-3:37,-5:153,154,155 Darius
6:82 David 2:46,48,-3:43,
-5:12,103,106,107,111,154,
156,-6:28 Dorothy 6:127 Edward 3:88 Elias 6:18 Elizabeth
2:30,31,-3:43,179,-4:69,89,
-5:12,107,-6:54 Elizabeth R.
6:86 Elsie 4:89 Emma 4:191
Eunice 6:18 Folsom 5:155
Gideon 1:167,-6:20,123,
127,185 Gilman 5:125 Hannah
1:167,175,176,-2:48,-4:86,
161,-5:125,-6:18,128 Hannah
E. 6:82 Hannah M. 6:18 Hannah R. 6:127 Hiram R. 4:189
Horatio N. 4:189 Huldah 3:167
Isabella 5:12 James 1:166,175,
-2:31,44,72,-3:40,183,-5:126,
-6:18,86 James R. 6:18 Jane
6:20 Jean 5:159 Jedidiah 4:182
Jemima 3:45 Jeremiah 1:168,
-2:129,-3:86,-5:174,-6:26,81,
86,185 Jethro 2:70 Joanna
4:132 Joel 1:166,168,171,176,
-6:18,86 John 1:171,-2:30,31,
-5:156,-6:86 Jonathan 2:68,
-3:42,-4:189,-5:12,110,154,
156,159 Joseph 2:43,45,65,67,
68,132,133,134,-3:88,91,
-5:103,104,106,107,110,153,
155,158,-6:26 Joseph C. 6:82
Joshua 1:167 Josiah 5:156
Judith 2:70,-3:87 Keziah 3:136
Lettice A. 4:189 Lois 6:18
Louisa 7:43 Lucretia E. 6:18
Lydia 1:163,-3:169,-5:125,
-6:18 Margaret 2:45,47,134,
-3:89,-5:104,107,-6:127 Martha 5:12 Mary 1:166,168,171,
176,-2:48,-3:39,91,-4:91,189,
-5:12,107,125,153,155,-6:18
Mary A. 4:189 Mary H. 2:30,
-6:86 Mary W. 6:82 Mehitable
2:68,-5:12 Miriam 2:65,

7

BEAN (continued)
-3:44,-5:158 Moody 5:103
Nancy 5:21 Nathaniel 2:67,
-5:106 Peace 5:125 Peniel 7:7
Rachel 1:63 Rhoda 5:12
Richard 4:88 Ruth 3:132
Samuel 2:43,45,47,48,
70,132,134, -3:37,-5:103,
106,109,153,154,156,159,-6:29
Sarah 2:47,48,68,72,129,
-3:40,44 -4:85,-5:22,109,
125,-6:28,127 Sarah T.
6:127
Seth 2:68 Sinkler 3:40 William
4:189,-6:29
BEAR, Jerusha 3:3
BEARD, Easter 4:13 Hester 4:12
Joseph 4:11 Mary 4:9 Thomas
1:179 William 1:178,-6:52
BEATLEY, Spencer 7:26
BECK, Abigail 4:125 Caleb
1:12,-4:58 Dorcas 5:90
Elizabeth 1:15,-4:51,53,-6:70
H 3:50,51 Henry 1:9,10,179,
-3:173 Joanna 5:134,-6:45
John 6:70 Joseph 4:76 Lucy
6:77 Mr. 1:13,-3:50,55,-5:90
Mrs. 3:176,-5:134,136,185,
-6:45,77 Samuel 4:125,-5:134,
136,185,-6:45,77 Sarah 5:136
Thomas 2:102,-3:55,174,176,
-4:50,53 Widow 3:176
BEDELL, Isabel 4:46 Robert 4:46
BEEDE, Aaron 5:125,-6:184
Abigail 5:125,172 Abigail H.
2:32 Abner 5:172 Anna 1:120,
-6:123 Anne 5:125 Beza 3:131
Caroline E. 6:180,181 Cyrene
M. 6:181 Cyrus 1:123,172,
-4:119,-5:172,-6:185 Daniel
1:118,121-124,-3:44,-4:68,
-5:63,160,171 David O. 6:181
David S. 6:180 Dorothy 1:123,
163,-5:63 Eli 2:32,67,-4:91,-
6:32 Elijah 1:163,-5:63 Elisha
5:63,125 Eliza A. 6:180 Eliza
J. 6:124 Elizabeth 2:69,-3:87,
-5:63,124 Eunice 6:124 Grace
5:63 Hannah 5:124 Hannah F.
1:175,-6:124 Hepzibah 6:26
Hezekiah 3:43-5:158,-6:26
Hugh J. 5:63 Huldah 5:124
James R. 6:124 Janathan

BEEDE (continued)
(see Jonathan) Jehoshea 3:131
Jeremiah 3:170 Joanna
4:131,-5:158 John 1:175,
-5:126,-6:124 John L. 6:124
Jonathan 2:69,-5:124,-6:123,
124 Judith 1:172 Kezia 3:130,
-5:172 Martha 1:121,-5:128
Mary 1:118,-5:121,124,125,172
Mary A. 6:124,180 Mary Ann
1:176 Mehitable 5:124 Miriam
1:176 Moses 1:175,176 Moses
H. 5:172 Mrs. 6:32 Nathan
1:122,163,-5:63,160,-6:184
Patience 1:118,121,123,124,
-5:63,172 Phebe 1:124,-5:173
Phinehas 5:158 Reuben 5:172
Reuben V. 6:180 Samuel 5:124,
-6:124 Sarah 1:118,-5:64,124,
-6:123,126 Sarah A. 2:32,
-6:124 Sarah J. 6:180 Stephen
1:172,-5:59,172 Susanna 5:124
Thomas 2:67,-6:32 William
5:63
BEEDLE, Susanna 5:98
BEGWORTH, Benjamin 3:97
BELCHER, Andrew 2:21 Governor
5:97,-7:83
BELKNAP, Mr. 1:100,-5:80,
-6:118,-7:12
BELL, Andrew W. 2:163 C. H.
5:81 Elizabeth 2:37,-3:43 F.
M. 5:100 George 2:36 James
6:38,-7:87 John A. 7:69 Matthias 3:29,71 Mary 3:87 Mary
Ann 7:87 Mesheck 1:22,-2:58
Mr. 4:2 Peter 5:41 Samuel 6:52
Thomas 1:22,-2:37,38 William
M. 2:58
BENMORE, Charles 1:11 Philip
1:10
BENNETT, Abigail 1:102,-4:93,
-6:172 Arthur 4:186 Deborah
4:183 Dinah 6:137 Ebenezer L.
4:182 Eleazer 1:157 Elizabeth
7:15 Elliott V. 5:86 Helen C.
6:59 James G. 7:58 Jeremiah
7:73 John 1:102,-2:98,6:79,172
John H. 4:186 Joseph 6:80
Josiah 6:137 Lydia 6:137 Martha 4:126,-6:137 Mary 4:57,80,
-5:39 Mehitable 6:159,-7:40

8

BENNETT (continued)
Miss 5:45 Mr. 3:175 Mrs.
3:175,-6:80 Nicholas 3:174
Phebe 6:137 Sarah 4:77,130
Stephen 7:14 William 2:104,
-5:86 William Sewall 7:12
Winthrop 6:79,80,-7:12,14,
15,73
BENNT, Francis 2:183
BENSON, Anna P. 4:112 David
7:23 Hannah 4:60 Henry 4:98
James 2:168,170,-3:160,-4:110
Jemima 5:43 Joanna 4:112
John 4:110,112 Joseph 3:3,
-4:112 Mary 4:98,107 Mercy
4:98 Noah 4:107 Sarah 4:110,
112 Susanna 3:160 William
3:160 William H. 5:142
BENTON, Jacob 7:36 William
6:136
BERDEAN, Mr. 5:140 Priscilla
5:140
BERJIN, Mary 5:56
BERRY, Abigail 1:40,83,90,
-2:137,-4:54,150,-7:45 Abigail
M. 1:144 Alfred 2:137 Ann
1:34,-6:68 Anna 3:154,
-4:146,-7:89 Benjamin 1:40,
-2:172,-4:99,152,186,-5:86,87,
117,-6:71,75,169 Brackett
2:137 Brackett M. 2:137
Charity 1:40 Charlotte 2:137
Clarissa L. 1:144 Daniel 6:68
Deacon 7:91 Deliverance 4:11
Dorothy 6:176 Ebenezer 1:40,
90 Eleanor 1:40,90,138,139,
-6:67 Elizabeth 1:144,-4:151
Elizabeth M. 1:144 Ephraim
1:34-6:75,115,116 Esther
1:45,46,144,-7:5 George 5:7
Gilman C. 2:137 Hannah 1:47,
89,90,95,137,138,-5:86,87,
-6:95 Hannah L. 1:136 Huldah
1:90 Ira 2:137 Isaac 1:92 Jacob
1:47,92 James 1:13,34,90,
-6:65,75 James T. 1:90 Jane
4:10 Jeremiah 1:89,90,138,139,
-2:137,-5:55 John 1:13,46,47,
-2:35,85,-6:67,70,-7:20 John
W. P. 1:144 Joseph 3:173,175,
-4:58,5:56,-6:68,72,120 Joseph
H. 1:144 Joseph J. 1:136

BERRY (continued)
Jotham 1:92 Jotham S. 1:144
Judith 1:139,-4:150,-7:91
Kezia 1:40 Leah 5:51 Levi
1:89,136 Lois 6:74 Love
1:137-139 Lydia 1:138,-4:40,
50,103,-6:115 Margaret 4:104
Martha 6:120 Martha M. 1:144
Mary 1:40,89,136,137,144,
-4:134,150,-6:114 Mary A.
2:137 Mercy 4:151 Merrifield
1:40,90 Miss 3:93 Mr. 3:154
Mrs. 3:56,175,176,-6:174
Nathaniel 1:46,144,-3:174,
176,-4:10,-5:42,-7:5 Nathaniel
F. 1:144 Nehemiah 1:47 Olive
1:90,136,-5:6,-6:116 Oliver
2:137 Patience 1:89,139
Rachel 1:40,92 Robinson F.
2:137 Ruth 1:40 Sally 2:137
Samuel 1:83,144 Samuel B.
1:138,-2:137 Samuel C. 2:137
Samuel F. 1:144 Sarah 1:47,
89,136,138,144 Sarah A. 2:137
Simon 1:40 Solomon 1:89
Stephen 1:34,-6:67,70,71,74,
115-117,-7:89 Susanna 1:40,
47,-2:85,-6:75,115 Thomas
4:31,-5:114 Triphena 6:71,115
Triphena D. 6:116 Walter 7:24
William 1:3-5,9,89,137,138,
139,-6:69 Zachariah 1:92
BESFORD, Elizabeth 3:171
BEVERLY, John 3:175 Mrs. 3:175
Sarah 3:181
BICKFORD, Abigail 2:167,-3:61,
109,-4:146 Abner 3:1 Alice
3:10,112 Andrew 3:106 Ann
3:88,-4:19,59 Anna 2:169,-4:17
B. 3:57 Benjamin 2:168,-3:60,
61,63,106,156,-4:88,-5:6,
-7:18 Bridget 3:59 Charles
4:125 Charles W. 3:48,139,
-4:144,-5:144,177,178 Daniel
3:2,-4:15 Deborah 2:168,-3:61,
63,106 Dennis 4:15 Dependence 3:61 Dodavah 3:110
Ebenezer 2:173,-3:160-4:14,
17,19,59 Edward 1:12 Eleanor
2:176,-3:156,-4:19 Elizabeth
2:168,175,-3:2,63,-5:53,147,
-6:75,117 Frances 5:178

9

BICKFORD (continued)
George 4:14 Gideon 4:86 Hannah 2:169,-3:2,58,59,61,62, 105,112,-4:97,148,-6:74 Hannah M. 5:177 Henry 3:171, -4:53,147 Huldah 5:151,-6:113 Ichabod 3:4,156 Isaac 5:8,147, -6:33,38,-7:88 James 1:103, -4:16,-6:72 Jane 2:39,40, -3:51,54,-5:5,-6:87 Jesse 3:183,-5:150 Jethro 3:57-59,61,63,105,108,112 Joel 5:116 John 1:178,-2:76,170, 176,-3:57,109,-4:10,16,19,129, 149,-5:4,114,117,-6:35,69, 73,74,-7:90 Jonathan 2:174, -3:160,-4:18,-6:70,146 Joseph 2:146,-3:156,-4:149,-5:26, -6:70,185 Joshua 3:160,-5:162 Lemuel 3:105,-4:142,-6:74, 115-118 Love 4:78,183 Lydia 4:15,18 Margaret 4:16 Margery 4:14,15 Mary 2:168,-3:60, -4:13,16,125,127,-5:2,-6:70, 75,113,130 Mary Sophia 7:88 Micah 4:181 Miriam 2:172 Miss 4:53 Moses 1:173,-4:76, -5:56,-6:39,73 Mr. 6:99,118 Patience 6:71 Persey 2:170, -3:110 Priscilla 1:173,-5:49 Rachel 4:57,-6:73 Rebecca 3:4,-6:66 Richard 3:59,-4:19, -6:70,75 Samuel 1:103,-3:60, 156,-4:59,-5:3 Sarah 2:176, -3:1,56,60,109,156,160,-4:16, 18,50,53,-6:65,74,115,-7:90 Susanna 3:1,58 Temperance 6:68,116 Thomas 2:168,170, -3:156,160,164,-4:17,53 Tristram 5:50 Winthrop 3:9, -4:78
BIDDLE, Capt 4:29
BIGELOW, Anne 6:44 Benjamin 5:185,188,-6:41,44 Elizabeth 5:188 Joseph 5:185 Lucy 6:41 Lydia 4:130 Mrs 5:185,188, -6:41,44
BIGSBY, Benjamin 6:167
BILLIARD, John 4:31
BILLING(s), Hannah 7:12 John 1:3,-7:12 Richard 7:12
BINGHAM, James H. 7:19

BINNS, Jonas 1:178
BISHOP, Jewett 6:170
BLACK, Elisha 1:93,94 Hannah 1:94 Mary 1:93,94 Samuel 2:182
BLACKBURN, Abigail 7:67
BLACKDEN, Mary 3:56
BLACKETT, Joshua 4:31
BLACKINGTON, Sarah 2:94
BLAGDON, Hannah 7:90 Ichabod 6:67 John 7:90,91 Lydia 6:70 Mary 2:17,-3:50 Rawlings 6:72 Samuel 2:17 Sarah 6:69
BLAIR, Henry W. 6:130 Phebe A. 7:37 William 7:37
BLAISDELL, Abigail 6:114 Daniel 2:130,132 David 3:184,-5:181,182 Dorothy 3:42,86 Eliphalet 4:447,-6:74 Elizabeth 3:42,132 Enoch 3:48 Ephraim 5:20 George 6:7 H. C. 3:48 Hannah 2:70 Henry 2:71, -3:130 Jacob 4:90 John 4:86, -6:114 Jonathan 2:70,-3:38,91, -4:31 Jonathan L. 6:111 Joshua 4:89 Judith 4:89 Julia A. 6:6 Lydia 3:44,131 Mary 3:42 Mary S. 5:182,-6:6 Miriam 3:91,-4:173 Miss 3:132 Moses 3:42 Nancy 4:175 Naomi 2:130 Nicholas 3:142 Philip 4:89 Ralph 2:44,133, 134,-3:88 Ruth 3:31 Sarah 7:18 Susanna 3:86 William 3:178, 184
BLAKE (see also BLEAK), Asahel 4:131 Chase 4:137 Dearborn 4:136 Deborah 2:84,85,87,89,91,106,109,110 Dorothy 2:106 Dudley 4:137 Eleanor 4:135 Elisha 6:173 Elizabeth 4:133,177 Elizabeth B. 5:150 Esther 6:33 Hannah 4:85 Henry 4:134 Hezekiah 5:154,-6:26 Israel 4:177,-5:111 Jasper 2:84,85,87,89,91,106, 109,110 Jedediah 4:137 John 2:84,-3:91,-4:133-6:173 Jonathan 3:130,-5:107,111,154, 156,-6:26,30 Lucy 3:168 Maria 2:110 Martha 4:137 Mary 3:136,-4:132,137,-5:111

BLAKE (continued)
Mehitable 3:88,-4:175 Michael
7:67 Nancy 7:71 Philemon
2:108 Robert 4:137 Samuel
2:91 Samuel O. 4:137 Sarah
2:85,87,-4:173,-5:111,152,
156,-7:69 Sarah F. 7:24
Stevens 3:170 Timothy 5:107
BLANCHANT, Elizabeth 4:12
BLANCHARD, Abigail 5:46 David
6:104 Ebenezer 5:46 Elizabeth
5:185,189 Hannah 6:166 J. S.
C. 4:142 John 5:185 Jonathan
5:161 Jotham 5:185,188,189,
-6:43 Moses 6:111 Mrs.
5:188,-6:43 Porter 6:164
Rebecca 6:43 Roscoe G. 5:82
Sarah 5:188 Thomas 5:46
BLANCHER, Mr. 3:146 Mrs.
3:146
BLAND, Anabel 2:190 Isabel
2:190 Joanna 2:191 John 2:190
BLASHFIELD, Hannah 4:103
BLAW, Janet 4:6
BLEAK, Abigail 5:66 Asal 5:66
Jonathan 5:66 Joseph 5:66
Mehitable 5:66 Sarah 5:66
Sherburne 5:66 Theophilus 5:66
BLIGDON, Katherine 6:1
BLIGH, Hannah 3:88 Sarah 3:86
BLISH, Abraham 6:1
BLISS, Mary 5:47 Thomas 4:192,
-5:47,48
BLOOD, Mr. 3:147
BLUE, Daniel 4:169
BLUNT, Abigail 5:186 Arthur
5:138 Elizabeth 1:20,
-5:135,136,140 George 5:133
Isaac 6:161 John 1:23,28,
-2:35,-5:184 Mary 5:136 Mrs.
5:138,184,186 Robert 1:20
William 5:133,135,136,138,
140,184,186
BLYDENBURG, Clarissa 1:105
Hannah 1:105 John 1:105 Mar-
garet 1:105 Mary 1:105,-6:155
BLYH, William 4:153
BOARDMAN (or Bordman),
Andrew 4:115 Benjamin 6:187,
-7:23 Clarissa 6:187 David
6:187 Elizabeth 3:162,163
Hannah 3:162 Harriet 6:187

BOARDMAN (continued)
John B. 6:155 Jonathan 3:162
Langley 2:163 Lucy 6:135
Martha M. 6:155 Mary J. 6:155
Mercy 3:162,163 Stephen
3:162,-6:155 Thomas 3:162,
163 William 2:55,-6:155
BODGE, Andrew 4:128 Benjamin
3:41 Daniel 6:139 Hannah
4:125,-5:101 Joseph 7:55
Mary 4:128 Richard 4:78
Stephen 4:183
BOGWELL, Olive 3:113
BOHANNAN, Andrew 6:50
BOHONON, Benjamin S. 7:69
Louisa W. 7:25 Sarah 5:143
BOICE, James 6:184
BOISE, Sarah C. 7:71
BOLDERY, John 4:31
BOMMAZEEN, Sagamore 3:82,
146
BOND, Esther 1:84 John 1:84
Margaret 3:52 Mary 1:84
Nicholas 3:100 Robert 5:45
William 5:170
BONHAM, Hannah 1:149 Hezekiah
1:149 Mary 1:149 Nicholas
1:149 Samuel 1:149 Sarah
1:149
BOODY, Joseph 6:35 Moses 4:11
BOOKER, Jotham 3:65,74
BOOTH, Mary 3:52,-5:43
BOOTMAN, Amos 3:42,-5:155
Thomas 5:155
BORDEL, Isaac 5:44
BOSWELL, William 3:97
BOTHERICK, Olive 4:129
BOUDY, Edward 1:22
BOUFFARD, Nicholas 2:186,
-3:71
BOULTER, Elizabeth 2:106 Grace
2:83,84,86,89,90,106,110 Han-
nah 2:90 John 2:110 Joshua
2:83,84 Nathaniel 2:83,84,86,
89,90,106,110 Rebecca 2:86
BOUNDS, Abigail 4:98
BOUNTY, Francis 6:168
BOURDON, Peter 3:67
BOURON, Charles 3:68,75
BOUTELLE, Jedediah 4:76
Timothy 4:178
BOUTON, Nathaniel 6:14,15

11

BOWDEN, John 3:100 Sarah 3:142
BOWDON, Mary 4:76
BOWERS, John Stewart 7:19
   Philip 2:139
BOWLES, John 2:162,163,-7:77,
   78 Lydia 7:77,78 Mr. 3:50 Mrs.
   3:51 Nabby 7:78 Samuel 2:160
BOWLEY, Caroline 3:165 James
   3:165 Moses 4:116 Oliver S.
   3:165 Sergent 3:165 Zebediah
   3:165
BOWMAN, John 3:173 Mrs. 3:175
BOYD, Abigail 3:110,-5:188
   Andrew 2:22 Charlotte 4:118
   George 2:171,-3:110,-5:130,
   133, 134,136,139,183,185,
   188,189,-6:42,43,46 Henry C.
   6:43 James 2:22 Jane 5:134,
   139,183,185,188,189,-6:42,
   43,46 Joseph 3:8,-5:130 Mar-
   garet 2:22 Mary 5:183 Mrs.
   5:136 Phebe 5:185 Submit 6:46
   Supply 6:42 Thomas 3:164
   William 4:103,-5:136,189
BOYNTON, Alexander S. 2:119
   Anna B. 5:94 Barzillai 2:65
   -3:37 Dorothy 2:45 Hannah
   3:39 Joanna 2:67 John 3:5
   Joseph W. 2:119 Joseph J.
   2:119 Lydia 2:119 Mary 6:56
   Nathaniel 2:119 Rebecca 2:119
   William 2:130,-3:37
BOYS (see also Boice & Boise),
   Samuel 6:107
BRACE, Mary C. 3:186
BRACKETT, Abigail 4:181,-5:21
   Ann 1:26 Ann E. 7:44 Anthony
   1:3,5,9,12,-2:23,25,27,59,
   61-63,98,99 Benjamin 4:78
   Catherine 6:153 Charles
   Franklin 7:60 David 7:64
   Deborah 6:140 Ebenezer 7:15
   Eleanor 1:90 Eliza 4:116
   Elizabeth 3:3,91,-4:76,79,
   -6:139 Eunice 6:138 George
   3:122 Humphrey 6:185 James
   4:78 Jeremiah 6:139 John
   1:25,-2:169,-7:60 Joseph 4:116
   Joseph N. 5:35 Joshua 3:10,
   -4:75,-5:166,168 Love 1:26,90
   Lydia 1:25,26,-6:154,-7:39
   Martha 3:125,-7:60 Mary

BRACKETT (continued)
   1:26,-2:125,153,-3:123,125,
   -4:127,-5:98,-6:157 Mary A.
   5:35 Mary Jane 7:15 Nathaniel
   2:153,-4:76 Perney 6:154
   Phenney 7:39 Phebe 1:26
   Samuel 1:25,26,89,90,-5:54,
   -6:62 Sarah 4:78,-5:98 Simeon
   6:53 Thomas 1:13,-3:122,123,
   125,-5:98
BRACKINS, William 2:23
BRACY, Patience 6:149 Penelope
   6:149 William 6:149
BRADBURY, Abigail 4:85 Jacob
   3:132 James 2:181,-6:38 Jane
   3:130 Mary 6:143 Theophilus
   6:58 Winthrop 6:169
BRADEEN, Joseph 2:36
BRADFORD, Governor 4:191 John
   5:39,-7:61
BRADLEY, Abigail C. 6:161 Ann
   Ayer 7:19 Apphia 6:49 Asa F.
   7:68 Augusta 4:8 Benjamin
   3:114 Charlotte 7:19 David
   2:67 John 3:91,-6:111,162
   Jonathan 3:40,-6:58 Joseph
   3:101 Martha 6:107 Moses 6:54
   Moses H. 6:170 Nancy 6:170
   Richard 7:16 Ruth 6:111 Sabra
   6:169 Sarah 6:105 Sophia 6:162
   Susanna 3:91 William 3:168
   Winfield S. 1:109
BRADSTREET, Colonel 3:85
   Dudley 3:149 Hannibal 4:32
   Samuel 6:50
BRAGDEN, Arthur 3:100 Miss
   3:100 Mrs. 3:100 William 3:74
BRAGDON, Ivory 6:40 Samuel 5:6
   Sarah 5:44
BRAGG, Hannah 2:136
BRAMHALE, Martha 3:50
BRAMSCOMB, Arthur 4:128,
   -6:157 Charles H. 6:158 Lucy
   A. 6:158 Mary H. 6:157
BRANSON, George 1:179
BRASSBRIDGE, Catherine 4:158
   Edmund 4:158 Edward 5:73,75
   Elizabeth 4:158 George 5:74
   Hannah 5:79 James 5:75 John
   4:158,-5:73 Martha 5:158,-5:74
   Mr. 5:74 Mrs. 5:79 Rosemond
   5:73,75 Sarah 5:75 William

BRASSBRIDGE (continued)
3:16,-4:156
BRATTON, Mark 2:187,-6:105
Noah 1:23
BRAWN, Eleanor 4:12 Elizabeth
4:12 George 4:11 John 3:104
BRAY, Hannah 2:139 John 3:51
William 2:182,-3:71
BRAYNARD, Sarah 5:22
BRECK, Arnold 3:83
BREED, Benjamin 5:58 Daniel
1:165,-4:124,-7:6 Ruth
1:165,-7:6 Samuel 5:58
Zephaniah 1:165,-7:6
BRENNAN, James F. 5:96,-6:48
BRETTEN, James 2:186
BREWER, Jacob 3:6
BREWSTER, Abiah 5:3,140
Abigail 2:176,-5:116 Betty
7:30 Daniel 2:94,-5:4,136,
138,140,-6:42,46 David
5:139,185,188,-6:41,44,46,78
Deborah H. 6:33 Elisha 6:116
Eliza 6:39,-7:29 Elizabeth
5:56,-6:77,115,120,-7:86
Elizabeth H. 5:183 George
5:146,189,-6:42,44 John
1:10,12,-2:103,-3:174,175,
-5:3,6,39,136,146,-6:45,115-
118,120,174,-7:30,31 John Jr.
7:30 John F. 6:78 John G.
2:163,164,-6:78 Joseph 5:133,
136,183 Joshua 5:38,-7:29,86
Margaret 5:185 Margaret
Elizabeth Neal 7:86 Mark
6:46,-7:43 Mary 4:149,
-5:101,136,-6:46,78,174 Mrs.
3:175,-5:136,138-140,183-
186,188,189,-6:41-46,77,78
Nathaniel 2:94 Paul L. 4:186
Peggy 7:11 Phebe 5:133 Robert
Neal 7:86 Rosietta 7:29 Ruth
5:139,-7:11 Sally 7:31 Samuel
2:104,-3:2,165,-5:188 Sarah
6:43 Stephen 5:8,-6:118,
-7:29,31 Susan C. 4:188
Timothy 6:33 Widow 3:175
William 5:184,186,189,-6:43,
45,77,78,-7:11
BRIANT (see BRYANT)
BRIARD, Elisha 2:20 Elizabeth
4:104,-5:140 George 6:79 John

BRIARD (continued)
5:187 Margaret 5:43 Mary 6:44
Mrs. 5:137,140,187,189,-6:44,
76 Oliver 6:76 Samuel 5:137,
140,165,187,189,-6:44, 76,79
William 5:189
BRICK, Miss 3:56
BRICKETT, Barnard 6:110 Nancy
6:108 Thomas 6:108
BRIDDEN, James 3:22 Joseph
3:21,70
BRIDGE, Abigail 3:88 Samuel
2:183
BRIDGES, Joseph 1:63 Mary 1:63
Sarah 1:63,-4:74,122,-7:69
BRIDGHAM, Henry 4:102 Jacob
4:104 William 4:102
BRIDGMAN, George M. 3:141
BRIER, Abigail 2:12,-3:52,54
Elisha 3:174,176 Elizabeth
2:13,-4:132 John 2:12 Mary
5:67,72 Mercy 2:50 Mrs. 3:176,
-5:72 Peter 5:67,72 Rachel
2:12,13,-4:131,-5:67,72 Robert
2:186 Thomas 2:12,13
BRIGGS, Abigail 6:191 Ezra 1:176
John 7:72 Joseph 1:176,-6:90
Mary 1:176 William 2:37
BRIGHAM, Levi 7:19,20
BRIMBLECOM, Almira 4:118
BROAD, William 1:11
BROADERS, Bartholomew 5:90
Jacob 5:90
BROADHEAD, Almena J. L. 6:63
Ann M. 6:63,-7:44 Daniel D.
6:63 Elizabeth H. 6:63,159,
-7:40 Epapras K. 6:63 John
6:63,153,154,159,160 John M.
6:63 Joseph C. 6:63 Josiah A.
6:63 Mary 6:63 Mary R. 6:63
Mehitable S. 6:63 Olive N.
6:63 Thornton F. 6:63
BROADSTREET, Northern 4:32
BROCK, Elizabeth 4:147 Ezra
5:55 Mary 7:60 Simon C. 5:181
Stephen 4:151 Thomas R.
6:107
BRODHEAD (see Broadhead)
BRONSDON, Ann L. 7:20
BROOK, Oliver 5:149 Samuel
5:170
BROOKE, Charles 4:7

13

BROOKIN(G)(S), Miss 5:43 Mrs.
3:175 Samuel 5:41 William
1:9,12
BROOKS, John 5:144 Michael
3:40
BROUGHTON, Abigail 5:41
Daniel 3:165 James 5:134 John
5:131,132,134,-6:44 Jonathan
6:44 Margaret 5:134,-6:44
Samuel 5:131,132 Thomas 1:10
BROWN, Abel 4:89 Abiah 2:174
Abigail 1:85,93,127,165,170,
-3:119,164,177,181,-4:90,117,
132,-5:121,154,-6:171
Abraham 4:90,135,138,-5:11,70
Alice 1:165,-5:121 Amos
5:121,-6:106 Anna 5:121 Anna
H. 1:170 Anson W. 7:68 Bath
M. 4:135 Benjamin 2:70,
-3:8,120,134,-4:171,-5:65,
70,159 Betsey 7:26 Capt.
7:78,80 Charles 5:41,-6:40,
-7:85 Charles C. 5:181
Clarissa 4:138 Comfort 1:141
Cotton S. 3:165 Daniel 3:135,
-5:36,157,-6:29,32 David 3:65,
71,-5:39,44 David S. 5:121
David T. 6:86 Deborah 5:3
Delia 1:165 Dr. 2:69,134,
-5:103 E. R. 5:82 Ebenezer
3:86 Edmund 5:129 Edmund M.
3:128 Edward 3:86,-6:86 Edward A. 5:192 Eli 7:85 Elijah
4:178 Elisha R. 2:165 Eliza
2:139,-3:165,-4:118,-7:67
Eliza H. 7:72 Elizabeth 1:45,
85,93,-3:6,45,87,90,128,164,
180,-4:98,104,169,-5:65,66,
68,70,-7:61,78,80 Elizabeth I.
5:182 Elizabeth L. 6:6 Enoch
3:44,87,119 Enoch C. 3:128
Enoch W. 3:128 Ephraim 3:171
Ezekiel 4:169,-5:11,14,65,
66,68,70,-6:32 Fannie W.
2:166 Francis 5:159 Freath
5:68 George T. 6:86 Greenleaf
C. 3:128,-4:74,117 Hannah
4:97,132,135,-5:11,14,70,
107,113,-5:11,14,70,107,
113,-7:22 Henry 4:31 Hoppy
4:173 Jacob 1:186 James
3:49,134,-4:103,-7:42 Jane

BROWN (continued)
4:175 Jeremiah 1:165,-4:31,
131,176,-5:121 Joanna 3:90
John 1:72,93,140,165,-2:83,
84,-4:31,91,98,171,-5:39,
54,87, 88,90,121,129,-6:11,
86,112,172,-7:71 John C. 7:61
John S. J. 1:141 John Osburne
7:78 Jonathan 1:85,93,-3:90,
177 Joseph 1:45,85,93,-2:69,
-3:9,89,-7:24,78,80 Joshua
3:128,-4:85,-5:37,111,154,157
Josiah 3:128,165,-4:104,118,
-5:36 Judith 3:135,-5:3 Julia
A. 5:181 Lawrence 3:119
Lebna 3:40 Lieutenant 4:28
Lillis 5:58 Louisa 7:87 Love
5:114 Lucretia K. 7:22 Lucy
M. 5:18 Lydia 1:127,-2:174,
-4:101,-5: 116,121,159,176
Madlen 2:172 Martha 1:186,
-3:194,-5:90 Martha Thomas
7:85 Mary 1:45,85,93,186,
-2:83,-3:114,-4:51,97,98,134,
138,-5:65,70,88,-6:28,-7:67
Mary A. 3:128,-4:74,116,
-5:36,-6:86 Mary Bell 7:86
Mary L. 6:6,8 Mehitable 3:120
Michael 2:184 Miriam 6:29
Miss 3:135 Moses 4:147,
-5:121,-6:172,-7:85 Mr.
2:59,133,-3:39,82,149,-5:43
Mrs. 2:130,-7:87 Nancy
6:6,170,-7:21 Nathan
3:87,128,-6:106 Nathaniel
4:130,-5:17,18,65,83,157
Nathaniel H. 6:86 Nathaniel T.
5:111 Nicholas 5:40 Olive 7:80
Patience 1:72 Paul 3:120,
-4:132,174,-5:65,70 Rachel
3:44 Rebecca 4:171 Richard
1:85 Robert 3:41,-5:159 Ruth
5:157 Samuel 1:72,85,-3:177,
-4:101,103,132,-5:30,70 Sarah
2:46,83,84,-3:43,128,136,
-4:97,118,125,132, 136,138,
171,175,-5:14,66,70,103,-6:52
Scipio 4:31 Simeon 2:130,-
5:105,107 Susan 3:120 Susanna
1:85,-4:152,-5:54,-7:85
Thomas 2:84,130,183,-3:39,
-6:171,172,-7:21,57 Walter

14

BROWN (continued)
6:86 William 1:127,165,170,-
5:121, 6:52,184 William G.
4:74 William H. 6:86
BROWNE, George W. 3:141
BRUCE, Jeduthan 7:43 John 4:2
Sarah 4:128 Thomas 4:76,78
BRYAN, William J. 5:178
BRYANT, Anne 6:64 Elizabeth
6:57 James 1:22 John 2:185,
-6:62 John S. 4:185 Lydia A.
7:63 Mary 4:89,168,-5:5,-6:61
Mrs. 3:176 Nancy 6:112,137
Robert 3:174,176 Thomas
5:118 Walter 6:137,138
BRYAR or BRYER, Abigail 1:188
Charles 1:186 Elizabeth 1:192
Giles 1:186 Hannah 6:50 Judith
1:191 Mary 1:186 Mercy 1:191
Peter 1:188 Thomas 1:183,188,
191,192
BUCHANAN, James 5:7
BUCKER, John 1:13
BUCKLAND, Deborah 5:144
BUCKLEY, Richard 1:22
BUCKMINSTER, Elizabeth 7:75
Frances 7:80 Joseph 6:79,
-7:11,15,73,75,80 Joseph
Stevens 7:15 Lucy Maria 7:73
Mary 7:80 Mr. 5:80,-6:172
BUELL, A. C. 3:94-96 Augustus
C. 4:82
BUFFUM, Aaron 5:30 Abigail
5:124 Anna 5:124 Benajah
5:124 Caleb 1:68,69,122,123,
-3:35,-4:41,-5:24,26 Christopher 5:26 Dorcas 1:122,
-5:24,30,126 Elizabeth 1:61,
66,68,69,71,119,120,122,162,
-3:35,-4:162,-5:26,-7:8 Eunice
5:130 Hannah 1:123,126,127,
170,-3:35,-5:29 Huldah 5:26
Huldah D. 5:125 Isaac 1:127,
-4:120,-5:29,-6:17 Jacob 5:30
James 5:30 John 1:71,120,126,
127,-3:35,-4:42,67,-5:28,30,
125 Jonathan 5:30 Joseph 1:51
Joshua 1:61,66,68,69,71,119,
120,122,162,-3:35,-5:27,30,
-7:8 Lydia 1:122,-3:35,-5:26,
30 Margaret 1:126,-5:29 Mary
1:61,-3:35,-4:70,-5:26,-7:8

BUFFUM (continued)
Mr. 3:174 Patience 5:30 Peace
5:125 Samuel 1:119,170,-3:35,
-4:124,-5:30,-7:8 Sarah 5:30,
-6:17 Temperance 1:123,-5:26,
172 Timothy 1:170,-5:64,124
Zervia 5:125
BULL, Hugo(e) 2:5
BULLARD, Augustin(e) 3:153,
174,-4:10
BULLEN, Aynthia 6:167 Martha
6:168
BUNKARD, John 6:57
BUNKER, A. 6:92 Aaron 4:77
Adeline 6:93 Andrew 4:127
Eliza A. 4:185 Enoch 7:59 Es-
ther 2:77 Huldah 3:171,-5:175
James 3:149 John 3:149,-7:58
Jonathan 4:46 Joseph 2:77
Love 1:100 Lydia 1:126,163,
-2:77,-5:175 Mary 2:77,78
Mehitable C. B. 7:58 Paul
1:126,163,-4:121,-5:62,175
Peter 6:185 Remembrance 4:79
Sarah 2:77 Simeon 1:126,163,
-5:175
BUNTIN, James 6:168 Martha
6:111 Richard 6:52
BURBANK, Eben 6:105 Elizabeth
6:105 Hale 3:131 Jonathan
3:134 Mercy 3:132 Samuel 6:10
BURDEN, George 6:145
BURGIN, Joseph Y. 2:162
BURHAM, Enoch 5:52
BURLEIGH (or BURLEY), Abigail
6:137 Ann Augusta 7:59 Ben-
jamin 2:155,-4:88,-6:160 Bet-
sey 7:42 Betsey S. 7:41
Clarissa 4:129,-7:42 Deborah
6:63,-7:42 Drusilla 4:125
Eleanor 3:3 Elizabeth 4:126,
-6:62,134 Elizabeth R. 6:134
Elizabeth S. 6:160 Frederic P.
7:41 George W. 7:42 Henry
6:133,134,136,138,151 Isaac
6:138 Jacob 6:137,155,-7:41
James 4:77,-6:138,154 James
3rd 7:39 Jasper H. 7:41
Jeremiah 7:42 John 4:77,
-6:151,-7:44 John B. 4:187
Jonathan 4:188,-7:42,57
Joseph 3:17,-6:137 Joseph L.

BURLEIGH (continued)
6:138 Josiah 4:117,-7:42
Josiah Jr. 7:42 Judith
6:138,160,-7:40 Lavina 7:42
Lois 7:41 Lucy 6:137 Mark
7:42 Mary 4:184,-6:137,138,
-7:59 Mary C. 7:41 Mehitable
4:126,-6:136 Mehitable S.
6:151 Moses 4:77 Nancy 2:155,
-4:88 Nathaniel 6:138
Nathaniel E. 7:37 Nathaniel R.
6:151 Peter 7:42,59 Reuben M.
7:41 Sally 7:42 Samuel 4:129
Sarah 2:155,-4:125,-6:34,37,
155,-7:17 Sarah Jane 7:55
Susan 7:42 Susan W. 6:159,
-7:40 Susannah 7:42 Thomas
3:114,182,-4:88 Wheeler 2:155
William 2:155,-6:40,136,138
BURLEY (see also BURLEIGH),
Hannah M. 5:46
BURNAP, Jacob 1:152
BURNHAM, Abigail 1:101 Alice
4:182 Amos 4:19 Calvin S.
6:93 Deborah 3:183 Dudley
5:8,-7:28 Edward 3:130
Eleazer 7:28 Elizabeth 4:78,
-6:175 Elliot G. 1:106,-4:130
Enoch 4:19,-5:149,-6:161,175,
-7:27,28 Frances 5:191 Hannah
1:106,-4:13 Harriet 7:45 James
6:4,75,175 Jeremiah 2:175,
-5:191 John 1:102,155,-7:86
John A. 7:72 Joseph 1:102,
-4:18,80,128 Joseph S. 1:101
Lois 6:175 Mary 5:114,-6:175
Mehitable 4:18,19,62,-5:53,
-6:175,-7:28 Moses 3:182 Mr.
1:106 Nathaniel 3:160,-4:18,
19,62,-5:182,-6:6,-175,-7:28
Olly 7:27 Robert 1:101,-4:77,
-5:190,191,-6:139 Samuel
5:191 Samuel W. 3:30,72 Sarah
5:190,191 Sarah H. 6:93
Susanna 3:160 Thomas P.
6:175 Tryphena (Triphena)
5:120,-6:175 Winthrop 3:1
BURNS, Patrick 4:31
BURRILL, Augustus W. 7:53
BURROUGHS (BURROWS), Amos
5:146 George 3:171
BURT, F. 1:159 Federal 6:35

BUSBEE, Richard 2:171
BUSHNELL, Abigail T. 2:95
Benajah 2:95
BUSS, Joseph 3:80 Richard T.
6:57 William 3:80
BUSSELL, Benjamin F. 6:170
David 6:29 Elizabeth 6:67
Izette 6:66 Jonathan 6:29
Judith 6:32 Martha 6:27 Mary
6:32 Samuel 6:32 Sarah 6:27
Simmons 6:29 Simon 6:65
William 6:27,32
BUSSON, Louis 3:68,75
BUSWELL (see also BUSSELL)
(BUZZELL), Andrew 7:18
Anna 6:104 Benjamin 6:54
Carter 7:20 Hammond 7:25
Hannah 6:109 James 6:164,
-7:65 Martha 6:56 Richard 6:53
BUTLER, Dorcas 4:84 Edward
5:135,138,184,187,189,-6:43
Elizabeth 5:135,138,184,187,
-6:43 Enoch 4:183 Henry 4:78
James 5:138 Mark L. 5:187
Mary 4:90,-5:189,-6:160 Mrs.
5:189 Phebe 3:114 Polly 7:40
Sarah L. 5:135 Stephen 3:86
BUTTERFIELD, Lieutenant 3:147
Mrs. 3:147
BUTTERS, Samuel 6:108,163
Thomas 7:68 Timothy 6:112
BUTTERWORTH, John 4:191
Mary 4:191
BUTTON, Thomas 2:19 William
2:19
BUXTON, Edward 7:70 Samuel
2:77
BUZZELL (see also Bussell and
Buswell), Abigail 2:130,-
4:175,-5:158 Abraham 4:31
Ashbury 5:19 Caleb 3:91 Cor-
nelius 2:167 Daniel 5:154
David 3:136 Deborah 4:149
Deliverance 3:45 Elizabeth
4:80 Hannah 5:153 Huldah
5:155 Isaac 5:104 Jacob 7:2
James 5:106,-7:90 Jane 5:160
John 5:110,-7:21 John B. 5:152
Joseph 2:47,-3:135,-5:108
Mary 2:45,47,71,-4:149,178
Mehitable 2:47,-3:42,-5:157
Miles 4:125 Rachel 7:90

BUZZELL (continued)
Samuel 2:48,-3:38,87,-4:125,-5:104 Sarah 3:37,-5:53,111,158
Simmons 3:41,-5:108,111,153, 157,160 Susan 7:86 William 2:44,67,130,134,-3:3,37,42, -5:106,110,154,155,158
CABAN, Samuel 4:117
CADET, Mendes fils 5:170
CAIN, Deborah 3:94 Jonathan 5:43
CALDER, Anthony 5:41
CALDERWOOD, John 4:32
CALDWELL, Abigail 1:69,-5:26 Charles T. 4:48 Elizabeth 1:69,116,-5:61,-7:9 Hannah 3:86 Margaret 5:86 Mary J. 5:101 Mr. 5:86 Samuel 3:45 William 1:69,116,-4:184
CALEF, Abigail 5:56,-6:173 Daniel 4:149,-6:173 Dorothy 3:132 Hannah 3:86,-6:31 James 4:114,-6:173 Jeremiah 5:40 John 3:87,91,-4:175 Joseph 3:131,134,-5:109 Lois 3:91,-5:106 Lydia 5:112 Mary 3:131,-6:27,96 Miriam 4:178 Robert 3:171 Samuel 5:108 Sarah 5:158 Susanna 5:117 William 5:106,108,109,112, 158,-6:27,31 Winter 4:32
CALF(E), Daniel 7:28 John 7:28 Samuel 6:140 Susanna 7:28 William 7:28
CALL, Elizabeth 5:44 Eunice 6:167
CALLAM, Bethiah 1:117 Caleb 1:117
CALLEY, Abiah 2:16 Annie 2:42 Benjamin 2:16 Comfort 2:16 Eliphalet 4:132,-5:65 Elizabeth 2:16 Hannah 2:16 John 2:16,-5:16 Jonathan 2:14,-4:132,-5:65 Josiah 5:65 Mary 2:16,-4:91,-5:16,65 Mehitable 2:14 Rebecca 2:16 Richard 2:14,16,-5:65 Samuel 2:16 Sarah 2:14,16 Sewall 4:126 Thomas 2:16,-5:16,65 William 2:15
CALWELL (see also Caldwell), James 2:169

CAMBRIDGE, William 2:182,-3:71
CAME, Hannah 4:190 Tabitha 4:189
CAMERON, Mary 2:18 William 2:18
CAMMET, Ann 6:30 Silas 6:27,30
CAMORE, Nancy 6:164
CAMPBELL, Dorothy 4:174 Elizabeth 3:133 Hannah 3:168 Mary 3:86,167
CAMPION, Clement 1:7,8 Mr. 1:7,9
CANNEY, Abigail 2:29 Almira 2:29,-6:82,179 Amos S. 4:163 Anna 1:170,172,-2:147,-6:126, 150 Anne 4:145 Benjamin 2:80, -4:65,-5:28 Daniel 5:146,176 Daniel G. 5:176 Deborah 1:71, 168,169,-2:147,170,-5:29,174, -6:143 Eliza 2:80 Eliza J. 6:82 Elizabeth 1:51,69,115,168,170, -2:80,-5:59,174,176,-6:81,84 Elvira J. 6:126 Fox E. J. 6:126 Hannah 4:163,-5:80 Huldah 4:163 I. 4:39 Ichabod 1:64,66, 71,-2:147,-4:163,-6:47,143 Isaac 1:64,-2:147,-4:124 James 4:163,-5:176,-6:126 John 1:51,59,127,169,170, 172,-2:29,74,80,123,-4:65, 147,-5:26,59,102,150,174,176, -6:82 John F. 6:179 Joseph 1:51,168,169,-2:80,-4:11,65, -5:174,176 Joseph D. 6:126 Joseph H. 6:82,179 Judith 6:150 Julia 6:179 Louisa 6:179 Love 1:128,172,-4:65,-5:176, -6:24,122 Lucy F. 6:126 Lydia 2:77,-4:150,-6:66 Martha 2:80, -4:9,-6:67 Mary 1:51,69,-2:76, 80,-4:9,12,40,65,-5:27,47, 175,-6:130 Mehitable 4:189 Mercy 4:145,-6:150 Moses 1:66,-2:147,-4:65,163,-5:54,80 Nicholas 5:102 Patience 4:65, 189 Peace N. 1:175 Richard 4:9,-6:143 Rose 1:54,55,59, -2:80,-4:65 Ruth J. 6:82 Samuel 4:11,-6:101 Sarah 2:147,-4:163,-6:101 Sarah J. 6:101 Stephen 4:189 Susanna

CANNEY (continued)
1:55,64,66,71,-2:80,125,147,
-3:35,-4:65,-6:66,113 Thomas
1:54,55,59,69,115,177,180,
-2:76,80,-3:31,-4:65,-5:102,
-6:97,130 Thomas J. 6:36
Trueworthy 4:189 William
1:59,-2:80,-4:66
CANNON, Hiram 5:145
CANVEL, Louis 3:68,76
CAPEN, Albert G. 7:70 Ebenezer
6:110 Hannah A. 7:65 Lucinda
S. 7:66 Maria L. 7:69 Rosanna
E. 7:70 Thomas C. 7:66
CARBOULEZ, Simon 5:166
CARD, Abigail 5:6 Hannah 2:67
John 1:21
CAREY, Joseph W. 7:23
CARINGTON, Dorothy 5:41
CARIO, Abigail 1:15 William
1:15
CARLE, Amy 5:98 Timothy 4:12
CARLISLE, Rachel 5:83
CARLTON, Abigail 2:37 Ebenezer
6:104 Edmund 6:165 Gilbert
5:21 Hannah 3:129 Olive 5:19
Rhoda 2:41 Samuel 4:32
Samuel C. 7:43 Theodore 3:6
CARPENTER, Christopher R.
6:133 Elizabeth 6:64,133
Helena 6:133 John 3:20 Philip
3:149
CARR, Abiah 3:41 Andrew 7:53
Anna 6:31 Benjamin 5:13
Clarissa W. 7:53 Deborah
6:174 Elizabeth 3:90,-4:133,
-5:14,-6:31 Hannah 6:30 Hep-
zibah 6:94 Jacob 5:147 James
5:13,-6:30 Jane 4:133 John
3:27,73,-4:89,-5:13,-6:174
Joseph 5:13,14 Judith 4:85
Lydia 6:31,174 Margaret 6:54
Martha 5:13 Mary 1:181,-2:45,
-6:51 Moses 5:13 Phineas 4:32
Priscilla 6:31 Rhoda 4:133
Samuel 5:13 Sanders 6:31
Sarah 5:13,14,-6:31 Solomon
6:31
CARRELL, John 2:83,-4:32
CARRIGAIN, Martha 6:54
CARROLL, Anne 4:6 Charles R.
4:8 James 4:8 Mary C. 4:6

CARROLL (continued)
Nicholas 4:6 Rebecca A. 4:8
Rebecca P. 4:8 Sophia 4:8
CARTER, Aaron 5:20,-7:21 Abiel
C. 7:18 Abigail 2:48,-3:169,
-6:110 Andrew 3:3 Ann 7:20
Bagley 3:71 Bela 6:167 Ben-
jamin 3:41,44 Benjamin G.
7:78 Betsey 7:20 Daniel 5:150
Daniel R. 5:149 David 6:168
Deborah 3:62,-6:162 Dorcas
7:19 Edward 1:11 Elizabeth
2:168,-3:62,64,159,-6:165
Enoch 3:136 Ephraim 3:167
Esther 6:163 Eunice 3:182
Frances 3:47 Hannah 3:62,64,
159,-6:55,58 Hepzibeth 3:62
Jacob 3:41,-6:51 Joanna 6:54
John 2:132,169,-3:38,40,47,62,
64,159,170,-5:108,-6:170,-7:29
John, Jr. 7:25 Judith 3:44,
-6:110,167 Levi 5:112 Lois
5:21 Lydia 6:111 Mary 3:2,47,
62,-4:174,178,-6:58,163,168,
-7:78 Michael 3:111,159 Miss
4:176 Nathan F. 3:190
Nathaniel 3:159,-7:19 Orlando
3:42 Phebe 6:105,-7:21
Ploomy D. 5:22 Polly 7:20
Rhoda 6:55 Richard 2:168,
-3:62,-5:19 Robert 3:28,73
Ruth 5:42,-6:50 Samuel 3:159,
-6:168 Sarah 3:62,-6:55,110,
112,-7:24 Sarah P. 5:21 Sarah
R. 7:23 Seth K. 3:48 Shuah
7:44 Simon 7:24 Susanna 6:108
Thomas 3:40,159,-5:108,112
Timothy 6:57 Wells 6:165
William 6:163
CARTERET, Philip 1:145
CARTLAND, Abigail 1:115,-4:38,
125,187,-5:58 Ann 4:126 Anna
1:161,162,166,-6:20,-7:6
Caroline 5:124,-6:20,128
Charles C. 2:165 Charles S.
6:144 Elijah 4:38 Elizabeth
2:31,-6:20 Eunice 1:68,-4:38,
-5:25 Gertrude 6:20 Hannah
4:123,-6:20 John 1:56,-4:123
Jonathan 1:162,-2:31,-4:123,
124,-6:20,-7:6 Joseph 1:56,63,
68,71,113,115,161,162,166,

18

CARTLAND (continued)
-2:31,128,-4:38,123,
-6:20,88,-7:6 Lydia 1:56,68,
71,113,115,161,-4:123 Mary J.
6:20 Miriam 1:71,-4:38 Moses
A. 6:20 Mr. 4:173 Pelatiah
1:113,-4:38,39,-5:31 Phebe
6:20 Sarah 1:166,-4:123 Tobias
4:123,164
CASS, Abigail 2:111 Benjamin
5:180 Daniel 4:131 Ebenezer
2:109 Eleanor 5:180 Eliphalet
5:19 Elizabeth 2:91 Hannah
5:71 John 2:84,86,89,91,
106,109,111 Jonathan 2:89
Joseph 2:84,-5:71,180 Martha
2:84,86,89,91,106,109,111
Mary 5:71 Mercy 2:106 Moses
3:88 Nason 5:71 Philip 3:177
Samuel 2:86 Sarah 4:91,-5:180
Tabitha 2:41
CASTLE, John 3:19,72
CASWELL, Abigail 4:128 Albert
M. 2:140 Alfred S. 2:140 Almira 2:140 Anna 2:140 Asa
1:143 Asenath S. 7:64 Charles
G. 1:143 Charles R. 2:140
Clarissa 4:183 Comfort 4:128
Dorcas 1:143,-2:140 Elizabeth
A. 2:140 Elizabeth J. 2:140
Emily 2:140 John 1:142 Joseph
1:143 Maria S. 2:140 Mary
1:142,143,-4:65 Mary E. 1:142
Mary H. 2:140 Michael 1:43,
-2:140 Polly 2:140 Richard
1:142 Richard G. 2:140 Samuel
1:142 Sarah A. 2:140 Thomas
6:160,-7:41 Warren 2:140 William 1:143,-2:140
CATE, Abigail 6:44 Bridget
3:53,-5:40 Deacon 4:63 Edward
3:53,174,176,-5:38 Elizabeth
3:51-53,56 Frederick 5:52
George 5:187 Hannah 2:55
Henry F. 2:187 Henry T. 3:71
James 3:53,-5:43 John 2:107,
-3:55,174,-4:49,-6:172 Joseph
5:88,131,-6:40,69,79 Lydia
6:172 Margaret 3:53,-7:91
Mary 5:42,-6:42,68 Mrs.
3:176,-5:187,-6:42,44,79
Nathan 4:116 Nathan H. 7:24

CATE (continued)
Samuel 1:12,-5:36,131,187,
-6:42,44,79 Sarah 5:88,-6:172
Walter 4:79 William 5:88
CATER, Edward 4:100 Henry F.
1:109 John 3:54,-4:57,-5:51
Mary 4:55 Richard 3:50,52-
54,99 Sarah 4:53,98,-6:68
CATERAN, William 4:32
CAVENDER, John H. 5:142
CAVERLY, Asa 7:44 Elizabeth
5:43,88 Hannah 5:88 Jane 7:13
John 5:49,90,-6:44 John B.
7:53 Lydia 4:187,-5:137,-6:46
Margaret 5:89 Mary 5:151
Moses 5:43,88-90 Mr. 5:86
Mrs. 5:134,137,185,-6:44,46
Nathaniel 5:88,-7:13 Nicholas
4:134 Phebe 5:185 Richard
6:41,44,46 Thomas 6:41 Wil-
liam 2:175,-5:131,134,137,185
CAVERNO, Miss 4:46
CAVEY, Peter 4:32
CENTER, Abraham 4:102,103
Mehitable 4:104
CHADBOURNE, Abigail 5:186
Hannah 5:136,138,183,186,
188,-6:42 Humphrey 4:147,
-6:68 Lucy 5:40 Martha 6:42
Mary 5:183 Sarah 3:181,-5:188
Thomas 5:136,138,183,186,
188,-6:42,-7:18 William 5:136
CHADDOCK, John 4:32
CHADWICK, Edmund S. 5:21
James 1:21 Mr. 5:40 William
K. 2:165
CHALLIS, Abigail 4:174 Chris-
topher 3:131 Dorothy 5:20
Elizabeth 3:132 Ezekiel 3:132
Judith 3:87,168 Margaret 5:160
Martha 5:156 Mary 3:44 Wil-
liam 3:43,-5:156,160
CHAMBERLAIN, Abel 6:55
Abigail 7:86 Abraham 5:1
Alice 6:114,115,118,171 Anne
4:146 Comfort 5:1 Dorothy
4:146 Ebenezer 6:73,113,116,
117 Eleanor 6:71 Enoch 7:86
Ephraim 5:8,-6:67,114 Ex-
perience 4:146 George W.
3:96,-4:192,-6:191,-7:1 Jacob
6:114,115,117,118,171,174,176

19

CHAMBERLAIN (continued)
James 4:148,-6:74 Jason
4:149,-6:113 John 1:83,
-6:72,116,176 Joseph 5:6,-
6:115 Joshua 5:113,-6:117
Lucretia 6:73 Lydia 1:82,7:86
Margaret 6:115 Mary 1:82,83,
-4:149,-5:2,-7:86,90,91 Moses
4:152,-6:37,174,-7:86 Paul
5:6,-6:114 Penuel 5:8,-6:117
Samuel 1:83,-5:55,-6:35,116,
118,174,-7:86 Sarah 5:146,
-6:174,191,-7:86 Susan 6:73
Thomas 6:114,116,138 Wil-
liam 1:82,83,92,-6:71,74,
115,174,-7:91
CHAMPERNOWNE, Capt. 1:9,
-2:22,24,59,60,63,98 Francis
1:8
CHAMPION, Levi 4:188
CHANDLER, Anna 5:16 Anne
1:191 Captain 2:131 Caroline
3:95 Daniel R. 5:16 Dolly 7:66
Dorcas C. 7:71 Dorothy 6:112
Elizabeth 3:8 Ezra 6:112 Hannah 1:191,-5:15,-6:164 Henry
6:105 Jeremiah 5:15,-6:54,
-7:25 John 4:133,-5:15,-6:52
Joseph 2:143,-4:169,-5:14-
16,71 Josiah 7:25 Judith
6:52,57,106,-7:72 Lucy 6:161
Lydia 3:88,-4:91,169,-5:14,
15,71 Mary 5:14 Moses 1:191,
-6:61 Mr. 1:10,-5:42 Nancy
7:19 Nathan 6:110 Nathaniel
5:16 Olive 5:15,71 Rebecca
7:20 Rebecca A. 7:24 Rhoda
6:165 Robert 2:182 Ruth 6:54,
163 Sarah 4:169,-5:15,16,
-6:162 Stephen 5:16 Susan D.
7:68 Theodate 6:56 William
2:143
CHAPIN, Curtis S. 4:178
CHAPMAN, Albert Foster 7:60
Alonzo Y. 7:60 Ann Martha
7:60 Burleigh 4:76 Calvin
6:8,92 Charles Henry 7:60
Comfort 4:126 Daniel 6:156,
-7:41 David 6:156,-158,-7:41
Ebenezer 4:130,183 Ebenezer
L. 6:158,-7:42 Edmund 6:158
Edmund A. 6:158 Edward 5:37

CHAPMAN (continued)
Edwin Burtin 7:60 Eliza 4:183
Elizabeth 4:13,-6:138,156
Elizabeth P. 6:158 Emily
6:158 Emily Melissa 7:60
Emma 4:76 Falkner 6:158
Francis 6:158 George W.
6:158 Helen Mar 7:60 Hiram S.
7:42 James 4:185 James M.
6:158,-7:61 Jeremiah Y. 7:60
John 3:4,-4:75,-5:152 John F.
6:158,-7:58 John M. 7:41
Joseph 4:179 Joseph Jr. 7:3
Levi 3:17,-4:128,-6:137
Lorinda C. 7:58 Lucy B. 7:55
Lucy L. 6:158 Lucy M. 7:63
Lydia 4:181,-7:58 Martha Ann
7:60 Mary 4:78,125,-6:158
Mary A. 7:42 Mary J. 7:55
Mary Jane 7:58,60 Mary L. B.
6:158 Mary W. 4:186 Mercy
4:12 Nancy 4:77,125,-7:41
Nathan L. 6:158 Nathaniel B.
6:158 Olive H. 7:41 Paul 6:138
Rebecca 6:154,-7:39 Samuel
4:126 Sarah 3:184,-4:128,
-6:157 Sarah A. 7:58 Sarah
Augusta 7:60 Sarah E. 6:6
Smith 6:137,-7:44 Solomon
6:61 Susan 6:158 Susan
Matilda Marshall 7:60 Susanna
4:186,-6:137,154 Susannah
7:38 Thomas 6:154,-7:3,39
Timothy 7:64 Tryphena 4:91
Vranna D. 7:64 Warren 7:41
William F. 7:58
CHARLES, Deborah S. 7:72
CHASE, Abigail 4:166,-5:20,71,
-6:57 Abner 1:164,165,-5:57,
-6:95,96 Abraham 6:95 Adeline
P. 4:142,-5:47 Albert 6:191
Am. 6:190 Amasa 2:29,-6:182
Amos 3:129,-5:18,-6:95,96
Andrew 3:17,-4:22,23,-6:190
Andrew J. 6:192 Ann 4:113
Anna 4:91,166,170,-5:71 Anne
2:11,14 Barzillai 6:191 Ben-
jamin 6:95,191 Benjamin Tap-
pan 7:16 Bradford 6:95 Burgess
T. 2:29 Caleb 6:57,58 Calvin
6:96 Caroline A. 6:40 Caroline
Augusta 7:87 Carr 6:26,94

20

CHASE (continued)
Charles 3:131,-6:30,94,96,
190,191,7:68,79 Charles E.
6:191 Clara S. 6:191 Clarissa
7:25 Consider 6:191 Content
5:127 Daniel 6:95 David 6:95,
191,192 Deborah 6:159,-7:40
Dorothy 3:170,-4:177 Dudley
L. 2:14,-3:17,-4:23 Ebenezer
3:134,-6:191 Edith E. 6:191
Eliphalet 3:183 Elisha 6:95,
191 Eliza 3:165 Elizabeth
2:112,-3:17,126,-4:136,-6:30,-
95 Elsy 7:26 Emma 6:48
Enoch 3:43,-6:26,30,95 Enoch
W. 6:40 Ensign 6:95 Esek
6:190 Eugene 6:192 Ezra 6:95
Fidelia E. 7:25 Frances 6:95
George 6:191,192 George N.
6:191 Green 3:134 Hannah
2:110,-3:88,-4:88,-6:52 Hannah M. 6:191 Heman 6:192
Henry 6:95 Henry S. 6:191
Henry V. 6:182 Humphrey 6:95
Isaac 2:190,-6:47 Isadore
6:192 James 1:190,-2:11,
-4:166,173,-5:71,-6:192 James
M. 6:191 James W. 6:191
Jeremiah 6:34,48,191 Jeremiah
S. 6:56 Jessie 6:191 Joanna
1:190,-4:166,-5:71,-6:192 John
3:8,136,-4:135,-6:47,95,192,
-7:16,79 John C. 5:20 John F.
2:38 John G. 6:191 John N.
6:190 John W. 7:76 John Wingate 7:76 Jonathan 1:190,-
2:14,-3:30,72,178,-4:166,
-5:70,71,-6:192 Joseph 2:110,
112,-6:48,95,191,192 Joshua
5:163,-6:95 Josiah 3:115,
-4:98,166,-5:71 Katherine
6:191 Lena 6:192 Love 2:12,14
Lucy 1:185 Lydia 4:132,166,
-5:70,71 Margaret 6:192 Martha 6:191 Mary 2:12,14,190,
-3:17,4:88,89,166,-5:31,71,
-6:57 Mary E. 4:23 Mary J.
5:20 Mercy 4:47 Miss 2:144
Moses 1:85,-6:48,95,96 Mrs.
3:133 Nabby 7:76,79 Nancy
3:17,168,-6:26 Oliver 6:191
Paine W. 6:96 Pamelia 6:192

CHASE (continued)
Parker 6:95 Paul 4:174,-6:26
Phebe 4:120 Phebe M. 6:182
Philip 1:165,-5:121 Phineas
M. 4:113 Prudence 3:43 Rachel
2:110,112 Rebecca 1:164,165,
-2:29,-3:114,-6:95 Roger 6:191
Russell 6:191 Russell C. 6:191
Ruth 6:55 Samuel 3:45,-6:26,
48 Sarah 2:12,14,-3:90,-4:166,
176,-5:70,71,-6:95,130,-7:12
Sarah A. 4:23 Sarah M 7:68
Simeon 6:95,96 Simon 6:47
Stephen 1:28,-4:133,-6:47,
95,112,191,-7:12,16 Theodore
7:16 Thomas 1:190,-2:12,14,
-6:95 Trueworthy 6:48 Walter
W. 6:191 William 3:88,-6:47,
191
CHATTERTON, Michael 1:3 Mr.
1:3
CHEEVER, Amos 6:109 Benjamin
2:164,165
CHELLIS, Timothy 6:167
CHENEY, Daniel 6:32 Edward
4:179 Harry M. 1:30 Mrs. 6:32
Nancy 4:187 Nathaniel 6:32
CHESLEY, Abigail 1:104,-4:126,
-5:116,-6:173 Alfred 1:154,158
Benjamin 1:104,154,-5:114,120
Charles P. 3:48,-4:148
Clarissa 1:54,-4:185 Curtis E.
1:159 Debby 7:28 Deborah
1:104 Elisha 4:76 Eliza 1:159
Elizabeth 1:156,-5:55,-6:171
Elizabeth Dennett 7:30 Ezra
1:154 Hannah 1:104,155,-4:77
Harriet 1:159 Hester 4:12 Isaac
1:104 Isaac B. 6:175 Israel
1:104,-4:125 Jacob 6:175
James 1:104,-3:145,150,-4:12,
76,-6:171-176,-7:28,31 Jane
1:159 Jeremiah 1:154 John
1:159,160 John Brewster 7:30
Jonathan 4:127 Joseph 1:154,
155,159,-4:78,-5:114 Joseph
R. 5:154 Laura J. 1:154
Lemuel 1:67,-4:164 Mary
1:104,159,-4:11,-5:56,-6:171,
-7:7 Miles 1:104,-5:55 Mr.
5:44 Nancy 1:104,-4:80
Nathaniel 6:137 Octavia 1:158

21

CHESLEY (continued)
Paul 4:129 Philip 1:178,-3:150
Richard 5:116 Richard F.
6:172
Samuel 3:150,-6:160 Sarah
1:67,159,-3:145,-4:79,5:120,
-6:174 Sophia 1:154 Susanna
1:104,154 Thomas 1:104,154,
-3:84,-4:127,129,-5:56,-6:171,
-7:30,31 Valentine 1:104 Wil-
liam 4:185
CHESWELL, Caroline 4:186
Mehitable 4:179 Paul 4:76 S.
W. 6:59
CHICHESTER, Hugh 5:163,164
CHICK, Lucy 3:5 Richard 4:12
CHICKERING, Alpheus 6:165 El-
liot 7:18
CHILCOT, John 5:89
CHILD, CHILDE, or CHILDS,
Abigail 4:102 Hannah 5:93
Henry 3:81 Miss 5:39 Sarah
4:10
CHISHOLM, Hugh 5:163,164
CHOATE, Abigail 3:38,-5:155
Ammi 5:109 Ann 6:27 Ben-
jamin 2:43,-3:41,130,-4:85,
-5:109,112,154,156,159,-6:31
Elizabeth 5:158 Epps 7:59
Jeremiah 5:105 John 4:32
Jonathan 2:72,-3:40,-5:105,
108,110,155,158,-6:27 Joseph
5:154 Mr. 2:133 Robert 6:104
Ruhamah 3:43 Ruth 5:159
Simeon 5:156 Thomas 7:23
CHOMET, Nancy G. 7:61
CHRISTIF, Elizabeth 4:17 James
4:17,19,62 John 4:60 Peter
4:62
CHRITCHESSON, Sarah 4:183
CHRITCHET, Mary 6:62
CHUB, Pasco 3:85
CHURCH, Abigail 4:10 Deborah
4:12 John 3:83,-4:11 Joseph
3:80
CHURCHILL, Elizabeth 4:183
George Elbridge 7:57 Ichabod
6:138 J. W. 6:16 James 4:79
John 4:99 Joseph 6:140 Lydia
6:138 Mary 6:137 Nathaniel
4:187 Sarah 4:13 Susanna 6:61
CHURCHMAN, John 2:125
CILLEY, Aaron 4:76,-5:154

CILLEY (continued)
Abigail 4:166,-6:32 Alice 4:166
Anna 3:180 Benjamin 2:46,
-5:105,108,111,154,160,-6:29,
142 Cutting 4:47 David 3:182
Dorcas 3:42 Dorothy 4:126,166
Eliphalet 4:106 Elizabeth
3:183 Elizabeth A. 6:160 Henry
4:136 John 4:47,85,-5:105
Jonathan 4:84,166 Jonathan S.
6:6 Joseph 4:47,166,182 Mary
6:160 Moses 4:86,-5:111
Samuel 3:40,-4:166,-6:29
Sarah 3:184 Thomas 4:11,47
William 3:87,-6:32
CLAGGETT, William 7:65
CLAPHAM, Belvedira 5:115
CLAPP, David 4:139 Supply
2:159-161,-5:164
CLARAGE, Winthrop H. 6:160,
-7:41
CLARGE (see Clarage), James
3:26,72
CLARK, CLARKE, Aaron 5:148
Abigail 3:18,135,-5:8,107
Abraham 4:122 Agnes 4:52,
55,103 Almira 5:142 Ananiah
4:147 Andrew 3:155,-5:91
Anfie 2:70 Ann 3:50,186,
-5:10,136 Ann F. 3:126,163
Anna 2:116,-3:87,-4:88,
-5:39,54,-6:55,-7:79 Anne
1:188,189,-3:56,-7:31 Benjamin 2:116,-3:18,37,-4:24,
73,-5:10,153,-6:33,-7:77 Benjamin F. 4:73,74 Caleb 4:94,
-6:59 Catherine 4:152,-5:41
Charles 5:18 Daniel 1:113,
-2:116,-3:18,91,-4:73,-5:32,56
David 2:41,117,127,-3:166,
-5:114 David J. 4:73 Deborah
2:116,117,-3:166 Ebenezer
1:92 Edward 1:10,11 Eleanor
3:18,166 Elisha 2:192,-6:103
Eliza 4:24 Elizabeth 2:10,41,
67,-3:18,39,50,56,-4:52,88,
103,154,-5:39,55,87,110,139,
-6:59 Elizabeth A. 4:73
Elizabeth M. 4:127,-6:176
Enoch 2:121 Enoch M. 6:35
Ephraim 2:41 Ezekiel 7:56
Ezra B. 4:24 George 4:104

CLARK (continued)
George F. 4:74 George K.
2:188,192,-3:48 George L. 4:88
Gershom 4:164 Greenleaf
3:135,-4:88 Hannah 2:41,116,
-3:90,-4:131,-5:51,105,155,
-6:138 Hannah D. 5:150 Han-
niel 4:150 Hezekiah 5:146
Ichabod 5:132 Israel 5:142
Izette 1:113 J. B. 5:37 Jacob
1:21,22,-5:159,-6:36 James
1:62,63,68,-2:126,-4:24,122,
-5:54 Joanna 1:188 John 1:10,
11,14,22,188,189,-2:10,65,70,
116,132,175,-3:37,104,114,174,
176,-4:100,116,122,154,-5:87,
90,105,107,110,130,133,136,
139,153,156,159,-7:77 John W.
4:74 Jonathan 1:68,113,188,
-2:41,55,116,126,-3:186,-4:88,
169,-5:10,24,113 Joseph 1:189,
-2:40,41,55,116,117,122,161,
162,-3:21,73,166,-4:76,122,
-6:176,-7:27-29,31,32,73
Joshua 2:40 Joshua Paine 7:28
Josiah 2:175,-3:55,-4:51,
-5:43,87,89,91 Josiah B. 4:20,
24 Josian 1:12 Laura L. 7:66
Levi 3:18,-4:24 Lois 4:137
Louisa 5:19 Lucy Elvira 7:32
Lydia 5:148 Mahew 6:27 Margaret 5:155 Margery 7:73 Martha 1:62,-2:9,116,126,-4:121
Martha Burleigh 7:29 Mary
1:188,-2:10,72,3-50,56, 155,
166,178,-4:51,52,103,122,150,
177,-5:115,136,142,148,-6:34,
37,59,169 Maurice 5:156
Mehitable 3:18 Mercy 2:10,
41,-3:18,-4:73,134 Moses
2:9,-3:18,126,-4:24 Mrs.
3:175,176,-5:139 Nancy 6:107,
-7:27 Nathaniel 2:41,188
Nicholas 1:189,-2:116,-3:166
Paul 2:10,-6:55 Peter 4:32
Phebe 4:104 Polly 7:87
Prudence 6:118 Rachel
2:41,116 Rebecca 4:147
Remembrance 1:63,-2:126,-
4:78,122 Robert 4:134,-
6:159,-7:40 Roocksby 2:10
Rufus 2:143 Samuel 1:12,

CLARK (continued)
-2:9,10,183,-3:18,166,-4:88,
97,-5:132 Samuel B. 7:56
Samuel F. 6:167 Sarah 1:63,68,
-2:10,116,126,-3:128,-4:20,
23,24,72,100,122,136,-5:42,
122,133 Sarah Ann 7:31
Satchwell (Satchel, Sachwell)
etc. 1:188,-3:1,-7:24 Simon
7:31 Solomon 6:65,118 Stephen
4:132,-5:5 Susanna 6:59
Susannah 7:15 Tabitha 2:41
Taylor 2:116 Thomas 4:57
Thomas A. 6:34 Thomas I.
7:40 Thomas J. 4:24,-6:159
Valentine 4:168 Walter W.
4:24 Ward 3:37,39 William
3:155,-7:73,79 Zipporah 1:188
CLARKSON, Andrew 2:115 James
2:103,104, 5:39
CLARY, Joseph W. 1:159
CLATTERDAY, Ann 3:41,44
CLAY, Alphonso 4:200 David T.
6:93 Jonas 2:45 Margaret 2:70
Samuel 3:30,75
CLEASBY, Hannah W. 7:24 Isaac
W. 6:163 John 6:56 Mary 6:157
Melinda 7:69 Ruth 6:168 Sarah
6:56,164,167 Tabitha 6:57
William 6:58
CLEAVES, Samuel 2:164
CLEMENTS (CLEMENS, CLE-
MENT) ---- 7:6 Abigail 3:146
Abner 7:5 Almira 7:69 Anna
5:54 Benjamin 5:34 D. 2:148
Dorothy 4:173 Ebenezer 4:175,
-6:72,-7:1 Elizabeth 5:50,
-6:72 Hannah 6:72,-7:18
Joanna 3:101 Job 3:101,-4:9,
-6:72 John 7:20,21 Joseph
3:23,71 Joseph W. 6:167
Mabel 5:33 Moses Jr. 7:26 Mr.
4:123,-6:29 Pamelia L. 7:20
Phineas 6:29 Robert 1:12 Sarah
4:148,-5:34,-6:56 Susan C.
5:19
CLEMLUS, Miss 6:191
CLENDENING, Mary 6:166
CLERAGE (see Clarage),
Winthrop H. 7:41
CLEVELAND, President 5:177
Rachel 1:183

23

CLIFFORD, Abigail 2:46,68,
-3:38,131 Anna 4:88 Anthony
5:110 Benjamin 4:173,
-5:103,104 David 3:42,132,-
5:154,160,180 Deborah 2:72
Dorothy 5:160 Dudley 3:182,
184 Elizabeth 1:83,-2:67,70,
86,88,90,91,-3:87,130 Esther
2:88 Frances H. 5:69 Hannah
1:84,-5:69 Isaac 2:43,48,68,
70,90,-3:38,41,-5:105,111,153,
-6:29 Israel 2:48,-3:45 Ithiel
5:69 Jeremiah 6:32 Joanna
2:44 John 2:70,86,88,90,91,
109,110,134,-3:37,132,-5:104,
108,109 Jonathan 2:70,-3:45,66
Joseph 2:70,94,-3:38,40,
-5:104,109,112,156,159,-6:29,
32,185 Joshua 3:38 Lemuel
5:69 Lucy 4:131 Margaret 3:87,
-5:104,156 Mary 2:91,-3:40,
114,132,-5:156 Mehitable
5:68,69,143,-6:27 Melinda 5:17
Nathaniel 4:89 Peter 1:84,93
Rachel 4:90 Richard 2:43,70,
-3:129,-5:106 Samuel 4:84,
-5:154 Samuel Jr. 7:23 Sarah
2:109,111,129,-3:41,130,
-5:111,153,157 Tristram 5:105
William 2:47,69,70,-3:42,132,
-5:103,106,108,110,153,156,
157,-6:27 Zachariah 2:65,69,
-3:89
CLINTON, Edward 2:182
CLOUGH, Abel 6:165 Abigail
2:47,66,-3:37,-6:163 Abner
3:182,-4:172 Ann 6:30 Anne
3:42 Benjamin 3:42,86,130,
-5:155,-6:32 Brackett 3:183
Charles H. 7:71 Cornelius
2:43,47,72,132,-3:37,-6:32
David 2:65,132,-4:90,6:169
Dorothy 3:131 Duke 4:32
Eleanor 3:43 Elisha 2:47,
-3:40,-5:108,110,112,155,158,
-6:26,30,51 Elizabeth 2:70,
-3:87,171,-5:12,108,-7:7,56
Ezekiel 2:47,-4:133,170-172,
-5:12 Ezra 2:70,-5:103 Hannah
2:70,-3:90 Ichabod 2:44,47,65,
66,68,70,72,129,132,-5:104
Isaiah 4:90,170 Jabez 3:44,

CLOUGH (continued)
-5:110,111,153,159,-6:28
Jemima 4:174 Jeremiah 4:172
Joanna 5:155,160 John 2:45,
-3:89,90 Jonathan 2:66,
-4:89,-5:157,158 Joseph
2:44,72,131,132,-5:159,-6:51
Judith 3:45,-5:156 Levi
4:172,-6:164 Love 2:65,
-4:125,-6:30 Lucy 1:112 Martha 3:182,-4:171,-5:104,-6:26
Mary 2:72,-4:132,172,-5:103,
110,112,-6:29 Mercy 2:45
Miriam 4:89,170-172,-5:12,153
Moses 5:110 Mr. 3:37 Obadiah
3:43,-5:156,160,-6:29 Reuben
3:41,-5:112,155,157,160,-6:30
Richard 5:155,-6:51 Ruth 2:45,
68,-3:44 Samuel 3:91,-5:104
Sarah 2:44,68,-3:88,89,-5:12,
111,160,-6:104,106 Susanna
1:112,-4:180,-6:138 Tabitha
3:87 Theodate 5:155
Theophilus 5:104 Thomas
4:172 Zacheus 2:48
CLOUSTON, Thomas 3:67,71
CLOUTMAN, Anna 5:113 Easter
(Esther?) 5:51 Edward 4:11
Hezekiah 5:6 John 1:115,-5:52
Mercy 1:115 Sarah 1:115,-5:58
COATS, Hannah 3:129 Robert 1:22
Sarah 1:131
COBB, Rebecca 6:190
COBBET, Mrs. 3:56
COBURN, Lucy 2:94
COCHRAN, Robert 3:65,71
COCHRANE, George E. 5:85 John
5:140 Levi 6:38 Mrs. 5:140
Samuel C. 7:68 Sarah 5:140
CODDINGTON, Herbert G. 5:96
COE, Abigail 1:98,154 Anna 1:98
Benjamin 1:98 Curtis 1:98,102,
154,-6:156,159 Ebenezer 1:98
John 1:98 Joseph 1:98 Mary
1:98 Matthew 1:3
COFFIN, Andrew 6:3 Ann 4:142
Anna 4:134,-5:1,10,15 Ben-
jamin 1:72,118,3:101 Charles
N. 6:7,92 Daniel 5:16,46
Daniel A. 5:46 David 5:15
Dorothy 6:133 Elihu 1:72,118,
-5:29,122 Elizabeth 5:16,148

COFFIN (continued)
  Enoch 3:181,-5:10,15,16,-6:10
  Eunice 4:170 George 4:142,
  -5:46 Gilman 4:142 Grindall
  4:142,-5:47 Hannah 4:142,
  -7:16 Ira 4:142 James 3:101,
  -4:142,-5:46 Jane 2:41
  Jedediah 1:72,118 John 6:133
  Jonathan 4:142,-5:46 Jonathan
  T. 4:142,-5:47 Joseph 5:10,15
  Judith 7:67 Levi 4:142 Lydia
  3:45 Mary 5:10,15,16,-6:1
  Miss 4:190 Moses 5:46,-6:107
  Mr. 2:71 Nathan 3:8 Nathaniel
  3:101,-4:142,-6:10 Parnel
  4:142 Peter 6:98 Sarah 5:10,
  15,-6:10,154,-7:26 Silas 5:46
  Stephen 3:101,-4:142,-5:46
  Susanna 4:142,-5:10,15,16,-6:3
  Tristram 5:10,15 Weare 4:142,
  -5:15 William 5:15,16,-7:16
COGAN, Mary H. 1:153 Stephen
  1:153 Susan 1:153 William
  1:153,-4:80
COGSWELL, Mr. 3:142 Thomas
  4:180 William 1:183
COK, Jean 4:3 Thomas 4:3
COKER, William 4:32
COLBATH, Alice 3:10,-5:73 Anne
  4:110 Charles 5:117 Deborah
  4:19,154 Dependence 3:8
  Elizabeth 3:155,-4:106,154
  George (page not given) 2:?,
  -3:155,-5:51 George E. 3:106
  Hunking 3:8,-4:17,-5:147
  James 3:158,-4:15,17,19,
  64,110 Jane 4:106,109,112,
  154,156,157,-5:74 John 4:156
  Layton 3:4,158,-4:154 Lemuel
  3:155,-4:154 Lois 3:9 Marana
  3:9 Mary 3:63,156,-4:106,-5:74
  Miss 4:109 Nicholas 4:130
  Olive 4:15,17,19,64,110 Pitman 4:109,112,154,156,157,
  -5:74 Sarah 5:55 Temperance
  3:10 William 4:157 Winthrop
  4:64,-5:146
COLBY, Abiah 6:169 Abigail
  4:170,-7:23 Abigail D. 4:170
  Abraham 3:40,-6:112 Benaiah
  5:116 Benjamin 6:112 Charles
  S. 4:170 Clarissa D. 6:170

COLBY (continued)
  Daniel 3:130 David 3:89
  Eleanor 6:106 Elijah 7:25
  Elizabeth 6:162 Ephraim
  6:108,161 Esman 4:177 Hannah
  3:89,-6:31,51 Jemima 3:88
  John T.G. 6:38 Joanna R.
  4:170 Joseph 3:91,-4:177
  Judith 4:174,-6:95,166,-7:17
  Lydia 3:87 Margaret 7:19 Mary
  3:91,-4:176-178 Moses 5:174,
  -6:163,-7:19 Mr. 6:58 Nancy
  6:110,111 Rhoda S. 4:170 Ruth
  6:95,109 Sarah 4:176,180 Sarah
  T. 6:165 Simeon 3:171 Spencer
  2:174 Susanna 6:166 Thomas
  C. 4:170 Timothy 4:173,-6:111
  Willoughby 4:176 Zaccheus
  3:130
COLCORD, Abigail S. 6:133
  Andrew C. 6:133 Ann 2:87,90
  Aurelia P. 5:21 Caroline
  2:92,-4:126 Daniel 4:179,
  -5:21,155 Deborah 2:90
  Dorothy 3:135 Ebenezer 2:46,
  -3:44 Edward 2:87,90
  Elizabeth 2:63,134,-3:90,169,
  -5:105 Elizabeth A. 3:169
  Eunice 2:55,114 Frances R.
  7:59 Gideon 2:114 Hannah
  2:45,65,-5:160,-6:30 Jeremiah
  6:136 John 3:133,-4:80,-6:133,
  136 John C. 6:133 Josiah 4:131
  Lois 5:18 Lydia 3:43 Mary
  2:46,71,130,-5:111 Mary C.
  6:133 Mehitable 2:130,-5:160
  Mrs. 3:79 Peter 2:71,-4:89,
  -6:61 Rachel 2:55,114 Samuel
  2:43,68,134,-3:39,42,-5:105,
  107,111,155,158,160,-6:30
  Sarah 4:179,185,-6:136,-7:38
  Shuah 2:87 Tristram 6:133
COLE, Abigail 2:111 Abraham
  2:106,109,111 Anna 5:144 Benjamin 5:144 Caleb 1:163,
  -4:162 Christopher 1:122,
  -4:162,-5:128,-7:8 Clara A.
  5:46 Ebenezer 5:144 Edward
  7:28 Edward Bell 7:28
  Elizabeth 1:66,122,125,163,
  -4:132,152,-5:143,-7:8 Eunice
  1:125,-4:162,-5:174 Frank T.

COLE (continued)
1:182,-2:166 Hugh 5:143,144
Isaac 2:106 James 1:126,
-5:93,143,175 John 1:66,122,
125,126,163,3:35,-4:11,69,162,
-5:144,-7:8 Joseph 5:144
Joshua 4:162 Martha 5:144
Mary 2:106,109,111,-4:152,
-5:93,143,144 Mrs. 3:83
Nathan 6:164 Ruth 5:93,144
Samuel 2:185 Stephen 4:162
Susanna 5:144 Thomas 3:83
COLEBROOK, Miss 4:4
COLEMAN, Abigail 3:160,-4:15,
19,106,154,155 Alice 3:9,
-4:108 Ann 3:59,60,64,110,
155,157 Anna 1:110,-2:174,
-3:108,112,5:74 Anne 6:68
Benjamin 4:111 Eleazer 2:168,
172,-3:59,60,64,108,110,112,
155,157,-5:76 Eliazer 4:14,
59,61 Elizabeth 3:7,-4:19,155
Enoch T. 5:78 Hannah 5:75
James 3:62,-4:149,-5:75,
-6:73,159,160 John 3:110,
-4:108,110-112,155,-5:74,76,
145,-6:75 John W. 4:110
Joseph 3:108,-4:112,154,
155,-6:72 Kezia 4:14,-59,61
Lydia 3:10,157,-4:106,112
Mary 2:173,-3:60,160,-4:110-
112,155,-5:74,-6:178
Mehitable 5:74 Mrs. 3:62 Olive
4:155 Phebe 3:40 Phineas
2:172,-3:59,158,160,-4:19,60,
106,-5:75,78,79,-6:178
Rosamond 3:1,8,112,-4:60
Sarah 3:2,155,-4:60 Tem-
perance 4:59 Thomas 6:69
Widow 2:43 William 4:14
COLKET, C. Howard 4:142,-5:47
COLLINS (Collings), Charles 5:18
Dodge 3:23,73 Ebenezer 2:68
Elizabeth 2:68,-3:167 Ephraim
5:41 Gilman 5:19 Hannah 4:174
Henry 4:180 Israel 4:173 Jabez
4:173 John 2:17,-3:87,90,
-4:54,-5:40 Jonathan 2:44,
68,131 Laban 3:136 Lucinda
4:180 Martha 3:77 Mary 2:69
Mercy 2:69 Moses 4:180
Moses N. 6:93 Mrs. 3:98

COLLINS (continued)
Robert 2:68,-4:97 Samuel 3:136
Sarah 2:17,68,-4:54,-5:44
Thomas 2:17 William 2:172,
-4:57,175
COLMER, Abraham 2:1-6
COLOMY, Elizabeth 6:36 Mary A.
6:185
COLVERWELL, George 1:22
COMB(S), Abigail 4:52,-5:40
CONDON, Edward 1:22
CONGDON, George E. 2:42
CONNELL Betsey 7:54 Dennis
4:32 Henry 4:32 Patrick 4:32
Philip 4:32
CONNER (or CONNOR), Benjamin
1:64,-2:128 Elizabeth 7:29
George 1:64 Gideon 4:176
James 3:40,-6:166 Joseph
1:41,81 Martha 1:64,-7:25
Mary 1:41,81,-4:146,-6:52
Morgan 6:137 Patrick 4:32
Samuel 1:21,41 Sarah 1:81
William 5:51,-7:29
COOK, Abiel 6:72 Abigail
6:69,113 Abraham 4:146,148,
-6:71,72 Anthony 4:80 Bethena
6:72 Daniel 4:146,-5:151,
-6:154,-7:38 Elizabeth 5:143
Hannah 5:147 Jacob 5:143
James 5:115,118 Jeremiah
5:52 John 4:9,-6:145,146
Jonathan 4:149 Jonathan D.
6:71 Joseph 4:148,-6:69,73,115
Kezia 5:6,-6:115 Lucy 4:150
Lydia 3:114 Lydia T. 6:127
Mary 5:148 Mercy 4:149,-6:70
Nathaniel 6:74 Peter 2:175,
-6:71,72,113,145 Phebe 6:71
Rebecca 6:145 Robert 4:148
Valentine 5:151 Wentworth
5:53 William 6:115
COOLEY, Daniel 4:89,-6:62
COOMES, Abigail 4:11 Joseph
4:114
COONN, Harriet 7:43
COOPER, Daniel 5:45 Elizabeth
S. 5:17 J. Fenimore 4:27
James R. 1:11 John 4:10 Wil-
liam 3:44
COPELAND, William J. 5:84
COPP(S), Anna 6:70 Benjamin

COPP(S) (continued)
6:65 David 6:66 Elizabeth 5:3
Esther 5:5,-6:66,-7:90
Jonathan 5:148,-6:35,-7:90
Joseph 5:55 Mary 6:69 Moses
6:69 Roger 6:171 Samuel
6:68,171 Tristram 5:49
CORBAN, Elizabeth 2:47,-3:42
CORBETT, Abraham 1:11
COREY, George F. 5:182 Sarah
6:51
CORLISS, Abigail S. 7:72
Ephraim 5:119 James 6:106
John M. 6:105 Mary 7:66
Samuel 6:56 Sarah E. 7:72
CORNEY, Ann 6:43 John 5:186,
188,-6:43,45 Mary 5:188,
-6:43,45 Mrs. 5:186,188 Sarah
C. 5:186
CORNWALLIS, Gen 6:13
CORSON, Abigail 6:72 Anna 4:152
Anne 6:115 Benjamin 5:116,
-6:116,-7:85 Calvin 4:184
Charles 5:150 Daniel 6:34
David 4:150,-6:174,175,-7:27
Ebenezer 6:113 Elizabeth 6:72
Ephraim 6:33 Hannah 4:145
Ichabod 5:117,-6:72,115,116,
-7:31 James A. 5:149 Joseph
5:50,114,-6:116,-7:87 Joshua
6:74 Julia E.H. 5:182 Kezia
6:72 Lavinia 6:38 Louisa 6:37
Maria 5:152 Martha 6:38 Mary
4:147,-7:31 Mary A.H. 7:55
Mary McDuffee 7:27 Mehitable
5:3 Mercy 5:54 Nahum 5:151
Rachel 5:148 Ralph 4:30 Relief
6:34 Sabina 5:146 Sarah 5:5
Thomas M. 5:46 Timothy
6:174 William 6:174
CORZENAC, Francois 3:68,75
COSSA, Ezekiel 4:32
COSTELLO, John 4:32
COSWELL, Cary 1:22
COTTON, Abiah 2:107 Abigail
3:7,52,54 Ann 2:87 Benjamin
3:56,174,176 Comfort 1:93
Dorothy 2:85-87,89,91,92,
107,108 Elizabeth 2:91,
-3:54,-4:49,54,58,5:43 John
2:85,-3:54,174,175,-4:54,58,
-5:42 Joseph 2:184,-3:29,54,73

COTTON (continued)
Margaret 5:43 Maria 2:108 Mary
3:54,-4:99,-5:139 Mercy 2:92
Miss 5:40,43 Mr. 3:55 Mrs.
3:175,176,-5:139 Prudence
2:112 Roland 2:112 Samuel
5:165 Sarah 2:86,89,-3:54,
56,-5:43 Seaborn 2:85-87,
89,91,92,107,108,112 Solomon
4:58,-5:44 Susanna 4:104,-5:44
Thomas 3:54,-4:179 William
1:9,10,12,-2:22-28,64,98,
100-103,-3:54,55,174,175,
-4:50,56,-5:139
COUCH, Anne 5:40 Dr. 1:11
George W. 5:19 Mary 5:41
COUES, Peter 2:160
COUPE, John 4:32
COURSER, Thomas 3:131
COURTIE, Lois 3:54
COVINGTRIE, David 4:3
COWAN, Elizabeth 5:82 James
W. 5:82 Susan E. 5:82
COWART, Cornelius 4:32
COWELL, Edward 1:12 Isacc
6:37
COWREY, Alice 6:111
COX, Clarissa 7:37 John 4:10
Leah 2:87 Mary 5:41 Moses
2:87 Prudence 2:87
CRAFORD (see CRAWFORD)
CRAIGIE, Isabel 4:2 Magnus 4:3
Marian 4:3 William 4:3
CRAM, Ann 3:186 Anna 3:93 Ar-
chintine 2:89,90,105,107,
108,111 Asa 2:42 Benjamin
1:181,-2:41,89,90,105,-7:85
Charity 3:186 David 1:112,
-6:138 Ebenezer 3:179
Elizabeth 2:46,-3:144 Esther
2:41 Hannah 2:111,-6:136
Henry 2:41 Humphrey 2:41
James 6:139 John 1:181,
-2:41,90,-5:92 John G.
1:112,181,-2:42,-3:93,144,186,
-4:48,-5:46,92 Jonathan
1:112,-2:41,-3:93,177,-4:136
Joseph 1:118,-2:108,-3:135
Mary 1:112,-2:107,-3:144,
-4:91,181,-6:139 Mehitable
4:134 Mr. 3:144,-5:45 Nancy
P. 1:112 Nathan 1:181,-2:41

CRAM (continued)
Samuel 1:112 Sarah 2:41,89,
-3:129,178,-4:130,-6:137
Smith 4:130 Susanna 3:167
Thomas 2:41 Timothy 2:42
Uriah 1:181 William 1:112
Zebulon 2:41,42
CRANCH, Andrew 1:12 Francis
1:25 John 1:21
CRANDALL, Charles H. 7:26
Phinehas 6:156
CRANE, Benjamin 4:32 Elisha C.
2:164 Florence A. 3:47,94,144
Mrs. Edward M. 1:181
CRANFIELD, Gov. 6:144
CRAWFORD, Elizabeth 2:172
Festus Allen 7:89 Mary
Frances 7:89 Robert 3:88
CRAYTON,Hannah 3:170
CREASEY, Caleb 4:184
CREBER, Thomas 1:13
CREIGHTON, James B.
3:114,117,119 Martha A. 3:117
Sarah 3:117 Zebulon D. 3:117
CREWSY, Barnaby 1:21
CRIMBELL, Abram 4:116 Ben-
jamin 4:116 Sarah D. 4:117
CRITCHET, Edward 5:108 Elias
5:154,191 John 4:126,-5:110
Mary 3:113,-5:156 Mercy 4:80
Sarah 5:108 Thomas 3:40,
-5:108,110,154,156
CROCKER, John 3:3
CROCKETT, Andrew 2:117 Anna
3:180 Anne 6:79 Benjamin
6:79,-7:12 Betsey 2:117 Char-
lotte 3:178 Daniel 2:117 David
2:117 Deborah 3:57 Edmond
5:53 Elizabeth 2:55,-4:14,
15,135,-5:90 Ephraim 2:55,
117,122 George 2:55 Hannah
2:117,-4:80 Hezekiah J. 5:151
James 2:55 John 2:55,168,
-3:94,183,-5:39,-6:61,-7:12
Jonathan 2:117 Joshua 4:13,
14,15 Lydia 5:41 Margaret
2:117 Martha 2:117 Mary 2:55,
168,-3:181 Miss 5:41 Mr. 5:90
Nancy 2:117 Polly 2:117
Samuel 2:55 Sarah 2:117,
-3:108 Thomas 4:103
CROMMETT, Ebenezer 2:186

CROMMETT (continued)
Eliza 4:182 Love 4:126 Martha
4:130 Mary 4:127
CROMWELL, Mercy 4:13 Oliver
4:191
CROSBY, Abial R. 7:72 Cornelia
7:31 Dr. 6:4 Hannah 4:76 Mary
2:130 Oliver 7:31 Thomas
2:133 Widow 3:40
CROSS, Abigail 4:101 Abijah 5:22
Abraham 5:42 Anne 2:81 Ben-
jamin 5:44 Betsey 7:87
Charles 7:26 Gilman 6:7 Han-
nah 2:81 John 2:81,-4:102
Joseph 5:147 Lewis 6:37
Lucinda 5:102 Lucy 6:35 Lydia
5:151 Noah 6:71 Richard
4:104,-5:116 Samuel 4:103
William 4:101,104,-5:43
CROSSMAN, Daniel 4:142
CROSSWAIT, Elizabeth 5:38
CROUTHER, John 2:97
CROWDER, John 2:62
CROWELL, Christopher 4:32
William 4:32
CROWLEY, Bartholomew 4:32
CROWN(E), Elizabeth 4:52 Henry
3:174 Mrs. 3:176
CROWNINGSHIELD, Benjamin
4:27,28,32,37
CROWTHER, John 1:3,5
CROXFORD, Mary 5:88 Susan
4:127 William 5:88
CRUCY, William 3:65
CRUMEL, Jacob 3:4
CRUMMET, Joseph B. 7:70
Nathaniel B. 7:61
CRUMP, George 3:72
CRUMWELL, Philip 3:151
CRUSE, Thomas 2:5
CULLUM, Capt. 7:16 David 6:80
John 6:80 Sarah 7:16
CUMMING(S), Charles O. 7:59
Edward P. 4:24 Elisha 6:137
Elizabeth 5:102 Isaac 5:102 J.
3:165,-4:24,-5:35 Jacob
4:115-118 Mary 2:94 Mary C.
G. 4:14 Richard 1:9,10,12,
-2:23,63,64,98,99 William
2:94
CUNNINGHAM, Mary E. 7:24
CURRIER, Aaron 3:132 Abigail

CURRIER (continued)
4:173 Abigail M. 4:179 Anna
3:135,-4:136 Caleb 1:22,
-6:165,-7:78 Chalice 5:17
Charlotte 7:76 David 3:168
Elijah R. 5:21 Eliphalet 7:62
Eliza 7:77 Elizabeth 3:42,
171,-5:17,-6:106 Elizabeth F.
5:20 Ephraim 3:136 Esther
3:133,-6:110 Eunice 5:22 Ezra
3:170 Hannah 3:136,-4:78,
175,-7:75,76,80 Harvey L.
2:144,-4:189 Jedediah 6:163
Jeff 1:10 Jeremiah 3:38,-5:105
Joanna 6:162 John 2:67,-4:174,
-7:80 Judith 2:68 Lucy H. 7:69
Lydia 2:67,-7:77,79 Martha L.
6:168 Mary 4:89,174,178 Mary
Jackson 7:79 Mary W. 7:67
Mehitable 3:169,-6:53 Miriam
2:144,-4:176,-6:163 Moses
4:174,-5:17 Mrs. 6:45 Nancy
4:173 Nathan 2:144 Nathaniel
7:77,79 Rebecca 2:41,-6:107
Richard 4:78,-5:17 Ruth 3:171
Sally 7:18 Samuel 6:112 Sarah
4:177,-5:17,-6:45,112 Sarah E.
5:20 Stephen 2:144 Susanna
6:54 Susannah Mendum 7:78
Theodore Jackson 7:77
Thomas 6:45,-7:79 William
6:35,111,-7:75-80
CURTIS, Dodavah 3:104 George
6:138 John 4:100,-5:42
Jonathan 6:170 Robert 2:181,
-3:71 Sarah 2:36
CUSHING, Elizabeth 5:146 James
6:26 Jonathan 6:102,103 Mary
4:134 Mr. 6:72,103 Rev. Mr.
1:98 William 5:116
CUTLER, Dudley 5:67 Hannah
5:67 Prudence 5:67 Richard
4:85 Robert 5:67,72,180 William 5:67 Zara 7:67
CUTTER, Ammi R. 5:134-136,
139,183,186,188,-6:42,44,77
Anne 5:134 Charles 5:139
Daniel 5:186 Dorothy 5:183
Elizabeth 5:136 Hannah
5:135,136,139,183,186,188,
-6:42,44,77 Jacob 2:162,-6:42
Mary 5:134 Nathaniel 6:44

CUTTER (continued)
Ralph C. 2:165 Sarah A. 6:77
Thomas 4:32 William 5:188
CUTTS (or CUTT), Anna 6:42,
44,76,77 Anna H. 5:186 Anne
5:39,139,183,185,186,188 Benjamin 5:188 Camden 6:77
Charles 2:162,-5:188 Edward
2:161-163,-5:139 Elizabeth
3:53,-4:50,58,-5:87 Elizabeth
E. 5:183 George 6:42 Hannah
5:38,131 John 1:10,12,-2:25,
98-100,103,-3:49-51,172,173,
-4:191,-5:43,131,135.183,185,
188 John R. 2:63 Mary 3:51,52,
56,-4:4 Mr. 4:100 Mrs. 3:175,
-5:135,183,185,188 Priscilla
6:44 Richard 1:6,9,10,12,
-2:21-26,28,98,99,-3:49,51,
-4:104,191,-5:87,185 Robert
4:191 Samuel 2:159,160,
-3:85,-4:97,104,-5:139,183,
185,186,188,-6:42,44,76,77
Sarah 3:50-52,56,-4:103,
-5:44,131,183 Sidney 6:76
Susanna 4:100,102 Ursula 3:81
DAHNOR, Josiah 3:22
DAILY, Abial 4:142 John 1:22
DALLING, Elizabeth 6:44,79,
-7:13 John 3:69,76 Joseph R.
6:79 Samuel 6:44 Thomas
5:165,167,-6:44,79,-7:13
DALTON, Abiah 2:108 Abigail
2:111 Caleb 2:106 Comfort
4:91 Elizabeth 2:87,-6:62
George 6:93 Hannah 1:94,-2:83
John 2:92 Joseph 2:108
Mehitable 2:83-85,87,89,90,92
Michael 5:37 Philemon 2:90
Samuel 2:83-85,87,89,90,
92,106,108,109,111 Sarah 4:85
Timothy 1:89,-2:89
DAME (DAM), Abigail 1:157,
165,172,-3:4,57-62,105,106,
109,110,138,139,-4:9,59,60,64,
105,108,110,112,126,130,
146,153,155,157,-6:175 Abner
3:61,-4:146,-6:71,114-116,119
Alice 2:176 Anna 4:130,
-5:59,-7:30 Benjamin 3:28,
71,110,158,-4:112,-5:138,185
Bethiah 3:9 Celeb 7:30

29

DAME (continued)
Caroline 1:172,-5:59 Catherine
4:129 Charity 4:15,-5:52 Chase
4:129 Daniel 5:146 Deacon
3:80,109,112 Deborah 6:73
Dorothy 5:120,6:119,176
Eleazer 4:59 Eliphalet
3:59,4-59,60,64,105,108,110,
112,153,155,157 Elizabeth
2:175,-3:9,47,59,62-64,101,
107,108,110,111,155,156,158,
-4:64,106,108,152,-5:146,
-6:114,115,121,146 Elizabeth
Bumberry 7:79 Elma M.
6:121 Elnathan 3:64,-4:59,6:69,73
Elsie 2:168 Esther 3:2,10,
-5:130 George 3:105,-4:130
Hannah 1:165,-4:106,157,
-5:59,-6:23,122,-7:79 Hannah
B. 5:91 Hannah O. 6:121
Hatevil 4:48 Henry 4:157
Hunking 4:80 Israel 4:80 Issachar 2:174,-4:106,107 Jabez
3:110,111,-5:146,-6:34 James
C. 4:158 Jane 3:58,106 Jean
6:69 Jethro 4:64,-5:138 Joanna
4:157 John 1:177,-2:168,171,
-3:6,57-59,62,64,107,111,145,
156,158, 160,-4:64,136 John R.
5:59 Jonathan 1:69,-2:125,173,
-3:63,-4:48,146,-5:41,59,
-6:71,120, 121,184 Joseph
1:157,-3:59,-4:154,158,-5:74,
-6:37,66,114,119,120 Joseph
P. 4:153 Joshua 3:160 Keturah
3:61,-4:147 Lois 5:149,-7:29
Mark 4:157 Martha 3:108,4:11
Mary 1:69,-3:62,112,156,
-4:59,108,110,112,149,152,
157,158,-5:27,74,-6:34,66,75,
115,121 Mehitable 4:154 Mercy
1:69,-5:54,59,-6:116 Meribah
Emery 7:30 Miss 5:40 Moses
3:57-60,62,105,110,138,-4:86,
110,-5:42,59,-6:72,93,178 Mr.
6:115,117 Mrs. 5:138,185
Nancy 4:76,112,-7:79 Olive
3:156 Owen 6:121 Patience
5:74 Paul 5:51,-6:117,119
Phebe 7:90 Polly 7:30 Pomfret
2:76,-3:47,-4:13,-6:146,147
Rebecca 4:110 Rhoda 5:59

DAME (continued)
Richard 1:165,172,-2:169,
-3:62,63,108,110,111,155,
-4:64,156,-5:3,59,-6:121,184
Samuel 3:146,155,-4:154,
-6:147 Sarah 3:114,160,
-4:77,79,105-107,125,-5:3,
118,185,-6:69,73,119,147,175
Sarah P. 4:187 Silas 5:3,55,
-6:119,175,176,-7:29-31 Simon
5:6 Solomon 3:60 Sophia 5:116
Stephen F. 4:157 Susan
4:79,130 Susanna 4:79,155
Temperance 4:64,-6:138
Theodore 3:111,-4:108,
110,112,157,-5:74 Theophilus
3:62,-5:59 Thomas 4:107
Timothy 3:5,-4:64,156,-5:50
Valentine 4:108 William
3:109,-4:13,-5:91,130,-6:121
Zebulon 2:169,-3:58,61,154
DAMON, Mary Ann H. 7:66
DAMOREL, Edward 7:76
Elizabeth 7:76 John 7:76
DANA, Mary 4:146 William B.
4:116
DANE, John 6:165 Susan 4:183
DANFORD, Sarah 6:49 William
6:49
DANFORTH, Isaac 6:169 Rufus
6:170 Sarah 1:181
DANIEL - DANIELS, Benjamin
3:150 Charity 1:64 Earl D. 6:93
Ebenezer 5:42 Ephraim 7:53
Eunice 4:118 George Snow 7:53
Hayes 4:185 Henry 5:40 Jacob
1:64 John 3:149 Joseph 4:175
Lydia 4:77,78 Mehitable 4:185
Miss 5:42 Sarah 1:64,-4:124,
187,-6:156 Thomas 1:12,
-2:100
DANIELSON, Arthur 2:191 Hannah
2:191,-3:92 Joshua 2:191 Levi
3:92 Sarah 4:146
DARLING, Abigail 2:45,-6:142
Arnold 6:190 Benjamin 3:90,
-5:130 Carlos 6:190 Daniel
2:130,-5:103,-6:190 David
2:170 Elizabeth 2:94 Franlin
6:190 George W. 6:143 Hannah
6:190 Huldah 6:190 Isaac 6:190
John 2:70,94,129,130,-3:90,

DARLING (continued)
-6:142,143,190 Joseph 6:190
Josiah 6:190 Judith 2:46,
130,-6:142 Lydia 6:190 Mary
6:142,143,190 Mary S. 6:190
Naomi 2:130,-6:142
Onesiphorus 3:44,-6:141 Phebe
6:142 Philip 6:143 Robert
6:190 Ruth 2:48,131 Sarah 3:15
Stephen 6:142,164 Timothy
6:163 William 6:190
DAVENPORT, John 5:164,166,170
DAVIDSON, David 3:25,72 Harriet
W. 7:72
DAVIS, Aaron 5:129 Abigail 5:53
Alfred M. 5:22 Almira B. 7:65
Amos 3:45,-4:175,177 Anna
5:118 Benjamin 4:175,-5:131
Benjamin G. 7:70 Calvin 5:19
Clement 4:129 Clement M.
4:130 Daniel 1:103,-5:39 David
3:83 Dean M. 3:82 Deborah
4:188 Dorcas 6:107 Eleanor
4:97 Eleazer 6:166,-7:19 Eliza
4:185,-5:19 Elizabeth 4:79,97,
-5:42 Ellen 7:58 Enoch 3:21
Franklin 5:22 George O. 7:57
Hannah 3:45,168-4:89,104,
-5:6,-6:167 Henry 1:103 Isaac
3:91,180 Jacob 3:88,-6:174
James 6:98,-7:69 Jane 4:55
Joanna 7:32 John 1:103,
-2:170,-3:2,26,43,48,74,102,
159,-4:80,99,173,-6:27,31 John
S. 2:164 Jonathan 4:125,
-6:159,-7:40 Joseph 4:125,
-5:88,90,129,131,133 Joshua
4:77 Judith 6:27,111,-7:65
Lois 3:167 Lydia 3:185 Lydia
L. 7:60 Lydia P. 3:180
Malachi 3:87,135 Maria 7:37
Martha 4:183 Mary 2:40,
-3:17,159,168,169,-4:177,189,
-5:8,158,-6:57 Mary J. 5:36
Mercy 3:180,-6:173 Miss 5:41
Moses 4:76,188,-5:90,-7:22
Mrs. 3:175 Nancy 6:166
Nathaniel 3:168 Nestor W.
2:165,-5:144 Noah 4:127 Orpah
3:89 Philip 3:44 Phineas 6:31
Richard 5:39,120 Robert 1:4,10
Robert, Jr. 7:18 Ruth 3:87,

DAVIS (continued)
-5:36,88,-6:161 Ruth F. 3:119
Samuel 3:17,42,-4:77,78,
125,127,187,-5:158,-6:27,50
Samuel C. 7:60 Sarah 4:80,
130,-5:5,22,-6:112,164 Sarah
E. 7:71 Solomon 4:181 Stephen
1:103 Susan 3:113,-5:149
Susanna 3:44,-4:76 Thomas
4:32,174,-5:118,-6:70,7:32
Timothy 6:173,174 Tryphena
4:178 Wentworth C. 4:188
Widow 2:121 William 1:13,
-3:45,173,175,-4:32,-5:133
DAWLEY, Hiram W. 6:37
DAY, Annah 7:41 Ephraim 7:41,43
Joseph 4:45 Josiah 4:45,93
Mary Annah 7:41 Nancy 4:175
P. B. 6:15 Thomas 4:45 Wealthy 6:122
DEALE, Aaron 6:140
DEAN(E), Asahel S. 6:16 Bethia
5:62 John 2:176 Margaret A.
4:116 Virginia 6:16
DEANEY, Joseph 6:135
DEARBORN, Abigail 4:133 Almira B. 7:18 Anna 3:41,
-5:14,115,-7:28 Benjamin
3:127,-5:90,129 Bethiah 1:186
Charlotte 4:126 Charlotte M.
7:58 David 4:127 Ebenezer
4:80 Edward 4:75 Eliphalet
4:184 Elizabeth 2:91,107,110,
-4:179,-5:45,-7:68 Francis
4:128 George W. 7:60 Gilman
2:165 Hannah 1:186,-2:9,51,
-5:16 Hannah T. 5:22 Henry
2:91,107,110,-4:75 James C.
2:10 Jeremiah 5:3 John 1:186,
-2:10,12,51,91,111,-4:77,134,
-6:154 John C. 6:35 Jonathan
1:186,-2:9,10,-4:178 Josiah
3:167 Levi 7:28 Mahala 7:21
Martha 7:60 Mary 2:10,12,51,
111,-3:120,-4:185,-5:16,145
Morris 4:181 Nathaniel 3:134
Peter 2:46 Roswell Hutchins
7:60 Ruth 5:14,-6:139 Samuel
2:107,-5:16,20 Sarah 2:68,
-3:120,-4:131,136,177,179,
-5:14 Simon 4:132,168,-5:14
Tabitha 3:41 Thomas 3:41

DEARBORN (continued)
Thomas H. 2:165
DEARING, Clement 7:91 Hannah
7:91
DECATURE, Susan M. 7:62
DECKER, Abigail 3:60 Abraham
5:129 Daniel 5:88 David
3:59,-5:90,129,130,132
Elizabeth 2:171,-3:57 Hannah
2:171,-3:57 John 3:57,59,
60,108,-5:88 Joseph 3:57
Joshua 5:90 Mary 2:170,
-3:57,-5:130 Sarah 2:170,
-3:57,59,60,108 Thomas 5:132
DEE, Harrison 6:190
DEERING, Ann 2:105 Elizabeth
6:68 Henry 1:11,-2:99,105,
-3:51,-4:58 Mary 4:147,-5:1,
-6:65
DeJEAN, Andrew 3:67,75
DELAND, Abigail 5:83
DELANO, Bridget 6:47
DELANY, Cornelius 3:69,76 John
4:32
DELAP, James 5:108 Mary 5:108
DELMER, Thomas 7:56
DeLORME, Augustin 3:67,76
DELPHIN, Jane 7:15 John 7:15
DEMERITT, Abigail 4:181 Anna
4:76 Avis 1:105 Ebenezer E.
7:43 Edmund 4:80 Elizabeth
1:105,-4:127 Hannah 4:128
Hannah M. 5:177 Hopley 4:182
Jacob I. 6:37 James M. 1:106
James Y. 1:79,-2:165 Jane
1:105 John L. 1:106 Jonathan
1:104 Joseph 4:185 Lois 4:80,
-5:117 Mary 1:105,-4:129
Mehitable 6:160 Moses 6:63
Nathaniel 1:105 Samuel 1:106,
-3:30,73,-4:78,-5:99 Sarah
1:106 Sophia T. 4:184 Susan
1:105,-5:56 Susan Y. 4:184
Susanna 4:80 Thomas J. 1:106
William 1:105,-4:125
DENBOW, Richard 2:78 Ialathiel
2:169
DENMORE, Salathiel 2:173
DENNETT, Alexander 3:50,173
Amy 3:50,56 Anna 7:12 Annie
4:99 Charles 3:1,-4:112,
-5:130,132,147 David 2:176,

DENNETT (continued)
-4:105,108,110,112 Dorothy
4:108,110,112 Ebenezer 4:108
Elizabeth 3:32,-4:104,110,
-5:129,131 Ephraim 2:103,
-3:55,-4:58,102,-5:87,88,165,
168,-6:45,79,-7:12,14 George
5:131 Grace 3:50,52 Hannah
3:5,8,-4:112,-5:80 James
4:57,-7:14 Jeremiah 6:45,46,
79,-7:12,16,74,76 Jeremiah Y.
5:188 Jeremy 7:14 John 1:12,
-2:20,101,102,158,159,-3:50,
55,173,-4:49,54,56,100,112,
-5:87,88,129,131,133 John
Plummer 7:16 Joseph 3:55,
-4:49,55,56 Katharine 7:74
Lawrence 1:22 Lydia 4:105,
-6:45 Mark 3:5,-5:166,-7:14
Mary 3:5,6,8,-4:50,-5:39,
80,130 Mehitable 4:49,50 Miss
4:55,-5:40,44 Moses 3:55,
-4:51,-5:80,87,132 Mr. 3:51,
-5:43 Mrs. 3:50,51,174,-5:188,
-6:45,46 Nancy 5:115
Nathaniel 7:13 Nicholas 4:58
Phebe 6:45 Ruth 5:87 Samuel
4:108 Sarah 2:124 Shuah 5:133
Susanna(h) 2:169,-6:46,79,
-7:12,14,16,74,76 Thomas 4:56
William 3:5
DENNICK, Mary 5:79 Moses 5:79
DENNIS, Abigail 6:90 Albert W.
5:141 Amos 6:20 George 6:77
Hannah 6:20 Jeremiah 6:77
Joseph V. 6:180 Samuel 6:180
Susanna 2:92 Thomas 1:10
William 2:92 William W.
6:180
DENT, Acaicus 2:48,132 Anna
2:65 Daniel 2:67 Hannah 3:43
John 3:41 Martha 5:103 Mary
3:89,-5:106 Solomon 2:69
Thomas 2:44,47,67,132,
-3:39,-5:103,106
DEPOUZOLE, Joseph M. 3:67
DERBY, Mary 3:88
DERMONT, Usher 1:11
DeROCHEMONT, Charles H. 5:19
DEVERSON, Miss 5:42 Mrs.
3:175 Thomas 3:174,175
DEVON, Lewis 7:72

DEWEY, H. P. 6:16
D'FLAU, Pierre 3:68,72
DICKEY, Hannah 6:107
DILL, Peter 3:82
DIMAN (see Dimond), Abigail
4:85,-5:66 David R.
4:116 Dolly 7:19 Dorothy 6:53
Elizabeth 4:174,-6:169
Ephraim 6:26 Esther 2:116
Eunice 2:116 Ezekiel 3:43
Isaac 5:66,-6:105 Israel
3:88,-5:159,160,-6:26,55 Jacob
6:170 James 2:116 Lois 2:116
Mary 2:116,-4:174,-5:159,
-6:163,166,-7:20 Miriam 6:168
Reuben 4:177,-5:66 Samuel
2:116 Sarah 6:161 Zelphia 7:18
DIMMOCK, Capt. 3:85
DINDEL, John 3:88
DINSMOOR, Daniel J. 69
DITTEY, Sarah 3:158
DIXON, Hannah 4:11 Lucy 3:6
Peter 5:41 Thomas 3:6 William 7:79
DOBBIN, John 6:52
DOCKHAM, Ephraim 2:122 John
3:174,176 Jonathan 4:78 Mary
4:155 Mrs. 3:176
DOCSROW, Elizabeth 4:125
DODGE, Daniel 4:185 Eliza 6:93
Hampshire 4:32 Hannah L.
7:69 James 4:32 John 5:109,
112 Nathaniel H. 3:127 Simon
5:112 Thomas 6:154,-7:39
Zachariah 4:32
DOE, Andrew 4:187,-6:138
Andrew W. 4:128 Benjamin
1:155 Broadstreet 4:79 Deborah
4:136 Deborah W. 4:185 Desire
4:127 Ebenezer 1:155
Elizabeth 4:185,-6:138 Francis
4:127,-6:62 George 4:130
George G. 6:151 Hannah 1:155
James 4:126 John 1:103,
-4:78,-6:139 Joseph 1:155,
-4:78 Joseph R. 6:151,154,
-7:39 Joshua 1:155,-4:181
Louisa 4:186 Lydia 4:184 Mary
4:76,80,-6:61,137,140 Mary J.
4:184 Mehitable M. 7:45 Nancy
4:77,188,-6:139 Nathaniel B.
5:2 Nicholas 3:181 Reuben

DOE (continued)
6:61 Sampson 5:43 Samuel
3:4,185 Sarah 4:185,-6:151
Simon 5:2 Sophia 4:184 Sylvester F. 7:62 Theophilus 4:76
Warren 4:116 Wiggin 6:137
Zebulon 4:127
DOEG, George 7:80 Mary 7:80
DOEY, Augustua M. 3:115
DOLBY, Abigail 1:88,93 Daniel
1:38 Hannah 1:48,87,88,93 Israel 1:48 John 1:83 Jonathan
1:38,48,83,87,88,93 Mary 1:38
Nicholas 1:38,87 Ruth 1:48,87
Sarah 1:38,48 Stephen 1:88
DOLE, Doctor 3:149 Ruth 6:139
Sarah 6:10
DOLHOUGH, Christian 3:151
DOLLOFF (or Dollar), Amos
5:106 Clement 3:129,-5:106
Eliza 4:136 Elsie 3:181 John
3:150 Love 4:86 Sarah 3:86
William P. 7:72
DOLLY, Mary 5:43
DOLTON, Mary 3:180
DONALD, Thomas 3:8
DONNELL(S), Lucy 3:90 Ruth
4:78
DORE (or Door), Andrew 5:53
Anna 6:74 Benjamin 6:114
Elizabeth 3:106,107,-4:146,
-6:69 Frances 3:106 Hannah
5:5 Henry 3:106,-6:71 James
6:71,-7:2 John 3:110,-4:146,
-7:54 Joseph 6:73,-7:2 Lydia
6:69 Margaret 6:69 Mary 4:10,
-5:150,-6:69,113 Mrs. 3:175
Olive 4:147,-6:69 Phebe 6:73
Philip 3:106,107,110,-5:39,
-6:69,71 Richard 1:12,-3:174,
-4:147,-6:69 Sarah 3:106,110,
-5:8,115,117,-6:72,-7:54
Simon 7:54 William 2:173
DORNIN, William C. 6:143
DOUGLAS, Cornelius 1:122,-3:35
Elijah 1:122 John 4:9 Joseph
3:80 Nathan 7:51 Phebe 1:122
DOVRELL, Thomas 4:32
DOW, Abby 6:93 Abigail 2:31,
-3:43,177,-4:174 Abraham
1:61,63 Amasa 5:108,-6:27,32
Anne 3:32 Benajah 2:47

33

DOW (continued)
Benjamin 4:181 Betsey 7:21
Chalice 6:28 Charity 1:96
Cyrus H. 7:72 Daniel 2:112
Delia 3:179 Ebenezer 6:110
Elizabeth 2:112 Elizabeth F.
5:21 Ephraim 2:67 Ezekiel
2:46,66 Gilman 5:20 Hannah
1:96,120,123,126,163,173,
-2:86,88,105,109,110,-4:67,
90,-6:17,-7:19 Henry 1:96,
-2:84,86,88,105,109,112,-3:149
Isaac 1:96,-6:104,170 Isaac,
Jr. 7:22 Jabez 2:106 James
1:96,-2:108 Jedediah 1:63
Jemima 2:68 Jeremiah 2:84,
174,-5:1 Jerusha 2:66 John
1:85,173,-2:91,3:155,156,
-4:67,-6:17,87,184 Jonathan
1:61,123,-2:31,-4:67 Joseph
2:86,89,91,106,108,110,112,
-6:57 Josiah 4:129 Lydia
3:40,-4:126,-6:128 Lyford
4:133 Margaret 2:84,-7:25
Martha 1:96 Mary 1:85,96,120,
129,-2:89,91,106,108,110,112,
-3:183,-4:10,67,78,150,-5:125,
-6:28,111 Mary G. 3:114
Meribah 6:55 Miriam 3:116,
-4:88 Moody 6:107 Moses
1:120,123,126,163,173,-2:172,
-3:120,-4:67,-6:184 Nathaniel
6:56 Paul 1:163,-4:67,-5:27
Pelatiah 4:67 Phebe 1:61,63
Philip 2:66,68,72,131 Richard
4:67 Rufus 5:19 Ruth 2:144,145
Sampson 3:153 Samuel 2:88,
-3:178,-6:32 Sarah 2:149,
-3:156,167,178,-6:27,51,62,
-7:70 Sarah G. 2:31,-6:183
Simeon 2:105 Simon 6:138
Susan 6:37 Susan C. 6:160
Susanna 1:85 Timothy 6:162
Winthrop 4:91 Zilpah 6:17
DOWLEN, William 3:87,
-6:116,119,147,148,150
DOWNES, Aaron 7:5,49,50,52
Abigail 6:147-150 Abigail Ann
7:51 Ann 7:53 Anna 6:147,
150,-7:32 Benjamin 7:52 Bet-
sey 7:53,54 Charity 6:147,149
Charles 7:52 Cynthia 7:54

DOWNES (continued)
Daniel 6:148,150,-7:52,53 Dolly
7:54 Dorcas 6:150 Dorcas D.
7:53 Dorothy 6:150 Ebenezer
6:146-149,-7:51 Edmund 7:52
Elizabeth 6:67,119,145,147-
150,-7:2,49 Elizabeth Tripte
7:85 Ely 7:32 Ephraim 7:52
Esther 6:149 Frederick G. 6:38
Frederick Gates 7:53 Gershom
6:6,8,146-149,-7:49-51,53,54
Hannah 6:35,119,-7:32,49,
51,52,54 Hiram 7:52 Ichabod
6:150 Isaac 6:150,-7:51,52
Jacob 7:51 James 6:34,69,147,
148,-7:32,50,51,54 James, Jr.
7:50 James Door 7:54 James
M. W. 6:38 Jane 6:149
Jedediah 6:150,-7:51 John
6:119,146,147,149,150,-7:49-
51,53 John H. 6:36,-7:54 John
Jones 7:53 Jonas 7:32
Jonathan 6:150,-7:51 Joseph
6:146,-7:51 Joshua 6:149,-7:50
Judith 6:148-150,-7:51,53
Katharine 6:145 Levi 6:150,
-7:52 Lewis 7:52 Love 6:147,
-7:51 Lucy 6:150,-7:53 Lydia
6:150,-7:50,52 Margaret 6:119,
148,-7:51 Maria 7:54 Mark
7:53 Martha 6:146,148,149
Mary 6:145-147,173,-7:49,51
Mary Jane 7:51 Mehaly 7:53
Mercy 6:147,149,150 Molly
7:50,51 Molly Perkins 7:32
Moses 6:66,119,147-150,
173,-7:30,49,52-54 Moses R.
7:51 Mrs. 6:116 Nabby 7:31
Nancy 7:51,54 Nathaniel 7:52
Nathaniel Hayes 7:32 Oliver
7:52 Patience 6:147,149,-7:50
Paul 6:119,146,149,-7:32,49
Peggy 7:54 Phebe 6:148,150,
-7:53 Phineas 6:149,150,
-7:50,51 Polly 7:53,54 Pomfret
6:149,-7:51 Rebecca 6:145,
146,149,-7:51 Reuben 6:149,
-7:50,51,53 Richard 6:146,
147,149,-7:51 Ruth 7:51 Sabra
7:52 Sally 7:52,54 Samuel
6:146,148-150,-7:51 Sarah
6:146,147 Sarah T. 7:54 Sophia

34

DOWNES (continued)
7:54 Sophia R. 7:51 Stephen
6:150,-7:53,54 Susan 7:54
Susanna(h) 6:119,-7:49 Tamson 7:53 Thomas 6:145-150,
-7:30,32,49-54 Thomas, Jr.
7:31,32,85 Timothy 6:150 William 6:146,148-150,-7:51-54
William E. D. 6:150
DOWNING, Abigail 5:51 Alice
2:174,-3:5,60,63,-4:17-19,64,
107,108,111,156 Bartholomew
4:64,-5:78 Benjamin 2:169,
-3:63,105,107,-4:18,-5:8,119,
-6:175 David D. 4:109 Deborah
3:110 Dennis 3:84,-4:157
Dorothy 2:176,-3:109 Ebenezer
4:154 Eliza 3:62,-7:39
Elizabeth 2:175,-3:6,9,58-60,
63,105,107,109,157,159,160,
-4:18,108,109,111,112,154,
158,-6:154 Elizabeth H. 4:111
Elsie 6:157 Hannah 3:59,-4:16,
18,111 Iset 3:157 John 3:4,57,
58,60,61,155,159,160,174,176,
-4:18,19,156-158,-5:74,108
John H. 4:109,-5:78 Jonathan
2:167,-3:8,58,59,62,105,109,
155,157,160,-4:19,155, 5:108,
112,115,156 Joseph 3:60,
-4:111,-5:112 Joshua 2:169,
-3:9,60,63,107-110,154,157,
159,-4:16,108,157,-6:175
Josiah 3:63,-4:108,109,112,154
Lois 3:2,-5:7 Lydia 4:157,-5:5
Major 4:155 Mary 2:170,173,
-3:4,58,131,-4:156,158,-5:8,74
Mrs. 3:155,176 Nelson 3:62
Patience 2:176,-3:160,-4:19,
150 Richard 2:174,-3:57,58,
-4:17-19,64,107,109,111,-5:74
Samuel 3:105,160,-4:112,
-5:156,-6:175 Sarah 3:25,43,
60,-4:149,157 Susanna 2:170,
174,-3:4,63,64,105,107,109,
110,154,157,159,-4:16,19,157,
-5:5,-6:178 Theodosia 4:107
DOWNS, Aaron 4:147,-5:116,145
Abigail 5:4 Anna T. 1:140
Elizabeth 1:140,143,-3:47 Gershom 4:13,125,-7:90 Hannah
5:111 James 5:52 John

DOWNS (continued)
2:136,-5:8,56 Joseph 4:32
Joshua 5:147 Margaret 4:146,
-5:113,152,-7:90 Mary 3:83,
-4:9 Moses 4:149,-5:3,7 Mr.
5:43 Mrs. 3:99 Paul 5:54
Samuel 1:140,143,-4:145
Samuel W. 1:143 Sarah 5:152
Thomas 3:81,85,-4:11,-5:40,
54,114 William 2:184,-4:145
DOWSITT, Charles 3:66,73
DOWST, Abial 1:41,43,44 Comfort 1:41 Elizabeth 1:41,43,
44,88 John 1:41,88 Jonathan
1:88 Mary 1:41,44 Ozem 1:41,
88,137 Rachel 1:43,44 Samuel
1:43,44 Sarah 1:41,43 Simeon
1:44 Solomon 1:43,44 Thomas
1:43
DRAKE, Abraham 2:82,84,85,
87,88,90,190,-4:85 Elizabeth
1:149,-2:87 Elizabeth E. 4:83
Francis 1:149,-2:28,59-61
Hannah 2:88 Harriet E. 7:69
Jane 2:82,84,85,87,88,90 John
1:149 Judea 3:180 Judith 4:168
Mary 1:149,-2:85,-4:90 Mary
W. 4:83 Nancy 6:56 Nathaniel
1:12,13,-2:62-64,98-100,190
Robert 2:90 Robert E. 4:83
Samuel 4:83 Samuel P. H. 4:83
Sarah 2:84,-3:180,181,-4:83
Sarah H. 4:83 Simon 3:180,
-4:168 Simon P. 4:83 Theodate
4:89 William F. 4:83
DRAPER, Mrs. Amos G. 3:139
DRESSER, Almira G. 4:115,
-5:182
DREW, Abigail 1:70,-2:172,
-3:138,-5:28 Abigail B. 6:90
Anelietta 6:25 Benjamin
6:71,136 Catharine 6:177 Cle-
ment 2:77 Daniel 1:71 David
L. 6:25 Dorothy 1:71 Ebenezer
1:70,114 Elijah 1:154 Eliza
5:29 Elizabeth 6:4 Francis 6:5
Hannah 2:77,-6:71 Horatio 3:46
James 1:12,-2:77,-3:174
Joanna 6:159 John 3:146,
-4:12,-5:147,-6:145 Joseph
5:115,-6:64 Love 1:54,71,114,
-2:76,-3:33,-5:32,94 Lucinda

DREW (continued)
J. 3:46,95 Lydia 2:77,168,
-4:127 Martha 6:72 Mary 1:54,
-4:76,79,126,-6:65 Meshech
2:77 Patience 2:77,-5:99
Phebe 6:5 Rebecca 1:101
Samuel 6:68 Samuel C. 1:154,
-3:182 Sarah 1:70,114,-4:13,
-6:75 Susanna 4:78 Tamesin
2:77 Thomas 2:77,-3:149,
-6:72,-7:90 William 1:54,178,
-2:77,-5:113
DRISCO, Elizabeth 1:16 James
1:16 Sarah 4:12
DROWN, Daniel 2:98 Daniel P.
2:164 Ebenezer 6:68 Elizabeth
5:50,-6:66 Huldah 5:5 Jonathan
6:68 Moses 6:174 Samuel
2:161,-4:147,-6:66,68,174,
-7:91 Shem 6:67 Solomon 6:66,
68 Stephen 6:174 Tamson
6:174 Thomas P. 2:98
DUANE, Marianna 4:6
DUCHESNE, Mathurin 3:68,75
DUDA, Elizabeth 6:138 Joseph
6:139 Nicholas 6:138 Susanna
6:140 Temperance 6:138
Zebulon 6:62
DUDLEY, Abigail 3:39,-5:157,
-6:27 Anna 5:155 Anna C.
3:170 Daniel 5:107,109 Davidson 5:108,111,155,158,-6:30
Deborah G. 3:169 Eleanor 3:42
Francis 3:185 Governor 6:4
Hannah 3:129,-5:108 James
5:106,108 Jeremiah 5:155
Jeremy 6:32 John 3:185,-5:165
Joseph 4:137 Josiah 3:136
Judith 3:136 Lydia 3:185 Mar-
tha 4:137 Mary 3:115 Myron S.
3:48,185,186 Nancy 4:176 Paul
5:155,157,-6:27 Peter 3:185
Peter C. 5:158 Samuel 3:40,
113,-5:107,109, Samuel P.
3:42,-6:32 Sarah 4:76,131,
-5:111 Sarah E. 6:93 Stephen
3:185,-5:106 Timothy 5:108
Trueworthy 6:30
DUE, Thomas 1:12
DUMMER, Gorham 6:107
Reverend Mr. 3:81
DUNBAR, Mr. 4:5

DUNCAN, George 3:87 James
3:43,142 Joseph 3:80 Mary
6:110 Mehitable H. 6:166
Nancy 6:112 Samuel 2:37
Susanna 5:89 Thomas 5:89
DUNCKLEY (see DUNKLEE)
DUNHAM, Benjamin 1:175 Ed-
mund 1:149 Franklin D. 1:175
Mr. 6:90 Sybil 1:175
DUNKLEE (or DUNCKLEY),
Abraham 6:108 Elizabeth 6:169
Sarah 7:68
DUNLAP, Frances 4:6 Sarah A.
4:8
DUNN, Anne 1:150 Benajah 1:150
Benjamin 1:150 Elizabeth
1:150 Ephraim 1:148 Esther
1:150 Experience 1:150 Fran-
cis 1:149,150 Hannah 1:150
Hezekiah 1:150 Hugh 1:146,
148-150 James 1:150 Jeremiah
1:150 John 1:148,150 Jonathan
1:150 Joseph 1:150 Lokiah
1:150 Martha 1:150 Mary
1:149,150 Micajah 1:150
Nehemiah 1:150 Phineas 1:150
Rachel 1:150 Rebecca 1:150
Richard 1:148 Ruth 1:150
Samuel 1:150,-5:127 Thomas
1:148 William 1:148 Zacharias
1:150
DUNTLEY, Olle 6:169
DURANT, Anna 5:130 Cornelius
5:91 Rebecca 3:170 Sarah
5:132 Thomas 5:91,130-132
DUREN, Alexander 5:20
DURGIN, Benjamin 4:128 Charles
1:154 Charlotte 6:6,62,
154,171,-7:38 Clarissa 4:130
Comfort 4:77 Daniel 1:153,
-2:181,-3:25,71,-6:136,171
Deborah 4:181 Drusilla 1:180
Ebenezer 1:153,154,-3:184
Elijah 6:55 Eliza J. 5:36
Elizabeth 1:153,-3:2 Ezra
1:154,-5:149 Ezra S. 5:36
Francis 6:136 Gregory 6:54
Hannah 4:80 James 1:103,152,
153 Jesse 7:22 John 1:180
John F. 1:152 John H. 6:162,
-7:22 John W. 7:59 Joseph
1:153,-6:173 Josiah 6:171,

36

DURGIN (continued)
173,176 Lettice 1:152,-4:78
Lydia 4:76,80 Margaret 1:152
Martha 1:153 Mary 1:153,
-3:184 Mary F. 4:182 Nancy
6:105 Nathl 3:183 Phebe 4:77
Rebecca 1:103,-4:76 Samuel
1:152,153 Stephen 6:7 Stevens
4:187,188 Susan 1:153, -4:80
Susanna 1:153,180 Temperance
4:130 Trueworthy 1:153,-3:119
William 4:182 Winthrop 4:90
Zebulon 1:153,-4:150
DURNELL, Lemuel 5:117
DURRELL, Caroline 4:182
Deborah 4:126 John 4:77 John
N. 7:64 Newman 4:183
Nicholas 4:181 Sophia 4:79
DUSTIN (or DUSTON), Cyrus 7:67
Ebenezer 6:57 Eliza 6:170
Mrs. 3:84 Olive 4:179 Samuel
6:37 Sarah 6:165
DUTCH, Charlotte 4:129 Hannah
4:72 Jeremiah 3:27,70 Mary
4:128 Mr. 3:132 Samuel
3:113,181
DUTY, Nathaniel P. 3:113
DUVAL, Francois 3:67,75
DWYER, James 3:5 Mary 7:50
DYER, David 4:185 Hannah 4:10
Henry 3:153 John 4:182 Mary
7:50 Samuel 6:137
D'ZAGE, Pierre 3:68,75
EARLE, Gilbert 6:184 Henry 2:32
Ruth K. 2:32 Timothy K. 2:32
William 1:10,12
EASON, Captain 3:100
EASTERBROOKS, Abigail 4:39
EASTMAN, Abel 6:162 Abigail
2:129,-5:103,-6:53,112
Amanda 6:22,181 Anna 5:160
Asa 6:58 Benjamin 2:45,68,
70,-5:104,107,110,153,155,
160,-6:27 Bernard 5:17
Chandler 6:161 Charles 6:105
Chester C. 6:96 Clarissa 6:167
Dorothy 6:26,51 Ebenezer 2:44,
47,48,66,69,72,132,-3:91,134,
-5:107,154,-6:9,54 Ebenezer,
Jr. 7:66 Edmund 6:58 Edward
2:45,-66-68,131,-3:89,90 Eliza
7:23 Eliza L. 7:79 Elizabeth

EASTMAN (continued)
2:65,-3:169,-4:131,132,
-5:105,155,158,-6:53,107,109,
163 Emily J. 7:66 Esther 6:112
Ezekiel 3:38 George J. 7:19
Hannah 3:169,-5:107,-6:31,
54,104,-7:18 Harriet 7:59
Henry 6:55 Hiram 7:24 Jacob
3:168,-4:93,190,-5:153 James
6:57 John 5:107 Joseph 2:45,
65,69,-3:86,89,-4:178,-6:29,
31,165 Judith 6:54 Laban 4:190
Lucretia 6:56 Lycurgas 4:125
Lydia 3:182 Margaret 3:129,
-5:104 Martha 7:65 Mary 2:69,
70,-3:87,89,133,-6:30,162
Mary Ann 7:68 Mary Jane 7:67
Mercy 4:84 Miriam 1:28,-6:170
Mrs. 6:29 Nancy 6:106,-7:70
Naomi 6:106 Nathaniel 3:89
Nehemiah 5:156 Obadiah 2:65
Olive 4:173 Patience 4:93 Per-
sis 6:107 Peter 4:177,-6:31
Phebe 6:111 Philip 7:24,70
Phineas 6:110 Reuben J. 2:48
Rhoda 3:169 Ruth 6:53,165
Ruth B. 7:71 Samuel 2:43,44,
47,71,131,-3:38,43,87,-4:177,
-5:105,107,111,154,156,158,
-6:26,30 Samuel G. 6:166
Sarah 4:175,177,-5:110,111,
-6:29,51,111,164 Sarah (or
Susan B.) 7:66 Seth 7:26 Shuah
2:66,131 Simeon 6:58 Sophia
6:169 Stephen 4:190,-5:107,155
Susan 7:25 Susan B. (or Sarah)
7:66 Susan F. 7:20 Susanna
3:89 Thomas 2:67,69,129,
-3:39,-5:103 Timothy 6:27,31
William 2:69,-3:91
EATON, Abigail 1:166 Abram
5:20 Anna 6:106 Benoni 3:87
Experience 7:2 Ezekiel 3:86,
-6:32 Hannah 3:130,-6:104 J.
M. R. 6:15 James 6:32 John
7:66 John B. 5:181 Jonathan
6:27 Maria 4:179 Mary 3:42
Miss 4:177 Moses 5:17,-6:57
Osgood 6:56 Patience 3:45
Ruth 6:109 Samuel 6:104 Sarah
6:104 Susanna 6:107
Theophilus 6:27

37

EDDY, Hannah 5:144 Henrietta
6:191
EDGERLY, Abigail 5:83 Alice M.
5:85,96 Anna A. 5:85 Clarissa
3:178 Daniel 5:83 Daniel C.
6:93 Elizabeth 1:102-104,
-4:126,-5:83 Elizabeth T.
1:104 Emeline 4:187 Hannah
4:146,-7:91 Jacob 4:186 James
3:7,-5:83 James A. 1:29,31,
-2:165,192,-3:188,-5:83-85,92
James H. 6:40 John 4:79,185,
-5:83,-6:138,154,-7:39
Jonathan 1:103,104,-4:80,89
Joseph 7:91 Joshua 6:71
Larkin 1:103,104 Lydia 4:126
Mary 3:43 Mr. 6:68 Nancy 5:83
Olive 4:79 Olive O. 5:181 Oren
3:114 Rachel 5:83 Rebecca
4:79 Robert 1:102 Robert T.
1:104 Samuel 1:102,103,-3:3,
-5:83,-7:64 Sarah 1:103,104,
-3:116,181 Thomas 5:83 William 1:103,104 Zachariah 5:84
EDGGEREMMENT, Sagamore
3:83
EDMONDS - EDMUNDS, Ben-
jamin 6:163 Esther 3:54 Hannah 3:54 John 3:54 Jonathan
1:137 Katherine 4:103 Martha
3:54 Mary 3:51,52,54
Mehitable 3:86 Mrs. 3:176
Thomas 3:54,174,176
EDNEY, Peter 3:28,74
EDWARDS, John 5:41 John H.
5:48 Morgan 1:147 Ruth 3:41
Sarah W. 7:65
ELA, Mary 7:86
ELATSON, Elizabeth 1:17,-2:103
ELBERTSON, Mr. 5:44
ELKINS, Abel 5:160 Abigail
1:142,-2:170,-3:129 Achsa
6:24 Anna 2:47 Catherine
1:36,48,94 Deacon 2:134
Dorothy 1:165,-2:67 Eleazer
5:66,68 Elizabeth 1:36,
-2:48,65,131,-5:110 Ephraim
2:130 Esther 4:9 Gershom
2:106,108,112 Hannah 1:48,
-2:72,-4:178,-5:106 Henry
1:36,48,94,141,-2:134,-3:150,
-4:180,-5:156,-6:31 Jacob

ELKINS (continued)
2:67,68,133 James 1:141
Joanna 1:48,-2:46,130 John
1:175,-5:66 Jonathan 2:106
Joseph 2:44,48,68,72,131,
134,-3:37,-5:104,110 Mary
1:36,142,175,-2:68,106,108,
112,130,-3:129,-5:112,-6:181
Mary E. 1:175 Mehitable 2:46
Mercy 5:66 Miss 5:104 Moses
2:43,71,108,134 Mr. 6:24
Obadiah 2:45,66-68,72,133,
-5:104 Obed 2:130 Olive 1:141,
142 Peter 7:21 Richard 1:165
Robert 4:9 Samuel 1:94,141,
142,-4:131 Sarah 1:165,
-2:66,-3:91,168,-4:131,-5:104
Thomas 5:106,109,112,156,
160,-6:31 Widow 3:175 William 1:142
ELLATHIANS(?), Nathaniel 5:43
ELLESTON, John 5:44
ELLETHRAP, John 4:102
Nathaniel 4:102
ELLINGWOOD, Eunice 1:181
John 1:22
ELLINS, Anthony 1:4,5,9,10,12,
-2:23,-3:51
ELLIOTT, Abigail 1:24 Abraham
5:86 Benjamin 6:166 Captain
5:185 Charles 6:109 David
3:129,-6:109 Dolly F. 7:72
Dorothy 3:89 Elizabeth 4:130,
-6:55,168 Ezra 6:167 Frederick
6:111 Hannah 4:85,-6:70 Jacob
3:168 James 6:106,162 Jean-
nette 7:72 Joanna 5:42 John
3:54,-4:32,-6:137 John F.
6:170 Jonathan 5:68,-6:140
Joseph 6:105 Judith 7:19
Lucinda 7:20 Lydia 6:107 Martha 4:91,179,-5:68 Martha Jane
7:71 Mary 3:91,-4:49,50,91,
-5:68,185,187,-6:110,-7:19
Mehitable 6:56 Mr. 3:53,-4:174
Mrs. 3:50,-5:187 Naomi 6:111
Nathaniel C. 7:26 Richard
3:50,52,54,55,171,-4:50 Robert
1:10,-2:20,100 Ruth 4:190,191
Samuel 2:181,-5:185,187,-7:21
Sarah 4:90,-5:68,86,-6:56,57
Susanna 5:43 Thomas J. 7:26

38

ELLIOTT (continued)
William 5:161
ELLIS, Abigail 5:119,-6:68
Bertram 4:96 Charles F.
6:87 Dorcas 4:149 Flizabeth 5:54
Jacob 5:148 James 6:87 John
4:146,-6:68 Jonathan 4:147,
-6:68 Joseph 4:150 Joseph S.
6:33 Lawrence 1:22 Mary 6:67
Miriam 5:4 Mr. 6:114 Paul 5:7
Robert 2:186,-3:72 Sarah 5:55
William 6:67,68 William R.
6:87
ELLISON, Anthony 2:98,99
Elizabeth 4:79 Jane 4:79 Mary
4:75 Sarah 4:76 Thomas 2:35
ELLSWORTH, Eunice 3:46
Jonathan 4:91
ELMES, Elkanah 4:43 James 4:32
ELPHINSTONE, Alexander 4:2
Euphemia 4:2
ELY, Lois 5:133
EMERSON, Abigail 1:99,100,
155,-4:126 Andrew 1:55 Anna
4:79 Daniel 2:44,-6:160 Daniel
R. 4:177 Deborah 4:76 Dorothy
5:55 Eleazer 6:57 Elijah 4:76
Elizabeth 1:155,-4:75,182,
-6:163 Hannah 1:105,-2:67,
-4:79,125,-7:4 Harriet 1:153
Ithamar 6:57 James 1:153,
-6:161 John 1:26,-6:167,-7:25
John T. 4:128 Jonathan 4:130
Joseph 3:90 Joshua F. 1:152
Levi 4:130 Lois 4:127,129
Mary 1:153,155,-6:52,108
Mehitable 6:164 Mercy 4:94
Moses 4:76 Nathaniel 1:155,
-4:76,-6:168 Ruth 6:55,167 S.
1:105 Samuel 1:100,
-4:79,146,-5:146,-6:167
Samuel T. 1:152,153 Sarah
2:76,-4:65,-6:165 Sarah A. D.
6:7,8 Smith 5:99,100 Solomon
4:127,-7:4 Susan D. 5:181
Timothy 1:50,153,155,-4:130
EMERY, Abigail 6:108 Almira
7:72 Anthony 1:180 Benjamin
6:110,166 Caleb 6:108 Charles
6:110 Clarissa W. 7:26
Eliphalet 6:108 Elizabeth 6:53
Esther W. 7:24 Hannah R. 7:69

EMERY (continued)
Huldah 6:47 Huldah P. 7:21
Isaac Jr. 7:69 John 6:107
Joshua 7:23 Josiah 5:11,13
Lucy 6:48 Martha 7:52 Mary
6:166 Mary A. 4:144 Miranda
6:38 Moses 5:11 Nathan 5:13
Rebecca 5:11,13 Sarah 6:95,
165 Sarah Bailey 7:22 Thatcher
2:164 Timothy W. 7:71 Wil-
liam 7:53 William T. 7:72
EMMONS, Anna 3:88 Hannah 4:56
Jane 4:108 Maria 3:89 Martha
3:129 Mr. 3:132 Samuel 2:133,
134
ENDICOTT, Samuel 3:115
ENDLE, Mrs. 3:56 Wilmot 3:50
ENGLAND, Samuel 5:22
ENGLISH, Joseph 3:147 R. G. W.
7:64 William 4:102
ERVINE, George 4:85
ESTEN, Joanna 4:192
ESTERBROOK, John 7:25 Mary
6:161 William W. 7:66
ESTES, Abial 6:22 Albert 6:22
Alice 6:21 Alice N. 6:125 Benjamin 1:49,55,64,114 Caleb
3:36,-5:123 Charles 6:22 Edwin 6:22 Edwin T. 6:22 Elijah
1:50,55,70,120,-2:124,127,
-3:36,-5:27 Elizabeth 1:49,50,
55,64,70,-3:35,36,-5:27,28 Esther 1:173,-6:21 Hannah 3:36,
-4:160,-5:27,-6:125 Henry
1:49,50,55,64,65,70,-3:36,
-4:159 Israel 3:36 Jedediah
1:173,-4:159,-6:21 John 1:70,
173,-3:31,-5:28,-6:21,22
Joseph 1:50,51,55,61,120,
-2:75,124,-3:36,-4:120,-5:123
Judith 4:160 Keturah 1:114
Lydia 5:27 Mary 1:50,55,61,
65,70,-2:124,-3:36,-5:60,-6:91
Olive 3:164 Phebe 4:159,
-5:123 Rebecca 1:114 Richard
2:124,-3:36 Robert 1:70,
-2:124,-3:36,-4:42,160,-5:27
Samuel 2:124,-3:36 Sarah
1:51,65,70,120,162,-2:124,
-4:161,-5:123 Silas 4:160
Simon G. 6:22 Stephen 4:159
Susanna 1:55,-2:124,-3:35,36,

39

ESTES (continued)
- 5:27 Thomas 5:123 Timothy
4:160
ESTY, Isaac 6:164 Joshua 6:163
ETHEREDGE, Nathaniel 3:189
EVANS, Aaron 4:164 Abigail 6:50
Alcesta 4:190 Almeda 4:190
Ann 6:99 Asaph 7:17,65 Asaph
Jr. 7:69 Benjamin 1:63,
-2:150,-4:122,-5:50,-7:29,30
Benjamin H. 4:122,-5:50
Civilian 4:190 David 4:164,
-5:55,-6:12,50 Edward 1:174,
-6:22 Eldad 4:190 Elias 7:33
Elizabeth 1:63,67,-4:122,
164,-6:37 Ethni 4:190 Franklin
7:71 George 4:86 George
Frederick 7:33 Hannah 2:31,
-4:13,-6:21 Hanson 1:174,
-4:159 Israel 6:11-13,49,53,
57,58,104 James 4:127 Jesse
W. 6:183 John 2:98,-4:164
John Place 7:30 Joseph 1:63,
67,-4:12,122,-7:5 Levi 4:128
Mary 1:67,164,174,-4:122,
-5:23,-6:23,-7:68 Mary A.
4:190 Mercy 1:67,164,-7:5 Mr.
3:80,-6:23 Nancy 7:29
Nathaniel 4:142,-7:17 Oliver
6:36 Omrod 4:190 Patience
4:9,-6:22 Phebe 4:122 Robert
3:84,-4:151,-6:99 Rufus King
7:29 Sally Nowell 7:29 Samuel
6:12 Sarah 5:55,-6:21 Sarah F.
6:183 Solomon 1:67,-3:31,
-4:163 Stephen 5:100 Sylvanus
4:190 Tappan 6:53 Thomas H.
2:31,-6:183 Tobias 4:121,164,
-6:21 Wiggin 3:29,75 William
1:9,2:31,-4:122
EVERETT, Martha 6:146 Michael
2:186,-3:72
EWER, Dorcas 6:136 Drusilla
4:184,-6:138 Elizabeth 6:138
Mary 6:139 Mehitable 6:136
Mr. 6:133 Nathaniel 6:61,62,
136,139,140,153 Sarah 7:68
EWIN, Alexander 7:44
EYERS (see also Ayers), M. 1:10
Samuel 3:151 William 4:12
EYQUEM, Pierre 3:68,75
FABINS, George 2:18 Mrs. 2:18

FABYAN, Abigail 3:8 Anna 5:78
Elder 4:63,105 Elizabeth
2:169,-4:19,56,60,64,-5:80
John 3:50,52,53,55,57,61,154,
157,173,175,-4:12,56,157,158,
-5:75-77 Joseph 3:53,-4:56
Lydia 5:78 Mary 2:171,-3:4,
5,7,158,-4:56,-5:77 Mehitable
3:57 Mrs. 3:175 Nancy 5:77,80
Phebe 2:171,-4:97 Rosamond
3:157,158,160,-4:64,158
Samuel 2:171,174,-3:9,53,
154,157,158,160,-4:15,19,57,
60,64,-5:76-78,80,-6:178 Sarah
3:53 Widow 3:175 William
5:75 William B. 4:157
FADY, Jean 3:69,76
FAIRBANKS, M. B. 6:192
Windsor 7:72
FAIRWEATHER, Caesar 4:33
Nathaniel 4:102 Sarah 4:101
William 4:101
FALCH, Anna 1:163 Hannah 1:163
Jedediah 5:127 Parker 1:163
FALKNER (see Faulkner)
FALL(S), Anna 3:168 Susanna
6:114
FARIS, Jack 4:33 William 4:32
FARMER, Abigail 1:181 Daniel
D. 5:93 Edward 1:111 Gardner
5:92,93 Mary 1:111 Miss 5:93
Moses 5:92,93 Phebe 1:111
FARNHAM, Abigail D. 1:158
Andrew J. A. 1:158 Benjamin
7:54 Delia F. 1:158 Dummer
5:6 Eliza A. 1:158 John 1:158,
-4:127,130 John H. 1:158 Paul
4:146 Samuel 3:19,69,70 Susan
1:158 Susan G. 1:158
FARNSEY, Sarah 3:176
FARNSWORTH, Betsey 7:45
FARNUM, Abigail 6:176 Abner
6:161 Benjamin 6:54 Bridget
W. 7:24 Dorcas 6:105 Dummer
6:105,-7:28 Eliza 6:102
Elizabeth 6:57,74,102 Ellis
6:74 Emma 6:55 Enoch 6:107
Ephraim 6:51 Esther 6:54,
-7:24 Gershom 6:114 Hannah
6:57 Hannah C. 6:68 Hazen K.
7:71 Hepzibah 6:104 Isaac
6:107 Isaiah 7:68 Jeremiah

FARNUM (continued)
6:154 John 6:106,168 John W.
6:111 Joseph 6:102 Judith
6:54,108 Lydia 6:168,-7:28
Mary 6:74 Mehitable 6:109
Mercy 6:114 Morrill 7:17
Moses 6:55,163 Nancy 6:106
Naomi 6:108 Nathaniel 6:114
Olive 6:136 Patty 7:18 Paul
6:74,113 Peter C. 6:108 Phebe
6:105,109 Phebe A. 7:70 Ralph
6:113 Rebecca 6:164,169 Sarah
6:58,163,166 Susan D. 7:22
Susanna 6:107,108 Zebediah
6:50,163 Zeruiah 6:51
FARRAND, Arabelle M. 7:66
FARRAR, Jonathan 4:133 Martha
J. 3:47
FARRIEN, Mary 4:178
FARRINGTON, James 6:36 Nancy
4:176 Philip 6:107 Stephen
6:49 Thomas F. 7:69
FARWELL, Benjamin 7:89 Ed-
ward Sherman 7:89 J. E. 7:89
J. E. S. 7:89 Samuel Parris
7:89
FASSET, Elizabeth 6:43 Mary
6:43 William 6:43
FAULKNER, Enoch 6:154,-7:38
FAUTREL, Nicholas 5:162
FAVOR - FAVOUR, Anna 3:89,
-4:176 Elizabeth 4:176 Hannah
5:17 John 6:111 Mary 5:20
Miss 4:173 Narcissa 7:71
Samuel 4:173 Timothy 3:86
FAXON, Christopher 5:130
FAY, Sidney B. 3:96,141
FEA, Isabel 4:4 Patrick 4:3 Wil-
liam 4:4
FEATHERHORN - HOUGH,
Wharton 3:104
FEAVER, Jonathan 3:131 Samuel
3:131
FELING, John 2:175
FELKER, Dorcas 7:45 Elias 6:6
S. D. 5:85
FELLOWS, Abigail 5:158 Anne
2:68 Benjamin 2:66 Ebenezer
2:44,47,66,-5:104 Eleanor
3:133 Elizabeth 2:72,-3:171,
-5:104,105,112 Esther 3:167
Eunice 4:21 John 3:42,132,169

FELLOWS (continued)
Jonathan 4:175 Joseph 2:48,
-3:40,87,89,133,-5:105,106,
109,112,155,158,-6:28,31 Mary
31 Nathaniel 5:155 Samuel
5:105,-6:167 Sarah 5:109
Simon 3:168 Thomas 4:173,
-5:157,159 Timothy 5:157
William 1:20,-3:55,-4:51,
-5:44,159
FELTCH, Sarah M. 4:118
FERDINANDO, Deborah 5:40
FERGUSON, Gilbert 1:11 James
3:150
FERNALD, Abigail 4:57,-5:90
Abraham 2:173 Amos 4:99
Benjamin 5:185 Captain 3:146
Diamond 1:170 Edward 2:182
Elizabeth 4:48,56 Eunice
1:170,-6:85 Ezekiel 4:103,
-5:41 George 7:15 Gilbert 1:28
Hannah 4:76,127 Harriet 7:44
Henry W. 1:30,-2:165,-3:45
Humphrey 4:99,-5:86,88,
91,131,-6:78 James 3:55,
-4:50,56,98 John 1:11,-2:159,
-4:57,99,-5:87,90,130,132,
-6:78,80 Joseph 4:80,-5:138,
140 Joshua 3:24,72 Josiah
6:169 Katherine 6:80 Margaret
1:170,-7:73 Margery 4:49,50
Mark 1:28,-5:138,140,185 Mary
1:28,-2:176,-3:7,-4:52,56,101,
126,-5:91,185 Mary Griffis
7:75 Mary S. 7:15,73,75
Mehitable 4:181 Miss 4:98 Mr.
2:170,-3:50,-5:42 Mrs. 5:92,
138,140,-6:78 Nathaniel 4:12
Noah 5:38 Renald 1:3,4,6-9,
-2:23,25,26,59-63,97,98
Samuel 1:12,-2:98,-5:131
Sarah 2:36,-4:48,77,-5:41
Simeon 2:181,-3:71 Tem-
perance 3:56 Theodore 3:186,
-3:74 Thomas 5:130 Timothy
6:168 Tomp 3:50 Widow 1:10
William 4:48,58,-5:132,-6:80,
-7:15,73, 75 William H.
1:80,112
FERRIN, Abigail 6:170 Alice
6:165 Hannah W. 6:170 Jane
7:25 Moses 6:112,138 Philip

41

FERRIN (continued)
6:167,-7:24 Ruth 4:180 Samuel
4:78
FESSENDEN, Eliza 7:89 George
Russell 7:89 James M. 7:89
William Cumston 7:89
FIELD, Abigail 3:8,-4:11 Daniel
6:99 Darby 1:110,178 Elizabeth
5:44 Hannah 2:167,-6:99 John
4:13,-5:42 Joseph 1:2,-2:174
Joshua 4:75 Mary 4:12 Sarah
1:152 Stephen 1:110 Zachariah
3:149,-4:13,-6:99 Zachary
1:110
FIFE, Abigail 7:22,23
FIFIELD, Abraham 6:28 Alice
2:47,-3:44 Amos 3:136 Asa
7:69 Benjamin 1:190,-2:9,
109,111,-3:147 Coker 4:71
David 2:9,51,-4:88,-6:55
Deborah 2:87 Dorothy 1:190,
-2:130,-3:129,-4:7,-5:163
Ebenezer 6:27 Edward 1:183,
190,191,-2:68,69,94,129,133,
-3:38,-5:156 Eliza 4:72,-5:35
Elizabeth 1:190,191,-2:68,84,
133,-3:91,-5:108,-6:30 George
4:71 George B. 4:115 Giles
2:86 Hannah 2:9,86,152,
-3:136,-4:72,131,178,-5:65
Joanna 5:112 John 1:190,
-2:43,47,65,68,109,130,132,
-3:38,40,89,-5:103,108,110,
153,156,-6:28,30 John C. 4:72
Jonathan 1:190,-2:66,-4:71,
-5:65,153 Joseph 1:191,-2:43,
130,-3:91,-4:71,-5:17,106,110
Louisa 7:70 Lydia 2:83,-3:167
Margaret 2:46,130 Martha
3:40,129,-4:72,-5:110 Martha
A. 7:55 Mary 1:190,-2:72,83,
84,86,87,109,111,-3:87,-4:71,
176,-5:110 Mary H. 4:117
Mehitable 2:65,132,-3:91
Moses 1:190,-4:178 Mr. 5:173
Mrs. 5:65 Nancy 3:162,-4:22
Paul 2:70 Peter 5:106
Ruhamah 3:168 Samuel 2:44,
68-70,-3:38,89,91,134,-5:104,
106,110,112,154,-6:27,30 Sanborn 3:169 Sarah 2:9,46,65,
71,72,130,-3:39,91,-4:72,118,

FIFIELD (continued)
-5:104 Shuah 2:65,111,
-3:40,44,-6:55 Stephen 5:154
William 2:83,84,86,87,-3:88,
-6:51
FINLANSON, Nathaniel 4:103
Wallace 4:100,102
FINTASON, Margaret B. 5:39
Wallis (see above) 5:43
FISH, Charles H. 5:82 Hannah
5:151 Sophia 5:119
FISHER, Jarvrin (Janvrin?) 5:2
Robert 5:165 Susanna 5:116
FISK(E), Abira 7:23 Anna 6:170
Benjamin 5:13 Betsey 7:24
Clarissa N. 7:69 Cotton 5:14
Daniel 6:107 Ebenezer 5:13,14
Ednah P. 7:67 Elizabeth 5:13,
14 Francis N. 6:166 Isabella
5:13 Jeremiah 4:177 Joanna
5:13 Nancy 6:142 Phebe 7:24
Samuel 5:13 Sarah B. 7:65
Sarah B. 7:68 Ward C. 5:13
William 7:18
FITTS, Dorothy 5:11 John 5:11
Joseph 3:130 Josiah 4:179
Mary J. 5:101 Pamelia 5:17
Ruth 5:11 Sarah 3:44,-5:19
FITZGERALD, Abigail 7:79
Elizabeth 5:8 James 4:33 John
2:184,-4:33 Mary Yeaton 7:79
Mr. 5:44,90 Richard 2:175,
-7:79
FLAGG, Aaron 7:88 Abigail 5:49
Ann E. 6:45 Charles A. 4:141,
-5:141,-6:142 Charlotte 7:88
Elizabeth 5:88 Gershom 6:43,
45,77,79 James 6:142 John
2:162 Jonathan 5:6 Love 6:79
Lucy 6:38 Mary 6:77 Mrs.
6:43,45,77,79 Sarah 5:5 Sarah
O. 4:127
FLANDERS, Abigail 4:23,176,
185,-5:41 Asa 6:29 Charles
6:58 Christopher 3:171 David
3:90 Delia 5:20 Dr. 4:173
Ebenezer 6:154,168,-7:39
Elizabeth 3:135,136,-6:50,
-7:37 Ephraim 3:133 Ezekiel
2:47,-3:44,129,-6:27,31 Hannah 6:106 Hannah K. 7:23
Jacob 2:44,47,131,134,-3:37,

42

FLANDERS (continued)
167,-6:104,142,-7:18 James
3:134,-4:174 Jane 4:177 Jesse
2:47 John 2:47,-6:165 Martha
6:169 Mary 3:86,91,-6:31,-7:22
Mercy 2:47 Miriam 3:44 Mr.
4:174 Mrs. 6:27 Nancy 7:26
Nancy P. 7:25 Nathan 6:109
Nathaniel 6:27 Patience 6:52
Peter 6:112 Philip 6:107 Rhoda
4:180 Richard 6:51 Ruth 2:47
Sarah 3:86,-5:108,-7:18 Simon
6:29 Stephen 5:108,-6:29
Tabitha 2:47,-6:50
FLAY, Ann 6:1 William 6:1
FLEMING, Andrew 2:141 Mal-
colm 2:141 Samuel 2:141
Thomas 2:141 William 2:141
FLETCHER, Agnes 4:53 Daniel
3:88 DeBerruyer Du Vanrouy
5:168 Dr. 3:82 Joanna 4:173
John 2:97,100,101,-3:49-
51,173 Joyce 3:50 Levi 4:182
Maria K. 4:180 Miss 5:44 Mr.
1:12,-3:98 Mrs. 3:98,175
Pembleton 3:84,100 Samuel
2:182
FLINT, Rhoda 4:20
FLOOD, Anna 6:49 Daniel 6:52
Nathaniel 6:155 Sarah 3:170
FLORANCE, Abraham 5:87,89,
91,131,133 Gideon 5:87 Hannah
5:131 Michael 5:89 Susanna
5:133
FLOYD, Captain 3:80 Charles M.
4:96 Eunice 6:45 John 5:186
Joseph 7:56 Mrs. 5:186,
-6:41,45 Thomas 5:186,
-6:41,45
FODAR, Jacob 4:103
FOGG, Abiel 3:127 Abigail 4:131
Ann 2:83,85,87,88 Caleb 4:131,
172 Daniel 2:87 David 4:170,
172 Dudley 3:183 Ebenezer
6:109 Eleanor 4:89,172,-5:9
Elizabeth 4:84,137 Enoch 3:7
Eunice 3:5 Hannah 2:108 Henry
D. 4:84 James 2:106 Jeremiah
5:100 Jesse 4:170 John 2:85,
-4:84 Jonathan 4:84,172,-6:160
Jonathan, Jr. 7:40 Joseph 2:83,
-5:7 Josiah 4:7,84 Katherine

FOGG (continued)
4:170 Levi 4:80 Lydia 6:169
Mary 2:88,92,106,108,-3:119,
-4:84,91,-5:37 Nancy 4:84
Reverend M. 5:104 Samuel
2:83,85,87,88,92,106,108,-4:91
Sarah 4:84,133,172 Seth 2:92,
-4:172,-5:9 Sherburne 5:9
Simon 4:133
FOGGITT, Thomas 3:19,72
FOLLANSBY, Keturah 3:91
Thomas 1:12
FOLLETT, Abigail 4:11 Ben-
jamin 2:11,-4:76 Deborah
2:11,-4:135 Elizabeth 3:54
Hannah 3:50,56 Lois 4:75
Lydia 6:62 Mary 4:49,50,
-6:138 Mrs. 3:176 Nicholas
2:11,-3:101,173,-4:52 Robert
2:177,181 Samuel 4:52,54
Susanna 2:172,-3:111,156
Thomas 3:111 William 2:184,
-3:72
FOLSOM, Abigail 1:70,-2:29,
-6:137 Abigail N. 6:83 Andrew
6:138 Anna 3:125,-4:79,-6:138
Arthur 7:80 Asa 1:154 Benjamin 2:29,-4:126,-5:45,-6:61,
184 Captain 6:61 Comfort 4:80
David 3:124 Deborah 4:23
Dorothy 6:46 Elizabeth 1:154,
-3:125,-4:79,125,-6:45
Elizabeth M. 5:45 Ephraim
3:127,153 George 6:61 Hannah
1:166,-3:124,-5:45,52,-6:62
Issac 4:94 Jacob 6:138 James
4:79,-6:61 Jean 6:137
Jeremiah 3:87 Joanna 4:129
John 1:176,-2:155,-3:41,
124,125,-4:133,-5:24,59,109,
111,154,155,157,160,-6:29,
184,-7:38 John L. 1:176
Jonathan 3:180,-6:138 Joseph
6:126 Joshua 1:70,165 Josiah
3:88,127,-7:79 Josiah Gilman
7:79 Judith 3:179 Levi 6:137
Lewis 6:61 Martha 3:124,125,
-6:155 Mary 1:70,3:118,124,
177,-4:132,-5:27,111,-6:44-
46,61,80,139 Mead 3:179
Mehitable 1:175 Miriam 2:45
Nancy 5:146 Nathaniel 2:159,

43

FOLSOM (continued)
160,-5:157,160,163,164,166,
-6:44-46,80,-7:77,78,80
Nicholas C. 5:155 Olive 7:77,
78,80 Peter 5:45,-6:35,-7:86
Polly 7:79 Samuel 1:166,
-3:124,-6:184 Sarah 2:155,
-3:44,124,125,-4:134,137,
-5:154,-6:80 Sarah Ann 7:80
Stephen 6:61 Susanna 3:40,
-5:109 Thomas 3:116 William
7:63 Winthrop 4:78
FOOT, Captain 3:80 Mary 7:42
FOOTMAN, Deborah 4:76 John
1:103 Jonathan G. 5:116 Martha 4:182 Sophia 4:78 Thomas
1:179 William 1:103
FORD, Abigail 4:78 Elizabeth
4:75,78 Henry L. 4:115 John
4:12 Margaret 5:180 Noah 6:58
Sarah 4:78
FORDUM, Mr. 4:1
FORST, Benjamin 7:27 Patience
Seavey 7:28 Samuel Doust 7:28
Susa 7:27
FOSS, ---- 7:9 A. Melvin 5:82
Abiel 2:135 Abigail 1:47,
-5:137,-6:173 Alonzo M. 2:165
Anna 6:54,67 Benjamin 1:144,
-2:135,172,-4:55,-6:69,71,172,
173,175 Caroline 4:116 Char-
lotte 3:192 Charlotte D. 3:192
Daniel 6:37,66 Daniel M. 3:192
David 6:120 Dorcas 1:144
Dorothy 1:85 Elias 4:78 Eliza
2:136,-3:192 Eliza E. 3:192
Elizabeth 1:132,-3:16,-6:68
Ephraim 6:69 Eri 7:49 Esther
W. 7:64 Hannah 6:68 Harder-
son 3:192 Harriet 7:49 Henry
5:129 Henry D. 3:192 Hinkson
1:92 Isacc 3:16 Isaiah 4:150 J.
2:33 Jacob D. 3:93 James
6:120 Jane 1:92 Joanna 5:88
Job 1:85,-6:71 Joel 1:144 John
1:10,47,81,-3:17,93,97,174,
176,-4:80,-5:149,-6:68,70,175
John H. 2:136,-3:192 John O.
3:192 Jonathan 6:137 Joseph
4:55 Joshua 1:144,-2:135,
-6:71,-7:5 Joshua M. 2:139
Judith 7:49 Lydia 2:191,

FOSS (continued)
-3:93,-6:71 Margaret 3:192,
-4:152,-5:130,-6:120 Martha
5:36 Mary 1:44,81,144,-4:49,
50,55,90,146,152,-5:36,178,
-6:120 Mary Ann 2nd 7:9
Mehitable I. 2:139 Mehitable
J. 3:192 Moses 6:74 Mr. 5:90
Mrs. 3:56,93,176,-5:137 Nancy
4:115 Nathaniel 1:43 Olive
5:133 Oliver 6:20 Orin 2:136
Rachel 2:135 Rebecca 6:73,172
Richard 2:136,-3:192,-4:151
Robert S. 3:192 Robinson
3:192,-6:37 Robinson T. 3:192
Sally 2:135 Samuel 1:44,
-3:55,-4:49,50,55,151,-5:120,
-6:113,-7:49 Sarah 1:47,85,
144,-4:55,-5:7,147,-6:70,-7:5
Sarah A. 6:20 Susan 7:64
Susanna 6:70 Thomas 6:120
Wallis 1:44 Walter 3:107,
-4:55 William 1:50,144,
-2:135,-4:12,55,-7:49 Willis
1:81 Zachariah 1:22,-2:171,
-5:86,88,90,129,130,133,137
FOSTER, Adams 7:66 Albert 7:55
Anna 6:53 Benjamin 4:33,102,
-5:42,43 Charles 4:191 Charles
G. 2:165,-3:48,-5:33 Dorcas
6:49 E. W. 1:182 Eden B. 6:15
Eliza J. 3:191 George J. 5:33,
34 Hannah 5:130,133 Herbert
D. 3:141 Jacob 1:93 James
6:118 Joanna 6:3 John 5:41,
163,-6:118 Joseph 1:79,109,
-2:165,-4:140,141,144 Joshua
L. 5:33 Lucretia 5:33 Lucy
6:56 Luke 5:130,133 Lydia Ann
7:71 Nancy 6:108 Nicholas 6:3
Philip C. 5:34 R. 6:100 Sally
Gould 7:19 Sarah 4:190,191
Simeon 6:106 Susanna 6:108
Thomas 4:33 Walter H. 5:34
William 5:130
FOTHERINGHAM, Patrick 4:28
FOULIS, Marjorie 4:3
FOWELL, John 2:5
FOWLER, Abigail 2:35 Apphia
4:78 Benjamin 5:159 Clarissa
1:158 Daniel 1:157 Eliza 1:158
George 1:158 Hannah 3:89,

44

FOWLER (continued)
-6:159,-7:40 Jairus 1:158 John
1:147,158,-2:35,-4:130,-7:4
John C. 6:159,-7:40 Joseph
1:158,-2:35,-5:159,-6:30
Josiah 2:45,-3:42,-5:112
Judith 6:30 Lodowick 1:12
Mary 1:158,-2:35,-5:59,150
Miriam 3:43 Philip 6:137
Samuel 6:50 Sarah 4:86
Thomas 5:160 William 2:45,
-5:112
FOWLES, Lemuel 4:33
FOX, Edward 3:176 Hannah 4:130
Jane M. 6:126 Joanna 4:185
John 7:67 Lois M. 2:31 Mrs.
3:176 Roanna 2:31 Samuel W.
2:31 Sarah 3:2,87,-4:85
FOXHALL, Nathaniel 3:100
FOXWELL, Ann 5:143 Mary
5:143 Richard 5:143
FOYE, Deborah 4:126 Hannah
2:139 John 5:44 Jonathan 4:182
Sarah 5:150 Stephen 3:143
Tabitha 6:73
FRAME, Robert 4:32
FRANCIES, Nancy 3:171
FRANCIS, Colonel 7:52 Elizabeth
B. 7:64
FRANCOIS, Jean 3:68,76
FRANKLYN, Frederick J. 4:114
FRAZIER, Elizabeth 4:52
FREDERICK, Christopher 1:21-23
FREEMAN, Adam 4:33 Cuff 4:33
George R. 4:7 Jacob 7:12
Jonathan W. 6:38 Nero 4:33
Newport 7:12 Violet 7:12
FREESE, Dudley 4:133 Jacob
3:181
FRENCH, Abigail 2:45,-4:83,
169,172,176,-5:16,110,112,157
Abigail L. 4:73 Abraham 2:139
Abram 3:127 Amanda M. 4:73
Amos 4:83,132,511 Andrew
2:114,154,-3:16 Ann 6:28 Anna
2:119,120,154 Barnes 4:180
Barzillai 4:172,-5:15 Benjamin
2:67,129,132,134,-3:41,133,
-4:80,151,-5:108,110,153,155,
-6:28,155 Benjamin F. 6:156
Betsey 2:154 Caleb 4:169
Chase W. 2:154 Cheef 2:114

FRENCH (continued)
Daniel 2:119,122,-3:16 David
3:16,43,-5:8,157,-6:26,31,
-7:42 Deborah 5:51 Dolly M.
3:115 Dorothy 3:118 Ebenezer
3:183,-4:88,-5:51 Elijah
1:157,-2:114,154,-4:182 Elisha
2:121,122,-3:16,-4:86 Eliza A.
4:117 Elizabeth 2:44,66,122,
143,-3:16,45,129,132,-4:133,
177,182,-5:11,106,108
Elizabeth E. 3:113 Elizabeth
G. 3:118 Ezra 3:178,-4:83,138,
-5:11 Gilbert 4:152 Hannah
2:67,114,-3:41,171,-4:83,
-5:11,14,15,-7:63 Henry 3:132,
-5:104,154 Henry S. G. 7:70
Isaac 6:56 Jacob 3:44 James
3:118,-4:33,-5:11 Jane 3:133
Jean 3:44 Joanna 3:171,-4:138,
-5:16,103,-6:27 John 2:154,
-3:170,-5:51,56,107,109,-6:26
Jonathan 2:46,-3:132,-5:103,
104,106,111,112,154,158,
-6:27,30 Jonathan S. 7:59
Joseph 3:16,-4:131,172,178,
-5:16,112,154 Joseph Y. 6:156
Josiah 3:170 Judith 2:65,
-5:15,-6:158 Kezia 5:148 Leah
4:152 Levi 2:120,-4:129,-5:14
Lois 3:135,-4:174 Lucy 3:118
Lucy C. 2:119 Lydia 2:119,
-3:16,-4:125,129,172 Margaret
2:132,-3:183,-4:172,-5:15
Mark 2:120 Martha 3:16,-4:85,
129,-5:11,157 Mary 2:114,122,
154,-3:16,41,118,120,181,
-4:78,83,126,136,138,-5:11,16,
112,154,158,-6:155 Mary F.
3:16 Mary J. 4:186,-6:155
Mehitable 3:18,118,-6:30
Moses 3:118 Nancy 3:126
Nathaniel 2:43,66,70,72,
-3:90,-5:104,106,107,110,153,
154,157 Nathaniel Y. 6:155
Noah 3:16 Obadiah 3:39 Olive
2:119,-5:50 Olive W. 4:129
Patience 5:15 Polly 2:119
Rachel 2:154 Reuben 2:119,
-4:134,-6:138 Rhoda 3:170,
-4:180 Ruhamah 5:157 Ruth
2:134 Sally D. 7:23 Samuel

45

FRENCH (continued)
3:182,-4:183,-5:105,107,
109,112,154,157,-6:26,30,112
Samuel T. 7:24 Sarah 2:129,
-3:16,40,118,169,-4:85,134,
172,183,-5:15,110,155,-6:26,31
Secomb 5:107 Simeon 2:43,
129,134 Stephen 5:51 Susan
3:16 Susanna 4:80,169 Thomas
2:119,120,-3:18 Thomas G.
5:106 Timothy 2:154 Timothy
S. 7:54 Walter 7:22 William
2:119,121,122,143,-3:16,
-4:128,-5:104 William S. 4:76
Zachariah B. 4:73
FRIEND, Abigail 1:68 Abraham
1:68
FROST, Abigail 1:24 Andrew P.
1:24 Anna 1:32 Benjamin
2:33,36 Charles 1:24,-3:84
Cooper 6:168 Dorothy 4:49,50,
52,53 Elizabeth 1:17,-2:33,
-3:177 Elizabeth R. 6:36
George 1:105,157,-2:36 Hannah
2:41,-5:49 John 1:21-24,
-2:33,181,- 3:71,-5:164 Joseph
1:24,-2:34 Julia A. 7:26 Love
5:151 Margaret 4:13 Margery
1:23 Mary 1:23,24,-2:33,
-4:75,76 Mr. 3:50,-5:124 Mrs.
3:56 Nathaniel 4:56 Nicholas
4:53 Samuel 1:21 Sarah 1:24,
-4:127 Stephen 3:26,73 William 1:24,-2:33,-4:52
FROTHINGHAM, Richard S. 5:150
FRYE, Abigail 1:58,61,64,65,
115,-2:126,-4:161,-5:28,-6:17
Adrian 4:12 Alice 1:62,
-2:150,-4:120,164 Benjamin
1:62,67,69,70,163,-2:77,149,
-4:164,-5:58,125 Catherine 3:5
Comfort 5:28 David 4:164
Ebenezer 1:61,64,127,-2:30,
126,150,-4:43,70,159,-6:103,
-7:8 Edward 6:88 Edward A.
2:30 Elisha 5:28 Elizabeth
4:11 Eunice 4:164 Gertrude
6:88 Hannah 1:52,57,58,125,
-2:77,126,-4:42,-5:28,-6:107
James 4:164 John 1:127,-2:77,
126,-4:159,164,-5:176,-7:8
John F. 5:28 Jonathan 2:150

FRYE (continued)
Joseph 1:118,-2:77 Joshua
4:70,-5:28 Judith 1:125,
-2:150,-4:164,-5:32 Lydia
2:30,-5:28 Martha 1:58,
-2:126,-4:43 Mary 1:125,127,
163,-2:126,-4:164 Obadiah
4:159,-7:8 Rachel 4:164
Roland 1:67,125 Rowland
2:150,-4:164 Ruth 1:69,125,
-2:150,-4:164,-5:26,174 Sarah
1:57,62,67,69,70,118,-2:77,
-4:40,164,-5:122 Silas 1:70,
125,163,-2:150,-5:27 Stephen
4:164 Susanna 1:118 William
1:51,52,57,58,61,64,65,115,
-2:75,77,126,-5:98,-7:8
FRYER, James 1:11 John 1:22
Mr. 1:11 Mrs. 3:56 Nathaniel
1:11,-2:99,100,-3:104
FULLER, Elizabeth 1:34,36,39
George 1:82 James 1:34
Jeremiah 1:34,82 Joanna
1:36-39 Joseph 1:36-39,92
Love 1:34 Mary 1:34,37,82,
-2:41 Richard 1:82 Samuel
2:93 Warren 4:136
FULLERTON, Elizabeth 5:139
John 4:33 Mary 5:132 Mrs.
5:136,139 Samuel 5:136 William 4:127,-5:129,132,136,139
FULLINGTON, Agnes 5:45,134
Ezekiel 6:92,93 Lydia 6:160,
-7:41 Mrs. 5:134 William
5:134
FULLONTON, Anna 4:85
Deliverance 5:180 Franccs
5:180 John 5:180 Mary 5:180
FURBER, Abigail 2:169,-3:155,
157,159,-4:16,18,63,156,-5:73,
117,-6:172,173 Alice 4:153,
-5:51,-7:86 Alice C. 5:79,-
6:38 Anna 4:109 Benjamin
4:64,148,-5:50,-6:38,171-175,
-7:29 Bethia 3:58 Daniel 5:120
David 4:126 Deborah 3:4
Easter (Esther ?) 2:171
Edmond-Edmund 5:150,-7:27
Edward 4:56 Edwin R. 3:165
Eli 4:59 Elizabeth 2:168,170,
-3:1,6,145,155,-4:19,53,64,
105,107,109-111,153,-5:39,

FURBER (continued)
145,-6:35,60,174,176,-7:30
Frances 3:61,-4:110 Hannah
3:112,155,158,160,-4:15,17,19,
60,63,149,-6:172 Jerusha
2:172,-3:3,59,157 Jethro 2:17,
171,-3:112,155,157,159,-4:16,
17,53,59,61,154,156,157,-5:73
Joel 6:174 John 4:16,129,-6:21
John F. 6:172 John Wingate
7:29 Jonathan 6:171 Joseph
4:17 Joshua 3:112,-4:17,56
Katharine 3:155 Kingman 3:47
Leah 2:167,-3:159 Levi 3:7,
-4:63 Luke 7:29 Mary 3:63,
-4:111,156,157,-5:2,52,55,73,
-6:171 Mary Barnes 7:79 Mary
Wingate 7:32 Mercy 6:21
Moses 3:6,111,112,155,158,
160,-4:15,17,19,60,63,107,109
Mr. 5:44 Nehemiah 2:171,
-3:10,155,157,159,-4:18,60,63,
156 Phebe 3:112,155,157,
159,-4:16,17,59,61,156 Philip
6:163 Pierce 6:175 Pierce P.
7:32 Polly 7:27 Richard 2:175,
-3:9,61,63,-4:61,64,99,105,
107,109-111,153,-5:79,-6:173-
176 Richard, Jr. 7:29 Samuel
4:61,-6:171-174,-7:27,29,30
Samuel E. 5:55,-6:171 Sarah
3:2,3,58,59,111,158,-4:18,127,
-6:173 Theodore 5:118,-6:171,
-7:80 Theodore Pickering 7:80
Thomas 4:55,63 Thomas, Jr.
7:28 Wallis 4:57 William
1:178,-3:58,59,111,145,150,
160,-4:10,-6:97,-7:29,79,86
William A. 3:47 William K.
3:46
FURBUSH, Anne 5:55 John 4:89
FURLONG, James 3:24,71
Lawrence 4:33
FURNAL (see FERNALD)
FURNESS - FURNISS, Edward
4:129 Robert 3:23,73,-4:126,
-5:166,167
FURSON (PHERSON?), Thomas
1:8,9,179
GAGE, David 6:50 Elizabeth
4:148,-5:116 John 2:126 John
C. 7:72 Joshua 5:46 Mary

GAGE (continued)
5:118 Sarah 5:2,46 Thomas
5:118 William 4:146
GAINS, Elizabeth 5:187,189
George 2:159-161,-3:10,
126,-5:162,166,168,170,187,
189,-6:42,45,76,79,-7:15,16,
74,75,77,79 John 6:76 Josiah
7:15 Martha 7:79 Mary 5:166,
187,-6:42,45,76,79 Mrs. 5:187,
189 Nancy 7:75 Ruth 6:45
Samuel 7:77 Sarah 6:154,
-7:16,39 Theophilus 6:79 William Langdon 7:74
GALE, Amos 3:130,169,-5:21
Daniel 4:89,93,132,-5:105 Dent
4:125 Elizabeth 4:93 George
W. 6:159,-7:40 Gilman 6:138
Hannah 3:169 Israel 4:173 Israel N. 5:21 Jacob 3:90,-4:93,
175,-5:105 Joseph 4:93 Judith
6:110 Lucretia 5:33 Lucy 5:21
Mary 3:129,-4:3,93,133,-7:70
Rebecca 7:56 Ruth 6:55 Shuah
4:93 Stephen 3:170,-4:93 Susan
4:93,174,179,-6:163 Widow
3:129 William P. 5:22
GALLOWAY, Elizebeth 4:12
GALTEAU, Peter 3:27,72
GAMBLIN(G), Benjamin 3:55,
-4:50,98,-5:40 Mary 4:50
GAMBOL, Mary 5:41
GAMMETT, Jonathan 5:156 Silas
5:156
GAMMON, John 3:29,73,182
GARDNER, Andrew 3:103 David
2:18,-4:99,-5:39,42 Eliza
6:143 Elizabeth 4:102,-5:60
Frank A. 5:41 Henry 5:186
Hepsibah 5:93 John 4:99
Joshua 5:41 Margaret 2:18,
-4:103,-5:38 Mrs. 5:186 Sarah
7:14 William 2:160,-5:162,
163,168
GARLAND, Abigail 2:138 Abigail
P. 2:135 Ann 5:36 Anna 5:2
Benjamin 3:44 Calvin 7:55
Caroline H. 2:192 Charles
2:140 Daniel 6:115,116,119,120
Dodavah 3:44 Dodavi ? 7:29
Dorcas 5:6 Dudley 5:4,-6:116
Ebenezer 4:149,-5:119,-6:174

47

GARLAND (continued)
Elizabeth 1:103,-2:83,84,
86,112,-4:78,186,-5:147 Elvina
L. 2:135 Ephraim 5:115,119,
-6:174 Francis 1:103 Gilman
2:140 Hannah 4:78,-5:65 Hiram
7:86 J. 1:103 Jabez 3:99 Jacob
1:103,-2:84,-5:65 James
2:138,-4:77,-5:55,-6:120,174
John 2:83,84,86,112,138,
-4:77,-6:38,117,147,174
Joseph 5:17 Joseph W. 2:135
Lucinda 7:86 Lucretia 2:140
Lydia 4:147,-5:3,8,65,-6:115,
147 Mahala 3:48 Malvina G.
2:140 Margaret 2:135,-5:4
Mary 4:186,-5:54,-6:7 Mary A.
2:140 Mary L. 1:140 Mehitable
1:140,141 Mercy 4:147 Moses
L. 1:141,-2:140 Nancy 5:120
Nathaniel 5:5,-6:116 Olive
6:71 Patience 6:174 Peter
1:140,141,-2:86 Phebe 6:117
Rachel 6:117 Rebecca 5:56
Reuel 2:138 Reuel L. 2:135
Richard 5:120,-6:74,120 Ruth
5:65 Sally (?) 7:29 Samuel
1:94,-3:178,-4:118,-6:174
Sarah 1:103,140,-4:126,-5:65
Simon 5:65 Susanna 6:113
Thomas 2:138,-6:116,117
Thomas R. 2:135 Tristram
5:54 William 1:140
GARMINE, Elizabeth 4:10
GARRATT, John 4:33
GARVIN, James 6:52 Jesse 6:170
John 6:55 Miriam C. 7:20
GASH, Sarah E. 3:47
GASKILL, Content 2:75,128,-7:5
Samuel 2:175
GATCHELL, Benjamin 4:56 Sarah
4:58
GATES, Nancy 5:147
GAULT, Andrew 6:110 William
7:19
GAUTIER, Mathurin 3:68,76
GEAR (see also GEER),
Deliverance 4:128 Elizabeth
4:128 George 4:128 John 5:35
Mary 5:45 Sarah 4:58
GEARIS (?), George 5:170
GEE, Joshua 5:44

GEER (see also GEAR), Walter
2:191,-3:47
GEORGE, Darius 5:21 David
6:51,53 David B. 6:165 Dorothy
6:55,169 Ebenezer 4:178
Elizabeth 4:45,92,-6:105
Elizabeth C. 7:72 Gideon
3:131,-4:178 Hannah 3:170
James 4:133 Jennie 6:56 John
4:127,-6:111 Joseph 2:47
Joshua 3:169,-4:92 Lydia 3:90
Mary 2:47,-6:111 Moses 2:47
Sarah 3:86,167,-4:76,-6:29,
-7:25 Stephen 3:168 Thomas
2:44,47 Timothy 3:89 William
3:133,134
GERRISH, Abigail 3:8 Anna 3:137
Benjamin 1:14,-2:182,-4:57
Bridget 4:53 Captain 3:81,
83,150 Daniel 4:129 Elizabeth
3:137,-4:11,-5:95,96 Enoch
6:106 George 4:57,75,182
Grace W. 5:102 Hannah 1:151
James 6:34 Jane 3:175 Joan-
nah 7:57 John 3:137,-4:185
Joseph 2:183,-3:20,72,137
Mary 4:50 Mehitable 1:151
Miss 3:176 Paul 4:76,78,-7:59
Richard 3:173 Samuel H. 4:96
Sarah 3:80,84,-4:80 Timothy
5:6 William 4:55
GETCHEL, Benjamin 5:40
GIAUGUE, Mary M. 1:112,-2:166
GIBBONS, Ambrose 1:3,178,180
GIBBS, Daniel 4:26 Heman 6:37
GIBSON, Charles 7:68 Edah 3:184
Ezra 3:115 George 3:114
Richard 1:2,-3:49 William
3:133
GIDDING(S), Deborah 4:83
Nathaniel 5:164
GILBERT, Harry J. 7:72 Prince
4:33 Samuel C. 5:36,37
GILCHRIST, Albert 7:72
GILE, Luther 6:37
GILES, Abigail 2:46,108,-5:100
Andrew 5:45 Bridget 5:45
Caroline G. 7:23 Catharine
4:80 Daniel 5:109,155,157,159
Dorothy 5:111,154,156,158
George 4:130 Hannah 4:185,
-5:157 Jacob 5:109,153,155,

GILES (continued)
158 John 3:102,-4:12,
-5:104,107,109,112,156,160
John M. 5:109 John T.
5:161 Joseph 3:41,-5:164,-6:107
Josiah 5:164,169 Mark 2:76,
-3:102,-4:11 Mary 3:41,-4:78,
-5:159 Matthew 1:178
Nathaniel 5:107,153 Nicholas
5:165 Paul 4:78,126 Rachel
5:125 Samuel 4:89,-5:158
Samuel S. 5:160 Sarah 3:120,
-5:104 Susan 1:158,-4:127
Susanna 4:75
GILL, Perney 6:170 William 6:54
GILLARD, John 4:33
GILMAN, Abigail 3:40 Benjamin
1:80 Bradstreet 6:152 Charles
1:146 Chase 6:160,-7:41 Comfort 3:181 Daniel 2:45,-3:43,
-6:28 David 6:137 Deborah
3:170,-6:138,139,156 Deborah
H. 3:113 Dorothy 2:133,-3:130,
-6:32 Dudley 4:133,-6:139
Ebenezer 6:94 Edward 6:94
Elizabeth 1:25,-2:44,-3:44,
116,130 Frances 4:178 George
6:39 Hannah 3:120,130,-4:126
Henry 3:183,-6:153,159,-7:40
Israel 4:126,-6:137 Jacob 2:43,
94,129,133,-3:41 Jemima 6:94
Jeremiah 1:80 John 2:46,71,
-4:127,-6:28,32,94 Jonathan
4:132 Josiah 3:12 Lycurgus E.
7:60 Mary 1:80,-2:45,94,-3:86,
87,-4:175,-6:28,62,158 Mary
Ann 7:59 Maverick 2:46 Moses
6:97 Mr. 3:149,153 Mrs. 2:129
Nathaniel 2:46,-3:129 Nicholas
2:71 Phebe 6:94 Phineas 6:32
Robert 3:168 Samuel 3:135,
-4:91,-6:61 Sarah 2:45,-4:125,
-6:28,140 Stephen 3:41,-5:109,
111,153,155,158,-6:28 Susan
4:127 Theodore 5:119 William
3:41,-5:154,157 Winthrop 5:45
GILMORE, Margaret 3:44
GLANDFIELD, Peter 1:12
GLANVELL, Anne 2:12 Joseph
2:12 Judith 2:12 Mercy 2:12
Thomas 2:12
GLASGO(W), Richard 6:156

GLASS, David 4:185 John 4:181
Jonathan 4:128 Samuel 4:184
GLEASON, John 4:75 Mary 4:127
Simeon C. 7:26 Timothy
3:28,73
GLEEDEN, Charles 1:11
GLEER, Thomas 2:172
GLIDDEN, Abigail 3:44 Davis S.
7:58 Elizabeth 4:184 Hannah
3:132 James 4:181 Jeremiah
4:135 John 7:3 Lydia 6:40,153
Mahaloth (?) 6:123 Margaret
3:184 Mary 3:86,89 Mehitable
3:129 Nancy 3:183,-4:127
Peter 6:119 William B. 7:45
Winthrop 6:119
GLOAD, Mary 6:166
GLOVER, Eliza A. 7:65 Lois
4:181 Susanna 4:126 Thomas
4:80
GLOYD, James 3:41
GODDARD, Elizabeth Sewall 7:80
Harriet 7:76 Henry 7:16 James
1:114 Jane 7:75,76 Jane Boyd
7:75 John 1:177,-2:161,-5:190,
-7:14,16,74-78,80 John Heath
7:14 Lucy Maria 7:78 Martha
5:190 Mary 7:78,80 Moses 7:7
Samuel 7:74 Sarah 1:115 Silas
1:114 Susannah 7:16,74 Wil-
liam 7:75 Zeruiah 5:170
GODFREY, Charles L. 6:6,8
David 6:154,-7:38 Deborah
2:110 Elizabeth 1:183 Hannah
2:108-110,112 Isaac 2:44,67,
69,109,110,112,130,134,-3:39,
-5:105 James M. 6:7 John
2:86,87,89,90,106,108,110
Mary 2:47,86,87,89,90,106,
108,110 Mehitable 2:106
Nathaniel 2:69,134 Oliver 5:37
Sarah 2:90,112,-5:105 William
2:65,89,110,134
GODSOE, Elizabeth 6:138 John
2:173
GOE, Abigail 3:42
GOFF, Patrick 1:22
GOLD (see GOULD)
GONICK, Oliver J. 7:87
GOOCH, Ann 5:87 Betsey 7:79
Elizabeth 5:86 James 2:181,
-4:79,-5:86,87,90,129,131,133

GOOCH (continued)
John 7:15,74,77,79 Polly 7:15
Samuel 7:77 Sarah 5:90,129,
131
GOODALE, Lydia 1:111
GOODELL, David H. 5:82 Samuel
5:7 William F. 7:68
GOODHUE, Eliza 7:86 John 4:78
Joseph 4:76
GOODLIVE, Elizabeth 2:48 Mary
2:65
GOODRICH, Amos T. 2:165
Sabrina H. 7:64
GOODWIN, Bartholomew 5:89,
132,169 Benjamin 5:145
Catherine 6:137 Coleman 6:167
Daniel 6:177 Dorcas 1:127,
-5:175 Dorothy 4:180,-6:56
Eliza 7:43 Elizabeth 4:148,
-6:56 Hannah 4:173,-6:34,138,
169 Ichabod 2:163,164,-7:52
James 3:84 Joanna 2:144
Judith S. 7:68 Lawrence 6:140
Lydia 1:127 Martha 6:109 Mar-
tha H. 4:183 Mary 5:1,89
Mehitable 4:77,-6:39,137 R. J.
P. 6:143 Reuben 6:108,150,
-7:23 Richard 6:146 Robert
4:185 Samuel 6:35 Sarah
4:186,-6:61,166 Silas 5:54
Susanna 6:162 Thomas 6:177
Timothy 3:129,-5:21 William
3:84 Willoughby 1:127
GOOTAM, Edward 3:9
GOPELL, George 4:183
GORDON, Abiel 3:89 Abigail
3:42,135 Abraham 3:133
Alexander 3:86,-4:135 Anna
4:135 Benjamin 3:41,-4:176
Benoni 5:110,153,156,160
Caroline E. 5:102 Daniel
3:180,-5:14,110,153,156 Daniel
D. 5:14 David 5:14 Dorothy
4:85 Dudley 3:134,-5:14
Elizabeth 3:41,86,-5:102
Emeline E. 5:102 Enoch 5:153
George A. 4:1,-5:97 Hannah
3:116,-5:158 Ithiel 3:89 James
3:44 John 2:70,-3:135 Jonathan
5:14 Joseph 5:14,-6:51 Josiah
5:153,156 Lawrence 6:139
Mabel F. 5:102 Margaret 6:50

GORDON (continued)
Mary 2:44,-3:119,134,168,
-4:79,-5:107,-6:162 Mary E.
5:102 Miriam 5:14 Moses
4:180 Nancy 4:130 Nathaniel
3:89 Samuel 5:156 Samuel R.
4:89 Sarah 2:71,-3:88,-4:134,
135,-5:14 Scrivener 5:112
Susanna 5:110 Tabitha 5:110
Thomas 3:43,88,-5:107,108,
112,158 Timothy 5:102
Timothy T. 5:102 Timothy W.
5:101,102 William 3:133,
-6:162
GORHAM, Eunice 4:142
GORURDEN (GORDEN?), Mr.
3:169
GOSPETH, Nathaniel S. 6:77
GOSS, Abigail 1:48,85,-2:136
Daniel 2:136 Deliverance 5:111
Elizabeth 1:141,142 Esther
1:44,45 Hannah 2:136 James
1:142 James M. 1:142 Jean
1:183,-3:43 Jethro 1:44,45
John 3:17 John S. 2:136
Jonathan 1:47 Jose 1:137
Joseph 5:111,156 Levi 1:44,45
M. D. 1:142 Margaret 1:48
Maria 3:43 Martha 1:83 Mary
1:44,-5:38 Mary A. 2:136
Michael D. 1:142 Mrs. 3:175
Nathaniel 6:169 Rachel 1:48,
-5:156 Richard 1:47,48 Robert
3:174,-4:10 Salome 1:47
Samuel 1:44 Sarah 1:44,142,
-2:135,136 Sarah A. 2:136
Sarah J. 2:136 Sheridan 2:135
Thomas 2:135,136 Tobias T.
1:142 William 2:135 Winnifred
L. 6:48
GOTHAM, Edward 5:79 James
5:79 Mercy 5:79 Mr. 5:79
Samuel 5:79
GOTT, Joshua 4:33
GOUDY, Abigail 2:36 Samuel 2:36
Sarah 5:137
GOUGE, James 4:33
GOUGH, Sophia 4:8
GOULD, Abigail 5:61 Alexander
3:28,74 Anna 5:72 Bar-
tholomew 6:57 Daniel 3:168
Elihu 4:43 Elizabeth 1:118,

GOULD (continued)
127,167,-4:43,177,-5:72,122,
-7:8 Emma 2:191,-3:93,142,
-6:94 Ezra 4:43 Hannah 4:175,
-5:61 Isaiah 1:116,125,-4:43,
67,-5:61,174 Jeremiah 5:72
John 3:129,-4:176,-5:62
Katharine 6:95 Lydia 1:58,62,
66,-4:43,-5:20 Margery 6:100
Martha 1:116,125,127,-5:176,
-7:8 Mary 1:119,-4:176 Mussey 1:58,66,116,125,127,167,
-4:43,62,-7:8 Nathan 3:89,
-4:176,-6:56 Samuel 1:58,59,
62,66,119,-2:80,-4:43,65,70,
120,180,-5:72,-6:100 Sarah
1:62,167,4:120 Stephen 4:43
Tabitha P. 6:100 William
3:132,-5:61,125
GOVAN, Andrew 5:22
GOVE, Abigail 2:105,107,-6:47,
182 Anna 6:17 Charles 6:17
Daniel 1:71,117,161,-4:38
David 1:117,126,-4:67,
-6:17,184 Dorothy 3:177,-4:47
Ebenezer 2:109 Edmund 1:161,
-2:111,-4:123 Edward 1:68,
164,176,-2:91,105-107,109,
111,112 Eleanor 4:137
Elizabeth 1:176 Enoch 2:175
Hannah 2:91,105-107,109,111,
112,-3:134,-4:67,-6:17 Hiram
6:17 James 1:128,-4:70 Jane
4:84,85 Jeremiah 2:112 John
1:68,128,164 Jonathan 3:182
Judith 1:164 Lydia 2:23 Martha
1:126,128 Mary 2:91,139,
-3:183,-4:47 Nancy 3:183
Olive 4:135 Peniel 2:106
Rebecca 1:71,117,161 Ruth
1:68,-3:134 Sarah 4:86 Stephen
5:23,-6:23 Stephen M. 1:176
GOWELL, Timothy 5:151
GOWEN, Mercy 3:8
GRACE, Nicholas 6:140
GRAFFORD, Bridget 3:98
GRAFHAM, Caleb 4:97 Mary
4:104 Rebecca 4:51 Samuel
4:102 Stephen 1:10,11
GRAFTON, Agnes 4:52 Anna 1:80
Elizabeth 7:83 Joanna 4:54
John 4:56

GRAGE, William 3:131
GRAGG, Samuel 4:33
GRAHAM, Anna 4:3 Asa 6:57
Azubah 6:166,167 Godfrey
4:128 Isabel 4:3 Joseph 7:26
Mary 4:3 Sarah 6:54 Thomas
7:68
GRANDEN, Clement 1:22
GRANDY, Daniel 2:185,-3:73
GRANT, Daniel 5:139,140,188,
-6:42,46,80 Eliza 4:129
General 6:129 General U. S.
6:132 Gilbert A. 7:59 Hannah
1:15 Helen St. John 7:59 Hiram
5:148 James 6:42 John 1:15,
-3:73,90,-6:80 Joshua Jr. 7:21
Katharine 5:138,139 Martha
4:81 Mary 2:36 Mrs. 5:140,188,
-6:42,46 Nelson 3:26 Peter
1:21 Samuel 6:80 Sarah 5:140,
-6:46 William 4:10
GRAVES, Deliverance 2:45
Elizabeth 6:151 Francis 4:9
Israel 3:129 Jacob 3:136
Joseph 6:151 Margaret 2:45
Martha 6:136,139 Mary 3:89
Mr. 3:102,-4:173 Mrs. 3:56
Samuel 6:151 William 1:11,
-2:45
GRAY, Agnes 5:43 Charles W.
4:27 Eliza 4:80 Elizabeth B.
5:148 George 3:58 James 3:58,
61,-6:67 Jethro L. 4:17 John
5:190 Mary 2:170,-4:186,191,
-5:113 Miss 3:58 Mr. 7:75
Rev. Mr. 7:29 Robert 2:164,
-6:176,-7:29 Samuel 4:33
Simeon 3:25,74 Simon 1:22,
23,-5:119 Tamson 3:58,61,
-4:151
GREAVES (see also GRAVES),
Hannah 5:41 Nathaniel 4:90
GREELEY, Andrew 3:135 Anna
3:132 David 2:133 Elizabeth
3:40 Horace 7:36 Jacob 4:187
Jonathan 3:131,-4:176 Joseph
2:44,72,130,133,194 Josiah
4:177 Martha 3:134 Mary
4:173,-5:133 Moses 2:71,-7:69
Nathaniel 2:46,134 Noah 3:131
Peter 5:39 Rebecca 6:120
Reuben 3:132 Richard 5:133

GREELEY (continued)
Samuel 3:131,-4:100 Thomas
4:56,-5:39
GREEN(e), Aaron 5:20 Abial
1:163,170,173,-2:127,5:174,
-6:22,84 Abigail 1:190
Abraham 1:167,-2:67,106,111,
-5:109,111,154,158 Ann 5:130,
134 Anna 3:58 Anne 5:139,158
Bethiah 3:3 Charles 1:142,
-2:8,-3:192 Charles A. 3:192
Clarissa D. 7:18 Cyrus F.
3:192 Cyrus W. 3:192 Daniel
6:22 David 1:163,173,174,-6:21
Deborah 1:192,-2:8,-4:121
Dorcas 1:142,143 Dr. 5:156
Edmund 1:11 Eliza 7:17
Elizabeth 2:84,140,-5:127
Ephraim 1:122,142,190 Esther
2:106,111 Eunice 2:8 Ezra
2:7,8 Francis B. 2:189,-4:92
H. B. 3:46 Hannah 6:22 Henry
2:84,-4:10,33 Huldah 1:121,166
Isaiah 1:167 Jacob 6:51 James
2:7 John 1:142,-2:111,-5:88,
109,130,134 John M. 3:46 John
P. 5:137 Jonathan 1:121,166,
-3:100 Joseph 1:142 Judith
1:174,174,-6:21 Levi 1:166,
-4:123 Lois 1:167 Lydia 1:122,
-4:148 Mark 2:190 Martha 2:8,
-5:111,156,-7:21 Martha O.
3:192 Mary 1:142,190-192,
-2:84,-3:192,-5:154,-6:22,44,
111,170 Mary C. 7:20 Mary E.
2:140 Mary J. 3:192 Miriam
3:126 Mrs. 5:134,137,139,183,
186,-6:44 Nancy 3:181 Nathan
3:171 Oren S. 3:192 Patience
1:174,-6:22 Peter 2:95 Richard
1:142 Robert 2:38,-5:88,183
Rosillah 2:140 Samuel 1:190-
192,-2:8 Samuel A. 3:96,137,
139,-4:96,192,6:48,94,96
Samuel M. 1:142 Samuel S.
2:190 Sarah 1:122,170,-2:8,
190,-3:89,-5:109,128,174,-6:22
Simon 1:121,163,170,-4:44,
78,-5:174,-6:22,184 Simon P.
7:56 Susanna 2:8 Thomas
1:142,191,-2:140 Thomas L.
1:143 Thomas O. 2:140

GREEN(e) (continued)
Timothy 3:46 Vercilda M. 3:192
William 5:137,139,183,186,
-6:44,-7:24
GREENLEAF, Abner 2:164 Cap-
tain 3:82 Harriette 3:179 Ruth
P. 3:178 Sarah 7:6 Sarah L.
4:136 Stephen 2:103,104
GREENOUGH, Abigail 1:24
Daniel 1:21,24,25,-5:44
Elizabeth 1:25 John 1:25,
-6:108 Joseph 7:67,69
Nathaniel 1:24 Pelatiah 3:6
Robert 1:24 Samuel 3:4 Sarah
1:24 Symonds 1:25 William
1:25
GREENWOOD, John 6:43 Thomas
6:43
GREGORY, Captain 6:45,46,77
Elizabeth 6:45 Isaac S. 6:77
John 2:164,-5:167,-6:78,80
Sarah 6:45,46,77,78,80 Wil-
liam 6:80
GRESHAM, Judge 7:33
GREWARD, Ephraim 5:152
GRIFFIN, Adoniram 1:151 Chase
P. 6:163 David 6:158 Ebenezer
3:168 Elizabeth 2:48,91,-3:132
Ephraim 5:109,112,154 Hannah
1:151,-3:89 Isaac 2:66,69,
129,-3:86,87 James 4:33 John
1:151,-2:186,-4:78 Jonathan
5:154 Lydia 2:46 Margaret 2:91
Mary 1:151,-2:69,-3:133,
-4:176,-5:112 Mrs. 4:178
Nancy 1:151,-4:187 Peter
6:26,-7:22 Phebe 2:47 Philip
1:9 Sarah 4:175 Samuel 5:109
Theophilus 2:44,-5:158,-6:26
Thomas 5:158 William 1:151
Winburn 1:151
GRIFFIS, Esther 4:99 Wilmot
4:99
GRIFFITH(S), Abigail 1:17
Deborah 1:15,18 Edward 4:126
Elizabeth 5:40 Esther 5:44
Hannah 5:41 John 1:15,18,
-5:38 Mary 1:15,18 Miles W.
1:17 Moses 1:15,18 Mrs. 6:42,
44,46 Nathaniel 1:15,18,-6:44
Nathaniel S. 6:42,44,46 Samuel
1:15,17 Sarah 6:42 William

GRIFFITH(S) (continued)
1:15,18,-2:36,-6:46 Wilmot
5:43
GRIGNARD, John 3:67
GRINDAL, Alice 5:41 Ichabod
4:99 John 4:98,-5:41 Sarah
4:98,102
GROO, Mrs. Byron 5:46
GROSS, Mr. 4:30 Simon 4:32
Thomas 5:43
GROVE, Elizabeth 4:16 John
3:157,158,-4:16,107 Martha
4:107 Mary 3:2 Nathaniel
2:172,-3:157,-4:60 Samuel
3:157 Sarah 3:157,158,-4:60
GROVER, Catherine 6:156 Mary
4:130,-5:46,-6:156
GROW, Ebenezer 6:66
GUILFORD, Benjamin 1:111 John
1:111 Joseph 1:111 Mary 1:111
Rebecca 1:111 Robert 1:111
Simeon 1:111 W. W. 1:111
William 1:111
GUILLORET, Julien 3:67,75
GULETIA, Jacob 3:146
GULLISON, Elihu 3:150 Joseph
3:150
GUNNISON, Alice 2:143 Chris-
topher 5:134 David 5:130 Han-
nah 5:138 John 3:25,73,
-5:130,131,134,135,138 John
N. 5:135 Margaret 2:143,-5:137
Mary 5:135 Mrs. 5:134,135,
137,138 Rebecca 5:140 Samuel
2:143 Sarah 4:132,-5:140 Wil-
liam 5:135,137,140
GUPPY, Abigail 6:44 Abigail D.
6:122 Ann 3:138 Anne 5:134,
137,139,184,187,-6:41,44
Bethiah 6:78 George 6:41
George F. 6:122 Hannah E.
6:122 James 3:138,-5:133,
134,137,139,184,187,-6:41,44,
101 Jane 5:139 Jeremy B.
6:122 John 5:187,-6:122,185
John D. 6:122 Joseph J. 6:122
Joshua 5:186,-6:46,78 Joshua
D. 6:122 Margaret 5:186
Prudence 5:184 Sarah 5:133,
186,-6:46,78 Sarah A. 6:122
GUPTILL, Hannah 1:68,-5:25
Lydia 5:25 Mary 1:68

GUPTILL (continued)
Nathaniel 5:40 Thomas 1:11,68
GURDY, Judith 6:31 Mary 6:27
Meshech 3:45,-6:27,31
GURNEY, Caleb S. 1:32,79,109
GUTHRIE, George N. 7:70
GUTTESON, John 6:57
GUYLLOT, Louis 3:69,75
GUYOMART, Bastien 3:69,76
GWINN, Elizabeth 6:3
HACKER, Anna 1:170 Isaac 1:170
Isaiah 1:170
HACKETT, Judah 4:131 Mr.
2:177,-4:25
HADLEY, Dorothy 3:42 Enos
1:111 Josiah G. 2:164
Mehitable 3:190
HAGAR, John C. 7:71
HAGGETT, Joseph 3:40
HAINES, Alanson C. 7:63 Dorcas
2:171 Eunice 7:66 Jane 3:175
John 3:127,-7:59 John S. 3:120
Jonathan 3:83,85 Joshua 3:55
Mary 3:87,175 Matthias 2:102,
103 Samuel 2:22,60,98,169,
-3:49-51
HALE, Henry 7:32 Jane 3:186
John P. 7:32 John Parker 7:32
Joseph 3:86 Lucy 2:144 Martha
M. 3:186 Mordecai 3:186 Mrs.
7:87 Samuel Augustus 7:32
HALEY, Alice 4:135 James 3:65,
-7:50 Molly 7:50 Sarah 4:126
Thomas 3:82
HALL, A. B. 4:82 A. R. 7:79
Aaron 7:7 Abigail 4:11,181,
-7:7 Abigail A. 4:115 Andrew,
Jr. 7:60 Ammi R. 2:162,-7:77,
79 Anna 7:7 Anna Maria 7:77
Caroline 7:76 Daniel 3:96
David Sands 7:7 Dorcas 7:7
Dorothy 3:95,-4:44 Dwight
2:165 Edward 3:147,149 Elijah
2:161,162,-3:94-96,-7:13,15,
73,76-78,80 Elizabeth 2:44,
-4:9,12,-7:13,15,73,76-78,80
Esther 1:144 George W. 3:165
Harriet 7:20 Hatevil 1:70,
-4:13,-7:6 Ivory 7:20,70 James
7:73 Jedediah 1:70,-3:33,-7:6
Jeremiah 1:110 Joel 7:7 John
1:10,13,179,-3:84,-4:12,33,

53

HALL (continued)
-7:7 Jonathan 7:7 Joseph
1:93,144,178,180,-3:51,79,147,
-4:13,-7:7 Joshua Byron 7:80
Joshua Henshaw 7:79 Lydia
4:130 Mary 1:144,-4:151,-7:7,
45,70 Mary A. 3:95 Mary Ann
7:78 Mehitable 3:112 Mercy
7:7 Moses 7:7 Mrs. A. C. 3:92,
-4:48,144 Peter 7:7 Ralph
3:148,-4:11,-7:7 Rebecca
1:180 Robert 7:66 Samuel
2:163,164 Sarah 1:70,131,
-4:13,-7:6,25,68,77 Solomon
4:75 Stephen 7:19 Thomas B.
7:40 William Leonard 7:13
HALLET, Harry 4:14
HAM, ---- 7:80 Abigail 4:56
Anna Walker 7:78 Benjamin
3:108 Dorcas 2:169 Dorothy
4:103 Eleazer 7:27,29,30,89
Elizabeth 4:49,50,56,-7:89
Ephraim 2:159,-7:80 Hall
Jackson 7:16 Hannah 7:43
Henry 7:77 James 7:30 Jane
7:16 Joanna 4:151 John 2:185,
-3:108,-4:11,149,-7:11
Jonathan 7:29 Joseph 3:183,
-4:142 Joseph P. 7:64 Judah
3:107,108,158 Mary 3:148,
-4:101 Matthew 1:10,-2:27
Mercy 7:27 Moses 1:80 Mr.
2:27,-4:104 Mrs. 3:56,175
Nathaniel 3:108,-7:78,80
Phebe 7:11 Reuben 3:108 S.
3:50 Samuel 3:2,108,-4:56,
77,99,-7:16 Samuel 3rd 7:11
Sarah 3:56,-4:58,148 Supply
7:74 Susanna 4:150 Timothy
2:164,-7:11,13,16,74,77 Tobias
3:108 William 1:9,12,-2:23,26,
162,163,-3:9,-7:13,16
HAMILTON, Captain 7:50 David
3:81 John 4:2 Joseph 3:69,76
Patience 4:189
HAMMET, Elizabeth 4:103
Ephraim 7:32
HAMMOCK, Susanna 4:147,-7:49
Thomas 7:90
HAMMOND, Captain 3:82 Edward
3:82 Elizabeth 4:152 Hannah
7:21 Joseph 1:23 Mrs. 3:82

HAMMOND (continued)
Otis G. 3:82
HAMNON, Elisha 3:9
HANCOCK, Margaret 7:72
HAND, Orre 7:72
HANDESYDE, Robert 1:20
HANDLEY, Experience 3:90
HANNAFORD (Haniford, Hanford),
Anna 1:189,192,-2:9 Anne Hil-
ton 7:30 David 1:189 John
1:189,192,-2:9 John, Jr. 7:26
Levi Dearborn 7:30 Reuben
7:30 Sarah 1:192,-7:30 Thomas
1:189,-7:63
HANSCOM, Deborah 4:130
Ebenezer H. 7:37 Ivory 7:49
James 4:185 James P. 4:185
Joseph H. 4:186
HANSON, Aaron 1:69,-2:78,128
Abigail 1:67,113,115,124,
125,127,169,-2:80,-4:13 Abijah
1:176,-3:34,-4:161 Amos
4:130,160 Andrew 4:40 Ann
1:52 Anna 1:65,113,115-117,
119,-3:34,-4:40 Anne 1:55,57,
63,68,70,163,-2:128,-4:39,123
Benjamin 1:59,-2:77 Bitfield
4:42 Caleb 1:126,163,-2:78
Catherine 1:67,-3:31,-4:40,163
Daniel 1:162,-2:78,79
Ebenezer 2:78-80,-4:150
Elijah 2:147,-4:39,121 Elisha
4:66 Elizabeth 1:53,54,57,59,
62,71,116,-2:75,77,78,128,148,
-4:40,42,120,-7:5 Elizabeth M.
2:31 Ephraim 4:79 Eunice 4:42
Ezra 1:163,-4:160 George 3:33
Hannah 1:55,70-72,114,117,
162,-2:29,31,32,78,80,126,
-4:80 Huldah 1:67,-4:39 Isaac
1:53,55,67,125,-2:78-80,150,
-3:35,148,-4:40,-7:7 Jacob
1:113,-2:150,-3:34 James
1:59,124,162,-2:148,-4:40,67
Jedediah 4:39 Jeremy 1:170
Joanna 1:60,-4:67 John 1:53,
54,57,61,65,67,70,116,117,174,
-2:78,79,125,-3:31,-4:40,-7:2,
7 John, Jr. 7:67 John Burnham
7:32 Jonathan 2:80,-4:44
Joseph 1:59,116,-2:78,-4:44,
-7:31,32 Joseph M. 2:29,32

HANSON (continued)
Judith 1:52,62-64,68,
69,115,163,-2:78,126,-3:34,
-4:42 Kezia 1:58-60,-4:66
Lois 1:72,-4:42 Lydia 1:56,
59,113,114,-4:66,-7:7 Margaret
1:52,53,57,59,116,-4:44 Martha
1:56,-3:34 Mary 1:68,72,114,
116,117,122,125,127,128,162,
163,167,169,-2:29,127,128,
-3:34,-4:40,121,128,147 Mary
Elizabeth 7:13 Mary J. 2:29
Maul (?) 1:53,57,68,117,119,
-2:80,124,150,-4:40,66 Mercy
1:64,174,-2:75,77,78,124,128,
-4:11 Micajah 4:39 Miriam
1:117,171,-4:42 Moses 1:68,
122,124,128,163,167,169,
-2:29,129,-4:40,42,-7:4 Mrs.
3:80 Nathan 2:78 Nathaniel
1:56,-4:39,40 Nicholas 1:114,
-4:39,40,42 Otis 3:34 Patience
1:51,62,70,114,165,167,169,
170,-2:128,-3:31,-4:42,66,121
Peter 4:123,-5:5,52 Phebe
1:61,65,67,70,-3:31,-4:162,
-7:7 Priscilla 1:72,-4:39,-7:9
Richard 1:115,165,167,169,170,
-4:39,41 Robert 1:53,56,59,
113,171,-2:80,147,-4:40,121
Ruth 1:167 Samuel 1:60,-2:78,
80,-4:68,168 Sarah 1:51,57,61,
67,70,116,117,119,125,126,
163,165,176,-2:78,-3:31,34,
-4:39-42,69,70,160,164,175,
-7:7 Sargent 1:171 Silas 1:56,
67,113,115,125,127,-4:39
Solomon 1:55,65,68,70,113,
115,-2:75,80,-3:34 Stephen
1:56,72,114,125,127,-2:124,
-4:39,161,-7:9 Susanna(h)
1:122,125,-4:39,70,160
Thomas 1:50,52,53,55,57,
59,70-72,114,117,162,-2:80,
127,-3:148,-4:42 Timothy
1:58-60,114,116,127,-2:29,80,
-4:40,60 Tobias 1:50,52,55,57,
62-64,68,69,128,-2:29,31,32,
75,77,78,128,-3:80,81,83,
-4:11,40 Widow 3:80 William
P. 7:62 Zacheus 1:65,163,
176,-3:34,35,-4:160

HANWELL, Richard 3:100
HARBUT, Sylvester 1:11
HARD, Jane 7:90 Sarah 7:85
Trustrum 7:85
HARDAWAY, Susanna 3:88
HARDON, Henry W. 1:79,
-2:166,-3:96
HARDY, Asa, Jr. 7:17 Experience
7:17 Josiah 7:18 Judith 3:163
Timothy 1:92 William H. 7:70
HARMON, John 3:75
HARPER, George B. 7:83
HARRADEN, Daniel 4:33 Joseph
4:33
HARRAT, John 2:165
HARRIMAN, Abigail 3:43
Elizabeth 3:41 Jane 4:132
Joseph 3:43 Mary 3:86 Mr.
4:177 Naomi 3:43 Samuel 3:86
HARRIS, Abel 2:162 Elijah 7:58
John 4:33 Mary Ellen 7:57 Mr.
4:30 Sarah 3:107 Thomas 4:46
Timothy 2:183
HARRISON, Nicholas 3:151 William 3:30,73
HART, Abigail 1:15,111 Albert
Nathaniel 7:54 Alice 4:156
Bridget 4:185 Charles Cutter
7:74 Dl (Daniel ?) 7:14 Daniel
7:75 Daniel Quimby 7:54 Edward 7:15,74,75 Elisha Callender 7:74 Elizabeth 7:15,74,
75 George 2:159,-4:55,80,-7:75
Hannah Susan 7:54 Henry 3:5
James 7:11 John 1:9,10,
-2:158,-4:52,80,-7:74 John
Francis 7:54 Joseph Buckminster 7:74 Lydia 4:97 Lydia
Ann 7:54 Mark 7:54 Mark
Hunking 7:54 Mary 2:17,-3:10,
-4:52,-7:11 Mary Jane 7:54
Nathaniel 4:57,-7:54 Robert
4:52 Samuel 2:17,102-104,
157,-3:55,-4:50,52,53 Sarah
4:97,-7:12,75 Sarah Abigail
7:54 Sarah Elizabeth 7:54
Sophia Elizabeth 7:54
Theodora 7:16 Thomas 4:53,
-7:11,74 William 2:187,
-3:74,164,-7:14 William Callender 7:74
HARTFORD, Charity 4:146

HARTFORD (continued)
Fifield 2:38 Hannah 2:38 John
1:51 Mark 4:147 Mary 4:151
Nicholas 2:146 Patience 4:147
William 1:51
HARTSHORN, John 3:151 Mrs.
3:151
HARVEY, Ann 7:83 Daniel 7:68
Elizabeth 3:50,52,53,56,-4:10
Hannah 4:89,102,-7:15,73,
75,77 Jacob C. 7:64 James P.
3:113 Jane 3:186,-7:75 Jane F.
1:99 Joakim 1:11,-2:100 John
H. 1:99 Jonathan 4:126 Joseph
2:164,-3:90 Martha 7:15,75
Mary 4:11 Mr. 4:104 Nancy
Lang 7:75 Peter 1:22 Rhoda
4:136 Richard 1:11 Samuel
3:181,-7:73 Sarah 3:44,-4:135
Thomas 1:12,-3:50,51,-4:99,
-7:15,73,75,77
HASKELL, Clara W. 7:53 Delia
7:53 Moody 7:53 William M.
7:65
HASTINGS, Elizabeth Jane 7:57
John 4:135
HASTY, Lettice 2:171
HATCH, Anna 4:97 Anthony 7:69
Elizabeth 1:25 Grace 4:97 John
3:173 Mrs. 3:175
HATHAWAY, Charles 4:33
HATTEN, Mark 1:22
HAVEN, Ann Elizabeth 7:85 Dr.
7:11,13-16,74,75 George 7:31
James Willard 7:31 John
2:162,-7:31,85 Joseph 1:153,
-4:147,-7:27-29 Nathaniel A.
2:160,161 Noah 7:28 Ruthy
7:27 Samuel 1:137,-2:36,37
Sarah Fisher 7:29 Thomas
2:163
HAWKES, Moses 7:7
HAWKINS, Anna 4:152 Charlotte
4:129 Hannah 4:189 Lewis B.
4:115 Rachel 4:159 Sagamore
3:79
HAWTHORNE, Nathaniel 3:22,70
HAYES, Abigail 4:145 Abra C.
7:88 Andrew 1:22 Benjamin
4:147,-7:88 Ebenezer 4:151
Eliza Jane 7:89 Elizabeth
5:151 Enoch 4:149 Ezekiel

HAYES (continued)
4:152,-7:64 Ezra 7:31 George S.
4:152 Hannah 7:31,88 John
3:152 Jonathan 2:40,-4:126
Joseph 4:88,183 Joshua 4:150
Louis 7:87 Lucinda 7:31 Mary
7:86,88 Mary Joanna 7:89
Mercy 7:27 Moses 4:149 Nabby
7:31 Nathaniel 7:31 Sabra 7:31
Samuel 4:151,184,-7:27 Sarah
4:185,-7:89 Susanna 2:8
Wentworth 4:146 William
3:180 Zenus 7:31
HAYNES, Joshua 4:49 Kezia 4:54
Louis 7:25 Richard 1:22,23
Samuel 1:10,13,177,-4:118
Sarah 1:42 Thomas J. 4:118
HAYTE, John 4:10 William 4:11
HAYWOOD, Thomas 7:45
HAZELTINE, Eliza 7:21 Jonathan
S. 7:72 Lydia 7:17
HAZELTON, Peter 3:42
HAZEN, Moses 3:142
HAZLETT, C. A. 4:51 Charles A.
1:182,-2:165,-4:96 James H.
4:9 Maria 4:9 Maria W. 4:9
Peter 3:42
HEAD, Oren 7:63
HEALEY, Jane 4:179 Mary 3:40
Samuel 3:42
HEARD (see also HURD), Hannah
7:29 Henry 5:119 James 7:28
John 2:23 Joseph 2:169 Lydia
7:28 Nathaniel 7:28,29
Nathaniel Horn 7:29 William
B. 7:71
HEARL, Mrs. 3:51
HEATH, Bartholomew 3:102
Enoch 4:173 Lewis 7:65 Moses
3:86 Nehemiah 3:42 Rhoda
3:136
HECK, Francis 4:33
HEFFENGER, Arthur C. 4:8
Charles P. 4:8 Constance 4:8
Francesca P. 4:8 Jacob A. 4:8
Katherine 4:8 Mary S. 4:8
Priscilla S. 4:8
HEINES, Sarah 3:38
HEMINS, John 1:139
HENDERSON, Benjamin 4:33
Charles 7:87-89 Charles Wil-
liam 7:89 Ellen 7:88 Harry P.

56

HENDERSON (continued)
7:83 Howard 4:12 Joseph 4:33
Mary 7:88,89 Mary Ann 7:40
Mary Louisa 7:88 Nancy 7:88
Robert 2:164 Sarah 7:89 Wil-
liam 4:152
HENELY, Mary 4:52
HENGD, Sagamore 3:83
HENRY, Abigail 2:38 William
2:37
HENSHAW, John 3:66,73
HENTY, Mary 4:127
HEPWORTH, Mary 2:168
HERBERT, Belinda 7:67 Richard
3rd 7:20
HERMON, Thomas 3:98
HERRICK, Senith 7:22
HERRING, Michael 2:5
HERSEY, Mahala 7:40 Peter 7:38
HESLOP, Robert 3:22,72
HETHERSEY, Robert 1:179
HEULET, James 2:44,72
HEWKS, Solomon 3:55
HEWITT, Mathurin 3:67,75 Oliver
3:68,75
HEWLAND, John 3:104
HICKS, Elizabeth 4:46 Michael
3:174,176 Mrs. 3:176 Samuel
1:22
HIGGINS, Isaac 4:45 Lydia 4:45
HIGHT, Joseph 7:74 Mr. 7:74
HILDRETH, Jane E. 7:70
HILL, Aaron 7:74-77 Abigail 4:57
Albert C. 2:32 Amos 1:121,-
4:124,-7:8 Andrew W. 1:171
Ann 7:43 Benjamin 4:132 Bet-
sey 2:113,-5:98,-7:12,21,27
Captain 3:52 Catherine 1:120
Charlotte 4:182 Chase C. 3:120
Daniel 7:14,54 David 2:113
Dorothy 1:110,-4:99 Elisha
7:12,14,73 Elizabeth 1:171,
-3:60,-4:45,46,54,171,-7:12,
14,73 Eunice 7:12,14,16,73,
75,76-79 Fanny 7:77 George
3:179,-4:171,-7:73 George
Massy 7:75 Hannah 1:55,69,
70,110,-2:50,-4:10,51,54,55,
-5:98,-7:54,74-76 Harriet 7:75
Henry 7:79 Horatio 7:26 Huldah
1:55,-3:36 Ichabod 7:14,16,27
Isaac 1:70 James 1:154,

HILL (continued)
-2:113,-7:12,14,16,73,75,76-79
James S. 4:126 Jane 2:153
Jeremiah 7:16 Jerusha 1:68
John 2:40,122,-3:5,29,51,55,
74,116,174,175,-4:50,58,126,
171,-5:98,-7:12,54 Jonathan
2:113,-3:2 Joseph 1:120,121,
-2:113,-3:36,51,52,55,178,
-4:49,54,58,-5:98,-7:8 Joseph
Sherburne 7:11 Joshua 2:113,
122,153,-4:94 Josiah 3:114,
181,-4:171 Lucinda 2:32 Lydia
1:154,-2:113 Mark 4:181 Mary
1:120,121,174-2:113,173,
-3:60,-4:171,187,-7:8,11,14,74
Mehitable 4:171,-7:73 Miriam
3:36,-4:41 Mr. 2:177,-4:25,50
Mrs. 3:175 Nancy 2:113,-7:76
Olive 7:14 Oliver 2:32 Polly
7:16 Polly Plaisted 7:74
Rachel 2:113,122,-4:97
Rebecca 1:57,-4:40,132
Reuben 2:113 Robert 4:79,129
Ruth M. 4:188 Samuel 1:51,55,
56,69,70,110,-2:40,124,167,
-3:60,179,-4:85,125,171,184,
-5:98,-7:11,14,74 Sarah 4:125,
178,-7:54 Simeon 1:56,-2:124,
-4:38 Sophia 7:74 Susanna
2:169 Theodore 7:78 Thomas
Quincy 7:76 Timothy 4:181
Trueworthy 4:79 Valentine
1:10,-3:151 Warren 7:54 Wil-
liam 5:98,-7:14,77 Winthrop
2:122
HILLIARD, Anna 3:127 Benjamin
3:191 Elizabeth 2:171,-3:108
Joseph 7:50 Mary 4:188 Mr.
7:29 Mrs. 2:131 Nicholas 2:168
HILLYAR, Elizabeth 2:83 Emale
2:83
HILTON, Aaron 1:181 Abigail
1:181,-4:186 Ann 1:181,-4:128
Anna 3:169 Benjamin 4:94
Calvin 1:181 Charles 4:90
Charlotte 4:113 Clarissa 4:77
Colonel 3:148,153 Daniel 2:122
Ebenezer 1:181 Edward 2:6
Elihu 1:181 Eliza 1:158,-4:130
Elizabeth 4:181 Joanna 4:94
John 1:179 John T. 1:181

HILTON (continued)
Joseph 1:181 Joshua 1:181,
-3:149,150 Marcia F. 3:139
Martha A. 4:185 Mary 1:181,
-3:118 Mary Ann 7:37 Mercy
2:50 Morrill 1:181 Moses 1:181
Mrs. C. H. 4:48 Nancy R.
4:116 Rachel 1:181 Sarah
4:125,184 Susan 7:43 Theodore
7:40 Theophilus 1:181 William
1:181,-4:94 Winthrop S. 4:185
HINCKS, John 1:21
HINCKSON, Robert 1:13 Thomas
1:9
HINE, Frank W. 4:95
HINKLEY, William 3:100
HINKS, Elizabeth 4:97
HINKSON, Mrs. 3:176 Robert
3:174,176
HOAG, Abigail 2:147 Abner 1:60
Anna 4:68 Benjamin 1:58,
-2:13,14,-3:88 David 1:54,
-2:147 Elizabeth 2:13,-3:12
Enoch 1:60,116,119,121,123,
-2:13,125,-4:67,123,-4:67,123
Enos 3:12,126 Esther 2:15,
-3:12 Hannah 2:147,-4:68 John
1:58,60,-3:120,-4:68 Jonathan
1:54,68 Joseph 1:54,-2:13,120
Joshua 4:68 Judith 1:117,119,
121,123 Kezia 2:147 Levi 2:15,
-3:12 Lois 2:13,-3:12 Lydia
1:123,-2:147,-4:68 Martha
1:54,68 Mary 1:60,116,-2:13,
14,-4:67,69 Mercy 4:68 Miriam
2:13,15,-3:12,-4:119 Moses
1:174,-4:68 Moses J. 1:174
Nathan 1:68,-2:13,15,124,-3:12
Phebe 2:150 Ruth 1:174
Samuel 2:147 Sarah 1:58,-2:13,
14,-3:12 Stephen 1:121,-4:68
Susanna 2:13,-3:12 William
2:147
HOBART, Captain 7:75,76,78
Jane Stevens 7:75 John 7:76,78
Mary 7:75,76,78 Samuel
7:75,76,78
HOBBS, Abigail 2:90 Bethiah 2:85
Elizabeth J. 1:134 George S.
2:144 Hannah 2:88 James
1:133,-2:112 John 2:107,110
Jonathan 1:134 Lucy 1:133,134

HOBBS (continued)
Lydia 3:42 Mary 1:133,134,
-2:84,-3:89 Maurice 2:84,85,
88,90 Mehitable 2:110 Miriam
3:134 Nathaniel 1:234 Noah
3:90 Sarah 2:84,85,88,90,
107,110,112,-4:10
HOBBY, Anstrus 1:126 Remington
1:126
HODDY, Elizabeth 3:175 John
1:16,-3:50,51 Mary 3:50,175
HODGDON, ---- 7:28 Aaron 3:8,
-4:109,-7:12,14,74,75,78
Abigail 3:6,33,112,157,-7:6
Abner 7:28,29 Alexander 3:58,
61,110,112,155,159,-4:16 Ann
2:172,-3:109,110,-4:59 Benjamin 3:7,8,-4:62 Caleb 2:124,
127,-4:67 Charles 3:5,160,
-4:156,-7:74 Edmund 3:33
Eliazer 3:110 Elizabeth 3:1,2,
58,105,-4:12,59,126,156,-7:12
George E. 3:140 Hannah 4:17,
-7:75 Israel 1:55,69,-2:78,
126,-3:33,-7:6 Jane 3:58,106,
109 Jeremiah 2:169,-3:109,110
John 1:69,169,-2:170,-3:7,33,
105-107,109,111,155,158,160,
-4:17,19,61,62,64,107,109,-7:6
Jonathan 4:76,146 Joseph 3:60,
61,106,157,-4:107,151 Liberty
7:29 Lydia 3:157,-4:128 Mary
1:69,-3:105,107,109-112,155,
158-160,-4:16,17,19,62,64,
107,109 Mehitable 3:105
Moses 1:169,-3:33,-7:6,12
Nancy 7:14 Patience 1:171,
-3:59-61,106,157 Peter 1:171,
-3:33 Rebecca 3:155,-4:147
Richard 2:187 Samuel 3:110,
155 Sarah 1:55,-2:127,170,
-3:8,36,110,-4:64,78 Stephen
4:80 Susanna 1:169 Tem-
perance 3:5,158 Timothy 2:127
HODGE, Mrs. 3:56 Samuel
2:181,-3:20
HODGKINS, Abraham 3:120
Joshua 3:178 Sarah 2:174
HOEL, Mrs. 3:104
HOGG, Ebenezer 4:33
HOHN, George 3:27,74
HOIT (HOITT), Benjamin 7:18

HOIT (continued)
Cyrus B. 7:57 Elizabeth K.
7:66 Ethan 7:67 Fanny Jane
7:69 James 7:17 Jedediah, Jr.
7:21 Joseph 7:28 Olly 7:28
Prudence 7:26 Rachel T. 7:68
Ruth 7:66 Sarah 7:57 W. K. A.
7:57
HOLDEN, Elizabeth 3:106 Wil-
liam 3:106,107
HOLICOMB, Captain 1:21
HOLLAND, Captain 3:100
HOLLIDAY, John 1:33
HOLMES, Anna 1:81 Anne 4:52
Benjamin 4:56 Deborah 1:81
Elizabeth 1:81,82 Ephraim
(Eperham?) 1:81,82,-4:56,151
Jeremiah 4:10,52 John 1:12,
-3:173,175,-4:52 Joseph 4:56,
152 Joshua 4:181 Lazarus 4:56
Mary 3:50,56,-4:52 Mrs. 3:175
Ruth 4:52 Samuel 1:82,-4:52
HOLT, Adam C. 7:69 Almira
1:156 Daniel 1:156 Elizabeth
1:156 Enoch 1:156 George
3:170 George W. G. 1:156
Hannah 3:115,-4:86,87 Henry
1:156 Jeremiah 4:87 Joseph
4:130 Joshua 4:87 Mary 7:43
Mary E. W. 4:87 Nathan 4:87
Peter 3:114-116,119,120,177-
179,183,184,-4:86-90,135-137
Sarah F. 4:87 Stephen 1:156
William K. 7:69
HOMAN, Daniel 3:40 Joanna 4:10
Joseph 3:134
HONEYWELL, Jemima 4:18
HOOD, Elisha 4:177 Samuel 4:177
HOOK, Elizabeth 3:91 Humphrey
3:43 Jacob 3:133,168,170
James 4:176 Josiah 3:169,
-4:178 Mary 3:130,134,177
Mood M. 4:180 Moses 4:173
Nancy 4:176 Peter 3:133
Reuben 4:89 Samuel 3:168
Sarah 4:89
HOOPER, Catherine 2:36 John
7:15,51 Mary 7:15 Samuel 3:42
William 2:36,37
HOPKINS, Caleb 4:45 Nathaniel
4:33
HOPKINSON, George 3:119

HOPLEY, Elizabeth 3:50,51,56,
-4:12 Mary 4:12 Mrs. 3:175
HORN(E), Abigail 7:32 Alice 7:30
Anna 7:28 Anne 7:90 Betsey
7:86 Daniel 4:33,150 Daniel
Wentworth 7:31 Drusilla 4:146
Ebenezer 4:150,-7:3 Elijah
4:152,-7:28,29,31 Elizabeth
Downing 7:30 Hannah 7:83
Ichabod 7:90 James 4:79 John
3:84,-4:13 Jonathan 7:32
Jonathan H. 7:86 Margaret 3:84
Mary 1:53,-4:11,78,-7:32 Mary
W. 7:88 Matilda 2:143 Mercy
4:12,-7:2 Moses 3:4 Nathaniel
4:125 Noah 7:32 Paul 5:50
Peter 7:30 Rachel 7:29,30
Rebecca 4:152,-7:32 Richard
4:117 Sarah 1:53,-2:123,150
Thomas 4:11 Widow 3:150
William 1:53,-2:75,123,
-3:80,84,-4:150,-7:2
HORNER, Elias C. 7:67
HORTON, Hezekiah 4:191,192
HOULDEN, William 2:170
HOULTON, Benjamin 1:111
HOUSTON, James 4:10 Sarah 7:7
HOWARD, Edward 4:10 James
3:176 John N. 7:63 Joseph
2:183 Mrs. 3:176 Sally 7:60
HOW(E), Abigail B. 4:168 David
3:183 Dorothy 3:181 Elizabeth
3:45,86 James 7:28 Joseph
Willard 7:28 Sarah 3:181
HOWISON, John 4:3
HOYT, Abigail 2:171,-3:64,86,108
Abishag 2:172,-3:59 Anne
1:187 Barnard 3:89 Benjamin
2:114,120,185,-3:5,91,127,133,
-4:14 Catherine 3:42 Charles
3:108 Charles W. 1:30 Daniel
2:114,120,-3:6,-4:180 David
3:89 David W. 3:140,141
Deborah 2:120,154,-4:179 Dennis 4:17,157,158 Dorothy 3:43,
59 Eli 4:176 Elizabeth 2:120,
154,168,172,-3:111,155,-4:157,
158,187 Enoch 3:7,-4:62 Esther 1:186,-3:159 Eunice 3:8
Frances 3:59 George 1:128
Gorham W. 4:185 Grace 3:59
Hannah 1:186,187,-2:120,

HOYT (continued)
-3:6,89,135 Israel 3:59,159
James 4:175 Jemima 2:120
John 2:171,-3:2,59,83,106,
109,111,112,134,154,155,157-
159,-4:14,17,60,62,105,108,157
John H. 3:114 Jonathan 2:120,
153,154,-3:183 Joseph 1:186,
187,-2:120,122,153,154,-3:130,
-4:105,113,115 Lettis 3:155
Lois 3:136 Lydia 1:151,-3:9,
109,111,112,154,157-159,
-4:17,60,62,105,108 Martha
2:154 Mary 2:114,120,153,154,
-3:6,7,112,129,168,-4:60,177,
180 Mary P. 4:158 Mr. 4:46
Mrs. 3:147 Nancy 3:182
Nathaniel 2:153 Rebecca M.
7:26 Reuben 3:88 Rhoda 1:128
Robert 3:147 Sarah 2:120,153,
170,-3:62,109,-4:71,149
Solomon 1:128 Sophia 7:69
Susanna 3:170 Thankful 3:113
Thomas 4:80 William 2:171,
-3:158,159,171
HUBBARD, Abigail 2:47,48,
129,133,-3:43,131 Anna 2:44
Benjamin 3:170 Deacon 2:66
Dorcas 1:68,-3:134 Dorothy
2:47 Elizabeth 2:47,-3:170
Francis 3:132 Grace 2:66,-3:90
Hannah 1:68 Heard 1:68 James
4:123,-7:5 Jane 2:46,72,-3:42
Jemima 2:45 Jeremiah 2:43,71
John 2:67 Kezia 2:72 Mary
2:69,-3:88 Mary A. 4:115
Mercy 2:66,72,-3:90 Reverend
Mr. 3:54 Richard 2:44,45,48,
67,129,133,-3:39,129 Sophia
7:88 Widow 2:43
HUCHES (HUGHES?), Joseph 2:86
Mary 2:86
HUCKINS, Agnes 4:53 Archelaus
4:53 Ebenezer 4:129 John
4:151 Mary 4:184 Phebe 4:151
Samuel S. 7:63 Sarah 4:53,
65,-7:5
HUDSON, John 4:9 Thomas 4:33
HUESTON (see HUSTON)
HUGGINS, Anna 2:85 Bridget
2:82,85,87 James 3:80 John
2:82,85,87 Martha 2:82

HUGGINS (continued)
Nathaniel 2:87 Sarah 3:51-
53,56,145 Susan 2:82
HUGH (HUE), Catherine 2:175
Elizabeth 3:143 Margaret 2:175
HUGHES, Benjamin 4:99 Charles
4:55 Clement 4:55,56,58
Daniel 4:57 Elizabeth 4:102
George 4:57 Hannah 4:55,58,98
John 3:29,-4:33,56 Joseph 4:99
Mary 4:57,100 Robert 4:57
Samuel 4:101 Solomon 4:50
William 4:57,104
HUIT (see HEWITT)
HULL, Hannah 3:50 Henry 3:119
Hopewell 1:146 Mrs. 3:80,175
Phineas 3:80 Reuben 3:51,
-4:52
HUMBER, Humphrey 1:7
HUMPHREYS, David 1:147
HUNKING (HUNKINS), Ann
3:50,51 Hercules 1:7,9,10,
-2:23-25,28,99 John 1:10,12,
-2:24,26,99,100,-3:104,173
Mark 1:10,12,-2:101,102,
-3:94,172,173,-4:11 Mary
3:175,-4:146 Mr. 2:22 Mrs.
3:175 Patience 4:58 Thomas
3:43 Widow 1:12,-3:50,175
William 3:51,174,175,-4:10
HUNNEWELL, Anna 7:7
HUNT, Abel 4:131 Elizabeth
4:137,167 John W. 4:137 Lydia
3:90 Margaret 2:65 Mary 2:190,
-3:134 Miriam 3:86,133 Miss
4:177 Moses 4:167 Mr. 3:98
Mrs. 2:65 Penelope 2:65 Philip
4:176 Richard 3:165 Robert
3:170 Samuel 2:94,-4:137,167
Sarah 2:65,-3:41 Stephen
3:135,136 William 2:183
HUNTER, Alice 2:176 William
2:67
HUNTINGTON, Elizabeth 3:134
Hannah 1:124 John 1:124
Moses 1:124,-4:123
HUNTOON, Aaron 3:131 Benjamin
2:48,-3:45 Charles 2:46,-4:131
Daniel 2:66,134,-3:129
Elizabeth 2:44,69 Hannah
2:71,-3:41 John 2:43,47,48,68,
133,134,-3:87 Josiah 2:48,

HUNTOON (continued)
-3:88 Lydia 2:46,-3:40 Mary
2:68,71,134 Mary R. 4:136
Nathaniel 2:46,-3:40,120,134
Philip 2:43,48,131,-3:39 Ruth
3:41 Samuel 2:46,47,-3:41,42
Sarah 2:44 Scribner 2:131
Scrivener ? 2:67
HUNTRESS, Abigail 2:172,-3:58,
59,105,106,112 Anna 1:20
Christopher 2:176,-3:6,105,
108,110,112,157,-4:16,17
Daniel 1:17,20,-4:157 Darling
3:110,-4:64,106 David 3:157
Deborah 4:108 Dolly 7:29
Elizabeth 2:174,-3:9,61,
-4:14,17,109 Elizabeth Emerson 7:29 Enoch 4:59,158
George 2:173,-3:58,112,176,
-4:11,158 Gideon 4:106 Hannah
3:58,59,-4:106 Henrietta 7:29
Hipworth ? 3:62 James 4:125
John 3:58,59,61,62,105,111,
-4:157,-7:29 Jonathan 2:174,
-3:20,105,-4:59,61,64,106,108,
111,153 Joseph 3:112 Joseph
Peterson 7:29 Joshua L. 1:20
Lois 4:109 Love 4:64,106
Lydia 3:8,-4:60,64 Mark 7:29
Martha 2:176,-3:108 Mary
2:173,176,-3:58,61,62,105,106,
108,110,111,157,-4:10,16,17,
59,61,64,106,108,111,153,157
Mrs. 3:176 Nathan 4:157 Noah
4:16,153 Olive 4:61 Paul 3:105
Samuel 2:173,-3:58,59,61,105,
106,112,-4:62 Sarah 3:61 Seth
4:111 Solomon 3:59 Susanna
4:60,62,109,157 Tamson 2:173,
-3:59 William 2:174,-3:58,
-4:17,60,62,64,109
HURD (see also HEARD), Abigail
4:9,147 Benjamin 3:83 Charlotte 7:86 Edwin Folsom 7:88
Elizabeth 4:13 Emily Ann 7:86
Experience 3:83,87 Hannah
4:151 James 3:84 Jean 4:148
John 1:167,-3:84,-4:10
Jonathan 4:151 Joseph 7:90
Lucy 7:86 Master 3:79 Mrs.
7:87 Mrs. Joseph 7:87
Nathaniel 3:98,-7:87 Phebe

HURD (continued)
1:167,-3:84,-4:150 Rebecca
7:90 Sarah 4:12,151 Sarah Folsom 7:89 Sophia 7:86 Tamma
7:85 Tammy 7:86 Timothy
4:152 Tristram 3:102 Widow
3:148 William 7:85,86
HUSE, Abigail 3:91 Ebenezer
4:175 Hannah 3:86 William
4:131
HUSSEY, Abigail 1:55,64,164,
-2:127,150,-4:124,-7:5,6,8
Ahijah 4:162,-7:8 Andrew
2:164 Ann 2:107,-7:2 Anna
1:62,171,-7:2,6 Anne 3:33
Batchelder 1:55,67,125,
-2:127,-4:65,164,-7:8 Bath-
shuah 2:109 Benjamin 7:2,4
Bethiah 1:121 Charles Moses
7:9 Christopher 1:125,164,
-2:81,110,-4:162 Content 7:5
Daniel 2:40,127,128,-3:33,
-4:141,160,164,-7:5,7 Deborah
1:72,-2:127,-7:74 Ebenezer
1:55,119,123,174,-2:145,-3:34,
35,-4:70 Eldad 3:34 Eleanor
7:4 Elihu 3:34 Elijah 1:171,
-2:39,40,-7:6,7,9,10 Elizabeth
1:63,64,67,69,70,118,164,166,
-2:40,3:33,35,-4:123,-7:2,3,5,
8,9 Eunice 1:67,72,119,123
George 3:34 Hannah 1:64,65,
70,72,113,122,125,166,169,
-3:33,-4:160,162,-7:2,5,6,8,9
Hanson 7:10 Hepzibah 1:119,
-2:127 Hope 2:112 Huldah
1:113,117,118,-2:108,-4:160,
164,-7:4,5,7 Isaac 4:164,-7:4
James 1:123,-2:29,-4:162,164,
-7:8 James F. 4:141 Jane
1:164,171,173,-2:150,-4:141,
-7:3,4,9 Jenny 7:3 Job 1:62,
-2:76,-7:2,3 John 1:169,
-2:77,81,86,88,91,105,107-
110,112,-3:34,35,-4:70,160,
162,-7:2,3,5,8 Joseph 1:63,64,
67,69,70,164,-2:40,-3:33,
4:160,-7:5,6,8,9 Lydia 4:160,
-7:3,5,9 Margaret 2:127
Margery 1:62,-4:120,-7:3 Martha 7:3 Mary 1:64,117,124,
-2:81,91,150,-3:34,-4:65,141,

61

HUSSEY (continued)
159,162,-7:3-5,7-10 Mary
Elizabeth 7:9 Mary J. 2:40
Mercy 1:124,164,166,171,
175,-2:150,-7:6,8,10 Micajah
7:7 Miriam 7:10 Moses B. 2:40
Olive 7:86 Patience 4:160,
-7:2,5 Paul 1:113,117,125,
171,-2:40,123,128,150,-4:162,
-7:6-8 Pelatiah 1:174,-3:35
Peter 3:35,-4:164,-7:5 Phebe
1:64,122,123,-2:128,-3:33,
-4:124,-7:1,6 Priscilla 2:40
Rachel 7:2 Rebecca 2:77,86,
88,91,105,107,109,110,112
Reuben 4:38,-7:1,2 Richard
1:164,-2:150,167,-4:141,-7:1,
2,6-9 Robert 1:164,-7:2,3 Ruth
2:40,128,-7:6 Samuel 1:67,124,
164,166,171,-3:33,-7:5,6,8,9
Samuel F. 3:34 Sarah 1:125,
-4:160,162,-7:2,3,5,8 Sarah H.
2:40 Simeon 1:169 Stephen
1:67,72,119,123,-2:127,128,
150,-4:39,164,-7:9,10
Susanna(h) 1:69,-2:77,105,
-3:33,-7:3,6 Sybil 7:10 Sylvanus 1:50,55,118,125,-2:123,
-3:35,-4:164 Temperance 2:29
Theodata 2:81,86 Timothy
1:166,-2:40,150,-7:8-10 Walter 2:128 William 1:64,65,72,
122,123,125,166,-2:29,75,127,
150,-3:31,-4:162,-7:6-8 Zac
7:2 Zachariah 7:2
HUSTON, Jennet 4:102
HUTCHINS, Betsey 7:18 David
3:152 Enoch 3:85,104 George
7:19 James 4:126 Jane
Johnson 7:21 Samuel 1:100,-
2:161-163 William 4:33
HUTCHINSON, Annice 2:41 Enoch
3:146 Hannah 3:146 Isabel 2:41
Susanna 3:86
HYATT, Thomas S. 7:70
HYDE, George H. 7:61 Lorenzo D.
7:61 Mary L. 7:61
IDE, Mrs. 4:192 Nicholas
4:191,192,-5:47,48
ILLSLEY, Elizabeth 5:40 Eunice
G. 4:72 Sarah 4:97 William
4:72

INGALLS, Betsey 3:113 Israel
4:178 L. B. 4:47 Melinda 3:114
Nathaniel 3:91 Samuel 3:171
INGERSOLL, Joseph 4:34
INGRAHAM, Edward 5:38 Mary
4:101 Moses 4:58,-5:44 Mr.
4:57 Samuel 4:53
INGS, Ann 6:1 William 6:1
IRISH, John 4:33
IRVING, Elizabeth 4:3
IRWIN, Robert 5:162
ISAALTON, Miss 5:40
JACK, John 6:140
JACKLIN, Rosamond 4:11
JACKMAN, David 6:111 Jonathan
6:109
JACKSON, Ann 4:182 Anna C. 4:6
Benjamin 4:52,-5:185,-7:16
Clement 5:87,184 Daniel 1:19,
-5:45,185,-7:13 Ebenezer 4:80,
-5:135,137,140 Edith 4:100
Elizabeth 1:19,-4:55,57
Ephraim 2:103,104,-4:58 Es-
ther 5:184,189,-6:43,45,77,
-7:11,13 George 7:16 Hannah
3:50,56,174,-5:129,185,-7:66
James 4:55 Joanna 1:19 John
1:9,11,12,19,20,-2:23,27,62-
64,98,181,-3:51,71,173,175,176
Johnson 4:103 Jonathan 5:88
Jone 3:51 Joseph 1:18,21,22,
-3:29,74 Joseph L. 7:69
Louisa 5:35 Lydia 4:149,-7:11
Margaret 4:52,-5:90 Martha
5:42 Mary 1:18,19,-3:56,-4:10,
47,50,103,-5:43 Mr. 2:22,
-3:50,-7:77 Mrs. 3:51,56,175,
176,-5:136,138,140,185
Nathaniel 5:136,138,140,185,
-7:16 Phebe 4:89,148 Philip
4:151 Richard 1:10,12,-5:184,
189,-6:43,45,77,-7:11,13
Robert 6:136 Ruth 1:23 Salome
5:185 Samuel 1:16,19,-2:127,
-3:174,181,-4:10,-5:88,90,129
Sarah 2:17,-3:56,-4:51,52,
-5:87,135-137,140 Stephen
5:118,-6:34,-7:87 Supply 6:43
Susanna 3:134 Thomas 1:10,
12,-2:17,-3:173,-5:138
Thomas M. 2:165,-3:45 Widow
1:12,-3:51,175 William 2:184,

62

JACKSON (continued)
-3:84,167,-5:137,-6:38,77
JACOBS, Abigail 3:103 Daniel
4:11 Deborah S. 6:185 Dorothy
3:7 Joseph 3:85,-4:182 Mary
3:131 Seth 4:122
JAFFREY, Elizabeth 4:103,-5:91
G. 3:50 George 1:19,-2:101-
103,-3:55,148,172,-4:49,102,
-5:183 Hannah 4:49-51 Madam
5:40 Mary 5:91 Mr.
5:139,186,
-6:41 Sarah 5:38
JAMES, Benjamin 2:54,-3:94
Catherine 4:75 Edmund 3:94
Eleanor 4:100 John 3:45,
-4:102,-6:28 Mary 2:54,-3:142
Matthew 5:41 Mercy 6:28 Pad-
dison 5:39 Richard 4:97,-5:44
Susanna 2:54 Thomas 4:76
William 3:100
JAMESON, John 3:86 Susan 5:147
JANVRIN, Ebenezer 5:129
Elizabeth 3:105,-4:55,57,
107,-5:44 George 4:97,-5:129
John 3:7,185,-3:158,-4:12,
55,105-107 Mary 2:173,-3:158
Sarah 4:179 William 4:107
JANY, Jousint 3:68,75
JAQUES, Deborah 2:169
JAQUETH (see JAQUITH)
JAQUIS, Henry 4:12
JAQUITH, Daniel 6:57 Sarah
2:42,-5:93
JARIGE, Pierre 3:68,75
JEAN, Julien 3:67,75
JEANEG, James 1:83
JEFFERDS, Forest 5:20
JEFFERS, John 4:176
JELLERSON, Benjamin 6:33
JELLISON, Ichabod 5:42
JENKINS, Abbie J. 6:182 Abigail
4:127,-5:59,-6:21 Adaline E.
2:30,-6:90,91,182 Amos 6:21
Anna 5:123 Annie 3:32
Arabella A. 6:182 Asa A. 6:81
Augustus 7:54 Augustus F.
7:54 Caroline 6:25 Catherine
1:171,-4:188,-5:123 Charles
7:54 Charles E. 2:30,-6:90,
91,182,183 Content 6:81 David
6:81 Dorothy 6:119,128
Ebenezer 1:122,172,-3:32,

JENKINS (continued)
-4:119,124,-5:128,-6:119 Edward 1:173 Edward V. 6:183
Edwin L. 6:182 Elijah 1:58,59,
114,123,172,-2:30,80,124,
-4:42,66,124,-5:62,123,128,
172,-6:90,122 Elizabeth 1:53,
54,58,59,61,63,64,114,115,117,
119,162,-2:31,80,150,-3:31,
-4:66,70,122,124,-5:57,-6:21,
25 Ellen A. 6:182 Emma 6:182
Ephraim 1:168,-5:58,-6:25 Experience 3:97 George 7:54
Hannah 1:54,60,165,-2:80,150,
-4:43,66,68,124,-5:26,58,122
Hannah J. 6:25 Henry A. 6:90
Henry E. 6:183 Hope 1:172 Ira
T. 6:86,183 Isaiah 1:115,119,
174,175,-3:32,-4:38,40,-5:58,
123 Jabez 1:61,64,115,117,
119,-2:80,-3:32,-4:42,66
James 2:150,-4:124,-5:128
Jedediah 4:124 Jemima 1:54
Jeremiah 6:122 John 1:171,
-2:150,-4:42,-5:26,122,-6:119
Jonathan 1:115,168,171,
-2:150,-4:41,-5:58,-6:25,89
Joseph 1:54,55,113,171,-2:76,
150,-3:7,34,-4:185,-5:32,122,
-6:21 Joseph A. 6:81 Joshua
1:123,173,-2:128,-4:66,-5:172
Kezia 1:54,-2:147,-4:78 Lois
1:171,-5:122,-6:88 Lydia
1:122,162,-6:182 Lydia A. 6:91
Mary 2:80,-4:43,-5:122,-6:25,
81 Mary A. 6:25 Mary E. 6:182
Mary H. 2:30 Mehitable 1:114,
123 Mercy 1:171,-5:58 Mrs.
5:139,-6:41 Nathan 5:128
Nathaniel 1:171,-5:32,58,115,
-6:81,86,172 Nicholas 1:174,
-2:30,-5:51,123,-6:91 Patience
6:173 Phebe 1:60,63,69,113,
115,161,-2:150,-5:26,31,-6:80
Reynold 1:51,54,58,59,64,122,
162,-2:80,-3:32,-6:98 Richard
5:139,-6:41,80 Ronald 4:66,
124,-5:127 Rowland 4:11 Ruth
1:161,163,165,169 Sarah 1:123,
163,171,174,175,-2:80,-3:32,
-4:66-5:26,59,122,-6:21,25,119
Sarah A. 6:81 Sarah F. 7:54

63

JENKINS (continued)
Stephen 5:58,116,127,
-6:119,172,173,182 Sybil 1:173
Tabitha 2:124,-4:66 Timothy
1:168,-5:29,59,64,-6:21,81
Walter 6:122 William 1:60,63,
69,113,115,161,163,165,168,
-5:26,58,122,-6:81 William A.
6:182 William J. 6:90 William
P. 6:183
JENKS, Captain 3:104
JENNESS, ---- 7:90 Aaron
5:119,-6:69 Abigail 5:9,55,
-6:73,-7:90 Adaline S. 3:192
Ann 1:37 Anna 1:28,42 Anna Y.
2:139 Benjamin 1:86,-2:139
Charles 6:33 Cornelius 6:119
Cyrus 6:180 Cyrus L. 1:182,
-6:180 Daniel 4:119,-6:19,37,
66,185 Daniel F. 6:180 David
4:148,150,-6:73 David A. 3:191
Deliverance 1:43 Elisha 5:5,
-6:116 Elizabeth 1:40,46,48,
133,143,-2:139,-4:172,-5:9,
-6:113 Elizabeth H. 1:143 Ellen F. 6:180 Ellen K. V. 6:180
Francis 1:37,48,81,82,-2:108,
111,-4:172,-5:9 George 7:55
George I. 6:180 Hall J. 6:160,
-7:40 Hannah 1:36,37,39,41-
43,46,86,133,-2:108,111,-5:7,
-6:65,67,71 Hezekiah 1:37 Ira
H. 7:64 Isaac 1:81,129,-5:115,
-6:36,172 Jemima 6:65
Jeremiah 5:113 Job 1:36,37,39,
86,96 John 1:34,36,37,40,46,
92,-3:177,-5:9,118,-6:66,67,
119,-7:27,89,91 Jonathan 1:81,
129,-4:122,-5:54,-6:73,114,116
Joseph 1:33,129,134,-2:139,
-3:114,-4:133,-5:9 Joseph D.
2:139 Joses 1:133 Joshua 1:42,
43,92 Keturah 6:113 Kezia 6:19
Langdon S. 1:143 Levi W.
3:192 Lowell 1:143 Lucy 1:34,
-4:146,-5:2,-7:91 Lydia 6:21,
73 Mar'h (?) 6:71 Mark 1:36,-
6:65,75,-7:90 Mary 1:33,37,39,
40,81,96,126,133,134,-2:139,
-5:6,9,-6:69,140 Minerva S.
3:191 Moses 4:150,-6:68 Mr.
6:113 Mrs. 6:113 Nancy 3:191

JENNESS (continued)
Nathaniel 1:37,133,-6:21 Noah
1:133 Oliver 1:143,-3:191,
-4:182 Patience 6:119 Paul
4:147,-6:113,172 Phena 6:71
Reuben P. 2:139 Richard 1:33,
37,96,129,134,143,-2:136,139,
164 Rufus K. 1:143 Samuel
6:116,-7:27-29 Sarah 1:40,48,
81,82,86,92,129,134,-4:148,
172,-5:49,119,-6:67,114,-7:29
Sarah F. 6:180 Savell 1:33
Semira P. 3:191 Sheridan 2:140
Sidney L. 3:191 Simon 1:133,
-3:191 Sophia P. 3:192 Stephen
5:53,-6:36 Thomas 1:37,-2:108
William 1:36,-5:8,117,-6:65,
111,116,117,-7:28,90
JENNINGS, Anne 4:6 Richard 3:90
JENNISON, William 4:33,-7:69
JEPSON, Abner 5:28 Anna 1:67
Anne 5:24 Jedediah 1:116,
-4:69,-5:60 John 5:60 Judith
5:31 Lois 5:60 Mary 1:67,116,
-5:60 Susanna 5:60 William
1:67,116
JEWELL, Abigail 5:37 Asa 4:21
Benjamin 4:187 Bradbury 7:57
Bradbury F. 7:57 Clara M. 7:64
Daniel 1:185,-7:37 David
1:185,-4:21 Elizabeth 1:185,
-4:118 Hannah 4:20,21 Hannah
M. 4:20,-5:36,37 Joseph 1:185
Levi 4:20 Lydia 3:127 Mary
1:185,-3:182 Robert 7:62 Sarah
1:185 Susan 4:180 Susanna
1:185 Thomas 3:86
JEWETT, Aaron 2:57 Abigail
4:166 Andrew 2:15,16,-5:142
Ann 2:15 Anna 2:11,15,57 Anna
F. 3:163 Anne 1:192 Benjamin
4:94,-5:147 Benjamin H. 3:163
Dearborn 5:2 Deborah 2:57,
-3:163 Elizabeth 2:15,57,
-3:126 Hannah 2:11 Henry 2:67
Jacob 2:11,57 Jedediah 5:170
John 2:57,-3:126,163 Jonathan
1:192,-2:15 Joseph 1:192,
-2:11,15,16,57,-3:17 Mark
1:115 Martha 6:137 Mary
1:115,192,-2:57 Mary A. 3:163
Mehitable 2:11 Moses 1:115

64

JEWETT (continued)
Nancy 3:163 Paul 2:11 Phebe
2:11 Samuel 2:67,-4:166 Sarah
2:15,-4:71 Sophia S. 5:35
Stephen 2:15 Susanna 2:15
Thomas 2:15 W. R. 6:15 William 4:166
JOHNSON, Abigail 4:166
Alexander 6:139 Anna 4:135
Benjamin 2:67,-3:118,-4:33,
77,166,-5:93 Bethia 4:166
Charles 4:97 Daniel 4:134
Ebenezer 3:55,-4:49,57,-6:110
Edmund 2:81,82,109 Edward
5:93 El. 3:56 Elizabeth 3:88,
-4:166,-6:65 Eln. 3:50 Enoch
4:166 George 4:129 George W.
6:6 Hannah 3:134,-6:95 Henry
4:97,99 Jacob 4:182,-7:45
James 1:3,6,9-11,-2:23,25,27,
61-64,98,102,-5:161 Jeremiah
2:164 Joanna 4:10,-6:104 John
1:10,13,-2:82,102,-3:68,75,
173-175,-4:57,-7:38 John M.
4:166 Jonathan 3:101,-6:62
Joseph 2:68 Judith 7:66
Katherine 4:102 Lieutenant
3:151 Mary 1:134,-2:81,82,89,
-3:33,182,-5:93,6:33,156,-7:6
Mr. 5:44 Mrs. 3:56,82,175
Nathaniel 4:90,-5:2 Noah 6:159
Otis 6:39 Parker 6:156
Patience 2:146 Peter 1:134,
-2:81,89,91,109,112 Phebe
6:166 Philip 1:22 Rhoda 6:166
Ruth 2:89,91,109,112 Samuel
2:47,-4:79 Sarah 2:66,129,175,
-3:181,182,-4:166,-6:65 Seth
5:93 Susanna 4:175 Thomas
1:179,-3:82 Timothy 4:135
William 5:93,-6:179
JOHONET, William 6:165
JOHNSTON, Abigail 4:168
Alexander 3:70 Dorothy 3:136
Francis 3:173,175 James 4:168
John 3:55,84 John Paul 3:10,
94,96 Josiah 3:167 Martha 3:6
Mary 3:83,130 Mr. 3:149 Mrs.
3:145,175 Peter 3:20,73 Sarah
1:150,-3:184
JONES, Abby M. 6:123 Abiah 1:93
Abigail 1:101,-2:35,36,81,

JONES (continued)
-4:76,-5:7 Abigail M. 2:29,
-5:24,-6:83 Abner 6:90
Abraham 4:53,58 Alexander
1:5,10,11,-2:185,-4:33 Alice
A. 1:157 Amos 6:24,127
Andrew H. 2:164 Ann 1:45
Anna 1:167,176,-6:24,25 Anna
J. 6:24 Anne 1:82,93 Augustine
2:32 Benjamin 5:51 Benjamin
H. 6:81,123 Betsey 7:53
Catherine 1:82 Charles 6:88
Charles A. 6:127 Comfort C.
1:156 Daniel W. 6:127
Ebenezer 1:101 Elizabeth
1:19,-4:12,54,100,-5:17,40
Elizabeth B. 5:76 Elizabeth E.
1:156 Ephraim 6:29 Eunice A.
2:32 Ezekiel 1:121,-7:6 Ezra
6:29 Fanny 6:108 Francis 1:12
George 1:10,12 George H. 6:90
George N. 6:123 George W.
6:127 Hannah 2:63,-4:54,146
Hannah B. 2:30,-6:24 Hannah
J. 6:24 James 1:167,-4:93,
-5:59,-6:24,185 James A. 6:24
James E. 6:127 James L. 6:90
Jane 6:118 Jeremiah H. 5:36
Joanna 4:58 John 1:3,9,10,45,
82,93,101,-2:24-26,-4:49,54,
58,-5:76,-6:29,-7:75,76,78
John, Jr. 7:73 John G. 6:127
John P. 1:155,156,-2:7 Jonas
5:186 Jonathan 4:125 Joseph
4:13,93,-5:56,119,-6:104,118,
-7:76 Joshua 4:58 Leah 5:115
Levi 5:56,-6:38 Lucy T. 6:123
Lydia 5:117 Lydia A. 7:64
Lydia S. 1:101,121,157 Mar-
garet 4:77 Martha 2:38 Mary
1:45,93,-4:52,100,-5:53,145,
186,-7:86 Mary Jane 7:87 Mary
S. 1:156 Mehitable 5:118,186
Miriam 4:174,-6:29 Mrs. 6:29
Nabby Maria 7:78 Nancy 1:156,
-4:78 Nathan 6:29,30 Nathaniel
4:55 Nicholas 6:81,83,185
Oliver 4:184 Pamelia 4:184
Pelatiah 4:184 Phebe 6:90
Philip 1:121,-4:123 Richard
1:167,176,-4:93,-6:24, 185
Richard H. 6:24,-7:71 Richard

65

JONES (continued)
M. 2:32 Robert 4:126 Ruth 6:24
Samuel 1:32,155,-4:97,103,
186,-5:53,105,118,186,-6:118,
150 Samuel C. 5:55 Sarah 1:45,
101,184,-2:71,-5:38,50,76,114
Sarah H. 6:88 Stephen 1:101,
-7:43,45 Stephen M. 1:101
Stephen Parsons 7:73 Susan M.
1:156 Susanna 1:82,100,101,
176,-2:81,-5:105,-6:25
Thomas 1:11,101,156,-2:81
William 1:3,21,22,45,101,
-4:101,125,-5:186,-6:24 Wil-
liam J. 1:157
JORDAN, John 5:41 Richard 1:21
JOSE, Anne 5:42 Christopher 1:12
Hannah 3:56,-5:40 Jane 3:51
Joanna 5:40 Mary 5:41 Richard
2:17,101,-3:150,172
JOY, Alfred 1:152 Alice 5:119
Ebenezer 1:152,-7:45,59 Eliza
4:187 Elizabeth 1:152 Jacob
1:152,-5:113,-6:136 James
2:190 Mary 1:152 Mary S.
1:152,-4:186 Mehitable M.
7:59 Samuel 1:151,152,155
Sarah 1:152 Susanna 1:152,155
Tabitha 4:11 Timothy 4:78
Timothy M. 1:152,-7:59
JUDKINS, Abigail 2:46,-3:41,43
Andrew 4:174 Anna 3:90,
-5:111,112,160 Benjamin 2:43,
-5:154,157,158 Caleb 6:29
Deborah 3:134 Elisha 6:26
Elizabeth 3:135 Elizabeth I.
5:22 Hannah 3:87,115,-5:105,
-6:190 Hannah J. 5:19 Henry
5:160 Joel 2:46,71,-4:176,
-5:103,105,107,110,155,157,
160,-6:29,31 John 3:44,
-5:153,-6:26,29 Jonathan
4:91,-5:110,157 Joseph 3:43,
-5:110,155,158,-6:27 Josiah
3:41,-5:111,153,157,160,-6:30
Leonard 3:129,-5:107 Lois
3:135 Lydia 3:40 Martha 3:134,
-6:26 Mary 2:46,77,-3:43,171
Mehitable 3:132,178,-5:155
Moses 5:103 Mr. 3:132 Parne
4:134 Peter 4:179 Philip
5:153,-6:30 Rebecca 3:45,

JUDKINS (continued)
-4:174,-6:28 Rhoda 3:164
Richard 5:158 Robert 3:88
Ruhamah 3:130 Samuel 2:43,
47,71,-4:134 Seth 7:26 Stephen
3:132 Stephen S. 5:22 Susanna
3:88 William 5:153 Zachariah
3:41,44,-5:110,112,154,158,
-6:26,28,31
JUNKINS, Lydia 4:189 Sarah
4:189
JUXON, Benjamin 3:154 Bethia
3:157 Mary 3:157 Thomas
2:171,-3:154,157
KADRU, Patrick 3:67
KARSWELL (See CASWELL)
KASE, John 4:10
KEAIS, Mary 1:16,-3:54,56 Mrs.
3:174 S. 3:50 Samuel 2:97,100,
101,-3:54,55,173,-4:49
KEAY, James 5:147
KEEF, John 4:34
KEESE, Henry 5:44
KEITH, Henry C. 6:82 Mercy 6:37
Mr. 5:162 Robert 4:1,5
KELLEY (see KELLY)
KELLOGG, Minnie L. 4:140
KELLY, Abigail 2:11 Abigail M.
6:181 Addi(e) 3:123 Alfred
5:19,-6:18 Alfred D. 6:181 Anthony 4:180 Benjamin 3:123,
126,-4:80,118 Catherine 2:130,
-5:104 Charles 4:72 Daniel
3:123,125,-5:104 Deborah 2:66
Derbe (Derby?) 2:44,68 Edward
2:66 Eliza J. 7:67 Elizabeth
3:87 Elizabeth C. 4:74 Esther
3:123 George P. 7:38,43
George W. 3:123 Hannah 2:11
Hannah B. 7:71 Hannah W. B.
4:74 Houldridge 2:11 James
2:69,-3:123,126 James W.
4:74 Joanna 4:72 John 6:159,
-7:40 Jonathan 2:11 Joseph
2:11,-3:123,-4:72,74,-5:169
Kate 3:123 Laura L. 4:74 Levi
3:123 Lydia 3:119 Lydia A.
4:74 Mary 2:11,-4:72 Mary A.
4:74,-6:181 Mary F. 6:64 Matthew 4:34 Minerva S. 4:74
Miss 5:42 Nathan 7:17 Philip
2:69 Roger 3:142 Samuel 2:11,

KELLY (continued)
68,-4:179,-6:64,160 Sarah
4:7,72 Sarah J. 4:127 Stephen
2:45 Susan 6:159 Susan A.
6:181 Susanna 6:181 William
1:22,-3:133 William A. 6:181
William P. 6:181
KELSEY, Susan 7:40 William
7:71
KEMP, Pelatiah 7:19 Z. Willis
3:96
KENDALL, Abel 4:85 Henry 6:167
Lucy R. 6:170 Mary 5:142
Nancy 7:20
KENIST, James 3:176 Mrs. 3:176
KENNARD, Alkins 4:97,-5:138
Ann B. 7:59 Anne 5:39
Diamond 3:8 Edward 3:53,54,
173,-4:57 Elizabeth 1:57,72,
115,-3:4,50, 52-54,56,-4:53
George 4:100 Jane 5:45 John
3:53,-4:53,-5:138 John W.
4:55 Mary 3:53 Michael 1:54,
57,-3:31,34.53,-4:57,-5:41 Mr.
4:99,-5:138 Mrs. 3:175
Patience 4:104 Richard 3:54
Ruth 2:175 Samuel 1:57,72,
115,-4:41 Sarah 3:53 Susanna
1:72 Thomas 4:102 William
3:7
KENNEDY, Gilbert 4:2 Janet 4:2
KENNISTON, (KINISON), Aaron
4:128 Abraham 6:62 Anna
3:126,-6:140 Asa 4:75 Betsey
7:79 Bickford 3:122 Catherine
6:168 Christopher 3:176
Deborah 5:174 Ebenezer 3:113
Elizabeth 3:120,122 Farezina
3:13 George 3:174 Hannah
3:13,-4:188,-5:108,-6:137
Henry 3:13 Henry A. 3:13 Job
2:46 John 1:11,13,-3:89,
-4:79,-6:80 Joseph E. 3:89
Joshua 4:75 Judith 2:45,-6:138
Lydia O. 3:13 Margaret 3:180,
-6:80 Mark 7:64 Mary 3:13,
122,-4:79,-5:108 Mercy W.
3:13 Moses 3:122 Mrs. 3:176,
-6:27,46 Nancy 3:13,122,-6:61
Nathan 4:80 Peter 3:20,72,
-6:46,80 Phebe 4:79 Reuben
6:27 Richard 3:44,-6:27 Sally

KENNISTON (continued)
7:40 Samuel 1:183,-2:122,
-3:122,123 Sarah 3:122,
-6:46,159 Stacy 3:122,-7:79
Susan 3:122 Susanna 3:113,
-4:75 Usseljell 3:13
KENT, Asa 4:137 Caroline 7:20
Charlotte M. 7:19 Ebenezer
4:125,130 Henry Oakes 7:33,35
James 5:152 Mary 4:126,7:17
Mary Jane 7:26 Oliver 1:178
Rachel 3:7,-5:83 Richard
1:157,-3:145,-4:127,183
Richard P. 7:35 Robert 1:157
Thomas 7:35 William 6:170
KERNY, Joseph 4:78
KESWELL (see Caswell)
KETTLE, John 1:10,11
KEYES, David 5:142 Robert 5:142
Sarah 5:142
KEZER, Lemuel 6:54
KIDDER, William 1:112
KIELLE, Benjamin 5:5 James
6:102
KILBY, William H. 5:96
KILGORE, Trueworthy 6:106
KILLMANOCK, Alexander 4:34
KIM, Elizabeth 4:11
KIMBALL, Abigail 3:89 Alvah
7:66 Anna 5:114 Apphia 6:166
Asa 3:74 Benjamin 6:53 Caleb
3:130 Caroline 6:40 Charlotte
B. 6:23 Charlotte G. 7:25
Clarissa 7:86 Clarissa E. 7:67
Cyrus 7:25 Daniel 5:50 David
1:11,-6:58 Ebenezer 4:176 Ed-
ward 4:34 Eleanor Cooper 7:30
Eliza R. 7:21 Elizabeth 2:85,
-4:81,-5:6,-6:107,119,162 El-
len G. 6:23,180 Ephraim 5:118,
-6:119,120,171,173,174,-7:27-
30 Ezekiel 6:106 Hannah 5:114
Harriet 7:24 Henry A. 5:192
Isaac 3:134 Isabella Graham
7:88 Jane 6:107 Jane K. 7:70
Jesse 4:119,-6:171 John 2:142,
-3:48,-5:21,-7:29 Jonathan
5:93 Laura 7:23 Lydia 6:162
M. J. 7:88 Mahala 6:169 Margaret Jane 7:88 Mary 2:85,86,
-5:3,20,53,55,-6:55,58,105,
111,120,-7:24 Mary Ann 7:24

KIMBALL (continued)
Mary B. 7:22 Mary F. 4:41
Maurice 5:20 Mehitable 6:57
Melinda 7:87 Moses 6:52,126
Moses F. 7:55 Mr. 6:23 Nabby
7:27 Nancy 6:56 Nathaniel F.
7:60 Nehemiah 5:1,-6:175,
-7:28 Pamelia 7:22 Paul 5:55
Philip 6:49 R. 7:88 Reuben
6:56 Richard 2:86,-7:80
Richard M. 6:167 Robert 3:17
Rufus 7:20 Ruth 6:106 Samuel
6:173 Sarah 3:169,-5:18,
-6:52,55,58,105 Simeon 6:105
Susan E. 7:68 Susanna 5:7,
-6:56 Thomas 2:85,86,-3:42
William 6:108,170
KIMBREL, George 2:37
KIMMIN(G), Benjamin 3:43 Sarah
4:13
KING, Daniel 3:81,-5:19 Eunice
B. 5:19 George 2:159,182,
-5:163 Hannah 5:41 Mary 1:110
Richard 1:5,110 Sarah 3:144
Sophia 4:187
KINGMAN, Elijah 1:86 John 6:172
Mary 1:40,86 Olive 3:46 Ruth
1:86 William 1:86,-6:172
KINGSBURY, Abigail 2:143 Chloe
2:143 Daniel 2:40 Elizabeth
2:95 Frank B. 2:40,42,142,
143,-5:48 Hannah 2:143 John
2:95 Joseph 2:142 Mary 2:40
Nathaniel 2:40,142 Sergeant
3:147
KINGSLEY, Jonathan 5:93,144
KINKAID, David 3:151
KINNEER, John 2:37 Martha 2:37
KINSMAN, Ephraim 6:51 Thomas
1:22
KIRK(E), Eleanor 4:10 Henry
3:173,175 Mary 5:41 Mrs.
3:53,175 Ruth 3:50,53,56
KIRKNESS, Thomas 4:3
KIT, Sarah 5:40
KITSON, Richard (?) 5:168
KITTREDGE, Charles 4:83
Eleanor 3:184,-4:83 Eliza 4:83
George 3:184,-4:83,89 George
W. 4:83 Mary R. 4:83
Theodore 3:184
KIVEL, John 5:85

KNAPP, Mrs. 5:187 Samuel 5:187
Susan J. 1:182 Ursula 5:187
KNIGHT, Abraham 6:65 Alice
3:61 Amy 5:98 Ana L. 6:62
Anne 1:7,8 Benjamin 6:139
Bridget 3:60 Caroline 7:87
Catherine 5:98 Charles 4:60
Daniel 3:59,-6:104 Deborah
3:154,-5:185 Elizabeth 3:58-
61,107,109,110,154,-4:11,12,
-5:118,-6:65,69,-7:90 George
3:110,-5:134-136,138,140,185,
188,-6:41 Hannah 4:79 Hatevil
5:5.116,-6:35,115,176,-7:27-29
Henry 6:62 John 2:173,-3:3,
58-61,107,109,110,154,155,
172,-4:14,-5:138,-6:65 John
Smith Bryant 7:29 Joseph
6:115,176 Joshua 6:68 Kezia
4:147,-6:66 Lois 5:55,-6:171
Mary 2:168,-3:2,58,109,-5:51,
76,134-136,138,140,185,188,
-6:41 Mary Dole 7:28 Mary G.
5:134 Mr. 3:154 Mrs. 3:56,151,
176 Nathan 3:174,176 Nicholas
2:174,-4:19,60,63,107 Olive
4:149 Richard 6:65 Robert 5:7,
-6:66,-7:90 Robert Jr. 7:90
Roger 1:1,6-8,10,-2:22,28
Rose 5:76,-6:173 Samuel 5:98,
-6:41 Sarah 4:57,60,63,107,
-5:8,76 Susanna 3:8,107,-4:63,
150,-5:53,136,151 Temperance
5:79,188 Walter Briant 7:27
Westbrook 4:53 William
2:158,159,-3:29,62,74,-4:19,
-5:44,76,120,140,-6:171,173
KNOLEN, William 5:42
KNOLLYS, Hanserd 1:147
KNOT, Susanna 5:43
KNOWLES, Abigail 4:133,-6:109
Amos 1:36 Comfort 6:113
Daniel 6:119,175 David 1:36
Deliverance 1:44,87 Eliza
4:115 Elizabeth 5:140 Ephraim
6:175 Experience 6:114,117
Ezekiel 1:35,36,-2:89 Hannah
1:35,3:191,-6:119,162 Isaac L.
6:119 James 1:83,-2:91,-4:34,
146,-6:117,175 Jemima 2:88,
89,91,105,110,-6:119 John
1:42,87,-2:88,89,91,105,110,

KNOWLES (continued)
-6:73,175 Joseph 1:44,86,87,
-2:110 Love 1:86,87 Mary
1:35,36,92,-6:74,119 Mary D.
5:146 Mercy 1:148 Mr.
4:30 Nathan 4:115 Rachel 1:87
Rebecca 6:175 Ruth Anne 7:67
Samuel 1:87,-5:4 Sarah 1:87,
-3:183,-5:44,-6:111 Sarah B.
7:26 Simon 1:44,86,-2:105,
-4:115 Susanna 4:149 Tryphena
5:8 William 6:175
KNOWLTON, Abraham 1:12
David 1:180 John 2:164,-7:17
Samuel 1:181,-6:161
KNOX (see also NOCK), Anna
1:164,-3:113 James 1:164
Joseph 3:114 Mary 6:105,163
Sarah 6:52,110 Sobriety 7:51
William 3:113
La BONTA, Margaret 7:72
La COSTE, Peter 3:67
LADD, Abigail 7:78 Alexander
2:163 Benjamin 6:30 Catherine
2:50 Daniel 2:43,48,65,131,
132,-5:159,160 Dorothy 2:65,
-3:42,-4:185 Eliphalet 2:161,
-5:164,165,169,170,-7:78·
Elizabeth 2:45,-3:136,-6:40
Hannah 3:41 Harriet 7:78 Isaac
5:157 Jeremiah 5:109 Joanna
3:88,133 John 2:43,65,132,
-6:27,32 Jonathan 6:26 Kezia
6:53 Love 1:190,-2:48,3:39,
-5:154 Mary 3:40,131
Mehitable 2:72,-3:181,-6:29
Mercy 1:190 Nathaniel 1:190,
-2:50,-3:41,118,-4:86,133,
-5:109,111,154,157,-6:27,30
Olive Maria 7:71 Samuel 3:85
Stephen 2:48,-3:87 Trueworthy
2:46,-6:26,29,32
LAINGTON, Joanna 6:37
LAKE, Robert 6:167 Thomas 3:48
LAKEMAN, Aaron 5:135 Mrs.
5:135 Tobias 5:135
LAMB, Bial 1:11 Elizabeth 3:3
Franklin L. 2:142 Fred W.
2:96,142 Isaac 2:142 William
4:34
LAMBERT, Gershom 2:35 Mary
6:50 Sarah 6:50

LAMBETH, Philip 4:11
LAMOS, Abigail 1:57,63,65,121,
122,125,-2:148,-4:122,160,
-5:61,100,-6:19 Anna 6:18
Deliverence 1:57,-2:148,-4:41
Elizabeth 2:148 Elizabeth W.
5:61 Ephraim 6:18 Esther
5:100 George F. 5:61 Grace
4:52 Hannah 1:121,-4:160,
-5:126 Hannah H. 5:61 James
1:63,119,128,-2:148,-4:123,
128,162,-6:18 Jesse 6:18 John
1:128 Jonathan 1:125,-4:39,
122,160,-5:174 Joseph 4:123
Kezia 1:119,-4:123,-5:123,
-6:18 Lydia 4:160 Mary 6:18
Miriam 5:99,100 Moses 5:99,
-6:18 Mrs. 3:149 Nathaniel
1:57,63,65,121,122,125,-2:148,
-3:149,-4:160,-5:61,100
Samuel 2:148,-4:38,-5:100
Sarah 1:119,121,128,-2:148,
-4:160,-5:126,-6:18 Stephen
4:123
LAMOUR, Jacque 3:76
LAMPERILL, Benjamin 1:34,
-2:88 Deborah 1:34 Henry 2:88
Ilyen 2:88 Sarah 1:34
LAMPREY, Hannah 1:92 Sarah B.
7:44
LAMSON, Albert H. 2:42,165,192,
-3:45,47,139,-4:144,-6:48
Gideon 5:168
LANCASTER, Thomas 3:100
LANCTON, Joseph 5:54
LANDAL-(LANDEL), Elizabeth
4:102 Lucy 4:104 Mr. 5:43
Thomas 5:38
LANDER(s) John 1:3 Rachel
1:111
LANE, A. C. 4:22 Abigail 2:208
Abraham 2:56 Albert F. 4:74
Amanda M. 4:24,74 Ambrose
1:5,9,-2:24 Andrew C. 2:115,
-4:73 Ann Lucy 7:63 Anna
2:114 Bathsheba 2:15,54,55
Caroline E. 4:22 Charles
2:115,-7:63 Charles E. 7:63
Charlotte 4:23 Daniel 1:36,
-2:56 David 1:46 Dinah 4:113
Dorothy 3:183 Ebenezer 2:55
Edmund 5:101,-6:102,103

LANE (continued)
Edmund J. 2:115 Elizabeth
1:93,-2:56,115,-3:119,164,
-4:23,-5:101 Elizabeth A. 4:73
Enoch M. C. 4:22 Eunice
2:114,115,-4:21 Ezekiel 1:41,
-4:136 George 2:115,-3:165,
-4:24,116-118,-5:35,36 George
E. 4:73,74 Hannah 1:36,48,
-2:55-57,-3:127,-4:21,-7:63
Hannah C. 4:21,22 Henry S.
4:24 Isaiah 3:135,-4:136 Jabez
2:15,55,114,115 James 2:56,
-3:164,-4:23 Jane 6:102 John
1:36,41,46,48,81,92,-2:56,
-4:21,22,189 John H. 6:102,103
John William 7:63 Joseph Hilliard 7:27 Joshua 2:11,54-
57,-7:27,29 Joshua J. 4:24
Josiah 2:56,-4:24 Katherine
4:80 Levi 2:56 Lucy 2:115
Lydia 4:24 Mark 2:56 Martha
2:13,55,114,-4:23,128,-6:92
Mary 1:41,46,48,81,-2:10-
13,15,54-56,114,115,-3:94,
179,-4:181,-5:101,102,-6:123
Mary Elizabeth 7:63 Mary M.
4:22,116 Mr. 2:64 Nathan 1:81
Olivia E. 7:63 Ruth 4:91
Samuel 2:10-13,15,54-56,114,
-4:21,-5:101,-7:67 Samuel. G.
4:22 Sarah 2:13,54-56,3:127,
-4:24,118,133,-5:92 Solomon
4:132 Stephen 2:56 Susanna
2:12,54,55 Thomas 4:22 William 2:56,-4:21,182,-5:101
William F. 4:21,23
LANEY, Joel 7:45
LANG, Anne 4:49,50 Benjamin
1:96,-3:3,-5:35 Catherine 3:7
Clarissa H. 4:116 Daniel 1:20,
-3:66,71 David 3:165
Deliverance 4:50,-5:42 Eleanor
1:96 Eliza 4:181 Elizabeth
1:96 Esther J. 7:66 George
3:113,-7:78-80 Grace 4:57
Hannah 1:96,-4:76 Jeremiah
5:45 Jewett S. 6:166 John 4:54
John Collins 7:80 Joseph 5:35
Martha 4:127 Mary 7:20 Mary
C. 7:71 Mercy (or Marsy)
7:78-80 Meshech 6:109 Mrs.

LANG (continued)
3:175 Nathaniel 3:55,-4:54
Priscilla C. 6:159,-7:40 Robert
1:12,-3:65,173,175,-4:50
Samuel 4:55,-7:79 Samuel W.
6:162 Sidney 4:79 Stephen
3:55,-4:49,50,52,54,-6:169
Stephen, Jr. 7:20 Thomas
4:54,98 Thomas J. 4:118
LANGDON, Amelia 6:45 Ben-
jamin 5:134,137 Caroline 7:11
Dorothy W. 6:77 Dr. 7:12
Elizabeth 4:48,-5:89,131,169,
-6:43,78,80 Frances Emory
7:79 Hannah 1:92 Harriet 7:14
Henry S. 2:162,-5:184,-7:79,80
Henry Sherburne 7:78,80 John
2:158,159,162,-4:25,-5:87,162-
166,168,169,-6:78,80,-7:12
Joseph 2:21,104,157,158,-3:54,
-4:146 Joshua 7:15 Katharine
Whipple 7:74 Mark 2:17,19,21,
104,157,158 Martha 3:53,-4:51,
-5:43 Mary 3:50,52,53,56,95,
-4:101,-5:135 Mary A. 6:43
Mehitable 2:17,19 Mr. 3:172,
-5:42 Nancy 7:78,79 Paul 5:90
Richard 2:181,-3:53,71,-5:91
Samuel 2:165,-4:100,-5:86,87,
89,129,131,133-135,137,183,
-6:41,43,76 Sarah 5:38,184,
187,189,-6:43,45,46,77,-7:11,
12,14,15,73-75 Sarah S. 5:159
Thomas 5:133 Tobias 2:17,
101-104,-3:53,55,173,-4:49,
100,-5:42,91 Walter 7:73,75
William 1:22,-2:159,160,-3:9,
-5:87 William Eustis 7:78
Woodbury 2:160,-5:165,166,
184,187,189,-6:43,45,46,77,
-7:11,12,14,15,73-75
LANGLEY, Anna M. 5:140 Benjamin 5:45 David 4:128 Easter
(Esther?) 3:9 Elihu 5:137,140,
185,188,-6:42,80,-7:13
Elizabeth 4:130 Ephraim 4:78
Hannah 4:79,187,-6:42 Harriet
4:77,-6:6 James 4:79 Joanna
4:75 Job 4:130 John O. 7:58
Joseph 1:102,-4:75 Love 1:156
Lydia 4:76 Margaret 4:79 Mary
1:102,-4:184,-5:101,119,

LANGLEY (continued)
-6:154,-7:39 Miriam 4:75 Mrs.
5:137,140,185,188,-6:42 Nancy
4:129,184 Olando 4:184
Patience 4:126 Reuben 4:116
Samuel 4:125,-7:13 Sarah
4:80,-5:113,185,188,-6:80,
-7:13 Thomas 1:102,-2:173,
-4:79,129,184,-7:56 Thomas
B. 5:137 Timothy 4:78 Valentine 5:8
LANGMAID, Deborah 1:88 Elsie
6:112 Henry 1:21,22 Jacob
4:126 John 1:88,-3:114
Jonathan 4:183 Joseph 1:22,
-4:52 Priscilla 2:46 Sarah
4:125 William 1:88
LANGSTAFF, Henry 1:179,-3:104
LANGTON, Mary 4:45 Mercy 6:37
LANVEAT, Entwinett C. 7:37
LAPISH, Hardison 1:152 Lucy A.
1:155 Robert 1:152 Tem-
perance 1:152 William 1:22
LARBOUETTE, Claud 3:68
LAREY, Olive 6:92
LARRABEE (or LARRABY),
Abigail 4:101 Eleanor 4:99,
-5:43 Jane 4:99 Mary 4:52,
-5:40 Samuel 4:103 Sarah 4:99
Thomas 3:74,-4:98,101
LARY, Anna 7:79 Elizabeth 2:175
Martha 7:79 William 7:79
LASCO, Richard 6:137
LASKEY, Lois 4:78 Love 4:80
Mary 4:125,129 Susan 4:182
LATHROP, Mrs. 4:190 Thaddeus
6:109
LATTEFER, John 1:12 Mr. 1:12
LAUGHTON, Mary 4:45
LAVENDER, ---- 7:89 James
7:89 Robert 7:89 Rose Ann
7:89
LAVERS, G. 3:51 Jacob 3:174,175
Mrs. 3:51,175
LAW, Hannah 6:78 Henry 1:109
Joseph 6:78 Mrs. 6:78
LAWRENCE, Anna 4:135,-5:68
Caroline W. 4:87 David
4:87,88,135,167,171,5:68
Deborah G. 4:83 Edward
3:178,-4:135,167 Eliza
6:160,-7:41 Elizabeth P. 4:87

LAWRENCE (continued)
George W. 4:87 Gordon
4:185,-5:68 Hannah 4:86,167
Jennings 4:167 John 3:119
Joseph 4:135,167 Joseph S.
4:87 Josiah 4:88,167 Jotham
4:83,87 Lydia 4:87 Martha
4:132 Mary 4:167 Mary H.
3:115,-4:87 Matthias 4:167
Mehitable 4:135 Moses 3:182,
-4:167 Olive 4:87,88 Olive H.
4:87 Olive H. B. 4:88 Rachel
4:167 Ruth 3:182,-4:87 Samuel
3:184,-4:87,91,169,-5:68 Sarah
4:87 Smith 7:26 Solomon 4:167
Susan 4:181 William F. 4:83
LAWSON, John 2:141 Publius V.
7:42,141,142
LAWTON, Ida M. 6:192 Ida M. F.
2:95,96,166
LEACH, Benjamin 5:130 Daniel
6:45 Elijah 1:21 Elizabeth
5:132,134 James 1:9,11 John
1:21,-5:138 Joseph 2:175,
-5:88,90,130,132,135,138,186
Josiah 5:132,134,140,186
Lydia 1:111 Mary 5:135
Mehitable 6:45 Miriam 5:132
Mr. 5:142 Mrs. 5:135,138,
140,186,-6:45 Nathaniel 5:134
Rebecca 5:140 Richard 4:79
Thomas 7:45 Thomas C. 5:140
LEADBETTER, Increase 4:34
LEADEN, John 4:34
LEADER, Mr. 1:9,-2:24
LEAR, Alexander 1:131,-6:42
Casar 3:24,72 Catharine 5:186
Eleanor M. 6:77 Elizabeth
1:18,23,131,-5:186,187,189,
-6:42,44,77,79 Hannah 1:23
Mary 1:19,23,-4:128 Mr. 1:13
Nathaniel 1:23 Paul 6:44
Richard L. 6:79 Samuel 5:186,
187,189,-6:42,44,77,79,-7:78
Samuel Peverly 7:78 Sarah
1:131 Susanna 4:11 Tobias
1:18,19,23,-3:24 Walker 1:23
William 5:187,189
LEARY, William 3:66,74
LEATHERS, Elizabeth 4:148 Jane
4:130 John 6:152 Joseph
4:127,131 Lydia 4:75,125

71

LEATHERS (continued)
Philip B. 3:183 Robert 4:79
LEAVITT, Abigail 2:53,-3:90,
-4:143 Anna 2:55 Benjamin
2:9,10,155 Carr 3:191 Comfort
3:127 Daniel 3:87,-4:143
Deborah 2:67,-3:87
Deliverance 4:142 Dorothy
4:143 Dudley 4:143 Eben T.
3:191 Edmund 6:56 Edward
5:151 Eliza 4:142 Eliza J.
3:191 Elizabeth 2:9,10,65,
-3:44,-4:143 Elsie 2:10,42
Ephraim 2:53,-4:116 Hannah
2:9,122,-3:42,-4:142,143 Hez-
ron 2:106,108,110,112 James
2:110,-4:142,143 James S.
4:115 Jean 2:9 Jeremiah
2:10,-4:142,143 Joanna 2:9
John 2:9,46,65,108,-4:142,
143,-5:18 John S. 4:192
Jonathan 3:42,-4:118 Joseph
4:143 Josiah 2:122 Lydia 2:106
Martha 2:106,108,110,112 Mary
2:9,-3:41,-4:142 Moses 2:112,
-4:143,174 Mr. 4:143 Mrs.
3:175 Nathaniel K. 6:7,92
Nehemiah 2:65,-4:142,143
Patience 2:9 Reuben 4:143
Samuel 2:122,-3:149,-4:142,
143 Sarah 2:53,65,155,-4:143
Stephen 2:44,-4:143 Susanna
2:53 Thomas 2:190,-4:142
Timothy 4:143
LeBLANCH, Lewis 4:34
LeBOSQUET, John 5:181
LEE, Abigail 5:18 Abraham 4:9
Caesar 4:34 Mary 4:92 Samuel
4:92 Sarah 4:45 Tryal 5:43
LEFAVOUR, Robert 2:164
LEGRO, Eben 7:53
LEGROSSE, George 4:16
LEIGH, Mr. 3:80 Mrs. 3:80
LEIGHTON, Abigail 1:67,98,
114,164,-2:171,-3:159,-4:79,
-7:27 Ambrose 5:32 Amos 7:27
Anna 6:74,117 Anna A. 6:127
Anne 1:98,-5:32 Catherine 3:6
Charles W. 3:94 Daniel 6:127,
176,182,-7:27 David 2:30,
-4:109,146,-5:51,-6:74,115,
117,118,124 David B. 2:30

LEIGHTON (continued)
Deborah 1:67,-2:172,
-3:4,156,-4:16,163 Dorothy
4:147,-6:74 Ebenezer 1:98 Edward 4:46 Elijah 6:176
Elizabeth 1:98,-2:169,-3:9,
-4:108,149,-5:3,32,78,118,
-6:115 Emily 6:25 Ephraim
2:30 George 4:44,-5:78,-6:25
Hannah 2:30,-6:113,127 Harriet
4:183 Hatevil 2:171,-3:156,
158,159,-4:15,64,109 Isaac
3:156 Jacob 6:114 James 1:98,
-4:80,-6:127 Jane 5:49 Jane A.
3:94 Jemima 3:158 Joel 3:9,
-5:80 John 1:67,98,114,-2:163,
164,-3:94,156,158,159,-5:2,32,
-6:66,75,113,182,-7:28 John S.
4:59 Jonathan 1:114,-4:40,75,
152,-5:32,-6:184 Joseph 4:64,
-5:78 Kezia 2:172,-4:148 Luke
4:105 Luke M. 2:161,162 Lydia
4:145,-5:5,-6:67 Mark 3:158
Martha 1:98,-3:94 Mary 1:98,
-3:7,94,-4:16,18,19,59,61,64,
105,108,-5:7 Mary S. 5:78
Mehitable F. 3:119 Moses
3:156,-6:118 Nancy 4:80,-5:7,
50,55 Paul 3:156,158,-6:94
Phebe 6:94 Samuel 2:163,
-4:109,-6:114 Sarah 1:98,
-2:126,-3:8,156,158,159,-4:15,
64,109,-6:67,113 Seth 3:94
Smithson 4:61 Solomon 2:146
Susanna 1:98,-6:66 Tem-
perance 4:90 Temperance P.
5:78 Thomas 1:177,180,-2:164,
173,-3:159,-4:15,16,18,19,59,-
61,64,-4:105,108,-5:80,-6:103
Tobias 3:156 William 3:156,
-5:4,80,-6:115,176,-7:27,28
William S. 6:182
LEMEE, Nicholas 3:68,75
LEMPRIERE, Clement 2:19
LENCEY, Hannah 2:175
LEONARD, John 3:2 Josiah 7:18
O. B. 1:145 Oliver B. 2:166
LESTUAN, Marc 3:68,75
LETHERS, Jonathan 2:174
LETTUCE, Ann 5:143 Elizabeth
5:143 Thomas 5:143
LEVERETT, Warren 5:36

72

LEVISTON, Daniel 3:82
LEWIS, Abraham 3:174,175 Benjamin 2:182 Ebenezer 5:86, -6:45 Elizabeth 1:62,-4:121, -5:131 Hannah 1:27,-3:51, -4:45,-6:45 John 1:11,27,62, 68,-6:108 Joseph 4:34 Lydia 6:78 Martha 5:40,139 Mary 3:176,-4:51 Mehitable 5:133 Miss 5:42 Mr. 3:50,-5:39 Mrs. 3:56,175,-5:134,139 Philip 1:10,13,-2:99,100,-3:173,175 Richard 1:12 Rufus G. 7:25 Sarah 1:62,68,-4:161,-5:129 Susanna 1:68,-5:23 Thomas 3:174 William 2:184,-3:55, -4:51,-5:38,86,129,131,133, 134,139,-6:78
LIBBEY (LIBBY), Aaron S. 1:136 Abigail 1:90 Abraham 1:40,90 Abram R. 7:70 Agnes 4:97 Anne 4:55,-5:187 Arter 1:35 Azariah 3:4 Benjamin 1:37,90, -5:56,130 Bethiah 4:97 Bethshua 4:98 Charles 7:70 Clement 5:7,95 Daniel 1:52,-2:127 Daniel R. 1:136 Deborah 4:77 Elizabeth 1:35,52,-2:172, -4:97,102,-5:88,137,-6:119 George 4:102,-5:86-88,132, 164,168 Hannah 1:34 Hanson 4:58,-5:49 Ichabod 4:100, -5:132,134,137,140,187 Isaac 1:35,37,-6:39,72,119 Jacob 1:33,34,37,40,90 Jane 1:35 James 2:103,170,-3:55,-4:18, 50,52,102,-5:86 Jeremiah 2:98,103,158,160,-4:100,101, -5:43,87,91,130 Jerusha 3:4 Job 1:37,90 Johammah 1:37 John 1:35,103,-2:18,-3:27,74, -4:10,104,-5:86,87,113,138, 140,-6:116 John C. 5:138 Joseph 1:37,90,-5:140 Lydia 3:1,-5:39 Mary 1:35,37,83, 90,-2:18,170,-4:52,104,-5:44, 56,86,87,90,134,140,-6:116,119 Mary R. 6:7 Matthew 3:1 Mehitable 1:136,-5:140 Meshech 5:50 Mr. 2:171,-5:44 Mrs. 5:134,137,138,140,187 Nancy G. 1:136 Nathaniel 5:91

LIBBY (continued)
Paul 4:123,-5:52,89,-6:116,-7:5 Rachel 3:119 Reuben 1:35,-3:1 Robert 1:103 Ruth 1:33,35 Samuel 1:37,136 Sarah 1:33,34, 37,40,90,136,-3:9,-5:52,132, -6:72 Stephen 3:5,-6:104 Theodore 5:89,90 William 5:87,132 William S. 1:136
LIDDELL, George 4:3
LIEVERE, Francois 3:26
LIGHT, Ebenezer 6:77,-7:12 Hannah 6:77,-7:12 Hannah B. 6:77 John 3:51 Margaret Meloon 7:12 Olive 2:57 Widow 3:175
LINCOLN, Charles H. 5:161 Edward 5:102 Zilpah 6:17
LINDSEY, Hannah Dame 7:79
LINKHORN, John 3:82
LISCOMB, William 4:34
LITCHFIELD, Mr. 7:78
LITTLE, Arthur 6:16 Benjamin 6:169 Francis 3:24,71 John 7:21 Judith 5:189 Mary 2:152, -6:43 Sarah 5:187,189,-6:43,45 Stephen 5:187,189,-6:43,45
LITTLEFIELD, Abigail 5:93 Annas 2:144 Anne 5:93 Edmund 2:144,-5:93 Francis 1:179, -2:144,-5:93 Hannah 7:56 Jonathan 5:93 Josias 3:83,149 Maybell 2:171 Mr. 3:150 Mrs. 3:83,149 Phebe 4:10 Richard 2:181,-3:71
LLINN, John 4:34
LLOYD, Allen 1:11,-3:174,176 Arthur 4:34 Mrs. 3:176
LOBDELL, Mary G. 4:144
LOBDEN, John 5:43
LOCKE, Abbie M. 3:192 Abby W. 7:59 Abigail 1:42,47,81,91,132, 135,141,-2:37,65,132,136, -3:119 Abigail B. 7:70 Abigail D. 1:133 Abigail P. 4:185 Abigail T. 1:141 Abner 1:43, 84,91 Albert C. 3:192 Alfred 6:39 Ann 1:133 Anna 1:33,86, 89,91,174,-6:23,123,124 Asa 3:191 Asa D. 2:140 Benjamin 1:133 Benjamin B. 5:149 Charles C. 6:180 Charlotte B. 6:23 Clara J. 6:93,-7:58

73

LOCKE (continued)
Clarissa 7:61 Daniel 1:91
David 1:42,86,89,91,133,139
Deliverance 1:33-35 Dorothy
7:4 Edward 1:165,174,176,
-5:26,-6:23,70,185 Edward F.
6:180 Eleanor 1:34,157,-6:119
Elijah 1:42 Elisha 4:78
Elizabeth 1:34,36-38,47,48,
83,86,95,135,174,176,-4:148,
-5:50,152,-6:23,172 Elizabeth
G. 2:140 Elizabeth J. 3:191
Elizabeth M. 1:176,-3-191 Ellen C. 6:23 Elvin 1:135 Enoch
6:92 Ephraim 1:34 Esther Y.
2:140 Francis 1:33-35,86
Gardner T. 3:191 Hall J. 2:37
Hannah 1:33,37,41,81,84,87,
89,133,138,-2:66,-4:150,-6:51,
66 Hannah W. 1:141 Harriet J.
3:192 Horace W. 3:191 Huldah
1:42 Ira 3:119 Isaac M. 2:140
Ivory 6:23 Jacob 1:43 James
1:33-36,38,81,165,-6:23,180
James H. 3:191 James W.
1:141 Jemima 1:87 Jesse
2:191 Jethro 1:91,135,-7:4
John 1:10,11,38,43,89,91,
135,-2:64,-5:7,54,-6:54 John
O. 3:191 Jonathan 1:42,84,91,
135,139,144 Jonathan D. 3:191
Joseph 1:41,81,91,138,141,
-3:191 Josiah K. 7:19 Lemuel
2:140,-3:191 Levi 1:91,137
Lieutenant 3:83 Louisa 6:23
Lucretia 1:141 Lucy 3:136
Lydia 1:38,-2:191,-3:93,-6:23
Lydia H. 7:60 Lydia M. 1:176
Margaret 1:42,-2:135,-3:42
Mary 1:27,35,42,43,83,89,131,
135,141,165,-3:2,191,-6:23,36,
72 Mary O. 7:61 Mercy 4:146
Meribah 4:147,150 Meribeth
1:36 Miriam 4:177 Nancy 4:130
Nathaniel 1:139 Olive S. 1:135
Patience 1:42,138,141 Perna
T. 3:191 Prudence 1:35,-6:113
Reuben 1:86,-4:93 Richard
1:43,81 Richard L. 3:192
Richard R. 3:192 Sabina 4:10
Sally B. 7:22 Salome 1:47
Samuel 2:48,129,131,133

LOCKE (continued)
Samuel J. 1:35 Sarah 1:33-
36,38,42,43,81,83,84,86,89,
-2:71,-3:20 Sarah A. 1:141,
-3:191,192 Sarah E. 3:192
Sarah H. 3:191 Sarah W. 6:23
Simeon 1:86,-2:191,-7:61
Simon 3:93 Sula A. 3:192
Susanna 6:65,68 Temperance
7:87 Temperance K. 6:119
Thomas 2:183 Tryphena 1:43
Ward 2:69 William 1:36-38,
42,47,48,83,87,92,133,138,141,
-4:187,-6:120,172
LOCKHART, Burton W. 6:16
LOKIR, Daniel 4:80
LOMES, Esther 4:186
LONG, Abigail 2:36,-3:133,-6:100
Alexander 6:52 Anna Maria
7:76 Benoni 3:87 Daniel 5:167
Ebenezer 2:77,-3:86,-6:29,31
George 2:162,-7:76,77 John
1:51 Lydia 5:153 Maria 6:31
Mary 6:29 Mercy 7:76,77
Mercy Collins 7:77 Mrs. 6:29
Patience 1:51 Peirce 2:159,160
Perry 1:22 Pierre 5:167
Richard 3:82,-5:111,153 Robert
1:22 Ruth 3:42,-5:111 Stephen
2:66,-3:88 William 2:43,66
LONGFELLOW, Mary 6:138
LOOKIN, Elizabeth 5:104 Hannah
5:110 John 5:104,106,110 Sarah
5:106
LOOMS, Widow 3:146
LORD, Amaziah 5:114 Ann 4:10
Anne 2:77 Benjamin 6:150
Daniel W. 7:53 Dorothy 4:10
Ebenezer 2:163,-6:135,-7:52
Edward D. 6:170 Elizabeth
6:135 Evelyn K. 7:63 Francis
B. 6:135 Gershom 6:185 James
7:53 Jeremiah 6:38 John 3:45,
-5:150,-7:53 John Jr. 7:53
John B. 6:135 John Calvin 7:53
Joseph 2:176 Lucy 6:135,140
Martha 4:12,-6:146 Mary
1:181,-5:119,-6:135,146,158,
-7:51 Mary L. 6:154 Mary
Louisa 7:38 Moody 7:53
Nathan 5:146,-6:146,-7:52
Nathaniel 6:135 Phebe 6:150

74

LORD (continued)
Rebecca 3:114,-4:89,-5:114
Robert 7:53 Samuel 4:150
Sarah 4:10,-5:113 Solomon
5:119 Stephen Downs 7:53
Susan 6:36,158 Susanna 6:135
William W. 4:151,-6:37
LOUD, Abigail 1:20,-3:138,
-4:58,-5:86,132,-6:44 Ann
3:138 Benjamin 5:39 Daniel
5:130 David 4:101 Edward 7:16
Edward B. 7:15,77 Edward
Brown 7:74,76,79 Elizabeth
5:135 George 3:25,74,-5:91,
-7:15,16 Hannah Mann 7:76
James Boyd 7:74 John 1:20,
-4:58,-5:88,91,132 John J.
1:79,111,-2:92,166,-3:139,
-5:144 Joseph 1:111,-5:129,
132,135 Margaret 5:130 Mark
5:87 Mary 5:88,91,129 Mrs.
5:135 Nathan 7:79 Peter Mann
7:77 Samuel 4:175,-5:132
Sarah 1:20,-6:44,77,80,
-7:15,16,74,76,77,79 Solomon
2:172,-3:138,139,-4:97,-5:86,
91,129,-6:44,77,80 Thomas
4:99,-5:87,130,132 William
4:58,-5:39,129,-7:79
LOUGEE, Anne 3:87 Gilman 3:86
James 7:21 Joseph 7:22
LOUTIT, Thomas 4:3
LOVEJOY, Chandler 6:167
Chandler, Jr. 7:23 Ebenezer
6:166 Henry 7:20 John 6:53
Martha 7:70 Mary 6:167
Miriam 6:58,-7:21 Peter 7:66
Phebe 6:51 Sarah 6:109 Warren
6:164
LOVELL, Elisha 1:22
LOVERIN(G), Abigail 3:115,
-5:107 Abijah 3:114 Anna
3:169 Apphia 4:176 Benjamin
2:70,-3:91,-5:103 Ebenezer
2:68 Elizabeth 3:169 Hannah
2:46,-3:44,90 Isabel C. 7:63
Jesse 3:167 Joseph 2:65
Lucinda 7:26 Mary 3:41 Moses
3:91 Richard 4:179 Samuel
2:65 Thomas 4:34 William
5:103,107
LOVETT (LOVIT), James 1:14,

LOVETT (continued)
-2:101,102,-3:174 John 4:10
LOVEWELL, Mrs. 3:176 Splan
3:174,176
LOWDEN, Anthony 3:83,-4:11
LOW(E), Abigail 6:43 Anna 2:155
Elisha 5:168,185 Elizabeth
2:155 Francis 3:79 Jacob
2:155,156,-5:40 Jeremiah
2:36,156 John 2:102,-5:189
Joseph 5:135,137,139,185,
189,-6:43,169 Lydia 5:135
Mary 1:112,-2:155 Mehitable
2:155 Mrs. 5:135,137,139,185,
189,-6:43 Richard 5:137 Sarah
2:155,156,-5:44
LOWELL, Abigail 5:12 Charles
4:6 Charles R. 4:6 Daniel
5:156,-6:185 David 5:12 Ezra
4:34 James 5:156,159 James
R. 4:6 John 4:6 Lucy 5:12
Mary 4:176,-5:12 Mary T. S.
4:6 Rebecca 4:6 Rebecca R.
4:6 Robert T. S. 4:6 Sarah
5:159 William K. S. 4:6
LOWNEY, William 4:91
LUBEY, Richard 4:34
LUCOMB, William 1:12
LUCY, Alexander 4:125 Caleb
4:177 Elizabeth 2:143 Hannah
4:185 John 3:121 Lucy 3:121
Lydia 7:58 Rachel 4:75 Sarah
3:56 Stephen 3:121,127
Thomas 3:173,-4:78,185
LUD, George 2:186
LUFKIN, Edward 3:44,-6:28,30
Hannah 6:28 John 6:30 Mrs.
6:28
LUNT, Daniel 3:80,-5:113,
135,139,183,187,-6:42 Henry
5:183 John 3:182 Miss 6:95
Mrs. 5:135,139,183,187,-6:95
Robert 5:133 Sarah 5:135
Stephen G. 6:42 Thomas 5:187
Timothy 4:34
LUSTHERS, John 6:152
LUTHER(S), John 6:152
Mehitable 5:144 Nathaniel
5:93,144
LYDSON, Martha 5:43
LYFORD, David 5:72 Edmund F.
5:72 Elizabeth 5:72 Francis

LYFORD (continued)
3:134,138 John 3:169 Love
6:138 Mary 5:72 Mehitable
4:91 Rebecca 3:177 Sarah 5:19
Thomas 5:72
LYMAN, Love 5:152
LYNCH, Patrick 3:19,73
LYNDSEY, Elizabeth 5:184 John
5:184 Mrs. 5:184
LYNN, William 7:18
LYON, Elizabeth 5:44 John 4:2
Lieutenant 5:40 Margaret 4:2
LYSSON, John 2:169
LUX, William 1:10,11
McCANN, Philip 3:19,71
McCLAREY, Andrew 6:166
McCLINTOCK, Eliza Ann 7:80
Elizabeth 7:80 John 7:80
Joseph 3:135 Mr. 5:80,-6:80,
-7:12,13,75 Samuel 2:181,
-3:3,71
McCLURE, James 5:169
McCOLLY, Alexander 6:163
McCONNEL, Samuel 3:28,73
McCOY, Charlotte 4:185 Comfort
4:80 Eliza 7:72 John 3:29,75
McCLUER, Alexander 3:119
McCRILLIS, Anne 6:173 Daniel
6:172 Elizabeth 6:73,114,172
Esther 6:172 Jean 6:70 John
6:35 John C. 6:173 Mary 6:172
Robert 6:71,172,173 Stephen
6:172
McDANIEL(S), Andrew 4:79,128
John 3:169,184 Nancy 4:183
Robert 3:28,73 Sarah D. 6:7,92
William 2:183
McDONALD, James 3:3 Jane
4:182 Lucinda P. 4:81
McDONNEL, Eleanor 5:45
McDOWELL, Edward 4:34 Moses
4:102
MACDUFF, Earl 4:4
McDUFFEE, Abigail 6:39 Anna
5:5 Daniel 5:2 David 5:54
Elizabeth 6:38 Hannah 5:3,
-6:115 Jacob 5:49,-6:117
James 5:3,149,-6:115,117,120
Jane 5:7 Jarvis 7:87 John 5:8,
113,148,-6:37,120 John F. 6:38
Jonathan 5:7 Louisa 6:40
Lydia 5:56 Martha 5:114

McDUFFEE (continued)
Marquis 7:64 Mary 4:145,
-5:116,-6:180,-7:86 Mercy
6:36 Richard 5:151 Samuel
5:150 Sarah 5:3,152,-6:40 Seth
5:152 Susan 6:36 Thomas
5:149 Thomas I. 6:36 William
6:115,116
McDURFEE, Elizabeth 6:119
James 6:119 Mary 4:150
MACE, Abner F. 4:188 Ithamar
2:136 John 2:136,-4:186
Joseph 2:38 Mary 1:59,
-4:65,-5:91 Rachel 2:136
Reuben 1:21 Richard 5:91,129
Sarah 2:36
McELROY, David 4:35
McFARLAND, Asa 6:13,105,161
Elizabeth 7:70 Sarah A. 7:70
Susan K. 7:70
MacFEE, Daniel 6:65 James
6:114 John 6:73,-7:89 Mary
7:89 Sarah 6:75 William
4:146,-6:73,114
MacGAFFEE, Eleanor 3:88
McGILL, Carroll 4:7 Lillie 4:7
Mary C. 4:7 Oliver T. 4:7
Rebecca 4:7 Roberta 4:7
McGLENNEN, Edward W.
3:48,139,189,-6:48
McGOUCH, Sarah 6:35
McHURD, Abigail 3:129
McINTIRE, Benjamin 7:11
Charles 7:12 David 7:24
Eunice 6:80 George W. 6:79
James 3:19,69,74 John 6:42,65
Joseph 6:65,-7:16 Katharine
6:77,-7:14 Mary 6:42,45,77,
79,80,-7:11,12,14,16 Mrs.
5:187,188,-6:45 Neil 5:164,
166,187,188,-6:42,45,77,79,
-7:11,12,14,16 Primus 3:65
Ruth 6:80 Thomas 6:45 Wil-
liam 4:33,93,-5:188,-6:80
McINTOSH, D. C. 5:48
MACKAY, Benjamin 5:167
McKENNEY, Robert 4:10
McKINNON, Charles 4:34
MACKRA, Margaret 3:87
McLAUGHLIN, Lawrence 4:34
MACLAY, Edgar S. 4:27
McLEAN, Sybel 2:42

McLINDON, John 3:66
McMANUS, James 2:38
McMILLAN, Gilbert 7:70
McMILLAR, Mary B. 6:52
McMURPHY, Alexander 3:45
James 6:93 Jane 2:45
McNEAL - McNEIL, Agnes 6:67
Charles 4:35 Daniel 6:67,73
Elizabeth 5:54,-6:113 Hannah
6:71 Hector 4:26,27,30,34 Jean
6:67,68 John 3:86 Malcolm
4:26 Mary 4:26,30,-6:69 Neal
4:26 Robert 4:34
MACOMB, J. M. 7:33
MACOMBER, John 5:141 Mary
5:141 William 5:141
MACPHEADRI (see McPhedris)
MACKPHEDERIS (see
McPhedris)
McPHEDRIS, Archand 2:18 Ar-
chibald 2:103 Hutchinson 5:38
John 4:102 Mary 5:39 Mr. 5:44
Sarah 2:18,-4:102
McPHREDIS (see McPHEDRIS)
McPHERSON, Daniel 5:159,-6:27
John 5:159 Mary 6:27
MACRENE, Margaret 5:112
MACTUER, Mr. 5:79
MACUBBIN, James 4:8 Nicholas
4:6
MAGEE, Katharine 3:86
MAGOON, Alexander 3:44 Ben-
jamin 3:38 David L. 5:22 Ed-
ward 3:131 Elizabeth 3:41
Hannah 2:67,-5:68 John 2:43,
47,131,-3:50,55,-5:68 Joseph
3:44 Mehitable 3:132 Miss S.
B. 5:22 Moses 2:47,-3:44,
-5:68 Sarah 2:46,72,129,
-3:87,-5:68
MAHARY, Thomas 2:184
MAHONEY, Michael 5:152
MAIN, Abigail 5:151,-6:68 Amos
4:145,-6:65,113,-7:86 Charles
E. 3:94 Elizabeth 5:149,-6:69
Hannah 6:66 Irene 7:54 Jacob
7:28 Josiah 5:54 Lucinda 7:54
Lydia 6:65 Lydia W. 6:34
Mary 4:146,-5:152 Mercy 6:69
Meribah A. 6:40 Stephen 7:54
Susan 6:39 Warren W. 7:54
William 7:54

MAKER, John 4:191 Mary 4:191
Reuben 4:191
MALLARD, Martha 7:61
MALOON, Abigail 4:99 Elizabeth
3:170 Jane 4:99
MANAHAN, Joseph 7:65
MANLEY, John 4:26-29,37
MANN, Anne 4:53 Benjamin 5:136
Edward 4:58 Elizabeth 5:184,
-6:80,-7:13,79 Emily 6:163
George Gains 7:13 Hannah 6:77
John 6:42,-7:79 Joseph 7:79
Mark 6:80 Mary 4:52 Mehitable
6:44 Mrs. 5:134,136,139,184,
187,-6:42,44,77,78 Patience
6:44 Peter 5:133,134,136,139,
184,187,-6:42,44,77,78,80,
-7:13 Sarah 5:134 Thomas 6:78
William 5:187
MANNING, Mary J. 5:35 Thomas
2:177,181,-3:71,-5:162,163,
165,166
MANSFIELD, Isaac 2:120 Mr.
6:80,-7:13 Roscoe 5:41 Widow
2:24
MANUEL, Sarah 6:52 Susanna
6:57
MARBLE, Abigail 1:111 Charles
3:161 Coker 3:164 Hannah
2:117,118 Isaac 5:161 James
4:72 John 3:161 Joseph H. 4:72
Joshua W. 4:72 Mary 3:161,
-4:45 Mary M. 4:72 Samuel
1:111,-4:72,93
MARCH, ---- 7:80 Caroline 7:87
Clement 1:15,-5:91,131,133,
135,137,140,185 Daniel 5:137
Eliza W. 6:36 Elizabeth
5:131,185,-7:75 Emily 7:87
Emily J. 6:38 Esther 5:134
Hannah 5:131,188,-6:35 Henry
5:89 Hugh 3:82 James 3:145
John 2:45,70,130,-3:38,81,
-5:86,105,107,111,135,154,
-6:30,-7:75,77,78,80 Jonas C.
5:50,140,148,-6:34,-7:85
Joseph 4:71,-5:87 Katharine
7:80 Lydia 7:85 Major 3:85,99
Margaret 2:130,-5:133 Maria
6:30 Mary 1:15,-2:70,71,
-5:86,91,130,134,136,137,188,
-7:75 Mehitable 5:111 Meriah

77

MARCH (continued)
5:154 Mrs. 5:135,137,140,185
Nathaniel 5:137,-7:75
Nathaniel Jackson 7:78
Nathaniel P. 5:91 Paul 5:86,
87,89,91,130-134,136,137,188
Reverend 5:109 Samuel 2:70,
-3:88 Sarah 4:71,-5:91,133,
-6:95 Sarah A. 6:38 Sarah Ann
7:87 Stephen 2:121,-5:107
MARDEN, Abial 1:89,-2:135
Abigail 1:38,45,46,82,87,
132,135 Abraham W. 6:63
Ahipzabah 1:129 Alice 4:97
Anna 1:95 Anna B. 1:143 Benjamin 1:46,85,87-89,91,95,96,
134,-2:135,-4:103,104,-6:112
Benjamin W. 1:141 Charity
1:46,87 Charles F. 6:48 Daniel
1:134,-2:137,-6:109 Dorcas
1:24,45,95 Ebenezer 1:45,82,
83,134 Elizabeth 1:46,82,87,
89,95,134,135,-2:36 Elizabeth
M. 1:135 Esther 1:45,82,83,134
George 1:82 Hannah 1:38,46,
83,95,132,134,143,-2:137,
-5:69,-7:80 Hepzibeth 1:44,45,
81,83,95,-2:36 Hinkson 6:172
James 1:37,38,82,83,87,132,
134,135,-2:138,-4:151,-6:172
John 1:10,13,37,81,83,96,
-4:135,-5:11,69,-6:70,172,
-7:57 Jonathan 1:24,44,81,83,
95,96,134 Jonathan T. 1:95
Joseph 1:44,134 Joseph W.
2:165 Judah 1:37,38 Judith
1:87,132 Kezia 1:95 Lavina
1:135 Lois 6:172 Lucinda 5:19
Lucy 1:134 Lydia 6:70,113,
-7:66 Margaret 1:96,129 Mark
7:71 Mary 1:24,37,45,46,82,
83,92,96,134,-2:138,-3:183
Mehitable 1:96 Mr. 4:99 Nancy
1:141 Nancy T. 1:134 Nathan
1:37 Nathaniel 1:44,81,82,95,
134,135,143 Noah 4:101 Olive
1:87,134,-4:88 Phebe 1:45,46
Polly 7:80 Polly Wendell 7:80
Prudence P. 1:95 Rachel 1:85,
87-89,91,-2:135 Rebecca 1:95,
96,134 Reuben 1:134,143
Rhoda 1:135 Ruth 1:46 Samuel

MARDEN (continued)
1:24,45,46,83,95,98,129,141,
-2:137 Samuel, 3rd 7:70
Samuel H. 1:134 Sarah 1:45,46,
81,132,135,-2:135,137,-4:183,
-5:11,69 Simon 6:37 Solomon
D. 1:85 Stephen 1:46,88
Thomas 1:92 Timothy 1:44
William 1:22,24,38,87,89,
95,96,132,-2:138,-5:150,-7:80
MARIE, Jean 3:67,75
MARION, Joseph 3:69,75
MARKES, Colonel 5:75
MARRETT, Avery 3:186 Eliza-
beth B. 3:186 Mary E. 3:186
MARRIFIELD, William 4:13
MARRINER, George 2:170 Mary
3:2
MARSH, Aaron C. 6:36 Gilman
4:89 Hannah 3:171 James 3:41
John 3:133,-6:154,-7:37,39
Mary A. 5:36 Matthew S. 2:162
Mr. 6:80 Nicholas 3:136 Susan
5:22
MARSHALL, Abigail 4:188 Com-
fort 4:188,-5:95 Elizabeth
2:19,-3:181,-4:50,56,58,-5:40,
44 Gideon 5:163 Hawley 1:25,
-3:177 Henry 1:25 Hipsibah
(Hepsibah) 3:133 James 2:165
Jane 4:101 Joanna 1:25 John
1:22,25,-2:174,-4:99 Joseph
1:25 Margaret 1:25 Martha 1:25
Mary 1:25,-4:178 Mary Ann
7:62 Nathaniel 1:25,-4:56
Obadiah 2:19 Thomas 1:21
William 5:20
MARSTES, Elizabeth 6:5 John 6:5
Mary 6:5
MARSTON, ---- 13 Abigail
2:111,-3:93 Betsey Coffin 7:16
Caleb 2:85,110 Comfort 6:137
David 4:131 Elizabeth 2:110,
111 Ephraim 2:82 Hannah 1:40,
-2:84,-4:20,21 Isaac 2:110,
111,-6:62 Jacob 2:85 James
2:84,-4:94,-6:138 Jemima
6:137 Jeremiah 2:192,-3:41,
-4:91 John 2:83,85,87,88,-6:62
John Caverly 7:77 Joseph 1:40,
-2:88 Joseph B. 7:71 Joseph S.
4:117 Lemuel 7:13,16,75,77

MARSTON (continued)
Lucy 2:90 Lydia 3:119,-6:61
Maria 2:109 Martha 2:83,85,
87,88 Mary 2:82-85,88,91,174
Nancy 4:86 Noah 3:164
Rebecca 2:84,85,88,90,105,109
Sabina 2:89 Sally 7:75 Samuel
2:88 Sarah 2:87,91,-4:94
Thomas 2:82,84,85,88,91
Thomas Meed 7:13 Triphena
2:89 William 2:84,85,88-
90,105,109
MARTH, Isaac 1:22
MARTHAN, Anne 3:43
MARTIN, Abra F. 5:189 Anna
5:86 Betsey 7:15 Catherine
1:112 Dan 1:104 Daniel 6:105
David 1:112 Dorothy 1:150,
-2:75,146 Edward 1:21,-2:36
Elizabeth 1:150 Elizabeth A.
5:181 Esther 6:56,-7:22 George
4:46 Hannah 6:42,107 Henry
7:22 Henry J. 4:195 Henry, 3d
7:18 Isaac 1:112,-6:43 Isabel
4:46 Jane 1:112,-4:55,58,-5:91
Jeremiah 7:21 Joanna 4:192
John 1:22,146,150,179,-2:37,
-4:192,-5:86,91,135,189,-6:43,
44 Jonathan 3:129,-4:175
Joseph 5:44 Kezia 4:102 Martha 3:50 Mary 3:50,51,56,88,
-4:14,191,192,-6:161 Mary
Bateman 7:12 Melinda 5:19
Mercy 4:192 Michael 2:173,
-4:14,-5:38,-6:178 Miles R.
2:165 Miriam 4:174 Miss
1:80,-5:44 Mr. 3:169 Mrs.
3:174,-5:135,189,-6:43 Mrs.
M. 3:51 Nathaniel L. 5:135
Peter L. 6:76 Priscilla 5:188,
-6:42,44,76,79,-7:12,15
Richard 1:10,12,-2:97,99,100,
-3:49-51,81,172,173,-4:46,
192,-5:131 Robert 4:191
Rosanna 1:112 Ruth 3:45 Sarah
4:177 Thomas 5:163,167 William 4:14,-5:188,-6:42,44,
76,79,-7:12,15
MASCALL, Stephen, Jr. 7:26
MASCOTT, Joseph 4:35
MASEY, Bethia 4:58 Mr. 4:58
Mrs. 4:58

MASH, Anna 6:137
MASON, Abigail 6:138 Albert C.
3:143,-4:192,-5:47,93 Anna
2:114,-6:137 Benjamin
1:187,-2:15 Captain 6:99
Catherine 2:76,79 Daniel
1:184,-2:122 Edward 2:42,122
Elizabeth 2:112-114,-4:12,
-6:136 Eunice 6:59 Hannah
1:184,187 Jeremiah 2:113 John
1:187,-2:112,114,191 Jonathan
2:113 Joseph 1:187,-2:15,113,
114 Lemuel 5:2 Levi 2:114
Martha 2:114 Mary 1:52,-2:15,
113,127 Mercy 1:183,187 Mr.
2:24 Nicholas 1:184,-3:17
Patience 1:52,-2:127 Peter
1:52,-2:127 Robert 3:1
Sampson 4:191 Samuel 6:62
Sarah 2:114 Shuah 2:114
Simeon 2:114 Susanna 3:4
MASTERMAN, James 4:34
MASTERS, Mary 6:152
MATHES, Abigail 1:154 Abigail
C. 1:103,106,154 Abraham
1:102,106,-4:78 Benjamin
1:106,110,111,159,-4:77,-7:45
Betsey 2:136 Daniel 1:102,103,
106,110,111,154,-4:79 Dorothy
1:102 Elijah 1:110 Elizabeth
1:110 Francis 1:110 Jacob
1:110,111 Jeremiah M. 1:154
Jessie I. 4:186 Joanna 1:110
John 1:106,110,111 Joseph
1:110,111 Lois 6:155 Lydia
1:110 Mary A. 1:154 Mr. 1:106
Phebe 5:51 Reuben 4:188
Robert 1:106,-5:50,114 Ruth
1:110,-4:79 Samuel 4:127,182,
-7:58 Sarah F. 1:154 Susan
1:155 Thomas 1:110 Valentine
1:102,106,154
MATTHEWS, Benjamin 2:174
Elizabeth 4:56 Francis 2:168
Harriet L. 1:111 John 3:181,
-5:162,164 Joseph 5:40 Miss
4:56 Mrs. 1:178 Peter 1:21
William S. 5:85
MATTOON(E), Hurbertas 3:147,
173 Mr. 1:12 Mrs. 3:51 Richard
3:147 Robert 1:10,-2:28
MAULE, Margaret 2:80

79

MAULINTOCK (see McCLIN-
TOCK)
MAUTIMORA, Mr. 11,12,14,16
MAVERY, Thomas 1:22
MAXEY, Hervey 4:175
MAXFIELD, Stephen 3:181
MAXWELL, Peter 3:69,76
MAY, Abigail 6:23 Elizabeth
1:173,176 Hannah O. 6:121
James 1:173,176 Lillian P.
6:23 Naomi 1:176,-6:127
Samuel P. 1:80,110 William
1:173
MAYNARD, John H. 7:70
MAYO, Augustus 7:15 Widow
7:15
MEAD, Benjamin 1:189 Elizabeth
4:54 Hannah 1:189,-5:186
James 6:41 Jeremy 6:155 John
1:189,-2:50,-5:40,-6:140
Joseph 1:182,189,-2:50,
-5:42,135,139,186,-6:41,144
Lettice 5:139 Lydia 5:44 Margaret F. 6:155,159,-7:39 Mary
6:155 Mrs. 5:135,186,-6:41
Sarah 2:175,-5:135,-6:137
Stephen 2:81 Susanna 1:189,
-6:144 Thomas 1:189,-2:33
MEADER, Abby V. 6:124 Abigail
1:127,128,164,-2:145,-4:66,
-5:63,122,-6:23,36,125 Albert
O. 6:124 Amanda 6:22 Anna
1:128,-5:26,176 Anne 4:66 Asa
5:25,-6:22 Benjamin 1:62,126,
163,164,-2:128,145,-4:121,
-6:22 Benjamin H. 6:181
Caroline 6:21,23 Charity 3:5,
-5:3 Charles 6:83 Charles H.
6:181 Content 1:173 Daniel
1:52,60,62,65,68,122,174,
-2:145,-5:32,-6:21,23,123,125
David 1:162,-4:39 Deborah V.
6:36 Deliverance 6:22 Edward
E. 6:85 Eleanor 1:52,-2:127,
145 Eli 2:29,-6:21,125,127
Elijah 2:145,-5:24,25 Elizabeth 1:60,62,65,68,122,165,
-2:78,-5:26,123,-6:23,122
Elizabeth Ann 7:60 Elizabeth
H. 6:85 Enos 5:122 Ephraim
2:30,-4:121 Eunice V. 6:83
Ezekiel 5:123 Ezra 5:122

MEADER (continued)
Francis 4:66,-5:50,-6:122
George 1:32,97 George E.
6:181 Hannah 1:126,128,152,
174,-2:29,-4:121,-5:64,175,
-6:17,23 Hannah E. 7:60 Hanson 2:31,-4:121,-6:22,125 Harriet 6:83 Henry H. 2:79 James
6:22 James J. 2:79 Jedediah
1:174,-2:29,145,-4:160,-5:26,
-6:125 Joanna 2:30 Joel
1:162,-4:70 John 1:164,
-4:42,126,-5:122,-6:124,136
John E. 6:181 John F. 6:22
John G. 7:71 John H. 2:30
Jonathan 1:171,-2:145,-4:44,
-5:32,-6:22,125 Joseph 1:60,
65,97,118,122,126,128,164,
-2:126,145,-3:8,-4:43,67,161,
-5:61,63,118,122,128,-6:23,40,
184 Joshua 5:29,64 Judith
1:163,-4:66,121,-6:21 Julia E.
6:181 Lemuel 1:166,-2:145,
-4:66,-5:53 Levi 5:24,-6:22,
125,181 Lois 4:66 Louisa
3:178 Lydia 1:171,-5:32,122,
-6:89,182,-7:4 Lydia A. 1:173,
-6:90 Lydia B. 2:29 Margaret
5:4 Maria 6:21 Martha 1:118
Mary 1:126,128,163,165,169,
-4:121,-5:64,-6:23 Mary G.
6:155 Mehitable 5:122,
-6:22,181 Mehitable S. 2:29
Meserve 4:126 Micah 5:29
Micajah 4:121 Miriam 3:126,
-4:66 Moses 2:80,-6:23
Moses, Jr. 7:4 Nathan 3:34,-
5:24 Nathaniel 1:52,68,128,
165,169,-2:145,-3:101,-5:25,
26,-6:85,125 Nicholas 4:39 Olney T. 2:31,-6:124,125 Otis
1:169,-5:25,26,-6:83,125
Patience 1:126,163,164 Phoebe
H. 2:79,-6:22 Ruth 1:97,
-5:32,-7:51 Sarah 1:162,166,
-2:29,30,-3:5,-6:22,122,125
Sarah F. 6:181 Sophia 6:23
Stephen 1:164,-2:29,-4:121,
-6:22 Stephen C. 6:181 Susan
L. 2:31,-6:22,85 Timothy 5:32
Tobias 2:79,-4:121,-6:22
Valentine 2:30,-5:64 Valentine

80

MEADER (continued)
E. 6:181 William 7:60 Wil-
liam F. 6:124 Winthrop M.
6:85
MEEDS, Stephen 3:71
MEHANEY, Jeremiah 4:34
MELCHER, Edward 1:10,12,
-3:173,-7:78,80 Elizabeth 4:54
John 4:56,-7:76 Maria 7:76
Mary 4:10 Mary Ann 7:78
Nathaniel 5:90 Sukey Ham 7:80
MELONY, Daniel 3:29,72
MELOON, Abraham 2:36 Ben-
jamin 2:36 Enoch 11,13,15,74,
75,77,78 Jane 2:35 John 3:109
Joseph 7:78 Lucy 7:75,77 Mar-
garet 7:11 Mary 3:108,109,
-7:74,75,77,78 Miss 1:92
Nathaniel 3:90 Olive 7:74
Peggy 7:15 Polly Libbey 7:13
Samuel 3:108,109 Sarah 2:38
MENDEZ, Cajar 5:166
MENDUM, Abigail 7:13 Ann 7:13
Charlotte 7:73 David 5:87,130
Elizabeth 5:186 Hannah 5:186,
-6:80 John 5:186,189,-6:45,
78,80,-7:13,73,74 Margaret
6:78 Mary 6:80 Mrs. 5:186,189
Nathaniel 2:103,157,-5:130,
-6:80 Phebe 6:80 Sarah 5:189,
-6:80 Susanna(h) 6:45,78,
-7:13,73,74 William 3:23,75
MENGUY, Pierre 3:69,76
MEREEN, John 4:45,92
MERRIAM, Delia Jane 7:87 Mat-
thew 7:87 Mr. 6:117
MERRILL, Abigail 2:52,-4:137,
-6:53 Alice 6:54 Ann 2:52 Ap-
phia 3:91 Asa 3:128,-4:118
Benjamin 4:136 Cassandra
7:55 Dorcas 6:52 Dorothy 3:128
Elias 2:52 Eliphalet 3:126
Eliza 3:183 Elizabeth 3:128
Enoch 2:52,53 Esther 2:9 Ford
3:128 Francis 6:166,178 Han-
nah 3:131,171 James 2:122,
-3:128 Joanna 4:75 John 4:177,
-6:10 Joseph 2:9,52,122
Joseph A. 6:63 Levi 2:52
Lucretia 3:128 Lydia 2:9,51,52
Mary 2:52,-3:128,-6:106 Mary
A. 3:161 Mehitable 2:53,-7:25

MERRILL (continued)
Nancy 3:126,-4:176 Nathan 3:38
Nathan 3:38 Nathan L. 5:35
Nathaniel 6:50 P. 3:11,126,
127,164 Paul 2:52 Phebe 2:52,
-3:161 Phineas 3:161,164
Rosette Jane 7:71 Samuel
2:53,-6:57 Sarah 2:52,53,66,
-3:128 Sarah J. 3:161 Susanna
2:52 Thomas 2:52 Wiggins
2:52 William 4:180
MERRITT, Elias 1:186 Esther
1:186 John 3:22,73 Joseph
1:186 Noah 4:45
MERROW, Esther 5:2 Joshua 5:4
MERRY, Abigail 2:88,-6:66 Bathsheba 2:90 Benjamin 6:66,70,
71,74 Daniel 6:74 Elizabeth
2:87,88,90,107 Hannah 2:87,
-6:73 John 6:71 Joseph 2:82,
87-90,107,-6:66 Mary 2:82,
-6:66 Moses 6:114 Samuel
2:107,-6:66
MESCHINET, John 4:34
MESERVE, Abigail 5:53 Andrew
6:108 Anna 2:176 Clement
2:170,-3:60,61,108,174,176,
-4:12 Colonel 5:130 Daniel
4:80 Ebenezer 7:37 Elizabeth
2:170,-3:60,61,-4:10,-5:131,
133 Esther 5:134,137 George
3:61,-5:88,130,131,134,137
Hannah 4:187 Henry 2:181,
-5:88 Jane 1:14,-5:133 John
2:45,-3:108,-5:117 John S.
7:43 Joseph 3:61,-5:129,130,
133 Mary 5:49,50,129 Mary E.
6:160 Mrs. 3:108,176,-5:133
Nathaniel 1:14,-3:6,64,-5:88,
90,129,133,-6:164 Peter 3:61
Philip 4:34 Samuel 4:77,78
Sarah 4:77,-5:90,134 Stephen
5:120 Tamson 3:102 W. S.
3:102
MESSER, Francis 2:17 Mary B.
6:63 Nathaniel 7:28 Sarah A.
W. 6:63 William 6:164,-7:28
MESSUERE, Peter 3:24,72
METCALF, Alfred 6:156
MEZEET, Isaac 3:3
MIDDLETON, Joseph 3:130
MIGHILL(S), Dorothy 6:72 George

MIGHILL(S) (continued)
    4:80 John 3:180,-6:74 Moses
    5:3,-6:74 Samuel 3:147
MILES, Elizabeth 6:156 Sarah A.
    6:93
MILLEN, Mr. 4:30
MILLER, Abigail 2:173,175,
    -5:183 Alice 4:99,-5:73 Anne
    4:98,-5:133 Anne E. 6:42 Ben-
    jamin 2:103,-4:101,157,-5:87,
    -6:42,44,76,78,80,-7:13,15
    Bridget 4:50 Elizabeth 4:101,
    -5:137 Elizabeth H. 4:156 Es-
    ther 6:80 Hannah 2:170,-4:98,
    -5:185,-6:44,78 Isaac 6:68
    Jean 6:68 Jeremiah 4:98 John
    4:98,-6:44,-7:22 Joseph 4:98,
    101,-7:15 Lydia 4:101,-5:89
    Margaret 3:5,-4:98 Mark 3:4,
    -4:156,157,-5:73 Martha 3:44,
    -4:12 Mary 4:81,101,-5:86,
    -6:78 Moses 4:104,-5:86,87,
    89,131,133,135,137,183,185,
    -6:76,-7:13 Mrs. 3:57,-5:135,
    137,183,185,-6:42,44,76,80
    Nicholas 5:135 Nicholas H.
    4:157 Patty 7:13 Peter 4:102
    Robert 4:192 Samuel 6:76
    Sarah 4:101,-5:87,-6:75
    Susanna 4:98,156,157,-5:73
    William 3:115,-4:104
MILLET, Lydia 1:98 Susanna
    1:101 Thomas 1:98,101
MILLS, Bethia 4:54 Captain 5:89
    Catherine G. 7:69 Charles 7:67
    Deborah 3:7,-4:157 Elizabeth
    5:4,-6:174 George 7:25 Jacob
    5:132,135,138,184 James 6:174
    Jeremy 6:174 John 2:187,
    -3:19,74,-6:174 Joseph 5:184
    Luke 3:4 Mary 4:77,-5:132,
    -6:174 Mrs. 5:135,138,184
    Peter 3:174 Richard 3:22,30
    Samuel 6:174 Susanna 5:135
    William 5:89
MILNE, John 4:34
MILTIMORE, J. 2:21 James
    3:126,127 Mr. 6:136
MITCHELL, Alanson 7:69 Anna
    6:80 Caleb 6:80 Christopher
    5:43 George 4:34 Jean 3:67
    John 4:34,-5:187 Joseph 4:34

MITCHELL (continued)
    Joshua 4:34 Mary 5:41 Mr.
    5:187 Mrs. 6:80 Nelson 5:102
    S. 1:159 Sarah 1:157,159,-6:52
    Stephen 1:157 Thomas 1:22
MITTON, Mary 5:98
MIXER, Charles T. 7:67
MOCARD, Miss 4:4
MOFFATT, Catherine 1:19 John
    1:19,-2:104,157,-5:45,185
    Mary T. 5:187 Mrs. 5:185,187
    Samuel 5:185,187
MOGRIDGE, Miss 5:42 Mr. 5:40
MONCTON, General 4:27
MONNETTE, Orra E. 5:143
MONROE, Hannah 1:157 Mary
    1:157
MONTGOMERY, Ellen D. 7:65
MOODY, Abigail 1:190,-2:70,
    -3:41,79,88 Alice 2:47,94
    Andrew 7:25 Ann 3:49 Anna 5:2
    Clement 3:90 Daniel 1:186,
    190,191,-2:47,70,94,-3:86,90
    David 2:45,70,-3:38,-5:104,
    107,110,153 Dorothy 3:89
    Elizabeth 1:186,-3:40 Esther
    3:54,90 George W. 7:70 Han-
    nah 1:105,191,-3:181 Jane 2:72
    Joanna 2:45,-3:42 John 2:47,
    70,94,-3:44,-5:22,104 Joseph
    2:171,-3:3,41,135 Joshua
    1:186,-3:49,54,77,84,-5:84
    Lydia 2:70,90 Martha 3:49,
    51,77 Mary 1:186,190,191,
    -2:70,-5:110 Mary Jane 7:70
    Mr. 1:11-13,-3:151 Mrs. 3:174
    Philip 2:43,47,70,94,-3:38
    Samuel 1:25,27,-3:54,88,177,
    -4:35,93 Sarah 1:191,-2:70,
    -3:43,44,77,-4:190,-5:107
    William 3:153
MOONEY, Abigail 4:80 Clarissa
    7:68 Daniel M. 6:39 Dorothy
    1:103 Jeremiah B. 1:103
    Samuel 6:107
MOOR(E), Abigail 6:151 Agnes
    1:184,185 Ann 1:184,-6:151
    Anna 1:185,-6:52 Anne 1:83
    Benjamin F. 4:115 Comfort
    6:151,-7:65 Eleanor 6:151
    Elizabeth 1:184,185,-4:55,104
    Elsie 6:54 Ezekiel 6:54

82

MOOR(E) (continued)
Hannah 1:185 Henry 2:182,
-5:170 Henry M. 7:22 Henry E.
7:65 Howard P. 2:94 John
1:184,185,-2:94,-3:119,-6:151
John W. 7:66 Jonathan 4:58
Lazarus 2:172 Lydia 1:185
Martha 1:185 Mary 1:185,
-6:52,-7:21 Mr. 4:57 Mrs. 7:76
Rachel 1:184,185 Robert 2:184
Samuel 4:46,54,55,94,102,
-6:109 Sarah 4:101,-5:7 Sophia
4:116 Sophronia 7:23 Taylor
1:185 Thomas 1:184,185
Widow 5:90 William 1:83,184,
185,-2:189 William, Jr. 7:68
MORDENT, Eleanor 2:35
Elizabeth 2:35
MORDOCK (Murdock?), Letus
2:169
MORDOUGH, James 5:56 Nathan
3:93 Robert 3:93
MOREAU, Jack 3:26
MOREY, Caleb 6:52 Eleanor 6:29
Elizabeth 1:86,-5:157 Joseph
5:155,-6:26 Samuel 1:86 Sarah
6:32 Susanna 1:86 William
3:42,-5:155,157,-6:26,29,32
MORGAN, Abigail 1:191 Abraham
1:192 Abram 1:191,192 Amos
6:169 Charity 1:192 Damaris
1:191,192 James 6:165
Jeremiah 6:169 Jesse 7:22
John 2:66,69,132,133,187,
-3:72,-4:34,-5:104,106,107,157
Jonathan T. 6:26 Joseph 5:106
Judith 3:131 Luther 2:66 Mar-
tha 6:112 Mary 1:191,-3:42
Nathaniel 2:66 Parker 2:66,
133,-5:104 Paul 5:157,-6:26
Priscilla M. 7:70 Rebecca
2:69,-3:88 Rhoda 5:107
Richard 1:192 Robert 1:191
Thomas 4:34 Timothy 6:40
Trueworth(y) 6:166
MORIN, Guilleaume (William)
3:67,75
MORRILL, Aaron 3:41 Abigail
1:62,66,-2:130,-3:32,-4:44,86,
121,162,-5:23,-6:98 Abra
3:118,-4:91 Abra B. 6:93
Abraham 1:62,66,-3:32,

MORRILL (continued)
-4:86,121,162,-5:23,-6:98 Adah
4:12 Amelia 1:35 Ann M. 7:67
Anna 1:62,66,124,-2:149,-3:40,
-4:137,-5:14,23,173 Anne 1:64,
67 Apphia 6:28 Archelaus 5:23
Benjamin 1:33,42,-2:66,130,
-5:103 Benjamin, Jr. 7:23
Benoni 5:11 Comfort 5:23,27,
31,121 Content 1:125,-4:161,
-5:175 David 1:125,162,
-2:149,-4:161 David L. 5:14
Dorothy 3:113 Elijah 5:12
Eliza Jane 7:67 Elizabeth
1:161,-4:161,-5:31,-6:20,48
Enoch 4:44 Ephraim 1:62,
-3:43,-5:23,-6:20 Esther 4:161
Francis 6:166 Gilman 7:71
Hannah 1:53,56,62,128,161,
-2:66,145,-3:118,-4:38,85,132,
171,-5:31 Hannah B. 6:93 Harriet 7:59 Henry 3:40,-5:109,
111,154,157,-6:28,32 Hope
5:31 Isaac 3:6 Isaac B. 3:114
Jacob 2:44,65,131,149,-3:43,
181,-4:44,171 James 4:161
Jedediah 1:53,62,64,66,67,
119,-2:80,-3:31,32,-4:120,
-5:23,123 Joel S. 7:68 John
1:53,55,56,59,62,119,-2:65,
145,149,-3:44,-4:11,135,161,
-5:123,-6:27,32 John W.
3:118,-6:92,93 Jonathan
2:149,-4:161 Joseph 1:33,34,
42,183,187 Josiah 1:64,
-3:32,-4:124,-5:23 Judith 4:44
Kezia 2:145 Lavinia 5:31 Levi
1:34,-4:133,171 Lydia 1:128,
-3:133,-4:161,171,-5:31,-6:18
Marcellus 6:165 Martha 4:47
Mary 1:187,-2:145,-3:43,51,94,
132,-4:44,171,174,-5:9,11,12,
109,-6:20,32 Mehitable 5:24,
-6:27 Mercy 4:161 Miriam
1:55,-2:145,-3:34,-4:133,171,
-5:154,-6:32 Moses 2:68 Mrs.
2:131,-4:168 Nathan 5:23
Nathaniel 1:33-35,-3:118,136
Oliver 3:118 Parker 3:169
Patience 4:161 Peace 1:59,
-2:145,-4:44,-6:85 Peaslee
2:149 Pelatiah 2:145 Peter

MORRILL (continued)
1:62,128,161,-2:149,-4:44,
-5:31,-7:7 Priscilla H. 7:72
Rebecca 5:23 Rhoda 3:136
Ruth 1:55,56,59,62,-2:149,
-4:161 Samuel 3:181,-4:44,
137,-5:14,-6:57,107 Sarah
1:33-35,62,119,125,128,162,
-2:149,-3:129,152,170,-4:11,
44,161,-5:18,31,103,-6:18,178
Sarah K. 7:65 Stephen 2:149,
-4:44,-5:18 Susanna 1:124,162,
-2:145,-4:161,-5:111 Tabitha
1:33,34,42 Thaddeus 4:161
Theodate 5:31 Theophilus 1:34
Thomas 2:149,-4:44 William
3:134,-4:168,171,-5:9,11,12,
-6:34 William P. 2:145
Winthrop 1:67,124,162,-3:32,
-5:23
MORRIS, Thomas 3:149 William
1:9,-2:64
MORRISON, Abigail 5:66,-6:170
Agnes 5:68 Alexander 1:131
Anna 2:10,3:166 Bradbury 5:66
Daniel 2:11,-5:110 David 5:3,
-7:24 Ebenezer 2:10,-5:68
Ebenezer 5:66,68 Hannah 5:45
Joel 4:183 John 4:129,-5:66,
-6:174 Jonathan 5:66,67,116,
-6:172,174 Joseph 5:135 Lydia
5:66 Mary 1:131,-5:66,137
Miriam 5:66 Mrs. 5:135,137
Rachel 1:94,-5:130 Robert
5:133 Samuel 6:173 Sarah
5:66,-6:156,172 Susanna 5:67
William 5:130,133,135,137
MORSE, Abigail 3:131,-6:108 Anthony 4:190 Benjamin 3:54,
-4:190,-6:55 Charles 3:74
Daniel 3:133,-6:106 Ebenezer
3:169,184 Elizabeth 3:50,56,
143,-4:190 Ezekiel 4:134 Fred
W. 3:48 Hannah 3:53,169 Hugh
4:190 John 2:144,-4:127
Joseph Calef 7:21 Joshua
6:105,168 Levi 7:24 Lydia 3:53
Lyman 7:56 Mary 3:51,52
-4:11,190,-6:95 Mr. 3:173 Mrs.
3:174 Obadiah 2:101,-3:50,
53-55,-4:49 Philip 2:45 Rachel
6:110 Ruth 6:95 Ruth S. 4:190

MORSE (continued)
St. Luke 7:21 Samuel 3:143,
-4:190 Samuel F. B. 7:17
Sarah 3:143,-4:190,-6:160
MORTON, Bryant 5:171,-6:184
Elizabeth 5:171 Ephraim 5:143
George 5:171 James 5:171
Joanna 6:3 Love 5:171
Nathaniel 6:3 Thomas 5:171
William 5:171
MOSES, Aaron 3:173,175 Abigail
4:104 Ann 5:89 Benjamin 5:90,
130,132,135,138,184,187
Daniel 5:132 Elijah 6:166
Elizabeth 4:184,186,-5:130,
-7:74 Esther 5:184 George
5:86,88,89,91,134 James 5:42
John 1:4,9,13,-2:23,-7:74 John
M. 2:93,-3:45,48 Joseph 4:97,
-5:90 Katharine 5:131,187 Levi
2:164 Lydia 7:75 Margaret
5:138 Mary 2:175,-4:102,-7:75
Miss 5:40 Mrs. 3:175,-5:135,
138,184,187 Nathaniel 5:131,
134 Nehemiah 2:164 Rebecca
4:97 Robert 4:100 Samuel 4:53
Sarah 4:52,-5:135 Sergeant
3:173 Susanna 5:132 Sylvanus
6:51 Thomas 7:74,75 Timothy
4:184 W. 3:56 William 5:132,
-7:75
MOSLEY, Jonathan 3:179
MOSS, Joseph 1:10,11 Obadiah
1:12
MOTTE, Nathaniel 2:37
MOULTON, Abigail 1:16,-2:91,
-4:98,102 Abra 4:77 Alice 4:99
Anne 1:87,-2:81,82 Bar-
tholomew 4:34 Benjamin 4:117
Bethiah 1:33 Charles C. 5:22
Daniel 1:11,35,42,47,-2:19,
82,111 Edward A. 6:49
Elizabeth 1:35,36,85,86 Flora
G. 2:96,166,-3:48,-4:48,-5:144
Hannah 1:86,89,-2:83,-3:44,
-6:111 Henry 2:83,84,86,88,
89,91,-6:58 Henry, Jr. 7:26
James 6:58,104 James, Jr.
7:24 Jeremiah 7:56 John 1:16,
-2:81,82,86,92,107,109,111,
174,-4:98,104 Jonathan 1:35,
36,41,85,86,89,-2:89,-6:54

MOULTON (continued)
Jonathan B. 5:22 Joseph
1:16,33,-2:84,103,104,-4:98,
116,-5:40 Josiah 2:88 Lucy
1:85,86,-2:19 Lydia 1:42,
-2:92,107,109,111 Margaret
2:84,86,88,90 Martha 2:81-
83,92 Mary 1:47,-6:57 Miriam
2:83 Mr. 3:84 Nathan 1:42,
-4:118 Nehemiah 1:87
Patience 3:64 Phebe 1:42,47
Reuben 1:35,86,89 Robert 1:36,
2:88 Ruth 2:82,86 Samuel P.
5:182,-6:6 Sarah 1:42,87,-2:84
Simeon 6:138 Sobriety 2:83,84,
86,88,89,91 Stephen 6:138
Thomas 2:81-83 William 2:84,
86,88,90
MT. EDGCUMBE, The Earl of
1:109
MOUNTFORD, Timothy 5:170
MOWAT, Edward 4:3
MOW(E), Dorcas 1:85,87
Elizabeth 4:103 Ephraim 1:85,
87 Hannah 1:87 Mary 1:85
Miss 5:39 Mrs. 4:104 Peter
3:55,-4:51 Sarah 1:85
MUCHMORE, Joseph 2:182,-3:71
MUDGE, Miss 6:83 Mr. 5:61
MUDGETT, Abigail 4:134 Hannah
4:91 John 3:43 Richard 6:185
Sarah 2:41 Susanna 3:86
Thomas 3:43
MUGFORD, William 4:35
MUGRIDGE (MUGGRIGE), John
4:181 Samuel 3:90
MUIR, Samuel 5:116
MULLALY, William 3:2
MULLEAHEY, Michael 4:34
MULLING, William 4:35
MUNCHOR, Daniel 3:21,74
MUNDEN, Elizabeth 4:9
MUNDRO, Elizabeth 4:145
MUNROE, William 4:34
MUNSEY, David 4:45 Francis
3:93 John 2:190,-4:45 Margaret
2:190,-3:152,-4:45 Mary 4:45
Timothy 4:45 William 3:93,
-4:11,45
MUNSON, Abigail 3:143 Esther
3:143 Ezra 3:142 James 3:143
John 3:143,-4:190,191 Joseph

MUNSON (continued)
3:143,-4:190,191 Mary 4:104
Mindwell 3:143 Mr. 3:50 Mrs.
3:56,175 Richard 1:12,-3:142,
143,173 Robert 3:142,143,
-4:190,191,-5:93 Samuel
3:143,-4:104 Sarah 4:104,190
Stephen 3:143,-4:190,191
Theodore 5:113 William 3:142
MURDOCK, Frances J. 7:68
MURPHY, Daniel 4:76 Mary 4:89
Michael 4:34 Pierre 3:25,70,73
Thomas 3:28,75
MURRAY, Abigail 4:184,-6:138
Charles Fabyan 7:60 David
4:182 Elizabeth 1:94,95,
-3:121,-6:139 Hannah 1:95,
-3:112,121,-6:137 Henry Han-
son 7:60 James 7:53 John
4:34,65,-5:117,-6:185 Lydia
6:139 Mary H. 7:60 Mr. 5:94
Orrin 7:60 Phebe 6:137 Samuel
1:94,95,-3:112,121 Susan 7:38
Susanna 5:55 Timothy 7:60
William 3:21,69,70,112,-5:1
MUSHUAY, Francis 3:6
MUSSELL, Robert 1:9,10
MUSSEY, Elizabeth 2:75,79,-3:34
Hannah 2:45 James 1:51,-2:79
John 3:134 Lydia 2:79 Mary
2:79 Ruth 2:79 Thomas 1:51,
-2:79 Widow 2:72,-3:100
MUSTELL, Mr. 2:28 Robert
2:24,27
MUTTLEBERRY, Ann 1:27 Enoch
1:27 Mary 1:27
MYRICK, John 4:151
NARRAMORE, Ann 2:92 Reverend
2:92
NASH, Phebe 4:101 Sarah 3:169
NASON, Abigail 2:144,-5:176,
-6:40 Agnes 5:86 Alice 6:76,79
Benjamin 2:144,-4:9,-5:40
Benjamin T. 6:79 Enoch 5:176
Hannah G. 5:114 James H.
2:166 John 6:76 Jonathan 4:12
Joseph 5:176 Joshua 4:116
Judith 5:176,-6:36 Kezia 5:176
Levi 5:176 Maria 5:176 Mary
4:152 Mr. 5:86,-6:76 Nathaniel
6:79 Reuben 5:176 Robert
3:28,73 Samuel 4:163,-5:86,

85

NASON (continued)
175,176,-6:185 Sarah 5:134
Shuah 4:9
NAQUANT, Nicholas 3:67,75
NAY, Abigail 3:120 Sarah
3:178,-4:116
NAYLOR, Lydia 4:149
NEAL (see Neil), Abigail 1:58,
191,-2:118,146,-4:43,-7:57
Andrew 1:51,61,63,167,
-2:118,123,127,146,-3:101 Asa
7:56 Asa, Jr. 7:57 Catherine
1:51,-2:123 Daniel 7:57
Deborah 2:118 Dominicus 7:51
Dorcas 1:61,63,67 Edward
2:146 Elijah 5:27,31 Elizabeth
1:127,-2:118,-4:104,116
Elizabeth Lewis Prentis 7:30
George 2:38,-5:125 Hannah
2:36 Henry 7:57 Hiram 5:125
Hubarteous 6:156 James 1:61,
69,120,127,163,167,-2:146,
-4:41,70,120,-5:27,124 James
Armstrong 7:31 Jeremiah
2:118,-3:54,-4:104,-5:44 John
1:58,69,120,-2:118,146,-3:54,
-4:75 John D. 5:37 John P.
5:181,182 John Prentis 7:30
Joseph 2:118 Joseph Lemmon
7:30 Joseph S. 6:156 Joshua
1:191,-3:54 Joshua W. 7:59
Kezia 1:127,-5:175 Lydia
1:163,-5:27 Lydia Ann 7:59
Mary 2:118,146,-3:7,178,
-5:39,-6:156,-7:59,80 Moses
L. 7:30,31 Moses Leavitt 7:30
Mrs. 3:175 Nabby 7:77 Olive
1:191 Patience 1:58,69,120,
-2:146 Phebe 2:175 Richard
1:21 Robert 2:162,164 Sally
7:78 Samuel 2:118,-3:50,52,
54,174,175,-5:27,-7:57,67,77,
78,80 Samuel Adams 7:30
Sarah 2:118,-4:80,-7:60 Sarah
A. 5:101 Sarah C. 4:188,-7:57
Thomas 3:54 Veline 7:57 W.
3:50 Walter 1:9,13,-2:23,59-
61,99-101,-3:50,54,55,172,173
Widow 2:122 William 2:36,37
William A. W. 7:65
NEALLEY, B. Frank 5:82 Benjamin 4:78 John H. 2:165,

NEALLEY (continued)
-3:189 Joseph 4:84
NEEDHAM, Mary 4:43
NEFF, Mrs. 3:84
NEIFERT, W. W. 5:143
NEIGH, Samuel 4:134
NEIGHBOUR, Francis 1:22,23
NEIL (see Neal), Abigail 4:129
Mary 6:156 Olive R. 6:154,
-7:39,41
NELSON, Anna 5:137 Elizabeth
2:167,-4:11,-6:77,-7:12 George
5:39 George F. 7:62 Hannah
4:9,-5:188,-6:41,44,45,77
James 4:100 John 4:103,
-5:136,188 Joseph 5:38,-6:74
Lade 6:73 Leader 2:176 Mark
3:28,75,-5:135,137,140,184,
188,-6:41,44,45,77,79,-7:12
Mary 2:167,-4:7,-5:38 Matthew
3:174,175,-4:98,-5:43 Miss
5:40 Mrs. 3:175,-5:135-137,
140,184,-6:79 Nathaniel S.
1:20 Samuel 2:93,-6:41,79
Sarah 5:136,146 Thomas 5:140,
184 William 1:79,-6:44
NEVINS, John 7:19
NEWALL, Chauncey 6:163
NEWELL, Mary 3:93
NEWHALL, George 3:113 Mary
3:114 Matthew 6:93 Sarah 7:42
NEWMAN, Samuel P. 7:20
Thomas 3:69,76 William 4:35
NEWMARCH, Benjamin 4:97
John 2:104,-3:55,-4:50 Joseph
1:27 Nathaniel 4:57 Samuel
4:55
NEWTON, Esther 5:104 John
2:70,71,-5:104,106,110,153
Margaret 2:46,-5:106 Miss
5:143 Thomas 5:153 Widow
2:43 William 5:110,143
NICHOLS, Abigail 3:93,-5:26,
-6:17 Ann 3:44 Caleb 5:126
Catherine 5:18 David 1:66,
120,122,127,-4:120,-5:25,171
Dorcas 5:122 Ebenezer 3:90
Eliza Ann 7:25 Elizabeth 3:181
Enoch 6:168 Eunice 1:120,
-4:69,120,-5:123 Hannah 1:66,
-4:120,162,-5:25,171 Ichabod
5:25,164,169,170 John 3:114,

NICHOLS (continued)
-4:120,-5:28,-6:17 Jonathan
5:25 Lydia 5:26 Mary 3:135,
-5:25 Natthew 6:166 Mehitable
5:109 Nancy 4:174 Nathan
5:164,169 Nicholas 3:132,-5:18
Phebe 1:120,122,127,-4:120,
-5:25,171 Rebecca 5:127
Robert 4:35 Samuel 1:122,
-4:120,-5:24,126 Sarah
1:127,-4:120,-5:26,-6:17
Stephen 4:120 Stephen P.
5:25,26 Stephen W. 5:17
Thomas 4:120,-5:25,26,-6:184
Tryphena 3:87 Warren 7:67
William 3:93,-6:58
NICHOLSON, Henry 1:19,-5:43
Sarah 1:19,-5:39 William 1:19
NICK, Philip 1:11
NICKERSON, Solomon 2:85
NILES, Sarah 4:190,191
NIMROD, Amos 3:42
NISBET, John 4:3 Mr. 4:1
NIVEN, John 5:41
NIX, John 2:92 Urith 2:92
NOBEL (Noble), Comfort P. 6:76
Fanny 4:77 Hannah 5:134,136,
137,139,-6:76 John 1:182,
-2:160,192,-5:136 John H. 6:76
Joseph 5:137 Mark 4:35,
-5:132,134,136,138,-6:76 Mary
5:134 Moses 1:156,157,-3:20,
73,-5:132,134,136,137,139,
-6:77 Mr. 7:14,77 Mrs. 5:134,
136,138,-6:76,77 O. 2:36
Rachel 6:76 Rebecca 6:76
Reuben 2:185,-3:74,-5:138
Robert 5:139 Sarah 4:127 Seth
6:134 Silas 4:182 Tirzah 4:89
NOCK, Abigail 7:52 Anna 1:120
Benjamin 7:52 Elizabeth
3:102,-5:2 Hannah 7:50,52
James 1:120,-2:126,-4:35
Jeremiah 7:50 Judith 1:67,
-4:164 Love 3:40 Mary 1:67
Mercy 1:120,-5:123,-7:52
Nathaniel 7:52 Rebecca 5:5
Samuel 2:183 Sylvanus 3:102,
-4:12 Zachariah 1:67
NOKES, Cuffe 2:12,-3:122 James
3:122 Lydia 2:12,-3:122
Rachel 2:12 Timothy 3:122

NOLTON (see Knowlton)
NORRIS, Asa 3:178 Benjamin
1:183,-4:73,-5:67 Caleb 4:73
Caleb W. 6:155 Caroline F.
6:93 Charles 4:73 Coffin D.
4:170 Dudley 3:183 Elizabeth
4:89 Eunice 3:119,-4:170 Huldah 3:88 James 4:73,169,
-5:14,67 James D. 3:184 John
2:105,-4:169 John D. 3:120
Jonathan 3:133,-5:67,102
Joseph 4:73,90,131 Joseph P.
5:67 Josiah 3:177,184,-4:91,
132,137,169,170 Judith 4:132
Katherine 4:169,170 Lucinda
5:102 Lucy 4:170 Lydia 3:177,
-4:86 Maria H. 6:7 Martha 4:73
Mary 3:90,182,-4:73,169,-5:14
Mary P. 3:184 Mehitable 2:54,
-3:166,-4:73 Mehitable C. 4:73
Moses 4:170 Nancy 4:73,136
Nathaniel 4:73,-5:14 Nicholas
2:90,105 Rachel 5:67 Rachel
A. 5:101,102 Rhoda H. 3:184
Ruth 3:182 Samuel 3:88,-5:67,
-6:159,-7:40 Sarah 2:90,105,
-4:170,-5:16,67 Simeon 3:115
Theophilus 4:132 Thomas C.
5:21 William 4:73,134,170,187
NORTON, Benjamin 4:186,-6:60
David S. 4:184 Elihu G. 5:148
Elizabeth 3:44,-6:142 Hannah
6:60 John 6:60 Levi 4:128 Lil-
lian A. 4:188 Lydia 1:102 Mary
6:118 Mary A. 6:60 Nathaniel
1:102,-4:186 Nathaniel C. 6:60
Samuel M. 6:39 Sarah 2:128
Thomas 6:60 Winthrop B. 7:65
NORWOOD, Sarah 3:2
NOWELL, Abraham 4:189
Ebenezer 4:189,190 Esther
4:190 Increase 4:190 John
4:189 Mark 2:93,185 Mary
4:189 Paul 4:189 Peter 4:189
Samuel 4:35,-5:128 Sarah
4:189 Silas 4:190
NOWLAN, Richard 4:35
NOYES, Benning 6:110 David 7:20
Dorcas 6:112 Fanny 6:161
Hannah 6:167 Harriette E.
2:96,141,166 Humphrey 4:175
Jane 6:108 Martha 6:109 Mary

NOYES (continued)
4:180 Moses 6:52 Phebe 3:168
Sarah 6:161 Simon 3:41
Stephen 6:110 Tappan W. 7:23
Thomas 7:66
NUDD, Abigail 4:168 Clarissa
4:126 Hannah 6:157 James
2:91 John 2:88 Mary 2:111
Mary J. 4:115 Samuel 2:108,
-4:168 Sarah 2:88,89,91,
106,108,111 Simon 3:91
Stephen 6:154,-7:39 Thomas
2:88,89,94,106,108,111
NUTE, Abra 5:118 Abraham 4:12
Anna 2:168 Daniel 5:152
Elizabeth 4:10 Ezekiel 5:150
Israel 5:151 Ivory M. 6:35
Jacob 5:148 James 1:178
Jeremiah 5:120 John 4:148
John H. 5:82 Josiah 5:7 Lydia
5:113 Mary 5:113,147 Nicholas
5:118 Samuel 4:148 Sarah 5:4,
151 Stephen 5:55 Susanna 5:52
NUTTER, Abigail 2:31,173,-3:58,
64,109,155,156,160,-4:107,
111,148,157,158,-5:149,-6:101,
124,126 Alice 3:3,6,8,160,
-5:53 Ann(e) 3:64,-4:112,
-5:75,189,-6:101 Anna 3:10,
-4:62,64,106,108,109,112,153,
154,156 Anthony 2:173,-3:2,79,
156,160,-4:16,18,19,60,62,106,
109,154 Arabella 3:4,-4:153
Benjamin 3:9,-4:18 Charles
7:14 Charlotte 5:117 Christopher 3:7,-4:107 Clement 7:12
Deacon 4:156 Deborah 3:59,
-4:62,-5:78 Dorothy 4:106
Easter (Esther?) 4:109,111,158
Ebenezer 3:10,-4:109 Eleanor
4:16 Elizabeth 2:173,-3:4,7,9,
59,61,107,-4:59,108,153,-5:78
Esther 4:158 Francis 6:176
Grafton 5:138,183,186,189
Hannah 3:1,107,112,156,158,
-4:15,16,18,19,59,61,64,107,
108,156,-5:75 Hatevil 1:177,
180,-2:167,170,171-3:10,57-
61,106,107,109,111,112,154,
156-158,-4:15,18,59-61,64,
107,108,155,-5:79,80,-6:101
Henry 2:181,-3:155,-4:12,

NUTTER (continued)
158,-5:184,186,188,-6:43,
45,76,78,-7:12,14 Jacob 6:43,
78 James 2:169,-3:2,109,155,
156,160,-4:109,111,158,-5:2
Jethro 4:158 John 2:174,-3:1,
9,60,109,-4:15,19,60,62,64,
108,109,112,153,154,-5:8,80,
120,-6:76,124,176 John M.
2:163 Jonathan 4:106 Jonathan
W. 2:30,31,-4:106,-6:124
Joseph 3:156 Joseph S. 4:153
Joshua 2:175,-4:108,111,153
Jotham 3:6,-4:60,-5:138
Lavina 2:30,-6:124 Leah
3:58-61,110 Lemuel 5:158
Lois 3:7,-4:18,64 Lucy 2:30,31
Margaret 7:12 Margery 6:76,78,
-7:12,14 Mark 3:157,-4:186
Martha 5:149 Mary 2:94,168,
173,-3:3,106,111,154,155,158,
160,-4:16,18,19,60,62,106,
-5:53,147,183,184,-6:43,130,
159,-7:40 Mary D. 5:79 Matthias 2:94,176,-3:156,-4:16,
19,59,106 Miriam 3:1,110 Mr.
5:90 Mrs. 5:138,183,184,186,
188,189,-6:43,45 Nancy 5:119
Nathan 4:111 Nathaniel 4:158
Nelson D. 4:19 Olive 2:175,
-4:153 Phebe 3:3,-5:148
Rebecca 3:107,109,111,154,
157,-5:186,-6:43 Richard
3:64,-4:158,-5:4,50,116
Rosamond 2:171,-3:62,109,
-4:16,76 Samuel 2:170,-3:64,
107,110,111,158,-4:107 Samuel
N. 5:55 Sarah 3:2,3,64,110,
111,158,-4:107-109,111,153,
-5:4,87,188,-6:43 Stephen
2:31,-5:51 Susan 6:124,125
Susan H. 2:31 Susanna 4:106,
-5:79,80 Temperance 3:109,
-5:120,149 Thomas 3:59,156
Valentine 5:87 William 3:10,
-4:109,-5:152 William S. 5:79
Winthrop 5:3 Zebulon D. 5:78
OAK, Henry 6:123 Nathaniel 4:125
O'BRIEN (O'BRINE), Joseph 4:35
William 4:35,-7:60
ODELL, Charlotte 3:164,-4:113,
116 George H. 4:113 James

ODELL (continued)
3:164,165,-4:113 James E.
4:113,-5:36,37 Joseph 6:54
Mary 3:165,-4:74 Sarah W.
4:113 William G. 4:113
ODIORNE, Abigail 2:38,-6:70,
-7:78 Avis 6:3 Benjamin
5:132-134,137,138 Daniel 6:41
Deborah 2:37 Ebenezer 5:137,
140,185,188,-6:43 Elizabeth
4:57,-5:132,-6:43 Hannah
2:34,-5:134,-7:78,79 Jane
4:52,134 John 1:10,13,-5:119,
138 Joseph 5:185 Jotham 1:21,
-5:87 Katharine 5:140 Lydia
5:117 Martha 5:188 Mary 3:51,
52,56 Mary B. 2:35 Mehitable
2:191 Meletiah 5:87 Mr. 4:56,
-5:91 Mrs. 5:137,140,185,188,
-6:41,43 Nancy 5:118,119
Nathaniel 4:54,58,-5:131 Olive
5:91 Patience 5:56,91,133,134,
137,138,140 Philip 1:13 Robert
5:162 Samuel 2:186,-5:167
Sarah 5:137 Sarah A. 6:41
Susanna 5:140,152 Thomas
5:168,170,-7:78,79 Thomas E.
2:34,35 William 2:34,-6:3
ODLIN, Elizabeth 4:75 John
3:148,-6:55,105,112 William
W. 5:147
OGDEN, Mr. 1:159,160
OGILVEY, John 4:3
OHF, Fer. 1:13
ONION, Thomas 1:9,12
ORAM, John 3:186
ORDWAY, Bradshaw 6:51 Hannah
3:88 John C. 7:25 Joseph 6:32
Lucy 4:136 Mehitable 6:40
Moses 6:104,-7:68 Mr. 6:120
Nathan 3:40 Plummer 7:72
Samuel 6:32 Sarah 4:91
ORNE, ---- 7:77,79 Benjamin
7:80 Charles B. 3:164 Eliza
7:77 Henry 7:76 James 4:127,
-7:76,80 Sarah 7:76,77,79,80
ORUM, Abigail 7:75,77 Robert
7:75,77 William Hale 7:77
ORYANT, George 6:112
OSBORNE, Abby M. 6:180
Adeline E. 4:186 Arthur G.
6:180 Caroline 6:20,21

OSBORNE (continued)
Caroline A. 2:32 Caroline C.
2:32,-6:128 Daniel 2:32,
-5:124,-6:20,121,128 David
5:124 Elijah 2:29,-6:123 Eliza
4:79 Elizabeth 5:124,-6:135
Esther 1:116,120,-5:123,-6:21
George 3:2 George A. 6:180
George J. 3:71 George J. Y.
2:181 Hannah 1:173,-5:124
Jacob 2:29,-6:82,179 James L.
6:123 John 1:153,154,157,
-4:75,181,-5:61 John E. 6:180
John H. 6:123 Jonathan 1:116,
120,-5:61 Joseph 6:137 Leah
N. 6:123 Marble 1:116,120,173,
-4:40,-5:60,123,-6:184 Margaret 2:29 Mary P. 2:32 Mary
R. 6:121 Mercy 1:173 Mercy P.
6:128 Mr. 6:156 Samuel 4:183
Sarah 4:11 Sarah N. 4:183 William 2:32,-5:124,-6:121 William P. 6:121
OSGOOD, Apphia 4:137 Benjamin
6:50 Betsey 7:39 Chase 4:137,
138,165,169,-5:67,168 David
2:46 Ebenezer 4:85,91,-5:67
Edward 4:138 Elias 6:105
Elizabeth 4:133,137,165,
-5:16,-6:154,170 Enoch 6:68
Hannah 4:89,138,-5:181,
-6:50,-7:18 Harriett R. 7:63
Henry 3:20 James 4:90 John
5:68,-6:109 Joseph 5:70 Judith
3:178 Lucy 6:166 Lydia 7:26
Martha 4:137,169,-5:67 Mary
3:179,-4:89,165,-5:16,70,
-6:168 Mary E. 6:47 Nehemiah
4:35 Phebe 4:137,138,165
Reuben 4:91,-5:16,70,-6:169
Samuel 4:137,-5:70 Sarah
3:179,-4:138,-5:181 Shuah
3:178,-4:137 Thomas 5:170
True 3:119 William 4:133,
-5:16,181
OSHAW, John 1:21
OTIS, Elijah 7:4 Howland 6:40
Jane 6:101,-7:5 Joshua 7:4
Joyce 4:11,-6:130 Mary 2:75,
-7:4 Micajah 7:4 Mr. 6:101
Mrs. 3:80,83 Nicholas 2:77,
-3:83,-7:4 Paul 7:4 Phebe 6:37

OTIS (continued)
Rebecca 2:77,-5:1,-7:5
Richard 2:77,-3:80,83 Sarah
3:47,-7:4 Simon 4:188,-5:150
Stephen 2:77,-3:80,-7:4
Susanna 2:77,78
PACHREN, Hannah 1:83
PACKER, George 3:181 Mrs.
3:175 Thomas 2:101,-3:173,
-4:9
PAGE (PAIGE), A. B. 5:48,144
Aaron 3:183,-4:165 Abigail
4:89,136,-5:7,72,118,120,
-6:75,117,175,-7:27 Abner
4:173 Amos 4:179 Anna 6:171
Asenath 5:20 Benjamin 3:132,
133,142,-5:11,72,119,158,159,
180,-6:34,175,-7:27-31
Charles 6:6 Christopher 2:108
Daniel 3:134,-4:124,146,-5:4,
-6:75,116,117,122,175 David
4:90,131,138,-5:72 David C.
6:172 Deborah 4:138 Dorothy
7:19 Ebenezer 5:112,155,
158,-6:28 Edward 3:22,70
Eleanor 5:11 Elizabeth 4:133,
-5:3,11,180,-6:28,31,-7:31
Elizabeth F. 6:122 Elizabeth
O. 1:158 Ellis 6:122 Enoch
1:121,124,162,-4:123 Enos H.
6:122 Eunice 4:185 Fanny 5:21
Francis 2:108,110,112 Hannah
1:124,-4:123,180,-5:11,19,180
Henry 5:159 Israel 6:18 Jabez
3:169,-5:110,159 James G.
7:37 Jemima 5:69 Jeremiah
3:91,-5:67,-6:167 Jesse 5:69
John 2:110,-3:44,-4:138,165,
179,-5:11,159,160,171,180,
-6:28,31 John D. 4:165 John
M. 6:122 Jonathan 5:69 Joseph
3:102,-6:75,171-173,-7:27,28,
30 Josiah 5:15 Judah 5:180
Judith 5:10,11,180 Laban 6:166
Levi 5:69 Lucy 2:110,-4:150
Lydia 3:181,-4:138,165 Margaret 4:90,138 Maria 7:26 Martha H. 5:119,-6:173 Mary
1:162,-2:68,90,105,108,110,
-3:178,-4:10,91,124,138,178,
-5:11,53,67,69,112,180,-6:20,
57,142,143,171,190 Mehitable

PAGE (PAIGE) (continued)
A. 6:165 Meribah 2:108,
110,112,-5:15 Moses 4:165,
-5:10,11,19,70,180 Moses A.
6:122 Mr. 5:70 Nathan 3:120
Nathan C. 6:121 Olivia 1:158
Patience 3:131 Reuben 4:165
Robert 1:158,159,-2:105 Ruth
1:121,124,162,-3:91,-4:123,
133,165,-5:69,171 Samuel
2:108,-4:89,123,-5:171 Sarah
2:68,-3:132,178,-4:152,-5:72,
-6:55,161,-7:28 Simon 3:133,
-4:133 Susanna 2:112,-5:72
Taylor 4:183 Thomas 2:91,105,
108,110,-3:129,-5:110 Wealthy
7:29 William 4:131,-6:122
William C. 7:45 William P.
6:112
PAINE, Amos 4:55 Christian 4:54
Christine 1:41 Hannah 1:45
Henry 1:21 James 1:11 John
1:41,-4:55,188 Mary 1:41
Moses 1:45 Philip 4:55
Richard 4:35 Rowena 4:188
Sarah 1:41 Susanna 1:95 William 1:6,45,95,-4:55
PALMER, Aaron 7:25 Abigail
1:91 Ann(e) 1:37,45 Barnabas
5:6,-6:115-117,175 Barnaby
6:72 Benjamin 5:1,-6:115,175
Brackett 6:175 Christopher
1:34,95,139 Comfort 3:120
Daniel 2:15,-5:119 Deborah
7:32 Dodavah 5:152 Dudley
5:52 Dudley S. 7:26 Elizabeth
1:34,139,-4:151,-6:72 Groath
4:84 Hannah 2:15,53,-4:99
Isaac K. 7:69 James 1:91 John
2:15,-5:2,22,54,-6:165
Jonathan 1:34,37,91,92,139,
-6:72 Joseph 1:45,192,-2:15,
-5:56,-6:116 Marinda 5:22
Margaret 6:72 Martha 6:175
Mary 1:183,-2:120,-7:72 Mercy
6:117 Miss 6:191 Rachel 5:72
Richard 2:53 Robinson 6:175
Samuel 1:37,-5:2,18,-6:113
Sarah 1:192,-2:15 Susanna
5:150,-6:175 Thomas 5:42
Trueworthy 2:189,-3:93 William 1:3,8,45,92,-4:152,

PALMER (continued)
-6:113,-7:32 William L.
2:190,-3:93,-4:49,93,-5:48
PALMES, Richard 4:35
PARCHER, Catherine 4:61 Elias
2:175,-4:13,61,-5:129,134,137
Elizabeth 5:129 George 3:20,
74,-5:134,-6:43,-7:75 Henry
5:137,-7:75,76,78 Katharine
7:78 Mrs. 5:134,137,-6:43
Samuel 2:184,-3:20,71,4:61,
-6:43
PARK, Edward 6:80,-7:12,16
Jerusha 6:80,-7:12,60 John
6:165,-7:12 Mary 6:80 Samuel
7:16
PARKER, Abigail 6:42,45 Adaline
R. 1:158 Alberta T. 7:83 Anna
1:28,-2:33,-6:3 Anne 7:19
Benjamin 1:21,25,28,-2:93,
-4:89 Benjamin F. 5:21 Caleb
4:35,-7:69 Charles 5:129,133
Dr. 7:82 Elbridge G. 2:93
Elizabeth 1:25,-2:33,93,
-4:49,50,52,53,-5:42,-6:42
Emily C. 2:93 Hannah 1:25,
-6:42 Henry R. 1:29,31,-2:165,
-3:188,-5:92 Henry R., Jr. 7:83
Henry Rust 7:81,83 Jacob 2:93
James 2:185,-3:49 John 6:46,
-2:187,-3:72,-4:53,57,-5:164,
166,169,170,-7:74 John F.
1:158 John Tappan 7:83
Jonathan 5:169 Joseph 4:35
Katherine 4:52 Mary 4:54,
-7:74,76 Matthew S. 5:88 Matthew Stanley Gibson 7:83
Michael 5:133 Miss 4:53 Mrs.
5:189,-6:42,45,46 Nathalie S.
7:83 Nathaniel 4:52,-7:17 Noah
3:147,151,170,-4:53 Peter
6:190 Phineas 4:180 Robert
1:158,-4:77,-5:129,162,166-
168,170,-6:42,45,46,56,77,
-7:11,13 Robert W. 1:158 Ruth
6:166 Samuel 7:13,76 Samuel
G. 4:127 Samuel W. 5:85 Sarah
6:42,77 Sophia M. 6:164
Stephen H. 7:71 Susannah
6:77,-7:11 Thomas 1:11,25,28,
-2:33,-4:35,52 William 2:33,
104,-3:55,-4:50,53,-5:88,166,

PARKER (continued)
189,-6:42,-7:74,76,83 Zurviah
S. 2:191
PARKS, Anna 7:14 Edward 7:14
Jerusha 7:14
PARROTT, Captain 6:172
Deborah 5:186,189,-6:44,78
Deborah W. 6:172 Deborah
Walker 7:13 Elizabeth 5:189
Enoch G. 2:162 Enoch Green-
leaf 7:12 John 4:35,-5:186,
189,-6:44,78,-7:12,13,15 John
F. 2:162,163,-5:186 Martha
7:12,13,15 Martha B. 6:172
Martha Brackett 7:13 Mary
2:92 Mehitable 6:44 Robert
2:92 Sr. 7:15 William W. 6:78
PARRY, Abraham 6:63 Ebenezer
6:63 Miss 6:63
PARSHLEY (PARSLEY),
Elizabeth 7:4 John 2:173,
-6:178 John B. 7:4
PARSONS, Abby S. 2:173 Abigail
2:137,138 Abraham 6:137 Al-
bion D. 2:138,139 Charles G.
2:137 Charles H. 2:138,139
Charles L. 3:48 Charles W.
2:138,139 Daniel 6:85 Daniel
D. 2:138,139 Edward 3:72
Eliza B. 2:138,139 Eliza E.
2:138,139 Emily 2:137 J. W.
1:139 John 2:137 John W.
2:136-139 Josiah 6:85,137
Judith 6:85 Langdon B.
2:138,139 Levi 4:174 Mary
1:47 Nathaniel 1:47 Samuel
1:27,47,93 Sarah 6:139 Senira
2:137 Thomas 1:22,-3:21,
-4:183 Thomas H. 2:138,139
Thomas J. 2:137-139 Warren
2:137 William 2:137,-4:35
Zaccheus 4:35
PARTRIDGE, Ann 6:144
Elizabeth 3:53 John 1:11,
-2:101,-3:50,52,55,173,174,
176,-4:49 Mary 3:50,52,53,56
Mrs. 3:174,176 Nehemiah 1:12,
14 Sarah 4:10,-5:42 William
1:14,-3:50,52,53,172,174,176,
-5:41,-6:144
PASON, Mr. 3:55
PASSMORE, Thos 2:183,-3:20,71

PATCH, Benjamin 3:62,64 John
3:64 Lydia 3:64 Paul 3:62
Sarah 5:81 Timothy 5:169
PATRICK, Christopher 3:100
PATT, Abigail 1:191 David 1:191
Ebenezer 1:191 John 1:191
PATTEN, Aaron 4:176 Colcord
4:180 Isaac 5:21 Lois 3:170
Louisa 5:22 Susan 3:171
PATTERSON, Charles H. 2:166
George 3:44 Mr. 4:16 Nancy
7:30
PAUL, Abigail 3:5 Amos 6:152,
156 Andrew M. 6:152 Benjamin
4:40 Charles H. 6:152 Daniel
1:10 Elizabeth 3:5 George M.
6:152 George O. 6:152,-7:63
James C. 6:152 James M.
6:152 Margery 6:152 Mary 4:53
Mary A. 6:152 Moses 3:47,
-4:53 Mr. 2:177,-4:25
Nathaniel 6:152 Nicholas G.
6:152 Nina C. 4:185 Samuel
6:152 Sarah 3:5,-4:56 Sarah E.
6:152 Temple 6:159,-7:40
William M. 6:152
PAYNE, Solomon 7:22
PAYSON, Mary R. 5:19
PEABODY, Francis 2:82,-5:148
Lydia 2:82 Nathaniel 5:170
PEACOCK, John 5:44 Mary 5:39
PEARCE (see Peirce & Pierce),
Harriet 4:7
PEARL, Abraham 4:146,-6:73,
114,116 Daniel 6:113 Ebenezer
5:49,-6:116 Eleanor 6:116
Eleazer 5:55 Elizabeth 4:149,
-6:67 Hannah 6:113,114
Ichabod 6:72 Isaac 5:7 John
1:54,-2:76,-3:33,-6:73 Joseph
2:176,-4:152,-5:146,-6:72
Mary 1:54,-4:151 Nicholas
3:147 Paul 6:73 Rachel 4:150
Sarah 4:151,-5:120,-6:72,113
PEARNE, William 2:159
PEARSON, Captain 3:146 Deborah
3:181 Ebenezer 4:93 Edward N.
1:30,-2:165,-4:95,-6:48
Elizabeth 2:176 Ephraim 3:86
Hannah 4:93 John 3:45,-4:75,
183 Levi 5:182 Ora 5:18
Samuel M. 4:114

PEASE, Ebenezer 3:119 Elizabeth
3:180 Elizabeth B. 5:149
Joseph 5:45,-6:140 Leonard
6:93 Lucy 3:182 Lydia 6:138
Samuel 3:147,-6:137 Sarah
3:182 Stephen 3:181 Zebulon
6:138
PEASLEE, Abigail 1:168,-2:31,
-5:121,-7:6 Abraham 1:161
Alice 1:61 Amos 1:61,163,
175,-4:70,-5:26,-6:21,128,182,
183 Anna 5:24 Benjamin 5:24
Caleb 4:177 Caroline 6:128
Cyrus B. 6:128 Daniel 4:174
Ebenezer 1:168,-7:6 Elijah
1:161,163,165,-2:31,-6:182
Elizabeth 4:175 Enoch 1:67,
-5:24,-6:183 Esther 1:161,163,
165 Israel 1:168,-4:124,-7:6
John 1:64,117,165,-5:26
Jonathan 6:182 Joseph 1:67,
117,-4:162,-5:24,-6:184 Lydia
1:64,-3:168-6:128 Lydia A.
6:183 Maria 6:128 Martha
1:67,-5:24 Martha C. 5:22
Mary 1:117,175,-2:31,-5:24
Mary H. 2:31,-6:121,182
Moses 5:17 Moses G. 6:182
Nathaniel 3:87 Nicholas 4:70
Pelatiah 3:170 Rhoda 6:21
Richard 6:128 Robert 1:61 Ruth
4:123 Samuel 1:175,-2:31
Sarah 2:149,-4:44,-6:128
Simeon 4:180 Timothy 2:145
William 4:174,-5:19,24 William I. 5:22
PEAVEY, Abel 3:106,112 Abigail
5:151 Abraham 7:50 Anna 2:11
Anthony 4:152 Daniel 4:17,
-5:80,-6:74,171 Deborah 2:168
Edward 3:159,174 Elizabeth
3:8,-4:62 Ezekiel 3:112 Hopley
5:80 Hudson (Hutson?) 2:172,
-3:156,-4:17,59,61,62,105,107,
109 Jacob 6:171 James 4:61,
-5:76,78,80 James B. 5:76
Jane 2:168 Jelletson 3:160
John 2:11,-3:9,-4:103,109,
-5:151 John N. 5:76 Joseph
3:4,160 Joshua 4:149 Lucinda
4:184 Madlin (Madeline) 3:160,
-4:15,17,59,61,62,105,107,109

PEAVEY (continued)
Mary 3:112,-4:16-18,59,60,
100,-5:80 Mary I. 6:7
Mehitable 5:38 Mercy 3:9,
-4:105 Nathaniel 2:11 Olive
7:50 Oliver 4:15,-5:51,-6:171
Rachel 2:169 Sarah 2:168,
-4:60,100,-5:78,-6:171 Sarah
C. 6:132 Simon 5:118 Tem-
perance 4:18,107,-6:114
Thomas 3:106,-4:15,16,18,
60,-6:75 William 4:100,
-6:74,75
PECKER, Jeremiah 6:106,-7:20
Robert E. 7:66 William 7:68
PEDERSON, Hants 4:35
PEDIGROVE, Stephen 3:6
PEIRCE, Andrew 5:114 Ann S.
2:191 Augusta 3:95 Benjamin
4:35,-6:98 Daniel 2:104,
-3:101,-4:54,-5:87 Eliza 6:34
Elizabeth 1:14,15,-4:51,54
George 1:14,-2:172,-4:55,58
Hannah 5:129,149 Jane 5:89
John 2:160,-5:42 Joseph 3:55,
-4:51-5:87,129 Joseph W. 4:75
Joshua 1:15,-2:97,102-104,
134,-3:55,-4:49,57,-5:147
Lydia 4:174 Margaret 4:98
Mark W. 2:163 Martha 4:58
Mary 4:55,99,-5:134,136,
138,185 Mehitable 4:49,50,
-5:39 Moses 3:169 Mr. 5:129
Nathaniel 4:57 Peter 5:134,
136,138,185,-6:43 Rebecca E.
W. 4:186 Samuel 4:175,-5:134
Sarah 3:136,-4:181,-5:44,101
Stephen 5:6 Thomas 2:103,
-3:55,-4:50,56,80,-5:89
Timothy 5:87 Tobias 4:103
William 6:43 William E.
2:165
PELHAM, Edward 3:145
PEMBERTON, James 5:40
PENDERGAST (Pendergrass),
Ann 4:126 Deborah 4:181 Ed-
mund 4:183,-6:139 Hannah
4:79 James 4:79,189 John
4:182 Mehitable S. 7:62
Nicholas 4:127 Rachel 4:79
Sarah 4:77,78 Solomon 4:75
Thomas 6:154,-7:39

PENDEXTER, Alice 5:132
Charles 5:131 Drusilla B. 7:45
Edward 5:86,131,133,-6:178
Elizabeth 4:99,-5:89,-6:178
Frances 6:78 George 6:78 John
4:103,-5:86,89,91,130,132,149
Joseph 4:125,-5:130 Margaret
4:99,-5:86,-6:178 Mary 4:99,
-6:78 Mrs. 5:86 Philip 4:103,
-5:89 Samuel 5:86,89 William
5:89
PENDLETON, Brian 2:22,25,28,
98,99 Briant 1:6,9,10 Captain
1:11 James 1:10,-2:97,99,
-3:49,50 Joseph 1:6,9 Mr.
1:6,-2:23
PENHALLOW, Andrew J. 4:7 Ann
7:73 Ann Wendell 7:73 Benjamin 5:188 Charles L. 4:7
David P. 4:8 Deacon 4:51,
-7:77 Deborah 5:44 Dunlap 4:8
Elizabeth 4:51,-5:130,139
Elizabeth J. 4:8 Hannah 5:40,
-7:13,14,73 Hannah A. 4:8
Harriet 4:7 Hunking 2:162,
-4:7,-5:185 John 2:98,104,
-3:53,-5:89,91,130,132-136,
139,163,167,185,188,-7:77
John, Jr. 7:77,79 John P. 4:7
Joseph 4:55 Mary 5:40,136
Olympia 4:57 Phebe 3:54
Richard 4:100 Richard W. 5:89
Samuel 2:36,102,158,159,
-3:55,-4:50,-5:132,162,164-
166,168,169 Samuel, Jr. 7:73
Sarah 5:134-136,139,185,
188,-7:77,79 Sarah Ann 7:13
Sarah Wentworth 7:79 Susan P.
4:7 Susanna 4:3 Thomas 5:135,
-7:13,14 Thomas Wibird 7:14
(had dau. Lyora b1700)
PENN, William 1:148
PENNY, Henry 3:152,-6:97
PEPPER, Rebecca 4:92
PEPPERELL, Dorothy 1:24,27
Mary 1:23 Miriam 3:54 Mr.
3:52 William 3:54
PERDEAN, Rebecca 6:136
PERENESS, Maturant 3:66
PERKINS, Abigail 2:83,138,-5:41
Abraham 1:102,-2:81,83,85-87,
109,111,-4:16,75 Adam 5:54

93

PERKINS (continued)
Ann 5:21 Anna 4:152 Benjamin
6:139 Charles 1:103 Daniel D.
5:182 David 3:7 Deborah 6:135,
138 Dorothy 5:2 Ebenezer 2:86
Elizabeth 2:109,110,-4:167,
-5:1,-6:135 Ephraim 5:49,148,
-6:39 Esther 5:2 Frances
3:47,-4:11 Gilbert 4:146 Hannah 2:83,-4:150,-5:120,-6:135
Huldah 1:42 Humphrey 2:87
Isaac 2:81,83,85-87,109 Jacob
2:81,109 James 3:177 John
4:94,167,-5:163,-6:135,136
Joseph 2:87,-3:168,171,
-5:35,116 Judith 4:146,-5:6
Lemuel 7:43 Lucinda 6:33
Lydia 1:102,-3:171 Martha
2:94,-5:81,-6:176 Mary 2:81,
83,85-87,109,111,-3:14,-4:12,
167,-6:60,135 Mercy 2:109 Mr.
6:101 Nancy 4:78 Nathaniel
3:152,-4:167 Nathaniel T. 4:89
Polly 7:56 Robert 6:135 Sally
7:44 Sarah 2:86,-5:8,42,-6:34,
93,101,135,136 Shadrach 5:54
Solomon 6:173,-7:30 Susanna
2:81,83,85-87,-5:54,-6:135
Thomas 3:174,-4:35 Timothy
2:85
PERLEY, Allen 6:141 Martha
6:141 Sidney 2:166
PERMAT (PERMITT), Abigail
4:101 Hannah 4:97 John 4:99
Judith 4:50,-5:44
PERRIN, Susanna 6:26 Timothy
6:26
PERRUM, Lydia 6:52
PERRY, Christian 1:25 Elizabeth
5:44 Jacob 4:34 John 3:45,
112,155 Mary 1:23 Rebecca
3:112 Richard 1:22,25
Rosamond 3:155 Sarah 3:112
PERSON(S), Elizabeth H. 6:139
Mary 1:43 Oliver 6:54 Samuel
1:43
PESGRAUE, Peter 1:11
PETERS, Andrew 4:58 John 4:129
Mary 4:58 Master 3:83 Pomp
4:35
PETERSON, Mehitable 6:110
PETTE, Peter 2:45

PETTENGILL, Abigail 6:54
David 7:71 Elizabeth 3:89
James 7:65 Jefferson 7:25
Lorenzo S. 7:71
PETTIGREW, Thomas 3:4
PETTINGALE, Ephraim 4:35
PETTIT, Joseph 4:35
PEVERE, Joseph 5:19,20
PEVERLY, Abigail 2:175 Anna
4:102 Anne 7:12 Anne E. 5:183
Benjamin 5:91 Benjamin C.
6:79 Elizabeth 4:100 Frederick
5:89 George 5:87,137,183,-6:44
Grace 4:54 Hannah 6:41 James
6:46 Jeremiah 6:43 John 2:101,
-3:174,-4:42,-6:41 Joseph
5:86,-6:41 Katharine 5:132
Kinsman 5:165 Mary 5:87
Moses 5:89 Mr. 5:91 Mrs.
5:137,183,-6:41,43,44,46,79
Nathaniel 4:100,103,-5:43,
-6:41,43,44,46,79,-7:12
Samuel 5:39 Temperance 4:101
Thomas 1:9,10,-2:24,-5:39,86,
88,132,-7:12 Widow 1:13 William 4:104
PEVERTON, David 3:112 Mary
3:112 Mr. 3:111,112
PHAREZ, Aaron 1:12
PHELPS, Aholiab 4:35 Samuel
W. 7:69
PHILBRICK, Abigail 1:88,89,
129,-2:82 Ann 1:130,-2:82-
87,89,91,105,106 Anna 1:129,
133,-2:82,85 Apphia 2:83 Benjamin 1:130,-2:48,68,131,136,
-3:38,43 Benjamin P. 2:136
Bethiah 1:33,-2:82 Captain
5:157 Catherine 2:51 Charles
P. 1:130 Christiana R. 2:138
Clinton 1:134 Daniel 1:88,89,
133,140 Deacon 5:109 Deborah
5:46 Ebenezer 1:33,92
Elizabeth 1:37,38,48,-2:89,91,
105,3:168,-4:10,-5:158
Elizabeth B. 1:140 Emeline
2:136 Ephraim 2:83,138 Esther
2:84 Hannah 1:33,129,130,
133,-2:108,3:43 Ira 1:140 Irene
2:136 James 1:33,37,38,48,93,
133,-2:83-85,87,89,91,106,-
3:180 Jedediah 2:43,65,130,

PHILBRICK (continued)
131,-3:37,38,135,-5:103,106,
109,112 Jeremiah 3:41,-5:112,
155,158,-6:28 John 2:82,83,
-3:174,176,-5:155 John C.
2:138 John W. 1:140 Jonathan
1:48,129,140,-2:84,-3:5,53
Joseph 1:129,130,133,140,
-2:89,-5:157 Joses 1:89,129,
130,133,134,140 Josiah 3:167
Josiah W. 2:138 Judith 2:72
Julian 2:136 Levi 1:133 Lydia
7:19 Lyman 1:134 Mary 1:129,
133,-2:130,136,-3:50,52,56,88,
170,-5:49 Mary S. 2:136
Mehitable 2:106,-4:86,-6:28
Mercy 1:88 Moses C. 2:138
Mrs. 3:56,176 Nancy (see Ann)
Nancy 5:18 Newell 1:140
Oliver B. 2:136 Patience 2:51
Reuben 1:130,133 Ruth 1:33
Samuel 2:86,-5:106 Sarah
1:89,133,140,-2:87,138,-3:5,
-5:19 Sarah A. 2:138 Sheridan
1:140 Susan 7:25 Susanna
1:129,130,134,140 Thomas
2:46,65,82,84-86,89,105,108,
131,-3:37,-5:103 Titus 1:48
William 2:102,108,-3:26,50,
52,55,73,174,176,-4:49
PHILBROOK, Joel 4:35
PHILIPON, Augustin 3:68,75
PHILLIPS, Captain 3:85
Catharine 6:191 Mary 2:172
Samuel 3:83,-6:10 Sarah
2:172,-3:130 Walter 5:37
PHILPOT, John 6:47 Richard 5:40
PHINNEY, Edmund 6:5
PHIPPS, Bethia 5:38 Danforth
4:56 John 5:38 Mary 1:14
Mehitable 4:98 Sarah 4:100
Thomas 1:14,-2:102,-3:55,
-4:50,58,104,-5:41
PICKERING, Abigail 2:168,176,
-3:159,-4:57,112,-5:52,76
Abigail L. 5:75 Alice 3:10,
-4:109 Anna 3:9 Anthony
3:159,-4:61,63,105,-5:146
Benjamin 3:111,-4:63 Captain
3:101 Charles W. W. 4:8
Charlotte 5:77 Daniel 3:155,
-4:56 Deborah 3:64,109,110,

PICKERING (continued)
112,155,158,-4:153,154,
-5:75,77,79 Elizabeth 2:169,
-3:4,5,109,-4:17,56,61,63,
-5:52,74-76 Ephraim 3:112,
-4:112,153,154,157,-5:74,76,77
Eunice 4:157 Fanny C. 4:8 Gee
5:76 Guy 4:8 Hannah 4:112,154
Isaac 4:8 Issac W. 4:7 James
2:94,168,-3:4,8,158,159,-5:75,
114,-7:37 James, Jr. 7:32
James C. 5:74 Jerusha 4:112,
154-156,-5:74 John 1:3,5,6,
8-14,-2:24-28,61,63,64,98-
102,173,-3:6,172,173,-4:9,56,
112,157,158,-5:74,75,115 John
B. 4:112 John G. 3:7,154,159,
-5:74-77,79 John S. 4:8 Joseph
3:64,-4:108 Joseph W. 5:76
Joshua 2:169,-3:63,64,109,
110,112,155,158,-4:14,63,157,
-6:61,110 Levi 4:105,156,-5:4
Lois 5:114 Louisa S. 4:8 Lydia
4:112,153,154,157,-5:74,76
Maria L. 4:8 Mary 3:9,50,51,
56,109,111,154,158,-4:7,8,12,
17,18,49,50,61,63,105-107,
109,111,157,-5:74-76,79 Mary
A. J. 4:7 Mary Ann 7:32
Mehitable 4:182 Mrs. 3:175,
-7:87 Nancy 4:112 Nehemiah
4:155 Nicholas 3:2,-4:111,
112,154,158,-5:75-77,79,-7:14
Olive 3:2 Olive Jane 7:37
Olive R. 4:157 Patience 4:111
Rebecca 4:12 Richard 4:107
Robert 4:7 Rose 4:157 Samuel
3:91,110,-6:139 Samuel S. 7:44
Sarah 3:10,-4:53,106,-5:75,
79,147 Sarah F. 5:74 Sarah T.
4:112 Stephen 3:158 Tem-
perance 3:3,7,-4:111,-5:75,77
Thomas 2:170,173,-3:3,109,
111,154,158,159,174,175,
-4:17,18,50,56,61,63,106,107,
109,111,112,154-156,158,
-5:74,77 Tryphina Berry 7:32
William 3:8,-4:18,-5:56,-7:23
William W. 4:7 Winthrop 3:3,
159,-4:63
PIERCE (see also Pearce,
Peirce), Augustine C. 7:23

95

PIERCE (continued)
Ebenezer Jr. 7:2 Edward John
7:80 Mary 7:33 Peter 7:13
President 4:8 Rocksby Harris
7:80 William 7:13 William S.
2:165
PIKE, Abby J. 6:7 Abigail 3:77-
79,81,97,-4:58 Abigail Libbey
7:74 Abraham 4:79 Benjamin
4:54,-6:78 C. R. 7:88 Daniel
5:188 Dudley 5:94 Ebenezer
7:14 Elisha 5:53 Elizabeth
1:14,-4:134,-5:131,-6:46,-7:80
Elizabeth H. 5:188 F. V. 7:88
Francis Holmes 7:88 Francis
V. 6:40 Hannah 3:77,169
James 6:149 Jeremiah 3:180,
-5:137 John 3:77,78,145,183,
-4:9,12,85,99,-6:98 John F.
5:135 Joseph 3:82 Joshua 3:53,
78,-5:133,135,137,183,185,
188,-7:75,76,78,80 Joshua, Jr.
7:14,16,74 Margaret 3:78,97,
-4:50,53 Mary 3:77,-5:55
Mercy 5:41,-6:137 Miss 5:43
Moses 3:43 Mr. 3:55,-6:118,
145 Mrs. 5:135,137,183,185,
188 Nancy 6:160 Nancy D. 7:40
Nancy Wilson or Willson 7:16,
75 Nathaniel 3:77,79,147,151,
152,-5:131,135,185,188,-6:46,
78 Nathaniel G. 5:148 Oliver
M. 3:178 Reverend Mr. 6:134
Robert 1:14,-3:77,79,80,148,
-5:183,185,-6:98 Samuel 3:53,
78,98 Sarah 3:77,79,-4:53,
-5:185,188,-6:46,78 Solomon
3:78,-6:98 Theodore 4:102
William 4:181,-5:133
PILLOW, John 7:78,89 John
Mycall 7:78 Joseph D. 2:165
William 7:79
PILLSBURY, Abigail 2:174 Caleb
3:171 Edmund 6:154,-7:39
Eliza F. 5:150 Elizabeth Ann
7:18 Frank J. 4:144 George W.
5:21 Hannah 6:48 Harrison 5:22
John 3:132 Martha H. 6:154,
-7:39 Sally 7:38
PINDER, Benjamin 6:135 Comfort
1:156 Elizabeth 5:79 Hannah
1:156 James B. 5:79 Jeremiah

PINDER (continued)
1:156 Joseph 4:76 Joseph D.
7:43 Joseph L. 5:79 Mary S.
4:186 Nancy 6:154,-7:39 Sally
7:38 Sarah 4:80,-6:154
PINKHAM, A. 1:99 Abigail 1:52,
63,106,-2:125,146,-4:78,-6:19
Abigail J. 7:64 Abijah 1:105
Alfred 6:19,-7:45 Alice 5:115
Amos 3:152 Andrew 3:32 Ann
7:87 Ann M. 4:115 Anna 2:125
Augustus H. 1:105 Ballard 1:99
Catherine 3:32 Daniel 4:80,
-5:36 Ebenezer 1:54,-2:124,
-3:32 Elizabeth 1:105,168,169,
172,173,174,-5:7,127,-6:19
Elizabeth A. 6:82 F. L. 6:192
Hannah 5:127 Hannah G. 1:172,
-6:89 Hannah R. 6:19 Isaac
7:27 Jacob B. 6:20 James N.
6:19 Jeremiah G. 5:127 John
2:125,-4:185 John S. 1:105
John T. 4:126 Jonathan 5:147,
-6:174 Jonathan L. 6:19
Joseph 1:168,169,172,173,
-4:43,-5:127,-6:34 Katherine
3:152 Lavinia 6:19 Lois 4:147
Lydia N. 6:19 Margery 1:106
Mary 1:52,53,99,-3:132,-4:126,
-5:51 Mary A. 6:175 Mary W.
6:19 Nathaniel 3:32,-5:5
Nicholas 1:168,-3:32,-4:43,
-5:64,127,-6:19,82 Nicholas K.
6:82 Otis 1:51,63,-2:76,125,
-4:43 Pamelia 1:99,106 Paul
2:123,125,-4:43,44 Phebe 6:19
Rebecca 1:173,-5:127,-6:91,
-7:30 Rose 1:63,-2:79,125,
-4:44,122,-5:127 Sally 7:44
Samuel 2:125,-5:150 Sarah
1:53,99,105,169,-2:147,-3:32,
-5:127,-6:82,-7:6 Sarah A.
6:19 Silas 4:43 Solomon 1:52,
-4:12 Sophia 1:99,-4:78
Stephen 6:174 Susanna 1:99,
-4:149 Thomas 1:53,54,99,
-4:11,-5:124,-6:174,175,-7:27,
30 Timothy 4:126 Timothy B.
1:99 Vincent 7:30
PINNER, Thomas 3:9
PIPER, Abigail 2:57,-4:116
Deborah 2:57,-4:20 Elizabeth

PIPER (continued)
2:57,-115,-4:116 George 3:166
Harriet 5:37 Hepzibah 2:115
Israel 2:115 Jane 2:57,151,
-3:127 Joanna 2:57 John 2:151,
-4:117 John L. 2:57,-3:166
Jonathan 2:57,58 Josiah 3:16
Mary 2:58,115,151,-3:46,164
Mehitable 2:51 Mercy 2:151
Moses 3:166 Mr. 7:30 Nancy
2:115,151,-4:116 Nathaniel
2:115 Noah 2:57,-3:164,165,
-4:74,115,117,118,-5:35-37
Noah R. 2:151 Olive 2:57,58
Patience 2:115 Phebe 3:166
Sally P. 2:57 Samuel 2:57,
122,151,-4:10 Sarah 1:183,
-2:115,151,-4:23 Stephen 2:115
Susan 7:70 Susanna 2:115,
-4:116 Tabitha 2:12,115
Theodosia 4:117 Thomas
2:12,115
PITKIN, Esther 6:93
PITMAN, Anna 6:46 Benjamin
1:182,-3:63,-5:87,140,186,
-6:144 Daniel 7:14 Dorcas 5:87
Elizabeth 3:50,56,-6:144,
-5:88,187,-7:11 Ezekiel 4:102,
-6:42,44,46,77,79,-5:43,86,88,
91,-7:11,13-16,76 Fanny 7:13
Frances 5:39 Hannah 5:140,
-7:14 Henry 7:76 Henry
Seaward 7:76 James 3:63 John
5:86,-6:42,43,45,-6:45,-7:11,
13,14 Joseph 1:182,-3:63,103,
-6:78,148,-7:76 Lucy 7:11,13,
14 Lydia 7:15 Mark 1:182,
-2:187,-3:72,-5:186 Mary 1:80,
182,-2:175,-5:41,187,6:42,43,
46,77,79,144,148,-7:12,14,16,
76 Mary Ann 7:80 Mehitable
3:63 Mr. 3:173 Mrs. 3:175,
-5:140,186,-4:42-46,77-79
Nathaniel 5:187,-6:43,46,79,
-7:12,14,16,76 Nehemiah 7:12
Olive 6:79,-7:11 Sarah 6:44,
-7:11,13-15 Sukey 7:14
Susanna 1:80,182,-3:63,-5:140,
-6:144 Theodore 7:13,16 William 2:97,-3:63,-6:43,78,
148,-7:16,80
PITTS, Bolton 4:35

PLACE, (PLAICE), Abigail
2:169,-3:62,-4:145,-5:6,-6:67,
116,117 Abner 4:159 Abraham
2:174,-3:62,-6:69,113 Alice
4:107,111,158 Amos 4:149
Charity 4:150 Charles 7:31
David 6:67,115,117-120,171,
173 Deborah 6:73 Dorothy 5:4,
-6:73,113 Ebenezer 2:168,
-3:62,64,112,-6:69,74,115,119,
-7:27,90 Eleanor 3:157
Elizabeth 4:107,-5:50,-6:34,
117-119,175 Elizabeth Furber
7:30 Enoch 6:35 Eunice 3:62
George 3:112,-4:147,-6:117,
118 George H. 4:8 Hannah
3:112,-4:148,-5:145,-6:67,114
Isaac 6:173 Jacob 6:115 James
2:170,-3:108,109,112,157,
-4:147,-5:1,-6:67,73,75,115
James Horn 7:31 Jane 3:62,64,
112,-7:90 Jennie 5:151 John
2:167,-3:62,109,112,-4:146,
150,-5:3,-6:72,73,114-117,173
John M. 5:1,-6:116,175,-7:30
John Musset 7:27,29,30
Jonathan 1:172,-3:62,-5:1,5,
-6:73,115 Joseph 2:176,-3:62,
-4:107,111,-6:73 Kezia 6:75,
118 Love 6:74 Lucy 5:2,-6:72,
115 Lydia 1:172,-6:73 Martha
6:119 Mary 2:170,-3:62,109,
112,157,158,160,-4:60,151,
-5:6,55,-6:66,72,113 Mehitable
6:118 Miriam 4:60 Moses 5:5,
-6:74 Nicodemus 3:158 Olive
3:160,-6:118 Paul 5:3,-6:116
Phebe 5:146,-6:175 Richard
3:62,-4:19,-6:68,73,116,-7:29
Ruth 3:157 Sally 7:30 Samuel
2:170,-3:112,157,158,160,
-4:60,-6:116 Sarah 1:172,
-4:111,-6:73,-7:89,119,171,175
Simon 6:120 Solomon 5:115
Stephen 5:55,-6:117,-7:30,31
Susan 6:35 Susanna 3:109,
-5:3,-6:117,-7:30 Widow 6:116
PLAISTED, Captain 3:175 Elisha
3:53,-4:10 Elizabeth 3:176
George F. 1:182 Ichabod 3:52,
54,174 John 1:14,-2:103,
-3:52,53,55,172,-4:49 Joshua

97

PLAISTED (continued)
3:53 Mary 3:51-54,56,-5:43
Mehitable 3:53 Mrs. 3:175
Olive 4:53 Samuel 3:54,-5:44
William 5:168
PLATTS, Huldah 6:190
PLUM(M)ER, Abigail 6:38
Abraham 3:179,180 Anna 3:133
Beard 4:150,-6:75 Benjamin
5:152 Caroline 6:39 Daniel
1:124,-2:168,-3:114,115,179-
181,-5:23,173,-6:185 David D.
3:179,180 Ebenezer 6:117,139
Eliza 6:160 Elizabeth 3:42,
179,-5:49,56,151,-6:71
Ephraim 5:5,6,152,-6:115
George W. 4:86 Hannah 3:179,
-4:173 Henry M. 2:165 John
5:8,173,-6:71 John J. 4:86,
-5:181,182,-6:6-8 Joseph
4:148,-6:73 Joseph C. 3:179
Josiah 3:41 Lois 4:149 Lydia
5:120,-6:120 Mary 3:113,179,
-4:168 Nancy 3:179 Nathan
3:136 Olive 6:36 Otis 3:47
Patience 1:124 Quintus 4:86
Rebecca 3:179 Rhoda 6:34
Richard 1:124,-2:145 Samuel
3:115,179,180,-4:86,168,-5:1,
181,-6:115,117,118,120 Sarah
3:179,180,-4:86,-6:35 Sarah F.
4:86 Susan 6:120 Susanna 5:50
Thomas 7:32 William 4:86,-
6:159 William, Jr. 7:39
PLUNKET, Abraham 4:35
PLURIEN, Guilleaume (William)
3:68,75
POLLARD, Achsah 7:22 Barton
3:87 Elizabeth 3:170 Francis
3:42 Jacob 4:175 Mary 4:173
POLLY, Jonathan 4:57 Mr. 4:57
POMERY - POMMERY
(POMEROY), Leonard 2:1-6
Mrs. 3:176 Rebecca 4:9
Richard 4:11
POMFRETT, William 1:177,180
POND, Maria 4:8 Nathan G. 2:93
PONTE, Leonard 3:68,75
POOR, Ann 2:155 Charles 2:155
George 2:155 John 2:88,92,155,
-3:125 John F. 2:155 Lydia
4:173 Richard 2:192 Sarah

POOR (continued)
2:155
POPE, Hannah 5:25 Lydia 4:162
Sarah 5:171 William 5:42
POPKIN, Thomas 6:105
PORTER, Caroline 1:138 Huntington 1:138,-4:24 Isaac 7:17
John 1:138,-6:141 John L. 6:93
Juliet 5:192,-6:141,142 Maria
1:138 Martha 6:141 Mary B.
7:26 Mr. 7:76 Nathaniel S.
1:138 Robert 4:126 Samuel
6:141 Samuel H. 1:138 Sarah
1:138 Susanna 1:138
POTTER, Alvira W. 7:68 Ann
7:24 Anthony 6:54,56 Comfort
7:71 Ephraim 6:51 Jacob A.
7:23 John 4:35 Joseph 6:56
Lydia 6:57 Phebe A. 7:69
Sarah 3:135 Sarah F. 7:24
POTTINGER, Elspeth 4:2
POTTLE, Aaron 3:11 Aaron T. M.
4:71 Abigail 6:118 Bemsley
3:11 Benjamin 3:11,128,-4:125
Deborah 2:16 Dudley 3:11
Eleanor 3:165 Eliza J. 4:71
Elizabeth 2:16 George W. 4:71
Hannah T. 4:71 Henry 3:11,
165,-4:71 Jane 3:11 Jennie
2:156 Jonathan 6:118 Joseph
5:4 Judah 2:156 Judea 2:15
Levi 3:11 Lucretia 4:117 Lucy
4:115 Mary 3:11,-5:4 Mary A.
4:71 Samuel 2:156,-3:11 Sarah
2:15,16,-3:128,-4:71 Sarah M.
3:128 Simon 2:15,156 Susan M.
5:36 William 2:15,16
POTTS, Thomas 4:10
POWELL, Charlotte 6:168 James
7:26 John 3:25,73 Keyes 6:164
Mary 5:44
POWERS, Mr. 1:111 Walter 6:153
PRATT, Jennie 2:32 Joseph H.
2:32 Leonard 6:161 Lucy Ann
7:72 Martha E. 2:32 Onor 6:192
PRAY, Abigail 2:38 Charles 5:115
Ebenezer 2:183,-3:20,71
Elizabeth 2:170,-4:99 Frances
Farnum 7:88 Hannah 1:38
Joanna 4:58 John 2:104,-5:40
Joseph 3:85 Joshua 5:150
Richard 4:58 Sarah West 7:89

PREBLE, Abraham 4:152,189
Captain 3:151 Commodore 4:7
Humility 4:189 Jonathan 3:54
Mary 4:189 Miriam 3:54 Rufus
2:37
PRENTICE, Joseph 3:170
PRESBY, Anna 6:107 Elizabeth
6:32 Mary 5:143 Mrs. 6:32
Paul 6:32
PRESCOTT, Abigail 3:179
Adaline A. 2:35 Alice 4:85 Ann
5:103 Benjamin 2:34,36
Catherine 2:35 Chase 3:117,
-4:135 Daniel 4:85 Deborah
5:182 Dorothy 2:34,-4:134
Dudley 4:131 Elisha 4:89
Elizabeth 3:180 Elizabeth E.
2:34 George B. 2:35 George W.
2:34 Hannah 1:137,-2:69,
-3:117,118,184,-4:132 Hannah
H. 6:7,92 Harriet 2:34,35 Har-
riet G. 2:35 Harriet M. 5:20
Henry 2:34 Honor 3:178 James
2:43,71,109,111,131,-7:24
Jeremiah 2:65,69,130,-4:134
John 3:117,179,181,-4:91,131,
169,-5:81 John H. 6:7 Jonathan
3:117,118,-4:132,134,184
Joseph 4:90,133 Joseph N.
2:34 Joshua 2:43,133,-3:37,
-5:103 Judith 7:57 Lewis 5:18
Mary 2:34,109,111,-3:42,117,
134,-4:86,89,90,-5:81,103,
-6:163 Mary N. 2:34 Mary R.
6:7 Mercy G. 2:34,36 Miriam
3:117,181 Mr. 3:103 Mrs. 3:37
Nathan G. 4:134 Olive 4:131
Patience 3:44 Phebe 4:85
Rachel 4:90 Rebecca 2:111,
-3:117,119,183,-4:10,134
Reuben 4:86,134 Reuben A. 6:7
Ruth 4:180 Samuel 4:90,133,
-5:181 Sarah 3:117,179,182
Sarah S. 5:21 Simon 4:85,90
Stephen 4:134 Susanna 4:90
William 2:35,-3:117 William
H. 2:34 William P. 2:34,35
PRESLEY, Jane 6:192
PRESSON, John 1:12 Nathan
6:154 Richard 6:138 Robert
4:79

PRESSY, Elizabeth 3:90 Heph-
zibah 3:91 Paul 3:90
PRESTON, Nathan 7:39 Susanna
4:49 William 6:161
PRICE, Herman 7:17 Simeon 6:56
PRIDHAM, Isaac 2:36
PRIEST, Amos 5:139 Calvin S.
2:34 Charity 5:138 Daniel
5:139,-6:42 Eliza 2:34 Jane
2:34 Laura 2:34 Mrs. 5:139,
-6:42 N. 2:34,35,37,38 Nathan
2:34,37 Polina 2:34 Samuel
4:77 Susan A. 7:64 Thomas
5:44,138,139,-6:42
PRINCE, Benjamin 3:66,74
Elizabeth 6:109 Isaac 3:132
James 3:131 Joanna 6:3
Joseph 6:3 Lydia 6:3
PROCTOR, Eliza A. 7:67 Hial
7:25 Isaac 6:162
PROUT, Elizabeth 5:135 Margaret
5:135 Richard 5:135
PROWT, Barnes 3:147
PRYOR, Patience 2:169
PUCKLINHORN, John 6:177
PUDNEY, William 6:50
PUE, Rebecca A. 4:8
PUFFER, Lavina W. 7:70
Thomas 6:166 Thomas, Jr.
7:71
PUGSLEY, John 4:12
PULSIFER, Benjamin 4:91
Elizabeth 3:144,-5:45 Jonathan
3:144,-5:45 Susanna 5:46
PUMMARY (PUMMERY),
Elizabeth 2:169 Jane 4:103
PUNTY, Peter 1:22
PURINGTON, Abby M. 6:126
Abigail 1:68,-5:25 Abijah
4:161 Abraham 1:119,-3:35
Alice R. 6:91 Amos 4:161
Amos D. 6:20,126 Amy 4:9
Anna 1:118,124,-4:69 Benaiah
4:124,-7:8 Benajah 1:120,
-4:44,-5:125 Daniel 1:60,65,
72,174,-4:69,-6:20,25 Daniel
T. 1:174 Edward J. 6:91 Elisha
1:65,119,161,-4:161,-6:183,184
Elizabeth 3:184 Em 3:50
Hezekiah 1:119 Huldah 1:161,
-5:126,-6:19 Isabella 1:119

PURINGTON (continued)
J. K. 5:127 Jacob 4:44,-5:25
Jacob K. 1:173,-2:32,-6:20,91
James 1:127,-4:44,69,-5:175
John 1:59,68,121,124,-4:44,
69,-5:25,121,125,173 Joseph
4:136 Josiah R. 4:117 Lydia
1:174,-4:69,161 Mary 1:173,
-5:25,-6:20 Mary E. 6:91
Micajah 1:173,-4:68,-6:20
Moses 1:59,120,121,127,
-2:145,-4:44,-5:25,126,-7:8
Mr. 2:24 Patience 5:173 Peace
1:120,127,-4:69,-5:125,127,
-7:8 Pelatiah 4:44 Phebe 4:161
Rebecca 2:32 Robert 1:3-5,9,
10,12,-2:23,97,-3:51,-4:161
Ruth 1:65,72,-4:16,-5:29
Samuel 1:161,-4:161,-5:29
Sarah 4:69,-5:122,-6:25 Sarah
A. 2:32,-6:91,183 Stephen
1:68,-5:25,-6:183 Theodate
1:59,121 Thomas 4:10 William
1:119,-2:127 Zaccheus 1:60,
118,124,-3:31,-4:68,69
PUTNAM, Allen 5:36 John 6:164
Nehemiah 7:23 Samuel R. 4:6
PUTNEY, Jewett 6:54 Josiah
6:166
PYM, Mary 1:110
QUADREAU, Patris 3:75
QUELEE, Henry 3:68,76
QUICK, Chatiry 4:58 Daniel 4:56
Mr. 4:99 Nathaniel 4:56
QUIMBY, Aaron 3:91,-4:174,
-5:110,-6:31 Abigail 2:72
Abraham 4:174 Alice 2:47,
-3:42 Andrew 5:160 Benjamin
3:133 Daniel 3:44,131,-5:55,
-7:54 David 2:44,47,66,-3:39,
88,167,-5:103,107,110,154,159
Eliphalet 5:160,-6:30 Elisha
3:135 Elizabeth 5:102,107
Elizabeth B. 5:19 Fred E.
1:29,31,79,182,-2:42,165,192,
-3:48,139,186,188,189,-4:48,
82,96,144,192,-5:33,48,85,96,
179,192,-6:96,132,-7:83 Hannah 6:31 Henry C. 5:144 Jacob
3:44,133,-4:190,-5:110,6:27
Jeremiah 2:44,-3:88,-5:159
John 3:88,129,168,-4:177,

QUIMBY (continued)
-5:103,159,160 Jonathan 6:30
Laban 4:190 Lucinda A. 6:7
Lucy 3:135 Mary 3:41,134,
-4:177,-5:110,-6:30,51 Mary
Ann 7:25 Mima 5:159,160
Miriam 4:178,190,-6:27 Moses
3:87,-5:110 Mrs. 6:27,30 Paul
3:133 Rebecca 3:133 S. E.
4:190 Samuel 2:48,-3:89 Sarah
2:69,-3:133,-4:173,-5:154
Susanna 3:135,-4:178 Timothy
5:159 Trustram 3:86,-6:30
QUINCY, Anne 5:133 Edmund
5:91,131,133 Edmund H. 5:166
Elizabeth 5:91 John H. 5:131
QUINN, John 3:25,71
QUINT, Ann 2:173,-3:156,157
Anna 3:157 Anne 4:111 Benjamin 5:134,136,139,187,-6:43
Benjamin R. 4:112 Dr. 2:40,41
Eliza 1:157 Eliza A. 7:64
Elizabeth 3:156,-4:112,155-
157,-5:189 John 3:156,157,
-4:14,156 Jonathan 3:156,
-4:111,112,155-157 Joseph
4:111,-6:43 Joshua 3:156,
-4:157 Margaret 3:157,-5:139
Martha 3:156,-5:74 Mary
3:111,-4:155,-5:80,136,-6:42,
190 Mrs. 5:136,139,187,189,
-6:42,43 Rossa 4:157 Samuel
1:157 Sarah 3:157,-5:74,80,187
Susanna 5:189 Thomas 3:4,61,
157,-4:15,-5:74,80,134,189,
-6:42
QUORNON, Jean 3:68,76
RACKLEIFE, Mrs. 3:173 William
3:173
RACKLEIFT, Mary 4:134
RACKLETY, Mary 3:2
RACKLEY, Anna 4:142 William
4:10
RAGG, Jeffrey 1:6,179
RAINES (see RAYNES), Francis
1:7 Mr. 2:22
RAITT, William 3:8
RALLE, Sebastian 6:2
RAMSDELL, Bartlett 4:191
Elizabeth 4:191 Emma 4:191
RAND, Abial 1:39,45 Abigail
1:84,88,95,-4:46 Amos 1:38,

RAND (continued)
82,92 Amy 1:94 Anne 1:38
Aphiah 1:137 Bethiah 1:48,92
Blake H. 1:182 Caroline 2:136,
139 Daniel 4:126 David 1:91
Deborah 1:129 Dowst 1:88
Ebenezer 1:94 Elizabeth 1:35,
36,38,39,83,84,88,92-94,143,
-3:168,-4:46,54 Enoch 1:94
Ephraim 1:39,87,91 Esther
1:38,82 Francis 1:9,13,-2:25-
27,60,62 George 1:48,94 Hannah 1:39 Hannah G. 6:39 Hepzibeth 1:81 Ira 1:143 Israel
1:87 James 5:51 John 1:94,
131,-4:46,79 John P. 7:17 John
T. 1:136 Jonathan 1:91,-4:46
Joseph 1:38,129,143,-2:139
Joshua 1:35,36,38,39,48,81-
84,92 Kezia 4:130 Levi 1:143,
-2:135 Lydia 4:46,58 Margaret
2:135 Martha 1:94 Mary 1:39,
87,91-93,129,136,137,143 Mary
J. W. 1:136 Mehitable 1:137
Meribah 1:39 Micah 1:82
Moses 4:46 Mrs. 3:56
Nathaniel 1:35,36,39,45,82,92,
136,137,-5:52 Nathaniel M.
1:143 Olive 1:45,136,143
Phebe 4:46 Philbrick 1:38,129
Philemon 1:35 Rachel 1:88
Reed V. 2:164 Reuben 1:39,93
Richard 1:39,94,136 Ruth 1:35,
36,38,39,48,81-84,137,-4:46
Samuel 1:84,87-89,136,137,
-2:135,-4:46,-5:147 Samuel H.
1:143 Sarah 1:38,39,84,88,
89,91,131,137,-2:135,-4:46
Susan 1:143 Susanna 1:137,
-5:7 Temperance 1:38,-5:116
Thomas 1:38,39,84,88,93,136
William 1:89,131,-2:135
RANDALL, Abigail 1:132,133,
142,-4:78,125 Ann 6:36 Anna
3:96 Daniel 1:132,-3:5,136,
-6:36,-7:2 Deborah 1:132,-2:37
Edward 1:12,81 Elizabeth
1:132,-3:101,-4:12,183,-5:54
Elizabeth W. 1:142 Esther
4:183 George 1:81,-2:139 Hannah 1:67,81-85,87,91,93,132,
-4:126,164 Idella 6:39 Jacob

RANDALL (continued)
1:22,-6:138 James 1:13,165,
-2:101,-3:29,-5:117 James M.
1:82 Job 4:184 John 1:83,132,
165,-2:136,139,-3:29,-4:77,
185,187,-5:59 John D. 4:140
John G. 2:131 Jonathan 1:93
Joseph 1:85,-4:10,75 Joses
1:132 Josiah 4:127 Levi 1:142
Levi D. 1:142 Lois 4:126,
-5:101 Love 4:127 Lucy 1:91
Mark 1:132,133 Mary 1:83,142,
165,-4:129,-5:8,152 Miles
4:127 Miriam 6:34 Olive 1:132
Rachel 7:2 Reuben 1:132,142
Richard 3:101,-4:12 Samuel
1:87,132 Sarah 1:67,142,
-2:37,139,-4:126,-5:54 Simon
1:67 Stephen 1:84 Susan S. 4:7
Thomas 1:91,-4:7,-6:33 William 1:82-85,87,91,93
RANDLETT, Elizabeth 3:165,
-5:146 Jonathan 5:119 Sarah
3:164
RANKIN(S), Andrew 3:30 Betsey
7:54 G. Andrew 3:74 Martha
3:45 Sarah 4:11
RANO, Elias 5:110,112,143,
154,157 Elizabeth 5:112 Han-
nah 5:157 Mary 5:154 Miss
5:143 Samuel 5:110
RATCLIFF, Elizabeth 5:39 Jane
5:39
RATHBONE, Mercy P. 6:121
RAWSON, Warren 6:168
RAY, F. M. 5:192 Samuel 2:94
RAYMOND, Abigail 4:142,-5:46
Jeremiah P. 6:163
RAYNEL, John 7:27 Mary 7:27
RAYNER, Mr. 6:145
RAYNES (see Raines), Nathaniel
6:69
REA, Samuel 2:165
RECORD, Mary 6:191
REDEAUX, Charles 3:27
REDFORD, Lieutenant 3:176 Mrs.
3:176 Sarah 1:17
REDINGTON, Miss 6:90
REDMON, Benjamin 3:21,73 John
2:85,107,110,112 Joseph 1:183
Margaret 2:85 Maria 2:107
Martha 2:107,110,112 Samuel

REDMON (continued)
2:85
REED, Abigail 5:59,88,-7:12
Andrew 3:59 Anna 7:12,13
Benjamin 5:115,117 Deborah
2:106 Elizabeth 1:140,-4:39,
-6:55,-7:13 George H. 6:16
Hugh 1:21 James 6:79 John
5:87,-6:79,-7:12,13 John G.
1:140 Joseph 3:59 Mark 5:53
Mary 2:106 Mr. 3:152 Mrs.
6:16,79 Nancy 5:54 Solomon
5:87,88
REEVES, Joseph 4:80
REINY, Agnes 4:102
REMICK, Caroline 2:140 George
W. 2:140 Ham 5:21 Hannah
4:51,57,58,97,-5:42 James
4:79 John 4:58,-5:42 Joseph
2:140 Mary 4:57,-6:33 Rebecca
4:58 Rufus 4:130 Samuel 4:97
Sarah 6:136 Stephen 3:7
Susanna 3:6 William 2:140,
-5:147
RENALS, John 1:3,-2:97 Mr.
2:172
RENDON, Joseph 5:40
RENNEL, William 4:102
RENO, Elias 3:41,-6:28,32 John
6:28 Joseph 6:32 Sarah 6:32
REO, Francois 3:67
REYNELL-UPHAM, William U.
1:109,-2:166
REYNOLDS, Abigail 5:148 H. K.
4:48 Lydia 5:150 Martha 5:120
RHODES, Patience 5:42
RICE, Jane 5:41
RICHARDS, Abigail 3:106,-4:147,
-6:72,-7:27 Bartholomew 6:74
Benjamin 3:106,107,-4:12,17,
-6:74 David 6:69 Deborah 6:65
Elizabeth 3:105-107,110,-5:49,
-7:27 Esther (Easter) 2:174,
-3:106,-4:15 Hannah 5:115
Isaac 5:151 James 7:27 Jane
3:107,-6:69 Jean 4:146 John
2:169,-6:67,74,113,-7:31 John,
Jr. 7:27 Jonathan 5:5,-6:66
Joseph 3:106,107,110,-4:11,
-6:113 Joseph, Jr. 7:90
Joseph, 3d 7:89,90 Lois 7:31
Lydia 5:56 Mary 2:171,-5:151

RICHARDS (continued)
Mehitable 5:119 Mr. 2:37 Mrs.
3:175 Nancy 4:77 Olive 6:66
Rebecca 2:169,-6:68 Richard
1:12 Salome 6:65 Samuel 6:65,
69 Sarah 2:175,-3:106,-4:15,
-5:55,-6:65,67,68,75,-7:90
Susanna 3:110,-6:74 William
3:174,175,-4:10
RICHARDSON, Abigail 3:3,-6:33
Dorothy 6:33 Eliza P. 4:117
Elizabeth 3:6 Hannah 1:159,
-5:145,151 James 2:186,-3:12,
-5:152 Jeremiah 3:87 John
3:83,-6:35 John A. 7:68 Joseph
1:159,-5:118 Lydia 5:148 Mary
5:152 Nancy 5:148 Penelope
2:76,-5:94 Phebe 6:39 Rebecca
5:4,-6:113 Samuel 4:132 Sarah
5:119 Susanna 4:148 Thomas
5:118 Timothy 3:8,-4:90,152
William 4:145
RICHMOND, Charles A. 3:48
RICKER, Abby 5:149 Abigail 7:51
Benajah 5:147,-7:85
Charles 5:119,-7:54 Clarinda
7:53 Daniel Downes 7:53
Ebenezer 5:52 Edmund 7:53
Edward S. 6:34 Elizabeth 5:149
Elizabeth Jane 7:53 Esther
6:37 Ezekiel 5:2,-6:175,
-7:27,28 George 2:93,-3:146
Hannah 5:119 Jedediah 5:113
Jesse 7:53 John 4:35,-5:7,118
Jonathan 7:52 Joseph 4:152
Joseph P. 4:126 Judith 3:83,
-4:11 Lucy 5:55 Lucy Ann 7:53
Lydia 5:114 Maturin 2:93,
-3:146 Mary 5:115 Moses 7:51
Nicholas 5:120,-6:175 Paul
5:145 Phineas 7:28 Rebecca
4:128 Samuel 4:146 Sarah
5:147,148 Sarah F. 7:53 Tam-
son 7:52 Tamson Downes 7:53
Thomas 5:146,-7:27 Timothy
4:149,-6:33 Tobias 4:148 Wil-
liam 7:28
RIDGEWAY, Sarah 6:104
RIGBY, Sarah 7:5
RILEY, Anna M. C. 2:165 John
5:164 Mrs. A. M. C. 4:48
RINDGE, Ann 5:135 Anne 5:139

RINDGE (continued)
Gotham 5:135,136,139,183
John 1:22 Mrs. 5:135 Olive H.
5:183 Sarah 5:136,139,183
RINES, Hannah 1:117 Mary 1:117
Thomas 1:117
RING, Benjamin 3:58 David
3:89,154 Deacon 4:61,63
Eliphalet 3:111 Elijah 5:192
Elizabeth 2:174,-3:58-61,
105,111 Issachar 5:192 Jane
2:173,-3:59 Jarvis 5:192
Joseph 3:58 Lucinda 5:143
Mary 2:173,-3:60,88,-4:14,
-6:178 Moses 5:143 Mrs. 3:154
Robert 5:192 Sarah 5:86,143
Seth 3:58-60,105,111,154,
-4:16,-5:86,192
RINGE, Jane V. 6:76 Jotham
6:44,76 Sarah 6:44,76 Thomas
W. 6:44
RIPLEY, William 5:8
ROACH, Guy 7:25 Lydia 5:115
Thomas 5:165,168
ROADS, Jacob 4:12 Mary 4:12
ROBBINS, W. A. 2:191
ROBERSON, Aseneah 6:138 Bathsheba 2:50 Jonathan 6:138
ROBERTS, Aaron 6:185 Abby E.
6:124 Abigail 1:65,-4:53,
160,-5:8,55,126,158,-6:17,101,
120 Abigail C. 6:38 Achsa 2:32
Alexander 3:40,-5:155 Amasa
6:25 Amos 6:122 Andrew J.
6:126 Anelietta 6:25 Ann W.
6:39 Anna 1:168,172,-3:36,
89,-6:84 Anna A. 2:30 Anna M.
2:31 Anna W. 6:33 Anne 1:66,
-4:145,162,-5:50,173 Anne M.
6:123,183 Asa 6:40 Benjamin
3:152 Captain 6:94 Charles
5:168,-6:122,126,-7:14 Charles
W. 6:84 Charlotte G. 6:83
Clarissa 6:121,-7:88 Cyrus
6:89 Daniel W. 6:84 David
1:126,167,170,-4:121,-5:175,
176,-6:84,185 David S. 6:81
Edmund 5:168,170 Eliphalet
5:158 Eliza 1:175,-5:126,
-6:124 Eliza A. 6:126
Elizabeth 1:61,66,121,167,
168,170,172,-2:31,32,45,191,

ROBERTS (continued)
-3:36,-4:120,-5:54,112,119,
126,146,150,173,175,-6:83,90,
101,121,171,176 Elizabeth J.
6:121 Elizabeth M. 6:84
Elizabeth N. 5:63 Emeline
6:40 Emily 6:25 Ephraim
1:167,-3:36,-6:25 Eunice
1:166,170-172,175,-5:126,
-6:85 Eunice E. 6:181 Eunice
V. 6:89 Ezekiel 5:160,173 Ezra
6:171 Francis A. F. 6:83
George 2:45,-5:107,110,112,
158,-6:121 George K. 5:126,
-6:83 Hannah 1:63,166-168,
175,-3:36,-4:103,121,-5:126,
151,174,-6:18,25,121,146,-7:50
Hannah E. 6:83 Hanson 5:63,
175,-6:126 Hatevil 2:191,
-3:152 Howard M. 6:127 Isaac
5:115 James 1:120,166,170-
172,175,-3:36,-4:42,-5:7,115,
126,-6:89,150,-7:87 James H.
5:174,-6:37 James W. 6:181
Jedediah 5:175 Jeremiah
1:170,175,-5:126,-6:84,124
Jesse 2:31,-5:124,126,
-6:123,126 Joanna 4:10 Joel
5:126 John 1:72,-2:67,191,
-4:12,42,151,-5:7,50,149,155,
-6:89,101,120,126,146,176,
-7:87 John C. 3:24,72,-6:81
John L. 6:37 John M. 6:84
Jonas 6:84 Jonathan 2:192,
-3:43,-5:107,157,-6:176
Jonathan D. 5:117,-6:81,185
Joseph 1:7,117,168,172,
-2:144,191,192,-4:40,42,152,
-5:28,63,-6:83,98,176 Joseph
J. 6:81 Judah 5:107 Kezia
1:60,61,63,65,69,71,72,117,121
Levi 6:121 Lewis 6:181 Love
2:30,32,-5:157 Lucy F. H.
5:174 Lucy J. 5:152 Lydia
1:69,-5:27,63,-6:81 Lydia M.
6:37 Margaret 4:42,104,
-5:157,-6:120 Martha J. 6:40
Martha Jane 7:87 Mary 1:126,
-2:75,-3:36,40,152,-4:55,152,
-5:4,5,53,-6:69,101,103,120,
-7:14 Mary A. 6:122 Mary C.
6:127 Mary E. 6:181 Mary J.

ROBERTS (continued)
6:81 Mary L. 5:174 Mary P.
6:36 Mehitable 5:53 Moses
1:66,120,121,124,127,167,172,
-3:36,-5:28,126,173,-6:17,75,
89,99,171-173,-7:1 Mr. 3:82,
-5:41 Mr. (Thomas) 1:178
Nancy 5:63,-7:60 Nathaniel
1:126,-4:42,49-51 Nicholas
1:168,-5:99,126 Nicholas H.
5:63,-6:83 Olive A. 6:181
Olive L. 6:126 Olney T.
6:181 Owen 7:49 Paul 4:42,-5:28
Phebe 6:142 Procinda 6:84
Rachel 6:112 Rebecca 5:54,
-6:120 Relief 5:3 Ruth 4:151,
-5:173 Ruth Abigail 7:87 Ruth
E. 6:123,126 Ruth T. 5:174,
-6:38 Samuel 2:46,-3:36,
-4:80,-5:94,150,160,-6:147
Samuel H. 6:126 Sarah 1:60,
-3:98,-4:42,-5:28,54,110,117,
152,-6:36,68,173 Sarah B. 2:31
Shubael 5:56 Silas 5:5 Stephen
1:60,61,63,65,69,71,72,117,
121,172,-2:30-32,-5:126,176,
-6:99,121,122,182 Stephen N.
6:127 Sukey 7:14 Susan L.
6:122 Susanna 5:114,-6:171
Susanna C. 6:84 Thomas
1:121,168,175,-2:31,32,-3:36,
-4:42,-5:118,126,175,-6:83,121
Thomas A. 2:192 Thomas E.
2:32,-6:122 Thomas H. 6:126
Timothy 3:3,-6:66,75,120
Walter 1:175,-5:126,-6:83,181
William 1:179,-4:149
ROBERTSON, Andrew 6:111
Elizabeth 7:19 Ismenia 6:112
Mehitable 6:112 Nancy 6:109,
166 Nathaniel 5:120 Peter
6:106 Preserved 6:169 Robert
3:73 Susan 6:108
ROBEY, Deliverance 2:84 Henry
2:84,86,90,-3:177 Ichabod
2:44,71,90,132 John 2:109
Judith 2:109 Meribah 3:40 Mrs.
2:72,132 Ruth 2:84,86,90
Samuel 2:86,-3:40,88
ROBIE, John 6:110
ROBINSON, Abednego 3:11
Abigail 1:186,-2:75,121,123,

ROBINSON (continued)
-3:11,12 Agnes 2:10,51 Almira
6:154,-7:39 Anna 1:175,
-2:53,-6:90 Bathsheba 1:186
Benjamin 2:53 Bradbury 3:12,
17 Charles 5:39 Chase 3:17
Daniel 1:116,122,-2:149 David
1:184,186,-2:10,12,51,53,-3:18
David Y. 1:79 Ebenezer 3:11
Elizabeth 1:53,116,122,175,
176,-2:53,75,76,148,149,-3:12,
133,136, 165,-6:33,101
Ephraim 5:165 Esther 1:186
George 6:159,-7:40 Hannah
1:176,183,186,-2:75,150,-6:90,
103 Isaiah S. 7:23 James
1:122,188,191,-2:149,-5:20,
128,146 Jane 3:12,126
Jeremiah 3:18 Jesse 3:164
Joel 6:90 John 1:188,-2:53,
149,-3:40 Jonathan 1:191,
-2:53,-3:11,12,17,18,87,122,
127,163,169,182,184 Joseph
1:188 Joseph E. 2:163 Josiah
3:119 Laona L. 5:48 Levi 2:53,
-5:116 Lucy 1:186,-2:12,51,
-3:130 Lydia 1:186,-2:149
Lydia T. 6:90 Margaret 1:116,
-5:60,-6:58 Martha 5:42 Mary
1:51-53,62,66,71,166,188,191,
-2:75,121,124,149,151,-3:4,11,
12,17,183,-6:90,101,103 Mercy
3:17,18,122,162,163,-5:7,-7:49
Meshech 3:11,-5:2 Miss 3:169
Mr. 5:43 Nancy 3:122,167
Nicholas D. 3:167 Noah 3:12,
18,122,-5:182 Robert 3:66
Samuel 2:149 Sarah 1:52,66,
186,188,-2:51,75,126,149,
-3:136,184,-5:118 Sarah J.
5:35 Shadrach 3:11 Stephen
2:149,-5:32,-6:90 Thomas
3:18,181,-5:182 Timothy 1:52,
53,62,66,71,166,175,176,-2:75,
76,149,150,-6:90,101,103 William 2:149,-6:90 Winthrop
3:18
ROBY, Luther 7:24
RODGERS (see also ROGERS),
Elizabeth Pinkham 7:88
ROGERS (see also RODGERS),
Aaron 5:31,32,-6:183 Abigail

104

ROGERS (continued)
5:42,-6:71 Abner 5:29 Ann 5:86
Anna 5:31 Anstrus 5:29 Ar-
temas 5:150 Caroline 6:64
Charles 5:146,-6:70,74 Charlotte 6:64 Daniel 1:106,
-2:158,159,192,-3:118,-5:86,
88-90,99,130,131,137,140,
-6:33 David 2:159,192 Deborah
1:126 Dorothy 1:106 Dorothy A.
6:64 Elizabeth 1:17,56,128,
-2:41,-3:93,115,-5:31,-6:64,
71,133,138 Enoch 6:104 Esther
3:98 Eunice 1:126,-5:29 Francis W. 7:20 George 3:7,
-5:29,-6:64 Hannah 1:58,71,
-3:7,-5:28,29,118,-6:74,-7:31
Huldah 5:31 Isaac 1:58,71,
113,-2:128 James 6:73,115
Jean 6:71 John 1:16,-3:104,
-5:31,88,90,-6:70,154,158,-7:7
Jonathan 1:58,114 Joseph 1:10
Joshua 5:115 Josiah 1:56 Levi
1:113,-5:31 Lucinda 7:20
Lydia 1:71,72,113,116,-5:29,
31,61 Margaret 6:104 Mark
5:137 Mary 2:173,-3:183,-6:3,
53,70,73,114,191 Mary A. 6:64
Mary E. 6:93 Mary (K. or H.)
7:18 Mehitable 5:86,137,140
Miriam 5:29 Mr. 3:82,103
Nancy 7:87 Nathaniel 1:16,17,
-3:54,-4:42,49-51,-5:60,-6:5,
64 Olive P. 6:64,139 Patience
1:58,-5:30 Paul 1:71,126,
-2:127,-5:29 Phebe 5:29,64
Rebecca 7:87 Robert 1:56 Ruth
4:151 Sarah 1:16,17,114,128,
-5:29,32,44,-6:17,64,71 Silas
6:183 Stephen 5:4 Stephen S.
6:54 Susanna 2:46 Thomas
5:130 William 6:113 William
R. 5:140
ROLFE, Benjamin 3:151,-6:51
Daniel 6:50 Henry 6:162 Jane
6:110 Mary 6:54 Mary A. 2:144
Mrs. 3:151 Nathaniel 6:52
Nathaniel, Jr. 7:70
ROLLINS, Abigail 2:121,175,
-3:106,127,-4:11,15,19,64,111,
112,115,125 Agnes 4:60 Alice
3:61,62,64,110,111,154,157,

ROLLINS (continued)
-4:18,63,-5:73 Anna 5:152 Anthony 4:111,-5:2 Asa 2:121,
-3:127,128 Augustus 6:34 Benjamin 3:111,-4:111,-5:66,72,
-6:173-175 Benjamin Heard
7:29 Bethene 3:112 Clarissa
3:162,-4:22 Daniel 2:50,121
-3:127,170 David 1:187,-2:13,
-5:66 Deborah 2:168,-3:53,105,
106,111,112,160,-4:14,111,
-6:72 Edward 2:173,-3:106,
-4:16,18,59,61,148,-5:149,
-6:72,114,147 Elisha 2:121,
-3:127 Elizabeth 1:187,-3:1,
-4:14,15,18,59,61,63,153,156,
-5:51,-6:173 Elsie 3:107 Esther 1:187,-4:18,59-61,63,
105,107,-5:115,-6:174 George
3:21,24,74,-4:105 Gertrude B.
3:94 Hannah 1:183,189,
-2:14,121,-3:4,60,111,127,161,
-4:22,59,-5:73,-6:21 Hannah
Heard 7:29 Harriet 6:93
Ichabod 2:164,175,-3:106,149,
-4:12,61,64,109,111,154,156,
157,-5:73,-6:149 James 1:179,
-2:168,-3:106,111,112,160,
-4:22,61,116,-6:148 Jane
4:125,-7:3 Jeremiah 2:14
Jeremiah S. 4:118 Joanna
4:108 John 1:190,-3:61,65,
105,106,-4:19,109,149,-6:173,
-7:3 John A. 4:126 Jonathan
1:187,-2:14,50,-3:110,-5:9
Joseph 1:189,-2:50,172,-3:2,
105,110,152,-4:15,18,59,-5:9
Joshua 2:121,-7:28,29 Joshua
N. 4:154,-5:4 Joshua Nutter
7:29 Jotham 2:14 Lazarus 6:68
Leah 4:61,-6:74 Levi 2:121,
-3:127,128,-4:22,-5:9 Loma
4:59 Lorenzo 6:21 Lydia 1:187,
-2:14,-3:64,-4:153,-5:73,
-6:109 Mark 2:121,-3:127 Martha 4:22 Mary 1:187,189,190,-
2:13,14,50,121,174,-3:105,106,
127,159, 177,-4:15,22,78,90,
108,111,118,154,156,-5:66,73,
-6:173 Mehitable 2:14,-3:118,
-5:9 Mercy 2:50 Moses 1:187,
-2:50,-6:116 Mr. 6:116 Nancy

ROLLINS (continued)
2:121,-3:127,162,-4:22,
-5:35,-6:173 Nathaniel 7:3
Nicholas 2:121,-3:127,128,
162,-4:22 Noah 3:110,-4:153,
-5:73 Obed 4:118 Olive 4:64,
109,111,112,154,156,157,-5:3,
73 Olivia A. 7:62 Patience 7:3
Paul 3:154 Phebe 3:43 Phebe
Heard 7:28,29 Rachel 1:189
Rebecca 1:190,-3:50 Robert
1:190,-4:61 Samuel 2:168,174,
176,-3:53,60-62,64,109-111,
154,-4:18,59-61,63,105,107,
108,111,126,154,156,-5:73
Sarah 1:187,190,-2:13,50,
171,-3:3,105,106,110,-4:18,
181,-5:66,-6:116,173 Seth F.
4:118 Sherburne 3:113 Stephen
1:190,-5:115,-6:173 Susan
6:175 Susanna 3:159,-4:18,59,
63 Temperance 4:157,-5:7
Thomas 1:187,-4:89 Valentine
4:18 William 4:80 William W.
6:36
ROOKS, Elizabeth 6:61
ROPER, Mary 2:82 Walter 2:82
ROPES, Joseph, Jr. 7:68 William
4:35
ROSE, Roger 3:104
ROSS, Betsey 4:82 Elizabeth 5:39
Hannah 3:130 John 5:44 Martha
5:116 Simon 5:148
ROUNDS, Holmes B. 2:166 Sarah
E. P. 2:166
ROUSE, Miss 5:42 Thomas 4:10
ROUSELEY, Mrs. 3:221 Robert
3:173
ROWE, ---- 7:2 Abigail 1:91,
-3:119 Anna 3:108 Anthony
5:42 Aritlus 4:91 Benjamin
3:111 Charlotte 4:133 Comfort
3:111 Deborah 3:110 Elizabeth
3:42,64,-4:106 Eunice 2:167
James 4:106 Joseph 3:154,171
Joseph F. 3:169 Josiah 5:18
Margaret 4:52,-5:40 Martha
4:10,-6:137 Mary 2:170,173,
-3:61,-4:15,-5:49 Miss 3:168
Moses 3:110 Mrs. 5:186
Nicholas 1:3,9,10,-2:24,27,61
Rachel 3:60,61,63,64,111,154,

ROWE (continued)
157 Samuel 2:170 Sarah 3:135
Sarah K. 5:186 Simon 6:7
Smith 7:70 Susanna 2:170
Thomas 2:169,-3:57,60,61,63,
64,111,154,157 William 3:63,
-5:186
ROWELL, Abraham 3:114 Chris-
topher 6:104 Daniel 3:170
David 5:69 Dorothy 3:43
Elizabeth 3:132,-6:77,-7:11
Elizabeth R. 3:168 Fanny
6:165 Hannah 2:70,-3:118,
-5:10 Jemima 2:70,-4:134,
-5:10 Job 5:69 John 3:118,
-5:10,-6:46,58 Jonathan 5:10
Joseph 6:109 Judith 3:88,
-4:175 Mary 5:69 Meribah 5:69
Moses 2:44,132 Mrs. 6:46,77,
78 Nehemiah 6:46,77,78,-7:11
Phebe 2:70 Philip 3:80 Sarah
2:70,-4:84,132,-5:10,-6:78
Susanna 2:70 Thomas 7:24
Widow 2:70,-3:39
ROWEN, Margaret 3:43 Mary 3:86
RUMRILL, Clement 4:9 Rachel
3:88 Rebecca 4:10
RUNDLETT, Abby 4:113 Abigail
4:169 Abraham 4:86 Beniah
3:113 Benjamin 3:87 Charles
1:189,-2:172,-3:152,-4:16,126,
-6:184 Daniel 1:189 David
2:153,-3:126,-4:130,-6:185
Dorothy 3:180 Elijah 3:115
Eliza D. 5:181 Elizabeth
1:189,-3:120 George 3:30,74
Hannah 2:163 Harriet 7:80
Jacob 2:153,-4:169 James
1:189,-2:50,162,-4:90,-6:160,
-7:80 Jane 2:153,-4:126 John
3:113,180,-6:184 Jonathan
1:189,-3:116,-4:133,134,136
Joshua 2:153 Josiah 1:189,
-2:50,-4:134 Lydia 1:189,
-3:116,-4:89 Mary 1:189,
-3:182,-4:16,133 Mary A. 5:35
Mercy 4:16 Moses 4:90 Nancy
3:184 Nathaniel 4:125 Newhill
A. 7:62 Priscilla 4:85 Rachel
4:135 Reuben 2:153 Rhoda 4:89
Richard 5:2 Ruth 1:183 Sarah
1:189,-3:119,-4:85 Sarah A.

RUNDLETT (continued)
4:113 Satchwell 3:25,74
Simeon 3:119,-4:113,117
Susanna 4:90 Theophilus
1:183,189,-2:153 Thomas N.
7:64 True 3:177
RUNNELLS, Abigail 4:182 Alice
5:147 Elizabeth 4:125 Hannah
4:127 Hazen 7:65,72 John 5:51
Jonathan 6:53 Jonathan, Jr.
7:20 Mary 4:126 Michael 5:3
Nathaniel 5:146 Samuel, Jr.
7:24 Sarah 4:76 William 3:44
RUNYON, Anna 1:150 Benjamin
1:150 John 1:150 Martha 1:150
Samuel 1:150 Vincent 1:150
RUSS, John 6:10 Joseph 5:41
Sarah 7:20
RUSSELL, Achsah 6:54 Eleazer
5:38 Elijah 6:57 John 5:94
Leonard 7:25 Lucy 5:93 Mary
W. 7:18 Philip 1:11 Rebecca
4:6 Thomas 5:43,-6:94 William 6:94 William F. 4:48
RUST, Ann 5:90 Anna 7:83 Anne
5:135,136,183,186,187 Eliza
3:142 Elizabeth 5:133,-6:51
Hannah 7:83 Hannah Marble
7:83 Henry 3:55,-4:50,-5:90,
129,130,133,135,136,139,183,
186,187,-7:83 Jane 5:139 John
6:56 Margaret W. 5:187 Mary
5:136 Mrs. 5:139 Nathaniel
5:186 Rebecca 2:144 Thomas
5:135 William 5:183
RUTHERSON, Mr. 5:40
RUTLING, Mary 4:189
RYAN, Deborah 4:187 Edmund
4:77 Hannah 7:65 Jeremiah
4:184 Michael 4:35
RYMES, Christopher 7:43 Mary
3:50,52,53,56,-4:102 Mrs.
3:175 Samuel 3:53,54,173,
-4:102,-5:43 William 3:54
SABIN, Elizabeth 4:192 William
4:191,192
SADLER, Edward 1:22
SAFFORD, Alice 1:18 John 1:18
Mary 1:18 Moses A. 3:45
Sophronia 7:62 Thomas 1:18
William 1:18
SAGART, John 3:44

SALISBURY, William 5:144
SALMAN, John 2:92 Mary 2:92
SALONETTE, Claude 3:76
SALTER, Abigail 6:80,-7:12
Alexander 1:88 Benjamin 7:77
Dorothy 7:13 Edward S. 6:80
Elizabeth 1:88,-7:15 Henry
7:12 Jane 7:13,15,74,76,77,79
John 1:88,-6:80,-7:13,15,74,
76,77,79 John, Jr. 7:12 Maria
Jane 7:76 Richard 5:162,169
Sarah 5:43 Sarah Ann 7:79
Titus 5:167 William Frost
7:74
SALTONSTALL, Colonel 3:152
Nathaniel 3:149
SALTRIDGE, Miss 5:40
SAMPSON, Elizabeth 5:40 Gideon
5:170 John 1:12 Nathaniel 4:36
R. 3:51 Richard 1:12
SANBORN, Abigail 2:46,129,
-3:87,168,-5:158 Abner 3:134,
-4:89 Abraham 2:46,-3:177,
-4:84,-5:72,103,105,107,109,
112,154,157,160,-6:27
Abraham, Jr. 7:18 Alice 3:133
Ann 2:89 Anna 4:88,172,-5:10,
68 Apphia 3:40 Aremintha
4:180 Asa 4:187,-6:160,-7:40
Benjamin 2:106,-3:42,168,171,
-4:178,-5:106,154,155,157,
160,-6:27 Bradbury 6:60 Caleb
5:168 Caroline 7:70 Catherine
3:132 Chandler 4:90,-5:10
Charles 3:169 Corson 3:133
Daniel 6:6,61 Daniel T. 5:65
Date 2:72 David 3:130,168,
-4:46,-6:29 David J. 6:18
David L. 6:19 Dearborn 4:86
Deborah 2:68,-3:86,-5:109
Diadama 4:136 Dorothy 1:116,
-3:41,-4:179,-5:60,-6:27 Dudley 1:116 Ebenezer 3:167,169,
-6:53 Edward 5:158 Eleanor
5:10 Elijah 3:131 Elisha
5:107,157,158 Elizabeth 2:72,
-3:42,43,131,132,-4:172,-5:21,
22,45,72,154,157,-6:29,32
Elsie 7:157 Enoch 3:43,132
Enos 6:27 Ezekiel 4:85,-6:93,
-7:58 Farriene 5:18 Gulielma
6:19 Hannah 3:136,-4:91,176,

107

SANBORN (continued)
-5:106,107,112,-7:57 Hannah
P. 2:32 Henry 2:32,-3:182,
-4:89,136 Huldah 3:130,-6:28
Isaac 3:131,-6:27 Jacob 5:17,
49,-6:158 James 3:120,-4:88,
-5:10 James F. 6:160 Jane
5:18,68 Jemima 4:131,133,172
Jeremiah 5:65,-6:159,-7:40
Jesse 3:127 Jethro 3:42,129,
-5:157,-6:29,31,32 Joanna
2:71,-3:88,-4:180 John 2:67,
68,71,82,84,85,88,89,91,106,
109,129,133,-3:87,91,114,167,
-4:46,-5:65,107,110,111,158
John D. 5:68 John G. 3:177
John R. 1:99 Jonathan 2:43,65,
66,71,72,109,131,-3:37,38,89,
90,132,181,-4:10,88,-5:10,72,
104,109,111, 155,157,159,
-6:31,62 Joseph 2:85,-4:46,
78,-5:72,-6:27,60,63 Joseph C.
5:103 Josiah 5:157,159 Juda
5:157 Judith 2:65,131 Kezia
6:18 Lavina A. 7:44 Levi 4:178
Louisa L. 5:21 Love 2:47,
-3:41 Lydia 2:71,-3:115,-4:88
M. Ray 3:48 Margaret 2:109,
-5:157,-6:27 Maria L. 7:72
Mary 1:116,-2:45,46,72,82,84,
85,87-89,91,105,106,109,130,
131,-3:86,133,-4:46,133,-5:21,
157,-6:31,54,139,166 Mary A.
6:19 Mehitable 2:44,72
Mephibosheth 2:89 Mercy 2:87
Moses 4:179,-5:109,-6:32
Moses D. 3:179 Mr. 5:40
Nancy 3:113,120,-4:88 Nathan
4:172 Nathaniel 2:91,-4:10
Oliver L. 7:25 Paul 3:42,
-5:104,107,111,155,157,-6:28
Peter 2:45,68,69,71,130,133,
-3:38,132,-4:180,-5:106,108,
153,156,158,-6:27 Phebe 3:133
Phineas 3:167,-5:109,155
Rachel 4:172,180,-5:72
Rebecca 5:111 Reuben 3:41,
171,-4:46,-6:32 Richard 2:89,
-5:68 Ruth 4:90 Samuel 2:44,
65,-3:45,89,178,-4:118,-5:61,
72,-6:27,29,32 Sarah 2:105,
-3:41,114,120,136,-4:88,136,

SANBORN (continued)
182,-5:10,17,45,72,105,108,
112,154,-6:29 Shuah 5:160
Simeon 5:112,-6:27 Simon 2:32
Smith 6:93 Stephen 2:88,109
Susan A. 6:19 Susanna 4:133,
-6:109 Tabitha 5:65 Timothy
3:42,-5:155,158,-6:29 Tristram
2:43,67,129,131,133,-3:40,131,
-4:91,-5:106,109,110,112,153,-
157,-6:27,31 Victor C. 2:166
Widow 2:44 William 2:87,89,
105,109,-3:44,119,133,134,
-5:45,68,-6:27,28,31 Worster
2:69,-3:89 Zadock 3:88
SANDEMAN, Robert 6:64
SANDERSON, Moses 5:182 Peter
3:178 William 5:41
SANFORD, D. 5:119
SANKEY, Caesar 1:72,-5:30
Simon 5:30
SANNO, Peter 3:69,76
SARGENT, Aaron 3:44,-6:169
Abigail 4:91,-7:25 Anna 6:109
Benjamin 3:100 David 3:88
Edward 1:23,-3:82,-4:10
Elizabeth S. 7:72 Hannah 3:7
Isaac 6:169 Jemima 6:6,164
John 1:10,-4:133,-6:169 John
P. 7:22 Jonathan 4:176,-5:17
Joseph 1:23,-3:53 Margaret
5:53 Martha 3:88,-7:71 Mary
5:21,127,-6:106 Miriam 5:62
Moses L. 7:17 Nancy 6:163
Nathaniel 1:23 Parna B. 7:26
Rachel 3:129 Rufus K. 6:160
Ruth 1:23,-3:50,52,53,56
Samuel 3:89,134 Sarah 1:15,
-5:21 Sterling 3:45 Stephen
6:161 Tappan 4:179 Thomas
6:55 Thomas B. 7:70
SATTERLY, Miriam 3:91
SAUNDERS, Abigail 1:88
Elizabeth 1:130,141 George
1:130,-4:133 Hannah 1:130
John 1:88,141 Joseph 3:80
Martha 1:130 Mary 1:93,130,
-3:43,-5:44 Mercy 1:130
Richard 4:11 Robert 7:70
Samuel 1:130 Sarah 1:88,130,
141,-3:77,-4:11 Tryphena 1:88
Willard 7:70

SAUNDERSON, Lydia 2:81 Mary
2:81 Robert 2:81
SAVAGE, Benjamin 4:76,-5:136
Deborah 6:43 Elizabeth
3:51,52,56,-4:130,-5:136 Esther 5:40 Henry 1:10,12 John
3:174,176 Josiah 5:91,136,138,
189,-6:43 Mary 5:138
Mehitable 6:136 Mrs. 3:175,
176,-5:136,138,189,-6:43
Samuel 4:183,-5:189 Thomas
5:91 W. T. 6:15
SAVORY (SAVERY), Elizabeth
5:133 Josephine A. 2:142 Mary
5:91,131 Robert 2:142,175,
-5:91,129,131,133 Sarah 4:175
SAWTRIDGE, John 5:140 Mrs.
5:138,140 Richard 5:138,140
SAWYER, Abigail 6:181 Benaiah
5:57 Bilfield 1:113 Caleb 5:81
Charles F. 5:82 Charles H.
1:79,-2:166,-5:81,82,83 Content 1:167,-4:41 Dorothy 3:44
Edward 5:57,81,82 Elijah 1:175
Elizabeth 1:164,-3:89,-4:75,
-5:57,82,-6:20 Elizabeth C.
6:89 Enoch 4:41 Ephraim 4:45
Eunice 2:30 Francis A. 5:81
Hannah 1:66,-4:42,-5:80,81
Hosea 5:57 Huldah 1:66,72,
-4:163,-5:80 Jacob 1:51,55,57,
65,114,116,161,167,-2:124,
-3:35,-4:41,-6:20 James 4:45,
-5:18 James C. 5:82 Jason
7:41,42 John 2:30,-4:185,
-5:21,81,-6:20 Jonathan 5:81
Joseph B. 6:89 Josiah 4:180
Justin 5:57 Kezia 4:41 Levi
1:172,-5:57,127,-6:89 Levi N.
6:89 Lydia 4:41,-5:58,-6:89
Lydia E. 6:89 Margaret 6:162
Martha 5:81 Mary 1:72,164,
172,-4:41,180,-5:30,81,-6:190
Micajah 4:41 Miriam 1:175,
-3:36 Moses 1:55,65,66,72,
-2:30,-3:36,90,-4:36,160,
-6:127 Nahum 5:57 Nancy 4:76
Nathaniel 4:174 Patience
1:116,-4:41,-5:59 Peter M.
6:20 Phineas 5:81 R. W. 4:189
Robert W. 5:96 Ruth 5:57
Sarah 1:55,57,65,113,114,

SAWYER (continued)
116,161,167,-3:35,-4:160,
180,-5:157 Sarah A. 6:20,-7:41
Sarah Ann 7:41 Seth 5:81
Stephen 1:55,57,65,113,114,
164,172,-3:34,-4:41,-5:57
Susan E. 5:82 Susanna 1:65,
-4:41 Thomas 4:45,-5:81
Thomas E. 5:58 Timothy 4:41
Tirzah 4:174 Walter 5:57
Widow 5:157 William 1:175,
-2:93,-3:139,189,-5:48,81,
-6:18 William D. 5:82
SAYER, Benjamin 3:39 Joseph
5:153 Juda 5:153 Mary 3:90
Miriam 3:45
SAYWARD, Hannah 3:7 Henry
2:83 James 5:114 John 1:12
Joseph 2:83 Mary 2:83 Richard
2:23,61
SCALES, Emily 7:67 Hannah 4:16
James 4:99,-6:57 John 3:57
Mary 4:101 Matthew 3:57,-4:98
Mr. 4:102 Nancy 4:186 Samuel
E. 6:164
SCAMMON, Barnabas 1:192 Comfort S. 3:165 Elizabeth
1:52,58,192,-3:162,-5:37
Hezekiah 3:162 Humphrey 3:16
James 1:192,-3:127,162 John
4:96 Mary 3:162 Rachel 1:191,
192;-3:162 Richard 1:52,58,
191,-2:125,127,-3:162,-4:44,
115 Samuel 1:191,-3:162 Sarah
4:116 William 1:183,191,192,
-3:162
SCATES, Benjamin 5:152,-6:176,
-7:28 John 3:23,74,-4:145,
-5:53 Joshua 3:24,73 Lucy
5:54 Lydia 5:52 Norton 5:147,
-6:176
SCEVA, Hannah 5:2 Joseph 5:2,
-6:174
SCHEGEL, Benjamin 1:46 Christopher 1:39,40,46,85 Deborah
1:39,40,46,85 Jacob 1:40,85
Mary 1:39
SCHELLING, John 5:18
SCOLLEY, Elspeth 3:3
SCOTT, David 4:102 James 2:64
SCRIBNER (see SCRIVNER),
Aaron 5:63 Abigail 5:63 Anne

SCRIBNER (continued)
4:149 Benjamin 1:126,
-5:62,63,153,157,-6:184
Deborah 2:44 Dorothy 5:63
Ebenezer 5:143,156,-6:32 Edward 2:70,-5:103,106,109,
153,156 Elias 5:142 Elizabeth
2:45,-3:129,-4:175,-5:153
Grace 3:168 Hannah 2:70,
-3:129,-5:63,156 Huldah
1:126,-5:62,63 Iddo 5:143,
-6:29 John 3:44,136,-5:106,143
John M. 5:142 Josiah 5:143,
159 Margaret 1:126,-3:41,
-5:62,175 Martha 3:40
Mehitable 5:143 Ruth 5:63
Samuel 5:63,108,110,142,
143,156,159,-6:29,32 Sarah
5:63,142 Stephen 5:63 Susanna
5:108 Thankful 5:63 Thomas
5:103 William 5:153
SCRIEVNER (SCRIVENER -
SCRIBNER), Benjamin 3:41
Deborah 4:84 Elsie 3:89
SCRIGGIN(S), Abigail 6:140 Mary
4:130 Samuel 6:140 Susanna
6:139
SEAMAN, Richard 5:166
SEARL, Catherine 5:46 Elizabeth
2:50 John 2:50
SEAVEY, Abigail 1:35,36,38,39,
41,81,-4:103,-6:34,67,-7:88
Andrew 7:24 Anna Phips 7:13
Annie K. 6:144 Benjamin
3:92,-5:41 Captain 5:88,90
Catherine 1:86,-7:66 Charles
1:144 Comfort 6:73 Damaris
3:92 Deborah 1:39 Ebenezer
3:53 Eleanor 6:46 Elijah 1:86
Eliza J. 1:144 Elizabeth
1:40,41,92,136,143,144,-3:92,
-6:73 Elizabeth Moore 7:12
Eunice 3:2,48 Frederica 4:151
Hannah 1:38,39,92,136,-5:117,
-6:42 Helen 3:95,-4:82 Henry
1:35,40,86,-3:92 Ichabod 6:34
Ithamar 1:35,41,-6:67,70
James 1:81,-2:168 Jean 6:69
Joanna 1:38,92 John 3:92,
-4:49,-5:90,-6:42 John March
7:16 Jonathan 1:41 Jonathan T.
6:39 Jonathan Tasker 7:88

SEAVEY (continued)
Joseph 1:38,39,-5:87,88 Joses
1:136 Joshua 1:136 Katherine
7:77 Lydia H. 7:66 Margaret
1:96 Maria 7:75 Mark 5:168,
189,-6:42,44,46,77,79,-7:12,
13,16 Mark W. 6:79 Martha
7:75 Mary 1:35,41,86,-3:92,
-4:147,-6:44,67,-7:22 Mary A.
D. 6:39 Mary M. 1:136
Mehitable 1:41,140,-6:77
Michael 6:42 Moses 1:41 Mr.
6:114 Mrs. 3:50,56,-5:189,
-6:42,44,46,77,79 Nathaniel
1:136 O. D. 5:177 Olive 1:136
Oliver 1:144 Paul 1:140
Rebecca 3:92 Ruth 1:86 Sally
L. 7:83 Samuel 1:35,36,38,39,
41,92,144,-3:92,-6:70,-7:17
Sarah 1:36,136,140,-6:127
Shadrach 7:67 Sidney L. 3:191
Solomon 1:39 Sophronia 1:144
Stephen 3:92,-5:87 Tamson
3:92 Theodore 1:143 Thomas
1:9,10,13,-2:23,25,27,60,
-3:53,92,-6:61 William 1:4,9,
10,12,-2:23,27,59-63,97,98,
-3:51,92,-5:189,-7:75,77 Wil-
liam G. 1:143 William W.
5:36 Winthrop 1:136
SEAWARD, Anna 5:137 Benjamin
3:19,73 Henry 3:59,-5:137,167
John 5:167 Joseph 2:98 Mrs.
3:175,-5:137 Sarah 3:59 Wil-
liam 2:192,-3:59
SECOMB, Elizabeth 4:174 Joseph
5:103,153,-6:26 Mary 4:177
Richard 6:137 Sarah 4:175
SEDEY, John 3:66,74
SEELEY, Mr. 1:179
SEFERAT, Philip 1:12
SELLARS, Tobias 2:182 William
5:42
SENTOR, Mr. 5:44
SERINGER, Joseph 2:183
SEVEAT, Margaret 4:52
SEVER, Caleb 5:155 Martha 3:167
Mr. 3:137 Thomas 3:42,-5:155
SEVERANCE, Anna 3:167,-6:28
Anne 5:156 Benjamin 3:42,
135,-5:153,156 Catherine 4:177
Dudley 6:27 Ebenezer 3:89

SEVERANCE (continued)
Elizabeth 3:90,135,-5:153
Ephraim 3:44,-5:159,-6:27,30
Hannah 3:88,169 Jacob 3:86,
-4:180 John 5:159 Jonathan
3:87,-5:19 Jonathan B. 4:74
Joseph 6:26,28 Lydia 3:90
Mary 3:41 Moses 6:27 Mrs.
6:26 Nathan 5:20 Peter 6:30
Samuel 3:171
SEVERNS, Benjamin 2:47
Elizabeth 2:47 Ephraim 2:44,
47,72,-3:38 Hannah 2:67,70
Jacob 2:48 John 2:47 Joseph
2:47 Lydia 2:45 Mary 2:47,72
Mr. 2:44,133 Mrs. 2:72,131
Samuel 2:66
SEVRIL, Sarah 5:41
SEWALL, Levi W. 7:64 Thomas
2:143 William 2:143
SEWARD, Abigail 5:38,-6:177
Agnes 6:177 Elizabeth 6:178
George 4:101,-6:177 Hannah
4:101,-6:177 Henry 6:177 John
5:39,-6:177,178 Mary 4:99,101,
-5:43,-6:177 Mr. 2:25 Richard
1:7,9,10,-2:184 Samuel 6:178
William 5:43
SEWER, Henry 4:10
SHACKFORD, Abigail 4:101,154,
-5:77 Deliverance 4:85 Dorothy
5:88 Eleanor 2:21 Eliza A.
6:34 Elizabeth 3:107,-4:60,61,
64,101,109,111,153-157,-5:43,
73,76,90 Hannah 4:155 Harrison D. 4:18 John 1:19,
-2:158,-3:9,107,-4:100,105,
181,-5:76-78,80,86,88,90,129,
131,-6:101 John D. 7:57 Jonas
5:164 Joshua 3:111,-4:13,100
Josiah 2:180,-3:71,-4:19,156,
-5:163 Mary 3:111,-4:12,100,
111,-5:43,129 Miss 5:44 Mr.
3:28 Nathaniel 5:131 Nathaniel
C. 4:157 Patience 4:105 Paul
3:107 Ruth 5:80 Ruth W.
5:76-78 Samuel 2:163,165,174,
-3:55,107,-4:51,60,64,109,111,
153-157,-5:73,-6:101,139
Sarah 3:56,106 Seth R. 5:80
Susanna 4:18,19,61,109 William 2:170,176,-4:16,18,19,

SHACKFORD (continued)
60,61,100,105,-5:73 William A.
7:37
SHAFFEN, Patrick 3:2
SHANNON, Anne 1:84,86 Cutt
4:101 Edward 2:37 Eliza 2:38
Elizabeth 1:84,-5:116
Elizabeth W. 4:114 George W.
5:187,-6:41 Harriette 5:151
James N. 6:46 John 1:86 John
G. 4:46 Lilias 5:113 Margaret
5:138 Morris 1:22 Mrs. 5:138,
183,187,-6:41,46 Nathaniel
3:140,-5:42,138,183,187,-6:41
Richard 3:96,140 Richard C.
6:46 Sarah A. 6:34 Thomas
1:84,86,-5:187 William 1:86
SHAPLEIGH (SHAPLEY), De-
pendence 3:6 Dorcas P. 1:144
Henry 1:144 James 2:162 John
3:146 Martha 3:58 Mary 1:144
Nicholas 3:58,59,146,-5:43
Rachel 1:144 Reuben 5:164,
-6:107 Samuel 1:144 Samuel
B. 1:144 Sarah 3:58
SHARES, Robert 1:11
SHARP, Sarah 1:72,-5:30
SHARPLES, John 6:78 John P.
6:78 Mary 6:78
SHATEREDGE, Esther 2:88 Mary
2:88 Richard 2:88
SHATTUCK, Enos 7:24 Henry
7:58
SHAW, Abiah 2:88 Abigail 2:109,
-4:48 Abigail M. 4:93 Abraham
1:16,-2:162 Anna 4:142,-6:31
Benjamin 2:90,92,107,109,111,
-3:135,-5:158,-6:26,31 Caleb
2:108 Daniel 6:29 Daniel C.
4:165 Eliza 4:93 Elizabeth
1:16,-2:88,90,91,108,111,
-3:114,-4:142 Esther 2:90,92,
107,109,111 Fanny 4:187 Fol-
lingsby 6:26 George 3:30,73
Hannah 6:160 Harriet 4:165
Henry 4:165 Ichabod 5:112,
-6:29 James M. 4:93 John
4:89,133,165 Joseph 2:88,90,
91,106,108,111,-4:48 Joshua
4:142 Josiah 2:111 Margaret
4:165 Mary 2:90,-4:93,-5:158
Mary A. 4:118 Mary J. 4:165

111

SHAW (continued)
Nancy 1:16,-3:178,-4:88 Oren
4:165 Rachel 4:84 Rhoda 4:165
Ruth 2:111 Samuel 2:91,
-3:181,-4:165 Sarah 2:107,
-4:93 Susan L. 6:22,125
Theophilus 4:93 Thomas
2:183,-4:36 William 1:16 Wil-
liam S. 4:142 Zebedee 4:142
SHEAFE, Elizabeth 1:27 Henry
1:26 Jacob 1:26,158,-5:90,
166,167 James 2:160,-5:166
Mary 1:26,-6:137 Matthew 1:26
Mehitable 1:26,27,158-160
Sampson 1:21,22,26,27,-5:90
Samuel 1:26 Sarah 1:26,27
Thomas 2:160,-5:90 William
2:37
SHECKLEY, Elizabeth 4:98
Jonathan 5:43 Margaret 4:57
Mary 4:54
SHELLY, Judith 5:143 Mary 5:143
Robert 5:143
SHEPARD, Anna 5:42 Benjamin
3:90 Daniel 3:44 Dorothy 7:37
Ezra 4:129 Isaac 4:79,-6:54
James 3:88 Joanna 3:129 John
4:78,-5:40 Jonathan 3:135
Joseph 3:115,-4:84,85 Mary
4:84,125 Nancy 4:84 Samuel
3:126,127,164,-4:84,-6:62,84,
133,136 Sarah 4:84
SHERBURNE, Abigail 4:104,
183,-6:43,77 Agnes 1:19 Alice
5:39 Ambrose 4:58 Andrew
1:94,-5:184 Ann 5:87 Anne
4:52,-5:44 Annie 3:96 Atrah E.
6:79 Benjamin 4:99 Catherine
6:80 Charles 4:101 Dolly 7:16
Dorothy 4:52,58 Edward 5:39,
87-89 Elizabeth 1:94,-3:54,
-4:10,58,-5:90,135,186,-6:43,
77 Ephraim 7:77 George 4:98,
104,-5:87,91 Hannah 2:35,
-4:57,102,103,-5:86,130,-6:46
Henry 1:2-4,8-10,13,-2:23,27,
62-64,97-100,102-104,157,
158,-3:53,54,173,175,-4:47,57,
58,98,101,-5:40,131,185,187,
189,-6:43,46, 77,80,-7:12,16
Henry S. 2:162 Isaac 5:186,
-6:43 J. H. 3:95 Jacob 5:91

SHERBURNE (continued)
James 4:55,57,98,-5:40,
-6:79,162 Job 4:59,-5:132 John
1:4,6,9-12,-2:23,25,27,60,64,
98,99,101,102,-3:50,53-55,
173,175,-4:49,57,58,79,98,103,
-5:8,44,86,88,91,130-133,135,
139,189,-6:41,43,44,46,77,79
John H. 4:47 Joseph 2:103,164,
-4:54,57,98,-5:55,188,-6:41,
44,107,-7:11 Lovel 4:103
Lydia 4:102,-6:45 Martha
1:94,-5:86 Mary 3:51,52,56,
-4:54,55,57,104,-5:38,88,130,
187,-7:25 Miss 3:95,-4:98 Mr.
5:39,139,162,169,186,-6:41
Mrs. 3:56,175,-5:139,184-189,
-6:41,43-46,77,79 Nathaniel
4:57,-5:39,90,130 Olive 6:44
Phebe 4:99,-5:39,187 Polly
7:12 Priscilla 3:53 Rebecca
4:75 Richard 4:47,57,-5:88
Ruth 4:57,58,-5:42 Samuel
1:13,94,-2:103,157,-3:81,
-5:86,133,139,165,167,170,
184,187,189,-6:41,43,45,77,
79,-7:11 Sarah 3:51-53,-4:51,
55,-5:185,-6:44 Susanna 1:94,
-2:117 Thomas 1:94,-2:175,
-3:54,-4:36,56,58,-5:41,44,165
William 4:56,-5:188
SHERIFF, Abraham 5:134
Elizabeth 5:134 George 5:184,
186,188 Hannah 5:184,186,188
Mary 5:188 Samuel 5:134,186
SHERMAN, Caleb H. 6:164 Roger
1:182
SHERWILL, Nicholas 2:1-6
SHEVALIER, Elizabeth 4:12
SHIPWAY, Ann 3:51 John 2:100
Mr. 1:12
SHORES, John 3:22,74 Peter
2:180,-3:71
SHOREY, Edward 4:57 James
5:187 John 4:56,-5:138,183,186
Lydia 5:186 Mary 5:184,-7:86
Minnie E. 4:48 Mrs. 5:136,186
Peter 5:136,138,140,184,187
Rachel 4:56,-5:183 Samuel
4:12 Sarah 5:138,140,183,184,
187 Stephen 6:37 Susanna
5:140

SHORTRIDGE, Abigail 6:41 Alice
1:181 Dorothy F. 6:77
Elizabeth 5:39 J. H. 5:176
Joseph 5:188 L. E. 1:80 Mary
1:182 Miss 5:41 Mrs. 3:176,
-5:188,-6:41,44,77 R.
3:51
Richard 1:12,80,181,182,
-3:174,176,-5:188,-6:41,44,77,
144 Susanna 1:181 William
6:44
SHUAL, Abigail 5:45
SHULTIS, Mark 4:8
SHURTLIFF, Anna 6:165 William
5:42,143
SHUTE, Adam 4:36 Andrew B.
6:156 Andrew W. 6:156 Anna
6:58 Benjamin 6:136 Clara A.
7:71 Cynthia M. 7:69 Edmund
7:60 Elizabeth 6:5 George
6:156 Henry 6:60 Jacob 6:50,55
James 6:68 James G. 6:156
John 7:23 John E. 6:156 John
W. 6:130,-6:156 Jonathan
6:136 Joseph 6:137 Lydia
6:153 Mary 6:54,69 Michael
6:153 Nancy 6:61,138,-7:23
Nathaniel 6:60 Rebecca 7:24
Robert 6:60 Ruth 6:167 Sarah
6:60,-7:22 Walter 6:60 Welthen 6:153 William H. 6:156
SIAS, Hannah 2:94 Joseph 4:135
Lydia 4:87 Mary 4:129 Ruth
4:135 Welthen 6:154,-7:39
SIBLEY, Hannah 2:9 Jonathan 2:9
SILLOWAY, Mary 2:70
SILSBY, Ozias 6:108
SILVER, Deborah H. 7:70 Judith
6:167 Ruth 3:90 Ruth Jane 7:71
SIMES, Anna 2:174,-5:39,139
Eliza A. 4:184 Elizabeth 5:136
George 6:43 Hannah 1:16,
-4:103,-5:185 James 4:36 John
1:16,-5:134,164 Joseph 2:159,
-5:134,136,139,167,185,188,
-6:43,45,76,79 Mark 6:76 Mary
5:38,-6:79 Mrs. 5:134,136,139,
185,188,-6:43,45,76,79
Thomas 5:134 William C. 6:45
SIMMONS, Mary 3:42
SIMONS, Harrison 7:71
SIMPSON, Abigail 1:28 Alexander
6:53 Andrew 1:106 Andrew L.

SIMPSON (continued)
1:106 Benjamin 6:54,109
Caroline 1:106 Eleanor 7:23
Eliza 6:112 Elizabeth 2:176,
-4:183 Hannah 1:27 James
1:106 John 1:27,28,-3:27,72
Joseph 1:27,28 Lovey 3:114
Mary 1:28,-4:80 Miriam 1:28
Mr. 3:84 Nathaniel 6:170 Sarah
1:27,-5:138 Susanna 1:20
Theodore 1:28 Thomas 1:20,
-3:55,-4:51 William 6:170
SINART, Robert 3:2
SINCLAIR (SINKLER), Abigail
4:129 Ann 3:88 Charles 1:102
Ebenezer 4:68 Elebath 6:59
Elizabeth 2:16 Hannah 6:59
Jacob 4:90,-6:59 James 6:59
John 4:20,133 John H. 7:19
Lucretia 7:59 Martha S. W.
4:115 Mary P. 4:20 Noah 6:59
Rachel 1:184 Rhoda 4:20
Richard 1:102,184,-2:16 Robert
P. 6:59 Susanna F. 4:20
SIVERET, Philip 2:19
SKATE, James 1:12
SKILLIAN, Elizabeth 4:50 Sarah
4:104
SKILLING, Mary 4:102 Simeon
4:100 Simon 4:56
SKINNER, Hannah 2:35
SLADE, Abigail 5:135 Benjamin
1:23,-5:135,139,184,187,189,
-6:46,77,-7:11,13 Hannah 6:96
Jacob T. 6:77 John 7:13 Lucy
5:135,189 Mary 5:139 Mrs.
5:139,184,187,189,-6:46
Samuel 7:11 Susan 6:96
Susanna 6:46 William 5:184
SLATER, Mary 6:109
SLEEPER, Abigail 2:71,-3:40,
90,133,-5:154 Ann 3:132,
-5:110 Anna 5:156 Anne
2:47,70,131,-3:45,-6:31 Arom
2:43,71,87,132 Benjamin 2:66,
-3:90,-5:111,153,154,156
David 3:41,-5:111,153,156,158
Dorothy 3:132,-5:153,156,158
Dudley 3:136 Ebenezer 2:46,
67,69,71,72,131-133 Edmund
6:31 Edward 3:42,-5:155,159,
-6:30 Elizabeth 2:43,-3:41,

SLEEPER (continued)
132,183,-4:91,-5:160 Ezekiel
3:168 Gideon 5:111 Gilman
4:89 Hannah 3:88,91,170,
-5:107,-6:105 Henry 2:46,
-3:136 Hepsibah 5:108
Hezekiah 2:47,-5:160,-6:30
Jacob 3:131 Jedediah 3:178
Joanna 2:83,87,106 John
3:40,-4:36,-5:105-108,155
John B. 6:28 Jonas 6:30
Jonathan 3:40,-5:107,109,112,
154,156,160,-6:30 Joseph
2:44,72,131,143,-5:160 Levi
3:169 Love 3:40,91,-5:105
Luther 2:106 Lydia 4:89,-5:106
Margaret 2:72,-5:108,-6:30
Martha 3:168 Mary 2:43,44,48,
69,-3:44,132,134,171,-5:153
Mehitable 3:134,-5:112 Moses
2:43,66,70,71,132,-5:103,105,
108,155,156,160,-6:30,110
Mrs. 2:72,-3:38 Naomi 2:83
Nathan 6:31 Nathaniel 5:160
Nehemiah 2:131 Peter 5:153
Richard 5:103 Samuel 2:147,
-3:40,-5:105,107,110,154,160
Sanborn 3:168,-5:160 Sarah
2:47,66,132,-5:159 Sherburne
2:68,-3:90 Stephen 2:48,-3:45
Susanna 4:131 Thomas 2:67,
83,87,106,-5:155,159 Tristram
C. 5:110 William 2:47,-3:42,
170,-5:153,156,158,-6:28,31
SLOMMAN, Edward 5:41
SLOPER, John 2:187,-3:73,174
Lieutenant 3:173 Lydia 4:51
Mr. 3:175 Mrs. 3:175 Richard
1:10,13,-2:99,100 Samuel
4:101
SMALL, Elizabeth 4:12 Elizabeth
C. 1:100 Francis 1:179 George
S. 1:100 James 1:100 John
1:100,-6:94 Joseph 1:18 M. C.
2:41 Nathaniel 1:100 Thomas
4:104 Zachariah 6:94
SMALLCORN, Samuel 2:181
SMALLEY, John 1:149
SMART, Abigail 4:77,-6:138,
-7:45 Anna 6:136 Benjamin
4:85 Benning 6:56,138 Caleb
6:157,164 Calvin 7:70 Charles

SMART (continued)
4:126,-6:157,158,-7:59 Charlotte 6:154,-7:39 Clarissa
6:157 Clarissa P. 4:186 Comfort 4:78 Daniel 4:77 Dorothy
T. 4:80 Ebenezer 6:138 Eliza
4:187 Elizabeth 4:77,-5:67,
-6:61,138,157,158 Francis 6:55
Giles 6:156 James 4:181 John
3:89,-4:79 Joseph 4:94,-5:68
Love 6:138 Martha 4:131,
-6:157 Mary 4:94,-6:139 Mary
A. 6:157 Mehitable 7:43 Mercy
5:68 Moses 5:67,69 Moulton
6:139,158 Nancy 6:61 Richard
5:69 Ruth 5:67,69 Sarah 5:67,
-6:138 Susanna 6:139 William
H. B. 6:158 Winthrop 5:68
SMITH, Aaron 3:126,-5:182 Ab-
bott E. 5:142 Abigail 2:13,
170,-3:13,42,108,125,168,
-4:75,-5:69,-7:51 Abraham
2:66,69,-3:43,-5:17,110,153,
156,159,-6:28,32 Addison
1:160 Agnes 5:69 Alexander
3:91,-5:104 Alfred 1:155,160
Almira 1:159 Anabel 2:190
Andrew 4:36 Andrew G. 4:126,
-6:157 Ann 3:119 Anna 1:112,
-2:65,66,-3:125,-5:106,157
Anne B. 6:157 Anne M. 6:157
Apphia 5:69 Asa 3:162 Barbara
4:3 Benjamin 1:98,100,156,
160,-2:69,-5:69 Benjamin M.
3:119 Benjamin S. 6:157 Betsey 7:39 Betsey S. 7:39
Bridget 3:41,-5:107 Calista L.
6:157 Chad 1:172 Charity 3:186
Charles 1:160,-4:56,-5:148
Charles H. 6:157 Charlotte
1:160,-6:62 Chase 3:87 Daniel
1:102,157,-3:26,74,89,136,
-4:77,-5:35,-6:138 David
1:34,47 Deborah 1:47,-2:50,
158,-3:44,-5:106,-6:62
Deliverance 3:43 Dolly W.
7:24 Dorothy 3:125,126,
-4:86,-5:13,152 Ebenezer
1:98,158-160,-3:127,-7:59
Ebenezer C. 4:181 Ebenezer J.
1:151 Edward 5:111 Eleanor
6:186,187 Elias 3:58 Eliphalet

SMITH (continued)
2:13,-6:64,133,137 Eliza 7:56
Elizabeth 1:98,100,103,156,
160,172,-2:129,144,-3:5,13,42,
87,89,131,-4:76,78,133,-5:12,
66,69,154,156,159,-6:28,30,33,
137,154 Elizabeth S.
6:157
Emily 1:160 Eunice 4:135
Ezekiel 2:45,-5:104,107,
112,154 Forrest S. 2:166
Franklin 4:7 Garland 4:187
George 1:97,177,-6:46,-7:51
George F. 1:156 George Harrison 7:58 George J. 7:51
George S. 6:7,8 Gideon C.
1:172,-5:124,-6:90,184 Greenleaf 3:118 Hamilton 1:102
Hannah 1:157,160,-3:43,54,
134,-4:46,77,180,181,-5:12,
107,108,160,189,-6:42,44,46
Hannah B. 5:35 Harriet 4:169,
173 Harriet M. 4:118 Harriet N.
7:62 Henry 1:160,-4:175 Henry
B. 1:159 Henry C. 4:130 Hepzibah 3:43 Hezekiah 3:126,
-6:61 Huldah 2:105,107,108,
110,112 Isaac 3:42,-5:154,
157,160,-6:30,-7:31 Isabelle
2:190 Isaiah 3:186 Israel
1:34,-2:50,-3:43,53,-5:156,
158,159 Issacher W. 7:55
Ithiel 5:107,110,111,154,
157,160 Jabez 3:53 Jacob
3:45,168,-5:13,69,70,108,154
Jacob S. 1:160 James 1:100,
-2:172,-4:6,-6:44,187 James
M. 5:18 James S. 1:159 James
W. 4:187,-7:43 Jemima 1:98,
-3:89 Jennie 3:90 Jeremiah
1:160,-4:132,-5:66,69,82
Jerusha 3:126 Jesse 1:100
Joanna 3:89,130 John 1:97-
100,102,160,-2:13,48,67,68,
105,107,108,110,112,144,163,
172,190,-3:13,43,51-53,125,
126,168,-4:35,135,-5:13,20,
106,108,120,-6:6,7,27,42,44,
92,-7:51 John B. 5:82 John E.
1:156 John M. 6:62,156 John S.
5:142 John W. 3:86 Jonathan
3:170,-4:47,48,89,-5:66,69,70,
107,110,111,142,155,157,158,

SMITH (continued)
-6:28,32 Joseph 1:157,160,
-2:13,171,-4:36,134,187,-5:69,
154,-7:38 Joseph B. 6:64,133
Joseph E. 1:159 Joseph H.
6:37,157,-7:44 Joseph M.
6:157 Joshua 3:133 Joshua B.
1:156 Josiah 2:13,-3:6,13,
113,180,-5:113 Josiah, Jr. 7:63
Judith 5:19 Leah 1:183
Leonard 1:102 Louisa 3:178
Louisa S. 1:159 Love 1:98,101
Lycurgus N. 7:62 Lydia 1:98,
100,112,156,-3:41,-5:12,21,111
Lydia M. 4:125 Margaret
1:105,160,-3:40,90,-6:28 Maria
4:186 Maria M. 6:157 Martha
6:191 Mary 1:47,92,97,100,102,
151,157,160,-3:13,41,43,125,
127,167,-4:47,100,115,127,
133,-5:12,66,69,106,153-156,
189,-6:8,90,-7:7 Mary A. 6:157
Mary E. 1:156 Mary G. 6:160,
-7:41 Mary J. 1:157,-6:20
Mary P. 7:56 Mary W. 1:160
Matilda 1:102 Mehitable 1:159,
160,-4:134,-5:12,13,70,160
Mercy 5:112,147 Merebeth 1:47
Meribah 3:54 Millet J. 1:100
Miriam 2:94 Moody 6:62,154,
-7:38,39 Moses 7:66 Mr. 3:84,
154,-5:40,189,-6:42,46 Mrs.
5:47 Nancy 4:78,86,-7:63
Nancy V. 6:160 Nathan 4:183,
-5:107,-6:154,159,-7:39,40
Nathaniel 3:180,-4:169,
-5:12,13,19,106 Nicholas
3:89,150 Olive 6:159,-7:40
Oliver 2:48,-3:44,-6:27
Patience 1:160,-2:45,173,-5:18
Pearson 6:33 Peter 5:110 Priscilla 5:69 Prudence 5:120
Quince 1:10 Rachel 3:45,114,
162 Rebecca 3:53,171 Reuben
1:183,-3:134,-4:88 Rhea S.
6:157 Richard 2:67,-3:133,
-4:47 Robert 1:160,-3:89,135,
-4:47 Robert F. 4:180 Ruth
3:162 Sally 7:25,59 Sally P.
7:39 Samuel 1:156,160,-2:13,
110,182,-3:71,-4:13,46,47,77,
-5:67,69,153,-6:4,137 Samuel

115

SMITH (continued)
G. 3:13 Sarah 1:34,47,100,
102,159,160,-2:69,-3:12,13,
54,120,126,133,-4:80,100,129,
-5:13,21,66,67,69,107,111,154,
159,-7:56 Sarah A. F. 6:7
Sarah P. 6:154,157 Sergeant
3:149,150 Simeon 5:108
Simeon P. 3:170 Solomon
2:13,-3:162 Sophia 7:66
Stephen 1:102,-2:112 Susan A.
1:110,182,-2:92,166,-4:144
Susan R. 1:159 Susanna 3:41,
53,94,-5:66 Tabitha 5:69 Temperance 1:160,-4:41 Theodata
2:105 Theophilus 3:12,13
Theophilus W. 5:34 Thomas
1:98,102,-2:45,67,-3:23,72,86
Thomas M. 1:151 Valentine
1:98,99,101,102,104-106,151,
153-160 Warren 1:102,-6:154,
-7:38 William 2:65,67,69,129,
134,-3:13,40,169,171,-5:103,
111,142,153 William B. 1:156
William D. G. 2:166 William
J. 1:190 William W. 7:44
Winthrop 1:103,157
SMITHSON, Deborah 2:169 Mary
2:173,-4:14
SNELL, Abigail 4:182,-5:140,150
Alfred William 7:9
Deliverance 4:125 Edward
5:140,185,188,-6:43,46,79
Eliza 4:129 Elizabeth 3:51,
52,54,56,-7:9 George 2:101,
-3:50,52,54,55,172,173,-5:184
Hannah 3:50,51,56 Joanna
1:116 John 1:116,-3:54,174,
-4:75,-5:61,188,-6:184,-7:9
Lydia Jane 7:9 Magery 5:140,
185,188,-6:46,79 Martha 5:188
Mary 5:185,-6:47,-7:9 Miss
5:43 Mrs. 5:184,188,-6:43
Nathaniel 6:43 Reuben 5:184,
188 Samuel 6:46 T. 6:24 Tem-
perance 4:126 Thomas 1:116,
-6:47,-7:9 Timothy Hussey 7:9
SNIDER, Mark 3:19,74
SNOOKS, William 4:36
SNOW, Anna 3:89,-5:106
Elizabeth 3:91,-5:109,111
Joshua 3:40,-5:106,109,111,

SNOW (continued)
155,158 Juda 5:158 Leslie P.
2:166 Mary 5:155
SOLOMONT, Thomas 6:61
SOMERBY, Elizabeth 2:188 Henry
2:188 Judith 2:188
SOPER, John 1:13
SOUTER, Hannah 2:91,106,108,
110 John 2:91,106,108,110
Mary 2:106 Rebecca 2:108
Sarah 2:110
SOUTHER, Mary 6:112 Nancy
6:164
SOUTHWICK, Daniel 1:125
Elizabeth 1:125 Jonathan
1:125,-5:28 Mary 4:70
SPARHAWK, John 2:160
SPARKES, Rebecca 4:10
SPAULDING, Abel 7:87 E. A.
7:89 George 7:89 Olivia 7:87
Theodora Norton 7:89
SPEED, Abigail 4:188,-6:153,157
Alfred 6:153 Ann 2:54 Augus-
tus D. 6:157 Benjamin 6:153
Benjamin T. 4:188 Ebenezer
2:54 Elizabeth 2:53,54,
-4:126,-6:153,157,-7:55
George W. 6:157 James 6:157
James N. 6:157 John 2:53,54,
-6:153,-7:44 Lydia 2:54 Mar-
garet A. 6:157 Martha 7:38,43
Mary 2:53,-6:136,152 Mary A.
6:153 Nancy 3:183 Robert
6:153 Susan 6:157 Susan N.
7:60 Thomas 2:54 William
4:78,-6:152,153,-7:61
SPEARS, John R. 4:27
SPENCE, Ann J. 4:7 Carroll 4:7,8
Charles S. 4:7 Charlotte H. 4:7
Count de 4:5 David 4:5 Graeme
4:6 Graeme K. 4:7 Harriet B.
4:6 Henry de 4:5 Hugh 4:5
James 4:6 Janet 4:6 Jessica
4:9 John 4:5 Katherine S. 4:9
Keith 4:4,6,7,143,-5:165,169,
170 Louisa J. W. 4:7 Lowell
4:9 Mabel 4:9 Maria B. 4:6
Mary 4:143 Mary C. 4:7 Mary
T. 4:7 Mr. 5:162,169 Nicol de
4:5 Patrick (Sir) 4:5 Rebecca
C. 4:9 Robert 4:5,9 Robert S.
T. 4:7,9 Robert T. 4:6,7,143,

116

SPENCE (continued)
144 Roberta 4:7 Stephen D. 4:7
Susan S. 4:7 Thomas 4:5
Thomas de 4:5 William 4:6
William de 4:5
SPENCER, Elizabeth 5:6 Mary
3:101,-4:13,-5:78,151 Robert
2:184,-3:30,72
SPENLEY, John 2:186,-3:72
SPERING, Elizabeth 3:106
SPILLER, Josiah 3:114
SPINNEY, Alvah 6:39 Elizabeth
4:104 George 3:24,72 Grace
3:56 Mary 3:6,-5:40 Nathan
2:169 Susan 4:184 Thomas
3:98 Timothy 3:5
SPIWOOD, Nehemiah 2:185
SPOFFORD, Benaiah 4:178 Mar-
tha J. 7:62 Miranda 5:19 Oren
5:19 Pamelia 4:176 Samuel
3:168
SPRAGUE, Laban 4:36
SPRING, Candace 7:79 Mr. 7:12,
13 Pomp 7:79 Seth 5:115
SPRINGER, Samuel A. 6:105
SPURLING, Ella M. S. 4:47
SQUIRE (SQUIER), Bartholomew
1:10 James 5:125 John 5:102
STACKPOLE, Charles 3:26 E. S.
1:181 Ebenezer 3:28,72 Elidyr
(Sir) 2:39 Eliza 6:37 Everett S.
1:107,109,-2:39,166,-5:48,141,
-6:5 James 2:39 Joshua 5:167
Martha 6:148 Minerva A. 5:85
Otis 6:35 Philip 6:146,148
Richard (Sir) 2:39 Rosanna
7:87 Samuel 1:128,-7:87,88
Sarah 6:18 Sophia 7:86 Thomas
1:128,-5:31,-6:18,185 Zerviah
1:128
STACY, Catharine Spofford 7:42
Moody Kimball 7:42 Sarah 7:42
Sarah Ann 7:42 Timothy 7:42
William 3:145
STANDISH, Miles 4:191
STANFORTH, Hannah 4:51 Mr.
5:41
STANIEL(S), Dorothy 3:40 Edward
L. 7:71
STANLEY, Mary 7:53 Nathaniel
2:94 Zerviah (Lady) 7:83

STANTON, Benjamin 4:146 Isaac
4:147 Joanna 4:12 John 4:150,
-5:152
STANWOOD, Lydia L. 7:69
STANYAN (STANYEN), Ann
4:11,-6:143 Anthony 6:143
Jacob 2:107 James 2:105,
-6:143 John 2:90,105,107,
110,-6:143 Joseph 2:110 Mary
2:90,105,107,110,-3:39,-6:143,
144 Susanna 2:147,-6:47,143
STAPLES, Benjamin 3:4
Catherine 3:5 Henry 4:115
Henry H. 4:115,-5:36 Josiah
3:5 Jotham 3:27 Mr. 5:41
Robert 3:4 Tobias 3:5
STAR, Mr. 1:12
STARBIRD, John 1:156 Rebecca
6:146 Samuel 6:145,146
STARBOARD, Sarah 4:80 Stephen
4:149 Thomas 4:9
STARBUCK, Edward 1:178 Paul
2:76
STARK, Caroline 7:69
STAVERS, William 2:163
STEARNS, Abigail R. 4:168
Augusta 4:8 Dudley 4:166,
-5:180 Elizabeth 4:166,167,
-5:180 Esther 3:180,-4:167,168
Ezra S. 2:166,-4:139,144 John
4:8,133,167,-5:180 Josiah
4:166-168,-5:11,180 Josiah H.
4:168 Mary 4:167,168 Mary E.
4:168 Mary P. 4:8 Samuel
4:167 Samuel R. 4:168 Sarah
4:32,166-168,-5:180 Timothy
4:167 William 3:116,120,177-
179,184,-4:89,137,167-169
William R. 4:168
STEELE, William 6:109
STELLE, Jonathan 1:155
STEPHENS, Amos 7:20 David
7:20 James 7:20 Phinehas 7:18
STERLING, Andrew 2:66
STEVENS, Aaron 3:42,-6:10
Abigail 3:41,-4:176,181,
-6:51,-7:24 Ann 1:185 Anna
1:185 Apphia 6:137 Benjamin
1:188,-2:46,-3:135,-5:103,106,
108,112,-6:136 Bridget 4:91,
-5:72 Caleb 1:12 Catherine

117

STEVENS (continued)
1:184,188,-4:182 Chase 1:114,
-3:167 Daniel 5:109 David
1:185,188,-2:14,15,-6:55 Dr.
7:75 Ebenezer 2:43,46,48,
130,-3:131,-5:104,111,112 Edward 3:135,-4:179,-5:72
Eleanor 5:9,68 Elihu T. 5:19
Elizabeth 2:15,40,-3:135,
-5:50,72,108,-6:56 Eunice 6:53
Grace 6:111 Hale 6:160,-7:41
Hannah 1:114,-2:14,-3:41,120,
-4:97,179,-5:68,-6:33 Jane M.
7:68 John 1:21,114,188,-2:48,
-3:88,108,111,115,131,155,
168,182,-4:16,177,180,-5:18
Jonathan 1:188,-3:184,-5:68,
-6:55 Joseph 2:14,-4:79,80,
-6:111 Joshua 1:110 Judith
6:56 Julia A. 5:21 Lois 5:176,
-6:126 Louisa 5:18 Lucretia
4:16 Lucy 6:51 Lydia 4:78,
-6:61 Lydia A. 4:188 Mabel J.
6:104 Martha 3:54,-5:72 Mary
1:110,-2:173,-3:41,107,111,
131,155,-4:16,79,97,-5:9,46,
-6:139 Mary A. 7:25 Mary K.
7:26 Mehitable 1:183,188,
-2:47,-3:42 Moses 3:19,43,
86,-7:54 Mr. 6:80,-7:13,14
Mrs. 4:106 Nancy 6:139,-7:17
Naomi 4:157 Nathaniel 1:185,
188,-2:14,47,-4:79 Olive 5:17
Patience 2:66,72,-3:44 Paul
3:181 Phebe 5:72 Priscilla
7:24 Rachel 3:127 Rebecca B.
4:128 Ruth 5:36 Samuel 1:188,
-2:43,-3:40,44,132,153,-4:175,
178,-5:106,109 Sarah 1:185,
188,-2:14,15,46,-3:107,108,
127,131,134,-4:59 Sarah J.
4:130 Stephen 4:106 Susanna
6:51,58 Theodore 7:66
Theophilus 5:9,68 Thomas
5:41,54,-6:57 Timothy 3:135
William 2:184,187,-3:20,71,
107,120,-6:84,137
STEVENSON, Andrew 4:139 Bartholomew 1:103 Cato 3:22
James 1:97 John 1:97 Mary
5:42 Richard 1:103 Thomas
1:97,178

STEWARD, Anna 2:71 Daniel
3:72 Giles 4:101 Mary 5:105
Robert 3:39,-5:105 Sarah 2:67
STEWART, Charles 4:3 James
5:42 John 4:2,174 Robert 4:2,
-5:110 Ruth 4:173 William
6:109
STICKNEY, Ann 7:23 David 6:55
Harriet 7:19 Jennie 6:57
Jeremiah 6:10 John 5:15 Judith
6:55 Mary 5:15 Mary Frances
7:68 Miriam 6:50 Nathan 6:168
William 5:15
STILEMAN, Elias 1:11,-2:97,
99-101,-3:49,51,83 Major
3:176 Miss 3:176 Richard 1:11
STILES, Deborah 6:102 Ezra
4:51,-6:76 Jane 6:102 Richard
4:36 Samuel 6:102,103
Triphena 6:66 William 6:102
STILLSON (STILSON), Daniel B.
4:186 Hannah 2:33 Henry 4:78
James 1:21,-7:64 Lettice
1:153,-4:150 Sarah 4:185 Wil-
liam 4:77
STIMPSON, Andrew 4:139 Bar-
tholomew 3:153 Jane 4:140
Sarah 2:190 William 2:190
STINSON, Abner P. 6:154,-7:38,
41 Clarissa Meak 7:41 Hannah
Coleman 7:41 Harriet Fink
7:41
STIVERS, Andrew 1:131
STOCKBRIDGE, Abraham 1:187
Abram T. 4:113 Andrew D.
6:160 Henry 6:62 James R.
4:113 John 1:187,-4:71 Martha
4:71,125,-5:35 Mary 1:187,
-4:114,116 Olive A. 4:113
Reuben 2:121 Samuel 4:35
Widow 2:122
STOCKER, Miss 5:40 Sarah 3:168
STOCKMAN, Abigail 5:103
Dorothy 3:82 Joanna 5:108
John 5:108 Mary 5:107 Mr.
3:79 Robert 2:43,131,132,-3:37
William 6:137
STOKELL, John 5:169
STOKES, Abigail 4:183 Benjamin
4:15 Deborah 4:9,-6:143 Susan
4:183
STOKLE, Doeg 7:12 George 7:12

STOKLE (continued)
Mary 7:12 Robert 7:12
STONE, A. H. 2:95,-3:144 Abigail
6:96,100 Benjamin 5:45 Daniel
3:144 Elias 6:100 Elizabeth
6:100 Gabriel 3:23 Gotham
6:109 Mary 3:144 Mr. 4:178
Sarah 7:54 Simon 2:95
STOODLEY, Jonathan 6:177
STORER, Clement 2:162 Jeremy
3:83 Lieutenant 3:150 Mrs.
3:83 Samuel 5:168
STOREY, Hannah 6:110 Jeremiah
6:108
STORROW, Jethro 4:36
STORY, William 1:177
STOUGHTON, L. H. 3:138 William 3:98
STOVER, John 3:145
STRAW, Aaron 5:16 Benjamin
3:171 David 3:88 Dorothy 3:182
Ebenezer 3:117 Eleanor 6:32
Elizabeth 5:16 Elizabeth D.
3:117 Ezra 5:16 Hannah
3:182,-5:16 Hannah C. 3:117
James 7:22 John 5:16,-6:28,
31,32,52 Josiah 3:117 Lydia
3:117 Martha 6:31 Mary 3:117,
-6:161 Mehitable 3:117 Mrs.
6:28 Rhoda 3:181 Rosalinda
3:117 Sarah 3:117 William
3:117,181 Zipporah 3:182
STREAN, John 4:132
STRONG, Aaron 3:144 Elizabeth
2:40
STUART, Abigail 5:20 Ann 5:131
Anna 2:65,-3:89 Elizabeth
5:107 Grace 3:177 Jane 5:131
Jean 3:45 Margaret 5:41 Mary
4:26,178 Nathaniel 4:174
Robert 2:129,-5:107 Ruth 5:18
Samuel 3:90 Sarah 3:45 Walter
5:131
STUBBS, Albert R. 5:141 Benjamin 2:182
STUDELEY, Catherine 5:87
Elizabeth 4:104,-5:87,131,
132,135 James 5:75,88,89,
130,135,137 John 5:38,91
Jonathan 4:100,-5:39,88,
89,91,131,132 Mary 4:101 Mr.
4:101,102,-5:87 Mrs. 5:135,137

STUDELEY (continued)
Sarah 5:130 William 4:103,
-5:137
STUTLY, Elizabeth 3:8
SUDRICK, Michael 4:85
SULLIVAN, Anna 4:90 Ebenezer
3:7 James 3:19,73 John
1:102,-6:4,5
SULLOWAY, Abigail 6:30 Alice
4:175 Benjamin 4:179 Hannah
C. 5:22 Hezekiah 5:108 Jacob
3:43,45,-5:111 John 4:36,
-5:110,155,160 Joseph 5:17
Luther 5:22 Lydia 6:53 Mary
3:43,45,-5:111 Mary A. 5:19
Miriam 4:179 Sarah 5:110 Wil-
liam 3:50,-5:108,111,155,
-6:26,30
SUMNER, Eli 7:16,85 Elizabeth
7:85 Samuel H. 5:119 Samuel
Haynes 7:16 Seth 2:143
SUTTON, Judith 6:165 Michael
6:56 Sarah 6:165 Solomon 6:56
SWAIN(E), Anna 2:48 Basell 2:81
Caleb 4:91 Daniel 3:47
Deborah 3:143 Dorcas 4:54
Ebenezer 4:133 Elijah C. 7:58
Elizabeth 2:81,85,-5:145
Isaiah 1:71,-5:29 Jacob 3:178
Jane 2:86 John 1:70,-2:88,
-4:54,-5:28 John A. 3:47
Jonathan 4:136 Lydia 4:135
Margaret 1:65,-5:54 Martha
4:131 Mary 2:88,-3:114,
-4:188,-5:118 Nathan 3:182,
-4:132 Noah 2:82 Olivera Jane
7:58 Phineas 4:133 Prudence
2:82,85 Rebecca 1:65,-4:160
Reuben 7:61 Rhoda 4:134
Richard 1:65,70,71,-2:81,86,
126,-3:143,-4:77 Roger 6:65
Sarah 1:70,71,-7:61 Stephen
4:89 Susan 4:127 Susan C. 7:58
Widow 2:181 William 2:82,85
SWAN, Harriet 7:23
SWAZEY, Joseph 3:94
SWEAT (see also SWETT),
Abigail 2:67,129,-5:20,111
Anne 2:47,71 Benjamin 2:45,
67,69,71,72,129,132,-3:37,38,
91,-5:105,107,112 Bethiah
2:69,-3:44 Clarissa S. 7:65

119

SWEAT (continued)
Dearborn 2:69,-5:112 Dorothy
2:51 Elisha 2:46,65,67,68,
-3:37,39,-5:105,108,111,155
Elizabeth 2:47,-3:44 Elizabeth
S. 5:20 Ephraim F. 7:25 Esther
2:65,-3:44 Hannah 4:176,
-5:155 Huldah 2:68,-5:104,109
John 2:43,44,46,66,71,187,
-3:38,-5:104,107,110 John D.
3:130 Joseph 2:67,-3:88,-5:17
Juda 5:110 Judith 2:72
Lieutenant 3:39 Lydia 4:132
Mary 5:103 Moses 2:132,
-5:107 Moses B. 5:22 Mr. 5:40
Mrs. 2:72,-3:39 Naomi 5:105
Nathan 2:69,-3:38,39,-5:103,
106,109,112,155 Nathaniel
3:171 Nichols 5:22 Pomp 2:187
Pompey 3:73 Robert 2:88
Samuel 3:130,-5:112 Samuel
H. 5:20 Sarah 3:37,-5:108
Stephen 2:68,-3:39,-5:105
Thomas 5:155
SWEENEY, Richard 3:74
SWEET, Moses 6:55
SWEETLAND, Richard 4:36
SWEETZER, Henry 6:162 Stephen
2:185
SWETT (see also SWEAT),
Alexander 2:17 Benjamin
2:90,105,108,111,-5:159,-6:5,
31,142 Elisha 6:27 Elizabeth
2:105 Esther 2:90,105,108,111
Hannah 2:90,-6:5 Jane 2:17
John 2:108,-5:18,158,-6:5 John
D. 5:159 Jonathan 3:8 Joseph
2:17 Lieutenant 6:27 Mehitable
3:7 Moses 6:5,31,108 Nathan
5:158 Sarah 6:5,110 Stephen
2:111,-6:5
SYMONDS, David 7:25 Sally 7:65
TABOR (TABER), ---- 7:53
Elizabeth 6:90 Eunice 1:126
Jacob 1:121,-4:42,-7:5 John
1:126 Reuben 1:126,-5:29
Sarah 1:121
TALER (see TAYLOR)
TALFORD, John 2:45
TALKEY, Betsey 7:15 Sarah 7:15
TALLANT, Joseph 6:109

TANDY, Abel 3:45,-6:28,31
Abigail 5:108,160 Anne 6:31
Elizabeth 2:71,-5:154 Mary
5:158 Mrs. 6:29 Rachel 2:134,
-5:105,-6:28 Richard 2:130,
134,-3:87,-5:105,108,-6:29
Ruhamar 7:70 Samuel 3:45,
-6:29 William 3:42,-5:154,
158,160,-6:32
TANNER, Jane 5:152 John 3:22,
71,-5:4
TAPPAN (TAPPEN-TAPPING),
Abigail 4:178 Amos 7:78
Aurelia 7:78 Benjamin 4:36 Dr.
3:151 Samuel 7:78
TARBOX, Mark 7:26
TARLTON, Elias 1:22 James M.
7:68 John 5:22 Marcy H. 7:40
Martha M. 6:152 Mary 2:37
Mary Ann 7:37 Mercy H. 6:160
Richard 3:146 Samuel 6:61
TASH, Jone 3:51 Joseph 4:182
Lydia 4:79 Nancy 4:78 Sarah
6:140
TASKER, Daniel 5:54 Lois 5:7
Lydia S. 7:71 Mercy 3:9
Samuel 3:102
TATE, Elizabeth 1:104 John
1:104
TAYLOR, Abigail 2:45 Anna
1:184 Captain 3:102 Comfort
5:136 David 3:181 Deborah
2:111 Edward 1:184,-3:101
Elizabeth 4:90 Hannah 5:42
Henry 1:3,-5:40 James 4:36
Jeremiah 4:85 John 1:184,
-2:111,192,-3:17,147 Jonathan
1:184,-3:41 Mark 1:184 Martha
2:192 Mary 3:167 Mary E.
4:117 Nathan 1:184 Penelope
3:91 Phineas 3:182 Rachel
1:184 Sarah 2:192
TEAGUE, Isaac 7:3 John 7:3
Joseph 7:4
TEBBETTS (see also
TIBBETTS), Abigail 7:91 Edward 7:90 Lovicy 7:50 Mary
7:90 Noah 2:166 Sarah 7:87
Sarah Chase 7:89 Thomas 7:50
TENNY, Edmund 6:106 Gardner
6:66 Phebe 6:151,152

TENNY (continued)
Sophronia 6:20 William 6:151
William C. 6:150
TERRY, John 1:11 London 4:36
TETHERLY, Charles Henry 2:42
Margaret 7:42 Mary S. 6:159,
-7:40 Miss 5:41 Thomas 6:159
Wethern 6:156 William 5:40,
-6:156,-7:42
TEWKSBURY (TUKESBURY),
Abigail 4:178 Anna 4:177
Elizabeth 4:176 Hannah 4:173
Joseph 5:18 Mary 5:22 Peter
4:176 Sarah 3:167
THA(T)CHER, Joseph 1:51
Richard 1:22
THAYER, Elihu 4:174 Martha
5:17 Mary 3:171 Mr. 7:12
Nathaniel 5:21 Sarah 5:17 William 7:72
THING, Abigail 3:184 Anne 3:133
Bartholomew 4:136 Elizabeth
3:184 Gilman 4:137 Hannah
3:135 James 3:178 Levi 4:133
Susanna 2:45 William 3:167
Zebediah 3:136
THISTLE, Mary 6:52
THOMAS, Abigail 5:65,-7:37
Anne 5:65 Bradbury 4:80 David
4:12 Elizabeth 1:99 Hannah
3:91,-4:98 Harvey 4:57 Isaac
2:45 Jacob 5:65 James 4:56,
137,-5:190 Joanna 3:180,-4:86
John 5:190 Jonathan 5:65
Joseph 4:79 Marcus S. 5:142
Martha 5:191 Mary 4:93 Moses
G. 7:26 Phebe 4:117 R. 4:80
Rachel 3:182 Richard 5:40
Sarah 4:80,93 Stephen J. 3:10
Wealthen 5:190,191
THOMPSON, Abigail 1:100,-
4:111,175 Abigail J. 1:152
Abraham 2:155 Alfred 1:99 Ann
6:99 Anna 1:100,-4:106,107,
109,153 Anne 1:97 Anne H.
1:97 Anthony 4:106 Arnold
1:176 Benjamin 1:97,-3:46,
95,160,-4:109,-6:50 Catherine
2:11 Charles 3:160,-4:55
Charles W. 6:82 Daniel 7:54
David 2:1-6,11 Deborah 4:78
Ebenezer 1:97,-3:95,-5:170,

THOMPSON (continued)
-6:184 Edmund 1:99,100 Edward 3:103 Eleanor 7:9
Elizabeth 3:57,90,-4:53,
-5:76,-6:23,161 Ella M. 7:83
Elsie 4:79 Enoch B. 4:107
George 1:22,-5:42 George W.
4:115 Hannah 1:99,-2:153,154,
-4:77,79,111,-6:143 Hannah E.
W. 4:117 Hattie F. 5:93
Hyrena 1:171,173 Isaac 6:173
James 1:100,-4:11,-6:55,-7:64
Jane 6:61 John 1:99,100,152,
-3:8,51,-4:106,127,-5:76 John
B. 1:97 John E. 1:152 John W.
E. 1:99 Jonathan 1:99,-3:132,
-4:76,130,183 Joseph 4:148,
-6:75 Lewis 1:176,-6:23 Love
1:99 Lovey 4:79 Lucien 1:29,
31,109,-2:166,-3:144,188,-5:48
Lucinda J. 3:95 Lucy 4:150
Lydia 3:157,-5:146 Martha
1:97 Mary 1:97,-2:174,-3:95,
154,-4:19,78,109,153,-6:124
Mary N. 6:7 Matthew 2:11,55,
154,155 Moses 1:100,-2:69,
154,-4:184,-7:83 Mr. 4:25,
-7:29 Nancy 6:106 Nicholas
1:100 Noah 3:154,157,-6:66,
173,-7:40 Olney 1:171,173,
-5:32,-6:89,90 Paul 7:9
Pelatiah 4:130 Phebe 3:132
Phebe A. 1:176 Rachel 4:106
Richard 2:176 Robert 3:150,
-4:80,-7:68 Samuel 1:100,
-2:168,-3:2,57,132,160,-4:89,
109,111,153 Samuel W. 5:76
Sarah 1:97,152,-2:117,154,174,
-3:160,-4:14,22,106,-6:52,53,
66,162,-7:7 Seth 3:90 Solomon
4:109 Stephen J. 4:187 Susanna
3:154,157,-4:80,130 Sybil
(Sibbel) 5:62,-7:9 Thomas
1:99,-2:177-180,-3:70,91,
-5:162,169 William 2:44,174,
-4:15,63,106,107,109,-3:120,
160,-7:58 William S. 2:144
THORNDIKE, John 6:55 Mary
6:165,-7:21 Sarah 7:17
THORN(E), Abraham 6:31
Elizabeth 6:26 Jacob 5:155
James 6:26,31 Jemima 3:91,

121

THORN(E) (continued)
-5:104 Joanna 3:177 John
2:71,-5:104,155,-6:26,31,109
John C. 2:166,192,-5:48,
-6:9,48,49,144 Phineas 6:58
Sarah 5:17,-6:26 Sarah L. 7:20
THORNTON, Henry 7:72 James
4:36 Mary 6:86 Matthew 2:96
THORP, Edward 2:182
THRASHER, David 4:85
THRESHER, William 3:66,72
THURAL, Lucy 2:51 Patience
2:51
THURBER, Mercy 4:192,-7:77
Richard 4:192 Samuel 5:46
Sarah 7:77 Thomas 7:77
THURLA, Abisham 3:131 John
3:130 Sarah 3:91 Tristram
3:130
THURLOW, Stephen C. 5:22
THURSTON, Abigail 1:192,-5:71
Abner 5:70 Andrew 4:85
Andrew L. 4:72 Anna 4:138
Benjamin 3:130,-5:71,-6:176
Clarissa D. 4:72 Deborah 6:139
Dorothy 4:138 Ebenezer 6:106
Elizabeth 3:126,-4:138 Ezekiel
4:138 Gilman 4:138 Hannah
5:71 James 5:71,-6:7,8,159,
-7:40 John 2:42,-5:71,-6:140
Jonathan 4:91,134,138,-5:70
Joseph 3:17 Lydia 5:71 Mary
4:132,-5:71 Moses 1:184,-3:87
Mr. 7:28 Nathaniel 4:72,138
Rebecca 2:119 Samuel 4:138,
-5:70,71 Samuel D. 6:6 Sarah
1:192,-4:91,138,-5:70,71 Shuah
4:138,-5:70 Stephen 1:192,
-2:120,-5:71 William 3:183
THWING, Nathaniel 2:181
TIBBETTS (TEBBETTS), Aaron
2:76,-5:94 Abigail 1:51,-2:76,
125,-4:123,147,184,-5:1,54,
-6:67,69,-7:5,52 Abigail R.
2:30 Alice 1:124,-5:28,173
Amos 5:28 Ann 2:76 Anna
3:33,-6:74 Anne 1:118,-5:122
Benjamin 5:52,-6:67,68 C. W.
6:8,48,96,144,189,192 Captain
7:77,80 Catherine 1:55,-2:76
Charity 6:67,172 Charles A.
6:86 Charles H. 2:30 Charles

TIBBETTS (continued)
W. 1:29,31,32,79,109,182,
-2:42,96,166,192,-3:48,96,138,
139,188,189,-4:48,96,144,192,
-5:48,96,144,192 Daniel 6:67,
149 David 3:33,-5:92,94
Deborah 4:148,-6:72 Dorcas
5:94 Dorothy 4:152 Ebenezer
4:147,-5:52,-6:67,70,119,120,
172 Edmond 6:119,185 Edward
6:66,130,173 Elijah 1:54,
-2:76,149,-3:33,-4:70,-5:94
Elijah H. 6:36 Elisha 2:76
Elizabeth 1:54,57,66,118,
-2:76,-3:31,33,47,148,-4:10,
40,117,123,162,-5:1,94,-6:40,
100,101,129,146,-7:5 Elizabeth
K. 6:119 Enoch 4:123,-5:50,
-7:5 Ephraim 1:50-54,112,
-2:74,76,122,125,-3:33,-4:78,
148,152,-5:94 Esther 3:33,
-4:152 Eunice 4:148 Ezekiel
1:124,-3:33,-5:28,120 Gideon
4:119 Hall Jackson 7:76 Hannah 2:76,-4:123,-5:52,-6:36,
-7:5 Hannah C. 4:192,-5:192,
-6:48,96 Harriet Chase 7:80
Henry 1:53,178,-2:75,76,148,
-4:11,146,-5:89,94,117,-6:68,
74,75,101,129,130,172,173
Hipzibah 2:148 Huldah 5:150,
-6:55 Ichabod 3:26,74,-5:94 Ira
5:152 Israel 6:68 James 5:53,
-6:68,130,172 Jane 1:166,
-6:20,123 Jedediah 4:152
Jeremiah 2:76,-3:153,-5:94,
152,-6:129,130 Joel P. 4:182
John 1:166,-3:33,153,-4:148,
-5:50,169,-6:172 Jonathan
5:28,94,146,-6:66 Joseph 1:54,
57,59,61,63,-2:76,79,-4:65,
123,-3:31,33,148,-5:54,-6:100,
146,-7:3,5 Josiah 6:68 Joyce
6:68 Judith 2:76 Leonard 6:35
Leonora 6:39 Lois 1:166 Love
1:59,-3:33,-4:65,-5:28,94 Lucy
5:150 Lydia 2:76,-4:151,-5:2,
94 Margery 2:76,-6:100 Mary
1:54,68,-2:76,-3:33,-4:12,
-5:24,92,94,117,120,178,-6:75,
119,130,-7:87 Mary A. 6:37
Mary E. 6:129 Mehitable 5:4

TIBBETTS (continued)
Mercy 7:2 Mrs. 2:122
Nathaniel 3:145,-4:145,
-6:68,75 Nicholas 5:94 Noah
6:36,129-132 Obadiah 1:118,
-2:149 Patience 4:147,-5:28
Paul 3:25,74,-6:68,72
Penelope 5:94 Peter 2:148
Phebe 2:125,-5:7,95 Philip
2:30 Rebecca 5:28,116,-6:172
Richard 5:89,-7:76 Robert 3:33
Rose 1:50,53,54,57,59,61,
-2:76,-3:33,-4:66,-5:117 Ruth
1:124,-5:28,56 Sally 7:77
Samuel 4:9,123,-5:44,-6:37,
103,120,-7:5 Sarah 1:59,63,
-3:33,-4:13,65,123,-5:92,94,
95,113,115,-6:68,75,172,-7:5,
76 Silas 3:33,-4:151 Simeon
3:30,74 Solomon 6:67 Stephen
5:4,28,56,-6:74 Susan 5:95,
-6:35 Susanna 4:147,-5:5,118,
-6:172 Thomas 1:12,-4:13
Thomas W. 5:152 Wealthy
5:119 William 5:55,-6:68
TIFFANY, Humphrey 3:79
TIFFT, Matthew 4:36
TILDEN, Joseph, Jr. 7:72
TILLSON, Eunice 6:191
TILTON, Aaron 3:168,-5:21
Abigail 1:192,-2:9-12,14,108,
121,-3:127,-4:134,171,-5:9
Abraham 1:192,-2:9-12,14,
-3:120,180,-4:169,-5:9,181
Abram 1:161 Anna 2:12,119,
-4:171 Arthur E. 5:181 Bridget
4:171,172,-5:11,180 Daniel
1:191,-2:9,50,108,111,112,-5:9
David 2:70,-5:160,-6:27,30,32
Ebenezer 3:181 Elizabeth
1:191,192,-2:50,-3:131,-5:9
Esther 3:180,-5:11,181 George
F. W. 5:181 Hannah 2:12,55,
89,106,108,-3:180,-4:169,-5:9
Henry 6:139 Isaac 3:82
Isabelle 3:119 Jacob 4:94,95
James P. 6:7 Jemima 4:94,95,
-6:30 Jesse 5:180 Jethro B.
4:171,172,-5:11,180 John 2:10,
11,108,-3:16,182,-4:94 John T.
5:20 Jonathan 4:86 Joseph 4:94
Josiah 2:10,12,70,130,-3:182,

TILTON (continued)
-4:85,-5:103 Levi 4:84,-5:180
Lois 3:132 Lucy C. 6:30 Lydia
1:191 Mary 2:14,111,-3:177,
-4:94,-5:9,160,180 Mary B.
3:180 Mary D. 3:177 Mehitable
1:191,-2:108,111,112 Mercy
4:94,95 Meribah 5:103
Nathaniel 2:10,-4:86,94 Olive
5:180 Rachel 5:9,-6:27
Rebecca 4:91 Sally T. 7:41
Samuel 2:68,89,106,108,112,
-3:184,-4:94,95,172,175,-5:180
Sarah 2:130,-3:183,184 Sarah
T. 6:160 Susanna 5:10 Timothy
4:175 William 2:106 William
F. 3:179,180,-5:181
TINA, David 3:65,75
TITCOMB, Beniah 3:157 Charles
5:21
TITUS, Frank H. 4:192 Sarah A.
5:182
TOBEY, Abram 5:37 Experience
4:101 Isaac 4:97 James 3:104
Joseph 2:184 Katharine 4:100
Lydia 4:103 Martha 4:51,52
Peter 2:184 Samuel 5:87,89,90
Sobriety 6:178 Stephen 4:9
William 4:57,-5:89
TOBINE, Patrick 4:36
TODD, Henry 7:20 John 3:186
Mary C. 3:186 Mr. 5:43 Sarah
5:21 Sarah D. 3:186 Susanna
3:177
TOMB, Samuel 6:140
TONGUE, Stephen 3:86
TOOGOOD, Edward 3:55,-4:49,
-5:41 Hannah 4:51 Mary 4:58
Mr. 3:174,-4:102 Mrs. 3:175
TOPPAN, Abigail 3:90 Amos
3:130 Bezaleel 6:10 Chris-
topher 6:10 Enoch 3:2 Martha
3:41 Sarah 6:10
TORR, Abigail 5:113 Eliza 4:183
Elizabeth 5:50 John 1:177,
-4:184 Jonathan H. 5:152 Mary
1:197,-5:56 Nancy 4:181 Sarah
4:78,-5:115 Seth 4:186 Simon
4:148 Vincent 4:184,-5:115
TORREY (TORY), Bethiah
5:139,184,187 David 1:115
Elizabeth 1:115,-3:168

TORREY (continued)
Frances 5:187 James 1:115,
-3:34 John 5:139 William
5:139,184,187
TOWLE, Anna 3:86,-5:153 Anne
1:47,84,95 Benjamin 2:107,
-3:142,-5:153 Caleb 2:107,
-3:91,-5:106,112,156,-6:27
Charles D. 3:116 Daniel 5:106
Dearborn 4:136 Eben S. 7:24
Ebenezer 3:44,-5:158 Elisha
3:87,-4:131,169 Elizabeth 4:84
Francis 2:107 Gardner 3:116,
-4:84,137 George W. 3:116
Hannah 4:167,169,-5:45 Huldah
1:90 Isabell 2:86,87,89,91,
107,110,112 James 1:47,
-3:169,-5:156 Jennings 4:167
Jeremiah 4:132,-5:112 John
2:112,-4:169,-5:20 John M.
4:186 Jonathan 1:47,84,-4:118,
-6:104,167,-7:72 Joseph 1:47,
-3:116,117,184,-2:107 Joseph
W. 3:117 Joshua 2:89,-6:167
Judith 3:171 Levi 1:47,-3:116,
-4:134,-6:116,-7:64 Levi G.
3:116,-4:136 Lucinda 5:11
Maria 6:27 Mary 2:91,-3:91,
134,-4:85,-6:56 Mathias 4:167
Mehitable 5:22 Molly 4:167
Nancy 3:116,117 Nathan 1:84
Nehemiah 4:176 Panny 3:116
Phebe 4:176 Phielmon 4:85
Philip 2:86,87,89,91,107,
110,112 Samuel 1:47 Sarah
3:116,168,-5:182,-6:6,60 Sarah
A. 4:118 Simeon 3:120
Solomon 4:167 Stephen 6:116
William 3:131,-5:158 Zipporah
6:27
TOWNER, James 7:87 Lucinda
6:165 Mary 7:87
TOWNS, George 3:69,76
TOWNSEND, Colonel 5:40 Daniel
5:151
TRAFFICK, Deborah 2:92
TRAFTON, Penelope 6:149
TRAILL, Alexander 4:1,2 Anabel
4:3 Barbara 4:3,4 David 4:3
Eliz(a)beth 4:3 Elspeth 4:2,3
George 4:2,3 Helen 4:3 Hugh
4:2 Isabel 4:4 James 4:2,3

TRAILL (continued)
Jean 4:3 John 4:1-4 Margaret
4:3 Marjorie 4:3,4 Mary 4:4,
6,143,-5:90 Nicola 4:3 Patrick
4:2,3 Robert 4:2,4,143,-5:90
Thomas 4:1-3 Walter 4:2
Walterus 4:1 William 4:2-4
TRASK, John 3:116
TREADWELL, Ann 6:45,-7:13
Anna E. 6:64 Anne 5:184,186,
188,-6:76,77,-7:11 Benjamin
Franklin 7:59 Caroline 6:64
Charles 5:184,187,-6:63
Charles Cutter 7:11 Charles R.
5:188 Daniel 5:140,-7:13
Elizabeth 6:63 Frances M.
6:64 Franklin 6:64 George 5:87
George R. 6:45 Hannah 4:76
Jacob 5:87,167,184,186,188,
-6:45,76,77,-7:11,13 Jacob C.
6:76 Joshua Brackett 7:57
Louisa T. 6:64 Lydia 5:183,
-6:63,160 Martha 7:59 Martha
Jane Brackett 7:57 Mary 5:186,
187 Mehitable R. 5:188 Mr.
1:22 Mrs. 5:140,183-185,187,
-6:41 Napoleon B. 6:64
Nathaniel 2:160,-5:183,185,187
Richard 5:184 Robert O. 2:191,
-5:164,165 Samuel 5:140,187,
-6:41 Sarah 6:41 Sarah W. 6:64
Thomas 2:163,164 Thomas D.
6:63 William 6:77 William C.
6:64 William E. 2:191 William H. H. 7:59 William H. H.
M. 6:64
TREAT, Mrs. 4:190
TREDICK, Elizabeth B. 2:34 Jane
2:33 John B. 2:33 Lucretia
2:33,34,37 Mary B. 2:33 William 1:80,-2:33,34
TREDWELL (see TREADWELL)
TREE, Francis 4:36
TREFETHEN, Abigail 1:131,132
Elizabeth 1:131,132,-2:36
Foster 1:22 Henry 1:21,22,
131,132 John 2:36,37 Joseph
1:131,-5:132,134 Lucretia
1:131 Margaret 1:132 Mary
1:131 Mehitable 2:36,37 Mrs.
5:134 Nathaniel 1:132 Robinson 1:131,132,-5:132,134

TREFETHEN (continued)
Salome 1:131 Sarah 4:149,
-5:51 William 1:131,132,
-4:116,-5:166
TREWSDELL, John 5:188 Mr.
5:188 Mrs. 5:188
TRICKETT, Thomas 1:179
TRICKEY, Abigail 3:63,-4:18,60,
106,108 Alice 5:119,-6:115
Anna 4:153 Anne 5:189 Aveline
7:60 Benjamin 4:79,108,-5:52,
-6:120 Catherine 4:156 Comfort 5:145,-7:31 Deborah
3:11,-6:43 Dorothy 6:85,120
Easter (Esther?) 4:63 Elihu
3:64 Elizabeth 2:172,-3:63,
154,-4:12,61,63,64,106,108,
109,111,149,154,156,158,-7:49
Ephraim 3:63,-4:150 Frances
2:24 Frances Jane 7:60 Francis 1:9 Hannah 5:7,-6:120
Henry 7:60 Isaac 2:171,-3:63,
154 Jacob 5:151 James 4:150
Joanna 3:107 John 3:9,63,64,
111,-4:64,106,-5:55,189,-6:43,
45,115,120,-7:91 Jonathan
2:173,-3:63,-4:16,18,60,108,
111 Joseph 2:175,-3:63,-4:61,
63,64,106,108,109,112,154,
156,158 Joshua 3:1,-4:106,153,
155,-5:28,116,146 Keturah
2:174 Lemuel 3:3,111,-4:109,
153 Lois 4:81,153 Lydia 4:16
Mary 2:172,173,176,-3:63,64,
107,110,111,-4:75,-5:79,-6:45,
71 Miriam 2:176 Mr. 6:74 Mrs.
6:43,45 Patience 5:73 Rebecca
5:8,-6:72,120,-7:91 Rosamond
4:106 Ros(s)e 4:153 Samuel
4:128 Samuel G. 4:158 Sarah
2:171,173,-3:63,154,-4:152,
-6:114,120 Temperance 4:153
Thomas 3:63,107,108,110,
111,-4:61,-5:41,79 William
4:156,-6:69,120
TRIGAL, Julien 3:67,75
TRIGGS, Mary 5:137,138 Thomas
5:137,138 William 5:138
TRIM(M)INGS, Oliver 1:3,9,
-2:24,25,27,62
TRIPE, Anna 2:176 Hannah 5:42
Lydia 7:49 Richard 4:148 Sarah

TRIPE (continued)
5:3,-7:54 Sylvanus 5:166
Thomas 2:172
TRIPP, Lucy 3:4
TRUE, Abigail 4:132 Henry 2:106
Jane 2:106 John 7:19 Mary
2:106 Mercy 4:181 Reuben
3:133 Waity 3:114
TRUEWORGEY
(TRUEWORTHY?), Samuel
1:11
TRUEWORTHY, James 4:98 Ruth
4:98
TRULL, Judith 3:42
TRUMBULL, Sarah 6:168
TRUNDY, John 1:22 Sarah 1:95
TRUSSEL(LL), Amos 4:178 Jacob
6:107
TUBB, Benjamin 4:11 William
3:65
TUCK, Dr. 3:133 Hannah 3:169
Jonathan 5:19 Josiah 6:62
Nathan 4:180 Sarah 3:168,-7:44
Susanna 3:134
TUCKER, Abigail 4:180,-6:175
Angeline 5:19 Benjamin 3:167,
-5:108,158,-6:26,30,31,104
Captain 6:27 Cyrus 7:69 Daniel
3:134 Dorothy 6:105 Eben 6:28
Ebenezer 6:26,168 Eliphalet
6:54 Elizabeth 1:130,131,139,
-3:87 Elizabeth H. 1:139,140
Esther 1:46 Eunice 5:150 Ezra
3:42,91,-6:28,31 Francis 1:11
Francis W. 7:26 George 5:132
Hannah 3:45,-6:30 Isaac 5:130
Jacob 3:177,-4:179,-6:123,185
James 1:140,-2:175 Jane 5:7
Jenny 7:27 John 1:12,139,
-3:48,50,55,83,146,-4:150,
173,-5:90,108,132,134 John W.
1:140 Jonathan 3:39,-6:26
Joseph 1:131,139,140,-3:133,
-4:147,-5:130,-6:119,120,172,
173,175,176,-7:27 Joseph P.
1:139 Josiah 5:115,-6:120
Judith 3:130 Lucy 5:18 Lydia
6:173 Mary 1:46;82,130,-2:72,
-3:44,135,-6:27,31 Miriam
6:31 Morris 2:72 Mrs 3:174
Nathaniel 1:46,130,131 Olive
2:38 Payson 7:34 Phebe 6:119

TUCKER (continued)
Richard 1:11,131,-2:28,59,
60,63,98 Ruth 6:123 Samuel
2:43,48,131,132,-3:39,88 Sarah
1:46,131,-6:62 Sarah R. 7:19
Susanna 1:46 Thomas 5:158
Thomas W. 3:164 Tristram
(Trustrum?) 3:3,-6:172 True
3:168 Widow 3:51 William
1:46,82,130,131,-5:41,134
TUCKERMAN, Betsey 7:15
Elizabeth 7:14-16,76,77
George Washington 7:76 John
7:14-16,76,77 Nathaniel 1:21,
-2:103,-5:40,-7:16 Samuel
7:77
TUFTS, Fanny 7:67 George F.
6:96 Lovey 4:80 Mary 4:76
Sophronia T. 7:71 Susie B.
2:166
TUKESBURY (see TEWKSBURY)
TUKEY, William 4:127
TURKAN, John 2:185,-3:72
TURNER, Bela 6:54 Caroline 7:89
Elisha 7:23 George 5:167 John
4:179 Louis 6:40 Lucy 6:81
Major 3:151
TURVIN, Jonathan 3:136
TURY, Bridget 4:98
TUTTLE, Abigail 1:61,-2:125,
-4:79,119,163,-5:176,-6:85
Anna 4:120,-6:85 Anne 1:169,
171 Asa C. 6:82 Bathsheba
1:66,-2:125,-4:163 Benjamin
2:149,-4:126,-6:137 Comfort
4:129 Daniel 4:186,-6:158
Deborah 1:126,-4:127,-6:39
Dorothy 4:9 Eben 7:58
Ebenezer 1:67,126,-2:125,
-4:163 Elijah 1:63,116,118,
-2:79,148,-4:122,-5:122 Elisha
2:125,-4:120 Elizabeth 5:83
Esther 1:63,116 Ezra J. 6:82
Hannah 4:77,125 Henrietta 7:58
Hiram A. 5:82 Hope 1:58,
-2:125,-4:44,163 Ira 5:61
Isaiah W. 4:114 James 1:53,
63,118,-2:79,125,149,-3:152,
-4:122 James S. 4:114 Jesse
C. 6:162 Job N. 6:33 John
1:178,-3:7,-4:76,146,163,
-5:83,-6:145 John G. 6:92

TUTTLE (continued)
Joseph 1:169,-2:30,-4:125,
127,-5:61,127,-6:82 Joseph E.
6:82 Judith 4:120 Levi 4:80,
183 Lucelle W. 4:114 Lydia
4:120 Mary 1:56-59,61,62,
66,67,-2:125,-4:9,38,120,125,
163 Mary A. 4:186 Mary L.
4:114 Mehitable 4:120 Mr. 4:46
Nancy 7:21 Nicholas 4:75,122
Otis 4:122 Phebe 1:53,-2:79,
146,-5:61,92,-6:85 Reuben
1:62,-2:125,128,-4:120 Rose
1:53,118,171,-2:80,-5:56,61,
-6:86 Samuel 2:125,149,-
4:150,-5:149 Samuel A. 4:114
Sarah 1:57,-2:125,-4:11,40,90,
183,-5:61 Sarah L. 4:114 Sarah
P. 2:30 Sophia H. 7:58 Stephen
4:122,-6:82 Tabitha 2:125
Thomas 1:56-59,61,62,66,67,
-2:125,-3:31,-4:69,114,116,
163,-5:181 Thomas B. 4:114
Timothy 6:85 Tobias 1:126,
-4:122,163,-5:175 William
1:116,169,171,-2:149,-5:61
William P. 2:30,-6:82,89 Zurviah 7:68
TWEED, Elizabeth L. 4:157
TWING, Nathaniel 3:71
TWIST, Lydia 4:123 Mary 2:42
TWITCHELL, Chloe 7:88 Julia
Celeste 7:88 William 7:88
TWOMBLY, Abigail 4:148,-5:50
Allen 6:85 Anna 2:126,-3:31,
-7:30 Anne 1:60,-4:68 Benjamin 5:53 Benjemin H. 6:39
Betty 7:30 Daniel 1:56,-2:125,
-4:38 Ebenezer 5:6 Eliza W.
6:36 Elizabeth 2:127,-4:79,
-5:5,151 Esther (Easter)
3:47,-4:13 Eunice 5:150 Hannah 7:28 Isaac 1:170,-2:126,
127,-5:150,174,-6:84 Isaac H.
6:84 James 7:53 Joanna 5:117,
-6:39 John 1:52,53,56,60,
-2:75,-3:31,-4:9,10,-5:53 John
H. 5:83 Jonathan 2:126 Jotham
5:1 Judith 2:126,-5:53 Lois
7:85 Lydia 5:3 Martha 1:60
Mary 1:59,170,-2:127,-4:66,
-5:8,114,-6:84 Mehitable 5:116

126

TWOMBLY (continued)
Moses 5:115 Nancy 5:116,
-6:40 Rachel 1:52 Ralph 4:77
Rebecca 2:126 Samuel 1:52,
-2:78,126,-5:119 Sarah 1:53,
56,-2:150,-5:1,114 Simon G.
6:85 Stephen 5:3,-6:36,
-7:29,30 Susanna 4:152 Tobias
2:126,-5:56,-6:113,-7:85 Wil-
liam 6:127,-7:88
TYDIE, Hannah 4:12
TYLER, Lavinia 7:23
UNDERHILL, Betsey 7:17
Charles W. 7:78 John 5:102
UNDERWOOD, Abigail 1:28 Ben-
jamin 1:28,-2:144 John 1:21,
-2:144 Joseph 1:28 Lucy 2:144
Temperance 2:144
UPHAM, Albert 7:85 Alfred 7:30
Francis William 7:85 George
B. 6:110 Joseph Badger 7:31
Judith A. 6:38 Judith Almira
7:32 Mary 6:33,-7:30 Nathaniel
7:30-32,85 Ruth Cogswell 7:32
Thomas C. 6:33 Timothy 7:31
UPTON, Jeremiah 6:164 John
6:112 Sarah 6:58
URAN, Jonathan 6:56 Samuel 7:25
USHER, John 3:100
UTLEY, Samuel 7:67
VAN TEIL, Captain 3:145
VARNEY, Aaron 2:125,-4:68,
121,-5:60,125 Aaron R. 5:61
Abby M. 6:126 Abel 4:68
Abigail 1:52,54-56,60,119,
120,122-124,162,172-174,
-2:75,126,148,-4:39,41,42,67,
119,124,-5:23,173,-6:21,23,87,
-7:8,54 Abigail P. 6:128 Achsa
5:27,-6:24 Adeline 6:87 Albert
6:125 Alva 5:128 Amasa 5:27,
127,-6:91 Amos 1:69,162,167,
169,174,-3:32,-6:21,23,24,123,
124 Ann 6:87 Anna 1:128,172,
176,-2:30,75,-4:119,-6:21,
23-25,89,-7:4 Anna J. 6:24,
-7:71 Anne 5:27 Anstrus R.
6:179 Asa 5:64,-6:21,25 Beard
R. 6:128,179 Beede 5:64
Benajah 5:58,127,-6:91 Benjamin 2:146,-4:65,151,
-6:100,101,-7:1,4 Bethiah

VARNEY (continued)
2:128,-4:160,-7:5 Caleb
1:117,167,172,-4:65,-5:62,-7:4
Calvin 5:94 Caroline 2:29,
-6:21,87 Caroline D. 6:125,127
Caroline M. 6:125 Charles
1:165,173,-5:25,59,-6:23
Charles E. 6:91,124 Charlotte
1:169,-5:172,-6:82 Christopher
4:162 Content 1:56,58,60,121
Cyrus 5:64,-6:24,91 Daniel
1:62,122,126,169,-2:125,126,
-4:121,-5:24,64,128,-6:83
David 2:128 David T. 5:94
Deborah 1:161 Deliverance
1:115,117,121,122,124,164,
-4:42,121,-5:128,-6:22 Dilwyn
6:25 Dominicus 5:145 Dorcas
5:122,126 Dorothy 1:65,67
Dudley 5:120 Ebenezer 1:50,
52-55,60,61,69,71,114,116,
117,-2:75,78,148,-4:65,3,
-5:6,57,94,-6:38,-7:4 Edward
6:125 Edwin 6:128 Eli 1:169,
-5:64,172,-6:82 Elias 5:58
Elijah 2:146,-5:57,92,94,
95,113,173 Elijah H. 5:120
Eliphalet 5:125,-6:185 Eliza
6:87 Elizabeth 1:52-55,60,61,
69,71,114-117,119,123,124,
161,169,171,174,-2:123,146,
147,-3:35,-4:42,65,-5:6,62,
128,-6:21,38,83,89,180,-7:4,8
Elizabeth M. 6:179 Elizabeth
W. 2:32 Enoch 1:114,-4:163
Ephraim 4:42 Esther 2:148,
-4:128,147,-5:113 Eunice
1:121,165,170,-4:42,182,-5:126
Ezekiel 1:124,-2:147,-4:70,
124,-5:64,173,-7:8 Ezra 4:163,
-5:64,94 Festus 1:162,174,175,
-2:29,-5:27,62,-6:20,125
George 1:169,-5:27,94,128,
-6:83 George D. 1:168,174,
-5:122,124,-6:25 George E.
2:166 Gulielma 6:24 H. C.
2:93,-5:92 Hannah 1:69, 116-
119,125,162,173-175,-2:29,
123,148,-4:41,68,124,163,
-5:26,62,64,124,-6:19,20,23,
89,125,-7:8,86 Hannah D. 6:23
Hannah E. 6:128 Hannah J.

VARNEY (continued)
2:142,-6:24,179 Hanson
1:114,-2:148,-4:66,-5:57 Henry
A. 6:25 Herbert C. 4:190
Hezekiah 1:116,117,125,
-2:128,-4:68 Hope 1:122,
-4:119,-5:128 Hopley 5:147
Huldah 1:65,120,127,167,
172,-2:147,-4:124,163,-5:60,
125,175,-6:19,89,-7:8
Humphrey 1:118,-2:146
Ichabod 5:29 Isaac 1:116,117,
174,-2:148,-4:68,-5:23,29,61,
64,-6:82,183 Isaac W. 6:179
Isaiah 4:163 Ivory 6:21,24
Jacob 3:34,-6:128,185 James
1:123,126,169,170,-2:146,
-3:34,-4:70,121,-5:2,23,60,64,
172 James Noah 7:54 Jedediah
2:128,148,-4:121,163,-5:60
Jeremiah 4:159 Jesse 4:163
Job 5:62,-6:89,-7:4 Joel 5:119
John 1:49,52,56,60,117,162,
-2:32,75,78,126,148,-4:42,
-5:8,58,62,124,-6:21,38,86,87,
125 John F. 6:25 John H. 5:62
John Hanson 7:4 John Orrin
7:54 Jonas M. 6:128 Jonathan
1:50,115,116,119,124,161,
-4:44,68,-5:25,60,94,-6:23,
-7:8 Joseph 1:51,54,55,60,
66,69,118,161,168,-2:75,123,
125,-3:32,-4:41,119,163,-5:64,
128,173,-6:19 Joshua 1:66,125,
128,-2:125,-3:36,-4:42,70,119,
161,162,-6:87 Judith 1:52,60,
123,128,-2:75,125,128,-4:67,
119,-5:172,-6:19 Keziah 4:119,
-6:19,38 Lavina 6:21,125 Levi
4:163 Love 6:24 Love T. 6:24
Lucy 6:24 Lydia 1:53,58,117,
169,174,-2:128,146,147,-4:42,
68,69,-5:25,64,94,116,122,147,
-6:21,35, 83,184 Lydia E.
6:86,183 Lydia L. 6:125 Lydia
N. 6:180 Margaret 1:60,-2:128
Maria 6:21,126 Martha 1:53,
122,126,-2:75,147,-3:31,
-4:121,148,150,-5:149 Martha
A. 6:40 Martha C. 5:128 Mary
1:49,50,52-56,64,68,69,114,
115,117,118,124,125,128,161,

VARNEY (continued)
162,167-169,174,-2:30,75,
123,147,-3:31,32,34,36,-4:119,
124,159,162,-5:6,27,57,58,61,
62,116,118,122,128,173,-6:18,
23-25,82,83,87,89,91,100,101,
123,125,-7:4,8 Mary A. 6:38
Mary D. 6:24 Mary E. 6:91,125
Matilda 1:170,-5:172,-6:82,83
Mehitable 5:52,57,61,121
Mercy 1:57,60-62,66,115,121,
168,-2:125,-4:41,119,121,124,
146,-5:8,58,121,127,173,-6:21,
25,-7:8 Micajah 3:34 Miles
4:65,-5:27,-6:24 Miriam 1:162
Mordecai 1:127,-2:146,-5:175,
-6:128,179 Moses 1:52,61,118,
125,127,128,161,-2:79,124,
125,146,-4:119,162,163,-5:29,
92,94,122 Nathan 1:61,122,123,
162,-2:125,-4:119,161,-5:58
Nathaniel 1:56,58,60,121,
125,-2:75,128,-4:42,68,70,
-5:94,175,-6:183,-7:5 Newell
B. 6:91 Nicholas 2:148,-5:23,
50 Noah 5:64,-6:184 Obadiah
6:25 Obed 6:21,23,125 Olive
5:23,56 Oliver 5:173,-6:21
Othniel 1:167,176,-5:27,-6:24,
25 Otis 1:115,-2:128 Oziel
5:64 Pamelia C. 6:83 Patience
1:56,118,-2:128,-4:68,150 Paul
1:50,114,123,-2:75,79,-3:34,
-4:41,119,-5:62,128,-7:4
Peace 5:151 Peace P. 5:122
Pelatiah 5:25 Peter 1:52-54,
-2:128,146 Phebe 1:127,-
2:146,-5:26,92,94,121,-7:1
Phineas 6:37 Reuben 1:162,
174,-4:119,124,-6:21 Rhoda
1:175,-5:27,147,-6:21,128
Richard 1:115,118,-4:119,
-5:59,121 Richard D. 6:21
Richard I. 1:176 Richard J.
6:24,127 Richmond H. 6:128
Rufus C. 4:145 Ruth 4:119,
-5:60,122 Samuel 1:54,64,69,
115,118,124,168,-2:75,123,
-3:31,32,-4:41,68, 69,124,
-5:23,122,126,173,-6:25,-7:5,8
Sarah 1:49,54,56,60,119,124,
168-170,174,-2:75,146,147,

VARNEY (continued)
-3:31,32,-4:42,68,119,121,159,
-5:23,29,49,57,94,123,149,172,
173,-6:25,87,-7:54 Sarah A.
6:91 Sarah E. 6:179 Sarah M.
6:125 Sarah P. 1:174 Sarah W.
6:23 Sarah Jane 7:87 Shubael
1:115,168,-3:32,-5:58,-6:87
Silas 2:128,-5:23,113 Simeon
3:132,-5:64,125 Solomon
2:146,-3:32,-4:69,-5:58
Stephen 1:50,57,60-62,66,68,
115-117,121,124,164,168,
-2:75,77,124,125,148,-4:41,
-5:58,-6:25,185 Susanna 1:52,
61,113,161,169,-2:127,148,
-4:68,119,-5:29,-6:19 Tabitha
4:163,-5:175 Temperance 1:69,
118,-3:34,-4:41 Thomas 1:50,
65,67,69,71,161,-2:15,146-
148,-3:32,-4:39,159,-5:4,5,23,
27,29,95,-6:19,-7:8 Timothy
1:60,64,119-121,124,162,
-2:150,-3:32,-4:67,124,-5:61,
63,125,-7:5,8 Tobias 1:68,165,
169,-2:125,-4:38,-5:25 William 1:172,-2:30,-5:61,62,
-6:89,-7:4 William H. 6:91
William P. 6:25 Zaccheus
2:147
VARNUM, Abigail 3:88 Joel 6:55
Martha 3:119
VARRILL, James 6:78 John
6:78,79 Mary 6:78,79 Susanna
6:79
VAUGHAN, Abigail 4:55,-5:42
Anne 5:133 Benjamin 6:93
Elizabeth 2:20 Elizabeth C.
5:89 Elliott 4:56,-5:87,
89,90,130,133 George 2:20,21,
101,103,-3:55,-4:49,-5:87 Jane
5:90 Major 3:104,172,175 Margaret 2:20,21,-5:44,133 Mary
2:21 Sarah 5:44 William 1:11,
12,-2:20,21,100-102,-3:173
VEASEY - VEAZEY, Agnes 1:184
David 2:10,51 Elizabeth
1:183,-2:10,51,94 Esther
2:10,51 George 1:183,192 Hannah 1:186,192,-2:10,11,51
Jeremiah 3:135 John 2:11
Judah 1:192 Levi 4:179 Mary

VEASEY (continued)
2:11 Nancy 4:89 Samuel
1:183,186,-2:10,51,-3:124
Sarah 1:186,-3:124 Simon
1:192 Stephen 2:10 Thomas
1:192
VENNARD, Andrew B. 2:165
Dorothy 2:37 Jane 2:37 John
1:22
VENNIN, Elizabeth 5:91 Hannah
5:89,91 Mr. 5:89,91 Rebecca
5:89
VERRILL, Abigail L. 1:141
Elizabeth 2:136 Elizabeth M.
2:136 Jonathan W. 2:136
Joseph 1:141 Joses 1:141
Maria 2:136 Martha L. 2:136
Mary 2:136 Phena P. 1:141
Richard T. 2:136 Samuel 2:136
Sarah 1:141
VICKERY, David 6:19 Hannah
6:22 Joshua 6:22 Mary 6:22
Sarah A. 6:19
VINCENT, Anthony 4:107
Elizabeth 3:6,-4:107,108,
110,112 John 4:110 Margaret
2:171 Thomas 3:1,-4:107,108,
110,112 William 2:171,-3:10,
-4:108
VIRGIN, Abiel 6:170 Abigail 6:58
Abigail D. 7:69 Bethiah 6:56
Charlotte 6:169 Eliza T. 7:69
Elizabeth 6:110 Emily 7:64
Fanny H. 7:23 Hannah 6:54
Hazen 6:166 Jeremiah 6:56
Joab B. 4:182 Jonathan A. 7:68
Judith 6:161 Leavit C. 7:17
Martha 6:108 Mary E. 7:72
Miriam 6:108 Phebe 6:56 Sarah
4:184,-6:58,-7:17 Sarah (A. or
S.) 7:67 Simeon 6:112 Simon
7:67 William M. 7:23
VOSE, Francis 5:35
VRIN, John 3:174,176 Mrs. 3:176
William 2:22,-3:80
WADE, John 3:100,-4:11 Major
3:85 Mr. 3:85
WADLEIGH, Achsa 3:131 Anna
2:47,-3:131 Benjamin 2:43,
69,72,133,-4:135,-5:104,106,
-6:27 Edward 3:119 Elijah
4:135 Elizabeth 3:134,-6:111

129

WADLEIGH (continued)
Enoch 3:120,-4:85 Enos D.
4:179 George H. 2:166,-3:189
Hannah 3:43,-4:89,135,-5:22
James 4:132 John 2:66,70,
133,-3:89,-4:132 Jonathan
2:45,-6:27 Joseph 6:29 Juda
5:104 Love 2:69 Mary 3:88,
-4:90,131,135,-5:10 Rachel
3:133 Robert 2:50 Ruth 5:106
Sarah 2:58,-3:43,169,-4:135
Simon D. 4:135 Thomas 2:47,
-3:43,-6:27,29,32
WAGONER, Mary V. 6:191
WAINWRIGHT, John 3:151 Simon
3:151
WAITE, David 6:104 Mary 4:89
WAKEFIELD, Mr. 3:150
WAKEHAM, Caleb 4:79,148
Elizabeth 5:83 Miriam 5:113
Thomas 1:12
WALBRIDGE, Levi 7:63 W. H.
5:179
WALDEN, Abigail 7:12 Jacob
7:12 John 2:129 Joseph 7:12
WALDRON, Abigail 5:54,-6:78,80
Abraham 6:120,172 Ann 3:79
Anna 3:137 Anne 6:78 Charles
6:186 Colonel 3:79 Constant
6:186 Daniel 6:187 Elizabeth
1:137,140,-4:11 Elizabeth S.
1:137 George 1:140,-6:172,186
Hannah 3:79 Isaac 2:161,162,
-4:89 Jacob 6:50,78,80 Jacob
T. 6:78 James 5:52 John 4:11,
-5:88 John D. 5:148 Jonathan
B. 1:137,140 Joshua F. 1:137
Major 3:80 Mary W. 1:137
Mehitable 5:119 Mr. 3:102,137
Mrs. 3:137 Richard 1:179,
-3:137,172,-4:103,-6:186
Richard H. 1:137 Robert S.
1:137,-4:127 Sabra 6:34 Sally
W. 7:20 Samuel 6:186 Sarah
5:150,-6:36 Tamson 6:34
Thomas 6:80 Thomas W.
2:157,-4:104,-6:186,187 William 6:186
WALES, Mr. 5:44
WALFORD, Jeremiah 1:5,6,9,10,
21,-2:23 Mr. 2:24 Thos 1:2,
5,9,10,-2:23,59-62,64,98,99

WALKER, ---- 7:74 Abiel
6:111,-7:21 Abigail 3:62,
-4:49,50,146,-5:44,51,77,118,
-6:51,67,187,-7:90 Addington
4:102 Alcock 4:57 Amasa 7:68
Ann 3:9,-5:91,129 Ann E. 7:42
Anna 3:63,106,-4:55,154,-5:77,
134,-6:50 Benjamin 4:58 Betsey Briard 7:14,15 Bridget
3:63,-6:109 Bruce 6:53
Caroline 1:153 Catherine 6:50
Charles 7:21 Clarissa 6:168
Daniel 3:4,160 Davenport 4:99
Deborah 5:150 Deborah R.
4:155 Deliverance 3:64,106,
111,157 Dorothy 4:97,-5:114
Ebenezer 3:111 Edward 3:3,
64,106,109,111,158,160,-4:17,
60,108,155 Eleanor 3:8,
-4:107,110,154-156,-6:80
Eliza 7:80 Elizabeth 2:170,
172,-3:5,8,-4:110,-5:52,77,
-6:108,164,-7:73,80 Elizabeth
K. 5:77 Elle 4:157 George
2:101-104,-3:174,176,-4:10,
-6:112,-7:80 George Alfred
7:42 George R. 7:42 Gideon
2:176,-4:105,107,110,154-156,
158,-5:44,76,-6:45 Hannah
4:142,-5:47,77,-7:18 Harriet
4:184 Hazen 7:21 Horton D.
2:164 John 2:168,-3:57,174,
-4:55,107,-6:71,178 John K.
5:118 Joseph 1:9,13,-2:169,
-5:184,187,-3:51,62,109,155,
-4:146,-6:42,45,71,76,78,80,
148,-7:14,89,90 Joseph A.
4:184 Joseph B. 6:96 Joseph
Burbeen 7:33 Joshua 3:111
Lemuel 3:109 Lucretia P. 7:18
Lucy 4:156,-5:184 Lucy M.
4:182 Lucy Maria 7:76 Lydia
3:158 Lyman A. 7:72 Margaret
6:148 Maria 7:74 Mark 5:78,
-6:187,-7:13 Mark W. 1:152,
156 Martha 3:111 Mary 2:170,
174,-3:106,109,155,-4:16,99,
-5:78,80,151,-6:50, 76,110,178
Mary C. 7:69 Mrs. 3:175,176,
-4:60,-5:184,187,-6:42,45,76,
78 Nancy 7:73 Olive 3:109,
-4:108,-7:76 Philip 1:182

WALKER (continued)
Rebecca 4:99 Richard 1:182,
-3:155 Robert 4:100,147,
-5:41,-6:73 Ruth 6:80 Samuel
2:169,-4:101,105,-5:77,80,
-6:105,163,-7:11,79 Sarah
1:152,153,-2:170,-3:4,111,158,
160,-4:10,17,99,108,155 Sarah
Ann 7:14 Seth 2:161,162,176,
-3:64,-4:154,156,158,-5:91,
129,131,134,-6:78,79,-7:12,14,
15,73,76,77,79 Seth S. 1:152,
153,-5:78 Stephen Huse 7:14
Susan B. 7:21 Susanna 5:187
Temperance 6:78,79,-7:12,77
Timothy 6:10,11,49,50,52
Tobias 6:78,-7:11,13,14,
73,74,76 William 1:12,-3:173,
175,-5:77,134,-6:53,78,-7:12
William D. 3:141
WALL, Hannah 2:85 James 2:83,
85 John 1:3,-3:21,73 Mary
2:83,85
WALLACE (WALLAS -
WALLIS), Albert 2:166 Alice
3:115 Anne 5:41 George 1:11,
12,-3:182 Hannah 1:132 Jane
7:13 John 4:46 Mary 5:41 Miss
5:42 Mrs. 6:80 Robert 4:178,
-7:13 Samuel 1:132,-3:115,
-4:93,-6:80,-7:13 Sarah 1:132
Sumner 2:166 William 1:93,
-4:80,-6:80
WALLINGFORD, Abigail 7:28
Charity 3:59,62-64,108,154,155
Colonel 3:62,-6:38,114 David
5:5,-7:28 Elizabeth 5:148
Elizabeth G. 7:86 Frances
3:108 Jacob 5:8,-6:115,-7:86
Joanna 5:150 John 3:62-64,
108,154,155,-4:9,147,-6:147
Judith 3:155 Lydia 5:49,-6:117
Mary 2:173,-3:62,-6:75
Patience 3:62 Peter 3:64,
-4:146,-6:114,115,-7:28 Phebe
3:62,-4:14 Rachel 4:190
Rebecca 5:147 Samuel 5:149,
-7:28 Sarah 3:62,-6:38,114
Susanna 3:154 Thomas 4:190,
-6:98,99 Widow 6:117
WALLIS (see WALLACE)
WALMSLEY, John 5:164,168

WALTON, Elizabeth 2:171
Frances 3:57,61,158 George
1:6,8,9,117,-2:23,-3:57,108
Jane 6:149 John 4:63,-6:149
Joseph 2:37,164 Mr. 2:36
Patience 3:108 Samuel 2:170,
-3:64 Sarah 3:134 Shadrach
2:101
WANERSON, Sagamore 3:149
WAPLES, Paul 3:4
WARD, Carl(e)ton 6:111 Carleton
G. 7:26 Daniel 7:14 Dorcas
6:78 Eliezer 7:77 Elizabeth
7:16 Hannah 2:83 John 1:22
Margaret 2:83,91 Margery 6:78,
80,-7:14,16,75 Margery G. 6:80
Mary Ann 7:75 Nahum 5:166,
-6:78,80,-7:14,16,75,77
Richard 2:185 Robert 4:98
Samuel 6:62,136 Thomas 2:83,
91 William 2:182,-3:21,71
WARDALL, Eliakim 2:87,90
Joseph 2:87 Lydia 2:87,90
Margaret 2:90
WARDWELL, Jeremiah 6:107
WARNER, Adriel 4:38 Agnes 6:77
Alden 4:43 Alexander 7:12 Asa
4:38 Charlotte 4:39 Daniel
2:104 David 6:77 Elizabeth
4:158 George 6:44 Gideon 4:38
Jane 4:10 John 6:80 John M.
4:39 Kezia 4:38 Margaret 6:42
Mary 4:103 Mary A. 6:45 Mat-
thew 7:14 Mrs. 6:42,44,45,
77,80 Peace 4:38 Pelatiah 4:38
Phineas 4:38 Ruth 4:38 Tobias
6:42,44,45,77,80,-7:12,14
WARNERTON, Thomas 2:63
WARREN, Abigail 1:56,58 Alden
1:58,-2:146 Amos 5:130 Eliza
7:49 Elizabeth 5:140 George
3:1,-5:137,140 Gideon 1:56,
-2:145 Gilbert 1:56,58 John
5:137 Joseph 5:152 Kezia 5:30
Margaret 2:39 Mary 5:137 Mr.
5:42 Mrs. 5:137,140 Sarah 5:87
Thomas 7:54 Tristram 2:146
Walter 5:39 William 5:114
WARZ, Elizabeth 2:110 Hannah
2:110 Nathaniel 2:110
WASHBURN, Charles 4:9 Gideon
4:36

131

WASHER, Ismenia 7:20
WASHINGTON, General 6:12,13
WATERHOUSE, Arthur 4:57 Benjamin 5:150 Elizabeth 1:14, -4:103,-6:172 George 6:36, 120,172 Hannah 4:55 Jacob 4:58 Jeremiah 6:40 John 4:104 Lydia 2:174 Margaret 4:52 Martha 5:46 Mary 4:52,-5:149 Mrs. 3:175 Nathaniel 4:99 Richard 4:55 Ruth 4:50,52,55 S. 3:50 Samuel 1:14,-4:55,58 Sarah 2:171,-3:56,105,109, -4:52,55,101 Timothy 4:52, 55,99 William 2:170,-3:109
WATERS, Eleanor 2:92 Joseph 3:159 Thomas F. 5:141 William 2:92,-3:66,73,-4:36
WATKINS, Andrew 1:27 Dorothy 1:27 John 1:22,27 Thomas 2:187,-3:70,72 William 1:27
WATSON, Abigail 3:41,-5:3 Abraham 2:44 Alice 2:167 Anna 5:51,-7:60 Benjamin 6:154,-7:39 Betsey 7:40 Clarissa 6:154,-7:38 Daniel 3:90,-5:145 David 3:181,-4:125 Dudley 6:137 Ebenezer 3:90 Edward F. 6:40 Elijah 2:92 Elizabeth 3:132,-6:139,159 Hannah 3:87,-5:146 Henry 6:61 Horace P. 6:39 Irving A. 2:166 Jacob K. 4:79 Jane P. 7:56 John 3:116,-4:78 Jonathan 1:51,-5:7 Joseph 4:185 Josiah 2:92,-4:126 Martha 6:154,-7:39 Mary 1:51,-3:118,-6:137,154 Moses W. 4:127 Nathan 2:92 Philip 7:18 Samuel 5:116 Thomas 5:43,108,-6:38,138 Timothy 3:66,72 William 5:42 William P. 6:92
WATTS, Samuel 5:129
WAYCOME, Mrs. 3:174 Thomas 3:173
WAYMOUTH (see WEYMOUTH)
WEARE, Elias 3:149 Joseph 3:43 Mary 4:189 Meshech 5:136,165 Peter 4:10,189 Redford 5:168, 169 Samuel 5:168 Sarah 4:189 Thomas W. 5:169
WEAVER, Richard 2:187,-3:72

WEBB, Daniel 3:170 George 1:177 John 4:36 Mary 5:129 Mr. 5:129 William 5:88
WEBBER, Benjamin 4:146 Betsey 7:23 Daniel 4:36,-6:56 Elizabeth 3:59 Hannah 1:64, -4:124 Isaiah 6:167 James 1:64,-2:168,-3:59 Keturah 1:64 Lydia 1:17,-3:6 Maximiliam J. 7:65 Richard 1:12,17,-3:173, -4:37 Sarah 6:56 William 2:165,-3:59
WEBSTER, Abiah 1:45,48 Abigail 1:137,-2:68,-3:87,-4:179 Abraham 3:129,-5:103 Alice 3:43 Amos 6:109 Andrew 2:45, 68,132,133,-3:39,-5:103 Ann 1:45,-3:44 Anne 2:46,69 Benjamin 2:66,69,131,-3:39,87, 132,-4:177,-5:105,106,109, 112,155,160,-6:31 Burnham 5:108 Caleb 2:134,-3:130 Charity 1:92 Charles 2:67 Daniel 3:91 David 1:135,-5:104 Dorothy 2:70,-5:160 Ebenezer 2:44,72,105,129-132,-3:38 Elihu T. 5:21 Elizabeth 1:23, 48,137,-2:45,46,65,72,129,133, -3:40,41,90,129,170,-5:18,106, 112 Elsie 5:108 Ephraim 6:190 Esther B. 7:72 Ezekiel 7:22 Fanny 1:135 Gideon 2:69 H. S. 4:141 Hannah 1:138,-2:48,89, 129,-3:87,-4:174,-5:19,-6:28, 190 Henry 4:177 Henry S. 2:40, 96,143,-6:47,103,192 Henry Sewall 7:10 Iddo 2:48,-3:43, -5:156,158,-6:28 Isaac 2:47, 107,-3:43 Jacob 5:109,112 Jane 5:156 Jeremiah 2:45,67, 69,71,72,129,133,134 Joanna 2:189 John 1:5,8-10,45,83, 135,-2:22,23,25,26,44-48,61, 62,66,67,69,71,72,98,112,132- 134,-3:37,-4:176,-5:18,104, 106,112 Johnson 2:66 Jonathan 2:66,69,72,133,-3:39,-5:18, 103,106 Jonathan P. 6:163 Joseph 2:48,68,-3:43,45, -5:103,-6:27,51 Joseph S. 6:30 Joshua 2:48,68,-5:106,109, 112,157,-6:27 Josiah 1:23,45,

132

WEBSTER (continued)
48,82,83,85,91,135,-3:115 Levi
L. 1:135 Lois 4:177 Marah
5:104 Margaret 2:66,70,-3:87
Maria 5:158 Mark R. 1:138
Martha 1:45,48,82,83,85,91,
135,137,138,-3:42,-5:20,104
Mary 1:26,135,-2:85,-3:40,
167,171,-4:175,-5:104,105,155
Mercy 2:70 Miriam 3:44,-5:108
Nathan 3:40 Nathaniel 1:135,
-2:69,133,-4:177,179 Olive R.
1:138 Patience 5:110 Phebe
5:106 Rachel 2:130,-5:154,
-6:27 Richard 1:85,137,138,
-6:164 Ruth 2:69 Samuel 2:48,
68,70,129,-3:39,40,-6:27,30,
-5:104,108,109,112,154,157
Sarah 1:23,26,48,135,138,
-2:46,68,72,85,87,89,90,105,
107,112,-3:42,129,134,171,
-5:104,109,110,150,-6:31
Shadrach 1:21,26 Shuah 2:47,
133 Stephen 3:88 Susan 1:181,
-3:170 Susanna 2:45,-6:190
Thomas 2:44,71,85,87,89,90,
105,107,112,131,133,-3:170,
-5:104,105,108 Waldron 5:109
William 2:131,-3:169,-5:105,
157 William G. 7:25
WEDD, Joseph 2:45
WEDGE, Thomas 1:10
WEDGEWOOD, Elizabeth D.
1:100 John 1:100 Lot 1:103,
-6:137 Mishael B. 4:188 Nancy
5:83 Noah 6:138 Rebecca 4:186
Sarah 4:80 William 3:179
WEDGOOD, Jesse 3:25 John 3:75
WEED, Abigail 5:159 David 3:41,
-5:111,156,159,-6:29 Dorothy
3:43 Elijah 5:111 Hannah 5:11
Jonathan 6:29 Mrs. 3:149
Nathaniel 3:147
WEEDEN, Amos C. 6:88
WEEKS, Abigail 6:104 Adee 7:74
Daniel 2:38 Ira 3:163 Joanna
6:137 Jonathan 6:34 Joseph 7:3
Joseph T. 4:116 Joshua 1:92,
-3:55,-4:50 Leonard 1:10,13,-
3:173,-6:97 Mary 3:51,95,120,
121,-6:164 Mary W. 3:163
Miss 5:40 Nancy 3:123,163,

WEEKS (continued)
-6:168 Pelatiah 2:182 Prudence
6:138 Samuel 2:102,-3:24,
-6:53 Susan 3:163 Susanna
6:58 Walter 3:121,123,163
William 4:79
WELCH, Ashbel 3:189 Avery
3:132 Benjamin 2:70,-4:53,
-5:105,-6:28 David 2:65,
-6:26,44 David S. 6:44 Deborah
5:112 Ebenezer 4:187 Eleanor
6:28 Elizabeth 4:98,-6:44
Emma F. 2:166,-6:192 George
1:22 Hannah 2:44-4:182,
-5:107,-6:32 Hezekiah 4:37
John 2:65,-6:28,32 John T.
1:29,31,-2:166,-3:188,-5:92
Jonathan 2:69,-6:26 Joseph
2:44,65,66,68,-3:88,-5:89,105,
109,112 Lois 3:135 Lucretia
6:167 Martha 3:89 Mary 2:67,
-3:40,-4:55,56,185 Matthias
4:150 Miss 5:42 Moses 2:66
Mrs. 2:72,-6:28 Paul 3:25
Philip 5:105,107 Reuben 5:159
Richard 6:162 Samuel 2:44,69,
72,129,132,-3:43,-4:101,
-5:109,157,159,-6:28 Sarah
4:148,-5:105 Tabitha 2:45,129
Thomas 2:47 Walter 4:36
WELLMAN, Jubilee 7:71
WELLS, Charles 7:21 Dorothy
5:136 Edward 3:174,176
Elizabeth 2:171,-5:40 Hannah
2:169,-5:183 Jeffrey 4:57 John
3:119 Joseph 2:176,-5:134,
136,183 Luke 3:84 Martha 3:88
Mr. 3:132 Mrs. 3:176,-5:136
Nathaniel M. 5:134 Peter 3:176
Philip 6:26 Sarah 5:136
Stephen 6:26 Thomas F. 7:69
William 5:91,136 Zebulon 4:97
WENDELL, Abraham 2:163 Ann
E. 6:88 Dorothy 1:166
Elizabeth 1:137 Evart J. 6:88
Isaac 1:166,-5:124,-6:88,185,
-7:9 Jacob 2:163 John 1:166
Margaret S. 6:88 Mary S. 6:88
WENTWORTH, Abigail 5:7,51,
-6:67,176 Abigail M. 6:63 Abra
1:123 Amaziah 6:147 Anna
4:148 Anne 6:173 Benjamin

WENTWORTH (continued)
4:147 Benning 6:23 Charity
7:54 Daniel 2:18,-4:100,
-5:8,113,-6:65,147 David 6:173
Deborah 6:63,159,-7:40 Dorcas
4:149 Dorothy 5:6,-7:5 Dudley
6:176 Ebenezer 2:165,-4:103,
-5:49,-6:173 Edmund 4:181
Elias 6:175 Elihu 4:147
Elizabeth 4:56,81 Enoch 5:49,
51,-6:147 Ephraim 3:102,
-4:46,81,-5:151,-6:118,120,
147,172,173 Eunice 4:161
Ezekiel 5:117,150,-6:175,-7:44
Frank W. 4:81 George 2:98,
159,-4:103,-5:113,162,163,168
Gershom 6:69 Hannah 1:123,
-2:18,-5:44,52,-6:23,66,118
Hannah C. 6:63 Huldah 6:37
Hunking 2:97,104 Ichabod
5:6,151,-6:176,-7:27,28,50
Ichabod Hayes 7:28 Isaac
4:148,-6:73 Jacob 6:147 James
5:6,-7:27 Jane 5:51,-7:90
Joanna 5:3 John 1:123,-4:12,
152,-5:49,161,-6:50,115,118,
175,176,-7:54,90 John H. 4:81
Jonathan 4:46,81,-5:6,-6:63,
147,175,176 Joseph 6:176
Joshua 5:167,169 Josiah 4:113,
-6:70 Judith 6:63 Kezia 5:150,
-6:147 Lois 4:81,-5:56 Lucy
6:176,-7:54 Lydia 4:46,-5:55,
114,119,-6:173,176 Mark H.
4:55 Martha 4:81,-5:2,147,
148,-7:28 Mary 4:81,-5:2,8,
50,-6:147,-7:54 Matthias 6:176
Mercy 5:114,115,118,-6:118,
-7:27 Moses 4:46,-5:174,175
Mr. 5:41 Mrs. 3:150 Nancy
6:37,-7:87 Olive 5:117
Patience 5:8,-6:115 Paul 2:169
Phebe 4:81 Rebecca 4:57,-5:7,
116,117,-7:27,89 Richard 6:63,
69,75 Richard P. 6:63 Samuel
1:11,-2:18,100,-4:53,150,
-6:147,-7:54 Sarah 2:163,
-5:4,8,44,56,-6:147 Spencer
4:126,-6:120 Stephen 4:81,
-5:3,-6:34,71,118,-7:54 Susan
6:39,-7:87 Tamson 4:12 Temperance 5:56 Thomas 5:5,117,

WENTWORTH (continued)
-6:69 Thomas J. 6:63 Tobias
6:40 William 3:84,-4:46,81,
-5:149,-6:175,-7:28 William
T. 1:182,-2:166,-4:81,82
WEST, Daniel 3:41,-5:112,155
Deborah 6:54 Edward 1:11,
-4:173 Elizabeth 5:112 John
3:131 Jonathan 3:168 Joseph
Carter 7:18 Mary 6:51 Mary E.
7:72 Nehemiah 3:135 Presbury
6:37 Sarah 6:57 Susan 6:162
William 6:169
WESTBROOK, Alice 3:50,56,
-5:191 John 1:12,-2:101,
-3:173,175,5:191 Martha 3:51
Mrs. 3:175 Thomas 2:102,
103,-5:191
WESTCOAT, Daniel 3:173
WESTON, Elizabeth B. 3:186
James 6:154,-7:39
WETHERELL, Abel 4:36 John
4:147
WETHERLEY, Mariah 7:43
WEYMAN, Samuel 3:72
WEYMOUTH (WAYMOUTH),
Benjamin 6:98,114 Deborah 5:6
John 6:114 Joshua 1:59,68,
-2:76,124,-5:44 Lucy 5:44
Lydia 6:171 Mary 1:68,
-2:124,-5:2 Mehitable 1:59,
-2:124,-4:66 Moses 6:171
Nicholas 2:185 Rebecca 2:76
Robert 2:76 Samuel 2:76 Sarah
1:59,68,-3:103,-5:2 Susanna
4:77 Tabitha 1:55,-3:34
Timothy 2:76,-4:132
Washington L. 6:158 William
2:76,-3:103
WHALON, Andrew 4:36
WHEAT, Solomon 4:187
WHEATLY, Harry 6:111 Henry
6:111
WHEELER, Ann 3:182,-5:186
Benjamin 7:18 Elizabeth
3:135,-6:41,104 James S. 6:64
Jeremiah 5:105 Jeremiah Jr.
7:19 John 3:146 Jonathan 5:105
Judith 3:115,-5:186,-7:21
Kezia 6:167 Leonard 6:64
Lydia 6:164 Mrs. 3:146,-5:186,
-6:41 Nehemiah 5:186,-6:41

134

WHEELER (continued)
Phebe 6:167 Ruth W. 7:25
Sarah 2:176,-6:106 William
6:108 Zenas 6:55
WHEELOCK, John 6:12
WHEELWRIGHT, Charles C.
3:184 Jeremiah 3:144,186 John
2:180,-5:93,167 Mary 3:144,
186 Samuel 3:98
WHIDDEN, Abigail 4:54 Anne
5:38,-6:79 Elisha 5:188,-7:80
Elizabeth 3:56,-4:54,103,-6:41
George 5:139 Hannah 6:44,
-7:23 Ichabod 6:59 Jane 6:46
John 1:12,-3:42,-4:54,136,
-5:91,133,137,140,185
Katharine Rosseter 7:80 Margaret 3:54 Mark 6:59 Mary
3:50,56,-5:131,140,-6:79,-7:12
Mehitable 5:183 Michael
2:174,-3:55,-4:10,50,54,
-5:131,139,183,186,188,-6:41,
44,46,79,-7:12 Michael H.
5:186 Mrs. 3:50,175,-5:137,
139,140,183,185,186,188,
-6:41,44,46 Rachel 6:59
Samuel 1:12,-3:54,173,175,
-4:54,-5:91,-7:12 Sarah
2:172,-5:131,185,-7:19 Widow
3:175 William 5:137
WHIPPLE, Alexander 7:37
Emeline 6:132 Emeline F.
6:132 General 7:13,15 Joseph
7:75 Katharine 6:43 Mary 4:4
Orin 6:132 Robert 2:185,-3:71
William 2:96,-4:4,-5:162,
-6:43
WHIRRIN, John 5:42
WHITAKER, James 2:184 Moses
3:133
WHITAWAY, Elizabeth 2:92
WHITCHER, Abigail 4:132
Elizabeth 3:89 Isaac 5:104
Jonathan 4:175,-6:137 Joshua
4:173 Lydia 4:89 Mary 3:104,
170,181,-4:133,178 Mehitable
2:12 Morris 4:177 Peter 3:170
Richard 2:12 Robert 4:178
Tabitha 2:12 William 3:184,
-4:147,-5:104
WHITE, Abigail 4:44,50,57,
-5:38,133 Almira L. 2:42

WHITE (continued)
Daniel 6:168 Elizabeth 2:174
Frances M. 7:66 John 3:129,
-4:57,-5:133,-6:165 John H.
4:186 Joseph 1:27,-2:37 Maria
4:6 Mary 1:27,-4:131,-5:38
Mrs. 3:175 Nancy 6:163 Nancy
N. 7:66 Nathan 1:21,27,
-3:55,173,175 Nathaniel 1:12
Philip 3:173 Richard 3:55,
-4:57 Robert 2:36 Ruth 2:36
Salome 3:50,56,-4:57 Samuel
4:57 Sarah 5:1 Solomon 1:27
Stephen 2:143 Susan 6:165
William 3:55,-4:49,50,57,
-5:43,-6:138 William C. 2:37
WHITEAKER (see WHITAKER)
WHITEFOOT, Robert 1:22
WHITEHAM, Abigail 5:146
WHITEHOUSE, Aaron 5:1 Abigail
6:75 Alexander 5:8 Anthony 5:6
Benjamin T. 2:96,-4:48
Charles T. 6:75 Comfort
5:119,147 David P. 6:119
Ebenezer 3:23,75,-4:186
Elizabeth 3:36,-5:50,-6:40,
71,114 Esther 6:71 Experience
7:90 Isaac 4:126 Israel 5:56
Jacob 5:21,-7:51 Jeremiah
5:113 John 3:184,-6:114
Jonathan 1:164,-6:68,114
Joseph 6:114,179 Judith 1:51,
-2:79,-5:4,-6:114 Lucy A.
6:179 Lydia 5:117 Martha 6:73
Mary 5:147 Mehitable 1:164
Moses 5:53 Nathaniel 5:4,50
Nicholas 6:35 Rebecca 5:2,
-6:69 Richard 3:173 Samuel
6:67,-7:90 Samuel H. 6:70
Sarah 1:164,-6:22 Sarah E.
6:179 Stephen 5:7,-6:67
Thomas 1:51,-3:151 William
6:71,179
WHITELOCK, John 2:184
WHITING, Captain 3:85
WHITNEY, Abel 5:143 Amanda
7:9 Eliza Ann 7:9 Frank 7:9
George 7:9 Hannah 5:81 Hep-
sibah 5:81 Joseph 6:47,-7:9
Laurentia Amorette 7:9
Leonard 6:110 Lucinda 5:143
Oliver 6:162 Phebe 5:143

135

WHITNEY (continued)
William 7:9
WHITROW, James 2:185
WHITTEMORE, A. G. 5:48,85,92
Arthur G. 1:29-31,-2:166,
-3:188, 4:144,-6:96 Eleanor
6:111 James C. 7:66 Joel
2:171 Joseph 3:72 Mary 4:58,
-6:183 Richard 6:108 Ruth 6:51
William 4:56
WHITTEN, Rebecca 1:95
WHITTIER, Anna 5:124,-6:88
Anna A. 1:166 Charles C.
2:190,-4:139,140,144 Edward
S. 6:88 Elizabeth 5:20,-6:95
Esther I. 2:30 Esther J. 6:88
Eunice 6:88 Gertrude 6:20
Gertrude E. 2:31 Henry M. 6:88
John 1:164,-5:124 John G.
1:164,-5:179 John Greenleaf
7:6 Joseph 1:119,164,-4:91,
130,-5:124,-7:6 Lois E. 6:68
Lydia 5:124 Mary 1:172,
-5:124,-6:90 Mary C. 6:88
Mehitable 2:190 Moses 2:30,
31,-5:124,-6:88 Obadiah 1:119,
166,168,172,-4:124,-5:124,
-6:88,183,-7:6 Phebe 5:124
Rebecca A. 6:88 Reuben 2:190
Richard 2:190 Ruth 5:124 Sarah
1:119,164,166,168,173,-2:30,
31,-5:124,-6:25 Sarah E. 6:88
Susanna 2:45 Tabitha 2:190
William 4:91,-6:88
WHITTLE, John 6:110 Thomas
1:22
WHITTUM, Aaron 6:176 Amos
6:176
WIBIRD, Elizabeth 4:49,50,52,54
Richard 2:102,104 Thomas
2:104
WIGGIN, Aaron 2:52 Abigail
1:187,-2:115,152,-3:125,161,
-4:129,-6:138,153 Abner J.
4:21 Amy 6:153 Andrew 1:128,
187,-2:51,52,82,87,107,109,
112,-3:52,55,121,123-125,152,
-4:11,74,77,79,114,115,119,
-5:163,-6:19,185 Andrew M.
4:115 Andrew N. 3:166 Ann
2:58,-3:123,125,-7:16 Ann D.
7:61 Anna 2:12,118,-3:15,121,

WIGGIN (continued)
166 Asa 6:137 Augusta 2:153
Barker 6:140 Benjamin 3:14,
166 Benjamin F. 4:20,-5:36
Bradstreet 1:187,-2:112,
-3:14,124,163,-6:60 Caleb 2:52
Caroline A. 4:72 Charles 6:60,
153 Charles F. 4:20,21 Charlotte 3:15 Charlotte A. 4:113
Chase 1:128,-2:58,190,-3:14,
124,126,-7:59 Clarissa 2:152
Comfort 3:14,124 Cutler 4:77
Cynthia 4:72,-5:37 Daniel
3:126,161,-4:20,72,-7:57
Daniel H. 4:113 Daniel J. 4:20
Daniel W. 6:153 David 2:52,
118,152,-3:14,128,161,-4:128,
-5:56,-6:137 Deborah 3:15,
126,-4:21,78 Deborah T. 3:15
Dorothy 2:51,52,-3:123,127,
164,-4:114 Dorothy B. 5:37
Dorothy E. 7:64 Dorothy W.
4:114 Edmund 2:152 Edwin
4:21 Elijah 3:125 Eliphalet
3:122,123 Eliza 4:187,-5:36
Elizabeth 1:128,187,-2:58,
118,120,152,-3:15,124,161,
164,-4:21,73,77,-5:35,-6:125,
153,154,-7:39 Elizabeth Ann
7:61 Emma F. 4:20 George
2:58,122,-3:15,126,162,-4:114,
-5:35 George F. 6:39 George
Freeze 7:16 Gideon 3:162 Hannah 1:183,-2:87,107,109,112,
118,152,-3:122,125,126,128,
161 Hannah L. 4:72 Harriet
7:14 Harriet F. 4:72 Henry
2:156,-3:163,-6:138,140,153,
155,159,-7:40 Henry P. 4:185
Hiram 3:166 Horace 4:113 Ira
W. 5:35 Isaac 3:124,-4:129
Isaac S. 4:114 Issachar 3:8,
-5:76,77 J. B. 5:37,-4:115
James 4:74,119 James J.
3:166 James M. 3:162,-5:37
James W. 3:164,-4:21 Jane
2:118 Jewett 3:121,-4:20,71
John 2:12,112,156,-3:163 John
O. 4:20,72,187,-5:37 Jonathan
1:187,-2:51,-3:15,-4:21 Joseph
2:156,163,-3:14-16,124,-4:128
Josephine 4:20 Joshua 5:50

WIGGIN (continued)
Josiah B. 4:115 Josiah P. 3:14
Judah 3:15 Judith 3:164,-6:19
Justin 3:15 Katharine 2:82
Levi 2:52,-3:162 Levi J. 4:20
Lida 3:121,125,161 Loker 3:17
Love 4:24 Lucy A. 5:181,182
Lydia 1:156,157,-2:152,156,
-3:127,-6:153 Margaret 3:163
Marie L. 4:20 Mark 2:58,122,
153,155,-3:166,-4:79 Martha
2:58,-3:14,16,121,125,162,
-4:20,80,-5:17,-6:140 Martha
R. 3:14 Martha T. 4:187 Mary
1:187,-2:51,52,54,58,82,107,
152,-3:14,15,116,121,123-125,
161,163,166,-4:74,75,79,116,
-6:138 Mary Ann 7:16 Mary G.
7:21 Mary J. 4:20 Mary P.
1:156,157 Mehitable 2:51,54,
122,152,153,-3:15,166,-6:159,
-7:40 Mercy 3:127 Michael
6:138,153 Moses 3:124 Mr.
7:14 Nancy 2:58,-3:122,161,
163,170,183 Nancy P. 7:64
Nathan 2:54,-3:121,166 Nathan
B. 6:159,-7:40 Nathaniel
2:58,151,152,-3:162,-4:78
Nicholas 1:187 Noah 3:14
Olive 3:15,162,-4:20 Olive L.
4:117 Otis 5:77 Patience
3:14,15 Paul 3:14 Peirce L.
2:58 Phebe 3:121,161,163
Phineas 3:125 Rachel 3:15,
-5:56 Richard 5:124,-6:19,
-7:14 Richard R. 3:14 Samuel
2:122,153,-3:15,125,-5:116
Samuel P. 2:164 Samuel S.
4:71 Sarah 1:191,-2:58,118,
152,-3:15,161,162,166,-4:20,
21,77,78, 80,118,-6:106,153
Sarah A. 6:93 Sarah Ann 7:45
Sarah B. 4:21 Sarah E. 4:72
Selina 4:74 Shadrach 3:161
Sherburne 3:163 Simon 2:107,
117,118,-3:122,-6:153 Stephen
2:152,156 Susan 4:71,-7:63
Susanna 2:117,156,-3:14,
-4:186,-6:153 Theodore 4:117
Theophilus 4:79 Thomas
1:183,191,-2:52,82,87,107,115,
-2:58,82,87,107,115,151-153,

WIGGIN (continued)
-3:15,16,125,126,161,163,-4:71
Thomas B. 2:54,58,-3:126
Uriah 3:166 Walter 3:15,-4:77
Walter W. 3:166,-4:113,116
Walton 3:15 Welthen 6:153
William 1:156,157,-2:152,
-3:15,-4:79,125,-5:76 Wingate
4:21,-7:61 Winthrop 3:14,124
Zebulon 2:54,-3:164,166,
-4:74,7:14 Zebulon J. 4:74
WIGGLESWORTH, Colonel 3:142
Michael 3:104
WILBUR, Anna 1:173 William
1:173,-5:124
WILKINS, Asa 6:170,-7:66 Cyn-
thia 7:26 Erasmus 3:104 Es-
ther 7:26 George 7:23 Jean-
nette 6:163 Sarah 6:169 Sophia
6:165
WILKINSON, Anna 4:106 Hannah
4:106,109 James 4:106,109
Joseph 4:109 Mr. 5:43
WILLAND, Enoch 5:51 Lydia
5:152 Sarah 5:8
WILLARD, Samuel 6:52
WILLES, John 6:139
WILLET, Mr. 4:176
WILLEY, Abigail 5:74,-7:58
Alice 4:79 Andrew 7:20 Ann
4:186 Daniel 4:130 Daniel F.
6:34 Daniel Needham 7:87
Deborah 4:79 Elias Cornelius
7:87 Eliphalet 5:120 Elizabeth
5:187 George Freeman 7:87 I.
7:87 Isaac 6:35,-7:87 Jacob
4:179 James 4:148 James P.
2:166 John 3:2,-4:149,151
Jonathan 5:73 Josiah 5:185,
187,-6:119 Love 4:128 Lucinda
5:22 Lydia 4:80 Margaret
5:185,-7:49 Mark 1:103 Mary
3:102,-4:75,185,-5:74 Matthew
5:76 Mr. 5:76,-6:119 Mrs.
3:56,-5:187 Noah 4:126
Phineas 6:154,-7:39 Rachel
3:120 Robert 1:103,-4:182
Rufus 4:183 Samuel 3:102,
-4:12 Sarah 4:125,-6:168 Sarah
Flint 7:87 Sarah G. 5:78
Stephen 4:80,-5:7,185,-6:119
Stephen A. 4:183 Temperance

WILLEY (continued)
5:73 Thomas 1:178,-5:97,99,
-6:97 William 3:148,-5:2 Wil-
liam B. 7:21 Winthrop 5:73
Zebulon 4:75,-5:73,74,76,78
WILLIAMS, Anna 2:154 Benjamin
3:160,-4:36 Catherine 4:46
Charles 2:183,-4:188 Daniel
1:22 Edward 4:188 Elizabeth
2:40,-4:45,187,-5:98 Elizabeth
C. 3:170 Francis 1:3,9 Hamden
6:160,-7:41 Hannah 4:58
Hendrick 3:27 Henry 3:27,71
Isaac F. 7:23 Jacob 6:36
James 4:183 John 2:184,-3:5,
27,-4:46,125 John P. 4:134
Joseph 4:173,177 Judith 3:168
Lewis 3:173,175 Mary 2:40,
-4:45,76,182,188 Mr. 3:101
Mrs. 3:102,142,175 Nancy 4:79
Nathaniel 3:180 Rachel 4:10
Robert 3:65,73 Roger 1:147
Sarah 3:136,-4:45,179,183
Thankful 4:45 Thomas 1:3,5,
-4:77,125 Walter 4:188
Washington 7:67 William
2:40,-3:174,-4:45,46,-5:98
WILLIS, Apphia 6:156 John 6:156
Samuel 7:59 Susan 6:156
WILLOUGHBY, Mrs. 3:176 Wil-
liam 3:174,176
WILLS, Anne 1:84 Deborah 1:42
Deborah R. 5:101 Edward 5:42
Elizabeth 1:89 Isaiah 1:84
John 1:84,89 Mary 5:42 Pris-
cilla 1:42,84,89 Samuel 1:42,
84,89 Sarah 1:89 Simon 1:42
WILMOT, James 6:146 Rebecca
6:146,147 Sarah 6:146,147
WILSON, Ann 6:191 Benjamin
3:114,135 Deborah 5:140,185
Ebenezer 6:138 Edward 3:74
Eleanor 5:143 Elizabeth 4:10
Eunice 7:64 George 7:66 Gowin
5:42 James 4:36,-5:140,145
Jane 7:67 Job 6:106 John 1:22,
-4:36,-6:56 John K. 7:21
Joseph 4:13,-5:148 Mary 6:55
Miranda 7:26 Nancy 5:35
Nathaniel 4:89 Peter 5:140,185
Ruth 7:18 Samuel 6:88 Thomas
6:165

WIMBLE, Elizabeth 1:110
Rebecca 1:110 William 1:110
WINBORN, Ebenezer 6:3
Elizabeth 6:2,3 Joanna 6:3
John 6:2,3 Lydia 6:3 Mary 6:3
Prince 6:3 Susanna 6:1-3 Wil-
liam 6:2
WINCHELL, Joseph 6:45 Mary
6:45 Mrs. 6:45 Thomas 6:94
WINCHESTER, Josiah 3:66
WINCOLL, Deborah 4:54,-5:43
Isaac 4:57,-5:87 Nathaniel
5:87
WINGATE, Aaron 7:76,78 Aaron
Patten 7:86 Abigail Roberts
7:31 Amos 7:27 Anna H. 4:23
Benjamin 5:4 Caroline W. 4:23
Charles 7:78 Daniel 5:114,
-6:71,-7:27,29 Daniel, Jr. 7:27
Daniel Gardner 7:28 David 5:2,
150 Deborah 1:171 Dorothy
4:149,-6:72 Edmond-Edmund
6:175,-7:28,31 Elizabeth
2:156,-4:22,23,74,-5:138,184,
-6:113,-7:86 Elizabeth B.
5:138 Enoch 5:49,-6:73 Eunice
2:156,-4:22 George 2:156,
-4:22,23,-6:86 Hannah
Elizabeth 7:87 Henry P. 4:23
Hiram 6:86 James 6:86,-7:76
John 1:170,-2:156,-3:79,
-4:22,23,-6:74 John C. 6:39
John P. 4:23 Jonathan 1:171,
-5:126,-6:85 Joseph 6:114
Joseph C. A. 4:23 Joshua 7:28
Love 1:170,-6:84 Lydia 5:148,
149,-6:86,175 Lydia White
7:27 Mary 2:156,-4:22,23,
115,-5:4,43,120,-6:71 Meshech
5:152 Moses 5:138,184,-6:86,
116 Paine 2:156,-4:22,-6:135
Reverend Mr. 5:109 Ruth 7:76,
78 Sally 7:86 Samuel 3:33,
-6:70,113,116 Samuel D. 4:23
Sarah 2:156,-4:21-23,-5:50,94,
146,-6:34,116 Shadrach 7:86,87
Stephen 5:117,-6:175 Susanna
1:170 William 1:171,-4:149,
-5:184,-6:71,86
WINKLEY, Abiah 6:34 Benjamin
6:160 Charlotte C. 1:151
Daniel 3:47 Deborah 3:94

WINKLEY (continued)
Elizabeth 5:101,-6:173 Francis
3:94 James F. 1:151 John
1:151,-3:94 Martha 3:94 Martha A. 6:40 Mary 3:94,-5:101,
151,-6:173 Mary A. F. 1:151
Miss 5:42 Mrs. 1:19 Samuel
3:46,-5:38,41,101,6:173
WINSLOW, Anna 1:120 Anne
5:71,124 Benjamin 1:62,65,
70,-2:147,-5:108 Catherine
5:103 Charity 1:66,71,72,120
David 6:131 Ebenezer 1:72
Elisha 5:71,108 Elizabeth
2:48,-3:42,182,-5:43 Emeline
6:132 Ephraim 2:48,-6:32
Governor 6:132 Hannah 3:134,
-4:133,-5:31 Hope 1:62,65,70
Huldah 2:72 Jacob 2:66 James
1:66,-2:149 Jane 1:120 Jennie
5:71 Job 1:71,-2:149 John
2:65,-3:129,167,-5:44 Joseph
1:120,-3:116 Martha 3:134,
-5:72,-6:26 Mary 3:87,-5:72
Mary E. 6:93 Mary Jane 7:59
Mehitable 6:32 Nathan 1:66,
71,72,120 Nicholas 4:36 Oliver
1:70,-3:34 Samuel 1:62,120,
-2:44,48,66,149,-3:39,44,129,
-5:71,103,106, 108 Sarah 5:38,
39,71,125 Simon 3:119,-6:93
WINTHROP, Governor 6:4
WISDOM, John 4:36
WISE, Abigail 3:86 Jeremy 3:151
Mr. 6:68 William 4:36
WITHAM, Abner 3:6 Dorothy 5:88
Drusilla 4:185 Eli 4:127
Eunice 3:6 Henry 3:156
Jerusha 4:48 John 4:14 Joseph
3:156,159 Jude 3:64 Mark
3:156 Mary 3:6,61,108,156,
-5:145 Mercy 3:156,159 Peter
3:61 Ruth 4:11 Sarah 3:64,
-5:88,89 William 2:168,
-3:61,-5:89
WITHERELL, Hannah 5:5 Hiram
3:165 James 6:113 Judith 5:52
Lydia 5:114 Thomas 6:75
WITHEREN, John 6:171 Juda
6:171
WODDES, George 5:88 Susanna
5:88

WODIN, John 2:83 Martha 2:83
Mary 2:83
WOOD, Anna A. 5:85 Asa 3:177
Cato 4:36 Cuff 4:36 Elizabeth
4:77 Herbert 3:76 James 6:115
John 4:36,184 Mahala 6:154,
-7:38 Ruth 6:159,-7:40 Samuel
3:87,-5:94 Sarah 4:179 Zachary
T. 5:85
WOODARD, Huldah 1:181
WOODBURY, Benjamin 7:14 Cor-
nelius 4:36 Lemuel 4:37 Mary
7:14 Polly 7:14
WOODCOCK, Anna S. 6:144
WOODEN, John 5:44
WOODEY, Elizabeth 3:109
WOODHOUSE, Elizabeth 5:135,
-6:44 George 5:135,184,188,
-6:42 Jane 5:184 Jerusha
5:184,188 Mary 5:188 Mr. 6:44
Mrs. 5:135,-6:42,44 Nellie
4:76
WOODMAN, Benjamin 2:94,
-3:144,-4:36 Captain 3:153
Catherine 3:7 Charles William
7:32 Charlotte Cheever 7:85
Dana 7:67 Daniel 4:37 David
5:156 Edward 3:144,-5:192
Elihu 5:17 Esther 6:37 Eunice
3:90,-5:104 Hannah 5:20,159
Harriet Crosby 7:85 J. H. 7:85
Jeremiah H. 6:130,-7:32,85,86
Jeremiah Hall 7:32 John 2:171,
-3:104,144,148,-4:174,-5:45,
106,191 Jonathan 3:5,131,144,
-4:183,-5:154 Joseph 3:131,
-5:109,157 Joshua 5:104,106,
107,112,154,156,157,159,
-6:28,32 Josiah 4:184,187
Lydia 6:55 Maria Barker 7:85
Mary 3:136,-4:130,179,-5:42,
-6:32 Mary E. 6:36,129,130
Mary Esther 7:32 Moses 3:130,
-4:129,-5:107,109 Mr. S. 5:22
Samuel 5:112,-7:86 Sarah
3:132,144,-4:127,177,-6:28,130
Sarah Jane 7:85 Sarah Tebbets
7:32 Theodore Chase 7:32
Uriel 5:146 William 5:41
WOODRUFF, Ann 4:190,191
WOODS, John 7:21 Jonathan 6:57
WOODSTOCK, William 2:183

139

WOODWARD, Ann 6:42 Elizabeth 4:54 Joseph W. 6:76 Moses 2:161,-6:42:76 Mrs. 6:42,76 Sarah 4:178 Stephen 2:122
WOODWELL, Gideon 4:36,37
WOOLETT, Edward 5:43
WORMWOOD, Joseph 4:78
WORSTER, Benjamin 3:23,75 Dorcas 5:150 James 5:5 Mary 5:53,-6:179 Philip 3:23,73 Sarah 3:42,-5:149 William 5:42
WORTH, Abigail T. 7:24 Eleanor 5:69 Joseph 6:29 Lydia 5:69, -6:29 Mary 5:69 Obadiah 5:69 Sarah 4:39,66
WORTHEN, Apphia 6:104 David 6:106 Ezekiel 6:53 Ezra 3:129 Isaac 3:65,74 Miriam 5:182 Richard 6:164 Samuel 4:175 Susanna 6:106 Walter 5:19
WORTHYLAKE, Benjamin 2:92 Elizabeth 2:92 George 2:92 Joanna 2:92 Rebecca 2:92 Sarah 2:92 Susanna 2:92
WOTTEN, John 1:3,5,9,-2:24,63
WRIGHT, Elizabeth 1:110 Frank 5:102 J. Gordon R. 5:142 James 3:66,73 Nathaniel 3:52 Samuel 1:110 Thomas 2:104,-3:51,55,-6:40 William 4:37
WRISLEY, Jewett 6:39
WYATT, Eliza 6:35 John 4:103 Jonathan 4:99 Mary 4:99 William 4:101
WYER, Elizabeth 2:89,91,107 Mary 2:89 Nathaniel 2:89, 91,107 Sarah 2:91
WYMAN, Bridget 3:42 Mary 6:111 Phebe 5:93
YATES, Bartholomew 3:30 Mrs. Arthur R. 2:180
YEATON, Benjamin 1:22,-2:36 Comfort 4:189,-5:95 Elizabeth 1:152,-2:35,-5:95,96 George 5:95 Hopley 2:181,-3:71, -4:188,189,-5:95,96 John 1:21,152,-2:174,-3:71,-4:125, -5:95 John D. 2:181 Joseph 2:36 Lydia 1:152 Mary 3:30, -5:95 Mehitable 2:36 Nathaniel J. 2:36 Richard 2:36 Ruth 2:37

YEATON (continued) Ruth A. 2:37 Samuel 5:95 Sarah 4:130,151 William 7:22
YEUREN, Jean 3:44
YORK, Abigail 5:113 Benjamin 6:60 Charlotte 3:133 Daniel 4:130 David 6:60 Deborah G. 7:37 Elijah 4:126 Eliphalet 4:182 Enoch 5:118 John 3:44, -4:76 Josiah 6:33 Mary 3:119, -4:76,-6:60 Olive 4:89 Richard 1:177 Roxanna B. 7:59 Sarah 4:80,184,-6:152 Thomas 4:125, 130,-6:60
YOUNG(S), Aaron 2:67,70,133, -3:39,-5:104,108,111 Abigail 5:156,-6:69 Ann 6:72 Anna 2:45,70,-3:8,89,-4:148,-5:51, -6:66,72,-7:2 Asenath 6:38 Charles 2:45 Daniel 2:46,66, 70,-4:126,-5:104,107,109,112, 154,156,159 David 5:108,154 Dorothy 3:91,-6:26 Drusilla 4:128 Dudley 3:90,-5:104 Ebenezer 2:175 Eleazer 2:167 Eliza 4:78 Elizabeth 2:70, -3:40,130,-5:112,-6:72,75 Esther 6:74 Ezra 2:163 F. E. 3:47 Gideon 2:69,134,-5:140 Hannah 2:192,-3:88,-5:107,-6:66 Hannah D. 5:148 Henry 2:12 Hezekiah 3:43,-5:108,154, -6:30 Ichabod 5:160 Israel 5:111 J. E. 2:191 James 6:75 Jean 6:66 Jeremiah 4:77, -5:114,-6:137 Joanna 3:130, -5:156,-6:30 John 2:47,66,69, 129,132-134,-3:44,45,84,102, -4:76,-5:104,109,111,154, -6:26,29,30,137 Jonathan 3:41, 130,-4:13,145,149,176,-5:99, 108,111,154,157,-6:26,30,66, 72,74 Joseph 2:43,66,67, -3:43,90,-5:156,157,-6:29,136 Kezia 6:137 Levi 4:88 Maria B. 7:43 Mary 4:80,85,174, -5:157,-7:4 Mercy 6:113 Miriam 6:51 Moses 2:67,133, -5:52,109,-6:116 Mrs. 6:29 Nathaniel 4:181,-5:111,154 Patience 2:12,-5:51 Robert 3:80 Ruth 6:26 Samuel 5:104

140

YOUNG(S) (continued)
Sarah 2:129,-3:44,45,
-5:108,109,159,-6:62 Sophia
7:43 Stephen 2:70,-4:66
Stephen F. 6:34 Susanna 6:115
Thomas 3:103,-4:145,-5:147,
-6:72,74,113,115,116 Timothy
5:146,-6:74 William 3:88,
-4:80,-5:44 Winthrop 7:4

NEGROES MENTIONED

Archelaus 5:139,186,-6:41 Archibald 5:75 Benoni 5:111 Boston
6:79 Caesar 4:61 Christol 5:133
Coffee 5:111 Corridon 4:62 Dinah
4:61,62 Hannah 5:38 Harry 5:90
Isaac 5:90 Jarka 4:18 Marcia 5:90
Nancy 5:91 Nero 6:41 Peg(g)
5:139,183,186,-6:41 Peter 5:183
Pharoah 6:79 Phebe 4:16 Phillis
4:62,-5:186 Surranam 5:132 Violet
6:79

PLACES - Volume Seven Only

Albany, N. Y. - 70,72 Albany, Vt.
- 72 Allenstown (N.H.) - 18
Alstead, N. H. - 19 Alton, N. H. -
5 Amesbury, Mass. - 6 Amherst,
N. H. - 18,21 Andover, (N.H.?)
-70,72 Andover, Mass. - 66,69,
70,72

Barnard, Vt. - 18 Barnstead, N.
H. - 4,39,52,56,71 Barre, Vt. - 40
Barrington, N. H. - 4,22,29,41,
90,91 Bedford, Mass. - 70 Berwick, Me. - 5,8,9,21,50,51,52
Beverly, Mass. - 26 Biddeford,
Me. - 50 Boscawen, N. H. - 20-
22,26,67,70,72 Boston, Mass. -
19,25,26,36,42,59,63,65,67,68,70-
72 Bow, N. H. - 17,18,20-22,25,
26,65,66,71,72 Bowdoinham, Me.
- 41 Bradford, Mass. - 20
Brentwood, (N.H.) - 40 Brinton,
Mass. - 42 Bristol, N. H. - 65
Brookfield, N. H. - 40,86 Brooklyn, N. Y. - 5 Brunswick, Me. -
20 Burlington, Vt. - 53 Buxton,
Me.(?) - 50

Canterbury, Ct. - 22 Canterbury,
N. H. - 4,24,26,66,72 Canton,
Mass. - 26 Charlestown, Mass. -
7,18 Chester, (N.H.) - 68
Chestnut Hills - 86 Chicago, Ill.
- 69 Cincinnati, O. - 69 Concord,
N. H. - 17,18,20-26,33,65-72
Conway, N. H. - 59,69,70 Cor-
nish, (Me.?) - 50 Coxhall,
(Lyman) Me. - 50,51

Damariscotta, Me. - 2,3 Danvers,
Mass. - 18,23 Danville, Vt. - 23
Deerfield (N. H.) - 21,22,40 Deer-
ing, (N. H.) - 20 Detroit, Mich. -
66 Dixfield, Me. - 24 Dorchester,
(?) - 66 Dorchester Heights - 52
Dover, N. H. - 1-9,24,31,38,45,
49,51,58,63,64,67,80,83
Dunstable, (?) - 25,66 Durham,
(N. H.) - 4,5,30-32,37,39,40,43-
45,56,58,60-62,64,68 Duxbury,
Mass. - 3

East Bradford (Groveland) Mass.
- 3 East Kingston (N.H.) - 39 Enfield, (N.H.) - 20 Epping, (N.H.) -
39-41,58,63,64 Epsom, N. H. -
70,71 Exeter, N. H. - 3,38-41,
44,56,59,62,63,87

Falmouth, Me. - 6,9 Farmington
(N.H.) - 32,50 Fryeburg, Me. -
19,70

Gilmanton, N. H. - 4,56,71
Gloucester, Mass. - 22,35 Goffstown, N. H. 69 Grafton, N. H. - 25
Great Falls, N. H. - 64 Greenland, (N.H.) - 13,39,40,44 Groton,
(N.H.) - 19 Groveland (E. Bradford) Mass. - 3

Hamilton, Mass. - 38 Hampstead,
(N.H.) - 19 Hanover, (N.H.) - 72
Harvard, Mass. - 23 Haverhill (?)
- 19 Haverhill, Mass. - 6 Hollis,
Me. - 50 Hooksett (N.H.) - 25,
26,69,72 Hopkinton, (N.H.) - 19,
20,22,23,25,65,68-70

Jaffrey (N.H.) - 20 Jefferson - 3

Kennebunk, Me. - 53 Kensington, N. H. - 6,85 Kittery, Me. - 8,51

Lamprey River - 56,57 Lancaster, N. H. - 33,35,36 Lebanon, Me. - 1,2,51-54 Lee, N. H. - 6,9,39, 40,58,59 Littleton, (N.H.) - 66 Loudon, N. H. - 9,20,22-24, 26,67-69,71,72 Lowell, Mass. - 45,53,58,69,70 Lyman (Coxhall) Me. - 50,51 Lynn, Mass. - 43,44

Macon, Ga. - 68 Madbury, N. H. - 2,4,9,43 Manchester (N.H.) - 59,71,72 Medford, Mass. - 67 Meredith, N. H. - 26,69 Mexico, Me. - 26 Middleborough, Mass. - 67 Milton, N. H. - 16,31,32,53,54 Montgomery, Ala. - 68,69,72 Montreal, Can. - 83 Mount Vernon, Me. - 60

Newcastle, Me. - 2-4 Newington (N.H.) - 40,74 Newmarket, N. H. - 37-45,55-59,61-63 Newport, (N.H.) - 21 Newton, Mass. - 72 New Boston (N.H.) - 26,67 New Hampton (N.H.) - 25,67,72 New York - 68 Nobleboro, Me. - 3 Northfield (N.H.) - 26 Northfield, Vt. - 35 Northwood, (N.H.) - 21,39,59 North Brookfield, Mass. - 26 North Hampton, (N.H.) - 55 North Yarmouth, Me. - 24 Nottingham (N.H.) - 40,56,64,68 Norway Plain - 86

Ossipee (N.H.) - 23,70 Oxford, Me. - 65

Parishville, N. Y. - 4 Peeling (Woodstock) (N.H.) - 67 Pembroke (N.H.) - 17-19,21-23, 70 Phillipsburd (Me.?) - 50 Pittsfield, N. H. - 17,22 Portland, Me. - 33,35,39 Portsmouth, N. H. - 20,22,24,33,41,45,55,83 Putnam, O. (?) - 70

Quincy, Mass. - 68

Raymond, (N.H.) - 38 Rochester,

N. H. - 2-6,25,31,32,49,50,54,91 Roxbury, Mass. - 53 Rumford, Me. - 17,18,21,23,25,67 Rutland, Vt. - 21 Rye, N. H. - 4,89

Saco, Me. - 67,70 Salem, Mass. - 2,38,68 Salisbury (?) - 25,26,69 Salmon Falls, N. H. - 86,87 Sanbornton (N.H.) - 22 Sandown (N.H.) - 39 Sanford, Me. - 8 Savannah, Ga. - 72 Scarboro, Me. - 9 Scituate, Mass. - 3 Shapleigh, Me. - 2 Somersworth, N. H. - 1-3,5,6,8,37,43,51,53 South Berwick, Me. - 45 South Hampton (N.H.) - 39 South Newmarket, N. H. - 63 Springfield (?) - 72 Springfield. Mass. - 64 Stoddard (N.H.) - 26 Strafford (N.H.) - 43,54,64 Stratham (N.H.) 38,40, 42,43,55 Sutton (N.H.) - 66

Tamworth, N. H. - 64 Tuftonborough, (N. H.) - 45,55

Vanceboro, Me. - 34 Vassalboro, Me. - 5

Wakefield (N.H.) - 85 Warner, N. H. - 23,68 Waterville, Me. - 38 Weare, N. H. - 6,71 Wells, Me. - 8,56 Wendell, Mass. - 65 Westminster, Vt. - 71 West Point, N. Y. - 59 Weymouth (Mass.) - 45 Winslow, Me. - 2 Wiscasset, Me. - 66 Wolfeborough (N.H.) - 4,54,81,83,87 Woodstock (Peeling) N. H. - 67 Worcester, Mass. - 69

SUBJECT HEADINGS

ADAMS, Rev. Hugh & family 6:1
American Revolutionary Naval
  Service, Continental Frigate
  Boston 4:25
Continental Frigate *Raleigh*
  2:177,-3:19,65
extracts from the journal of Benjamin Crowningshield 4:37
launching of the Continental
  Frigate *Raleigh* 4:25

names of officers and men belonging to the Continental Frigate *Boston* 4:31
New Hampshire privateers 5:161
original draft of report of Capt. Hector McNeil to the Marine Committee of Congress 4:27
Answers to queries 5:47,94,143, 192,-6:143
BICKFORD, Hon. Charles Woodbury memoriam 5:177
Book Notices 1:32,107,182, -2:39,141,188,-3:46,92,140, 190,-4:92,139,-5:141,-6:141
BURNHAM, Sarah daughter of Robert, of Oyster River 5:190
CANNEY, residence of family 5:102
Change of date 4:13
Corrections 5:80,-6:47
David Thompson's indenture 2:1
Devon and Cornwall Records Society 1:108
Donations 1:109,182,-2:42,96, 192,-3:48,96,139,189,-4:48,96, 144,192,-5:48,96,144,192, -6:48,96,144,192,-7:48
Dover tax rate 1648 1:177
DUDLEY, Rev. Myron Samuel memoriam 3:185
Durham births, marriages, & deaths 1:97,151
Epping births, marriages, & deaths 3:113,177,-4:83, 131,165,-5:9,65
births, marriages, deaths, & intentions of marriage 5:180,-6:6,92
EVANS, George Frederick memoriam 7:33
Family record of Richard Hussey 5:179
First Congregational Church records, Concord, N.H., marriages 7:17
marriages by Rev. Israel Evans 6:53,104
marriages by Rev. Asa McFarland, D.D. 6:105,161
marriages by Rev. Timothy Walker 6:49
organization & pastors 6:9

First Congregational Church records, Rochester, N.H., baptisms 7:27
baptisms by Rev. Amos Main 6:65,113
marriages by Rev. Joseph Haven 1776-1824 4:147,-5:1,49, 113,145
marriages by Rev. Amos Main, 1745-1757 4:145
First Congregational... baptisms attested by the Deacon 6:114
baptisms by Rev. Avery Hall 6:115
baptisms by Rev. Joseph Haven 6:118,171
marriages by Rev. Francis V. Pike 6:40
marriages by Rev. Isaac Willey 6:35
marriages by Rev. Joseph Haven 6:33
marriages by Rev. Thomas C. Upham 6:33
FOSTER, Mr. Charles Gale memoriam 5:33
Friends records, Dover, N.H., Monthly Meeting family records 2:73,123,145,-3:31, -4:38,65,119,159,-5:23,57,121, 171,-6:17,81,121,179
marriages 1:49,113,161,-2:29
George Huntress of Portsmouth & Newington, N.H., his children & grandchildren 6:177
Gravestone inscriptions, N.H. signers of the Declaration of Independence 2:95
GREEN, Hon. Ezra inscriptions on gravestone 2:7
Hampton baptisms 2:81
births 2:82,105
HUNTRESS, George of Portsmouth & Newington, N.H., his children & grandchildren 6:177
HUSSEY, Richard family record of 5:179
In Memoriam, Col. Henry Oakes Kent, 7:35
George Frederick Evans 7:33
Hon. Charles Henry Sawyer 5:81

143

Hon. Charles Woodbury Bickford 5:177
Hon. Noah Tibbetts 6:129
Mr. Charles Gale Foster 5:33
Rev. Myron Samuel Dudley 3:185
William Trickey Wentworth 4:81
Inscriptions from tne Waldron Cemetery, Dover, N.H. 6:186
Inscriptions on gravestone of Hon. Ezra Green 2:7
Journal of Rev. John Pike 1678-1709 3:77,97,145
KENT, Col. Henry Oakes memoriam 7:35
Kingston First Church admissions 2:71:129
baptisms 2:46,65
baptisms by Rev. Joseph Secomb 5:103,153,-6:26
deaths 2:135,-3:37
marriages 2:44,-3:39,86,129, 167,-4:173,-5:17
Kingston families 1725 2:43
Legislation 4:95
Letter from Rev Joseph Gerrish 3:137
Library of the New Hampshire Genealogical Society 6:188
Marriages by, Rev. John Osborne, Lee, N.H. 4:75,125,181
Rev. John Pike, Dover, N.H., & vicinity, 1686-1709 4:9
New Castle, births, marriages, & deaths 1:23,-2:33
town tax 1720 (Island Side List) 1:21
New Hampshire Genealogical Society 5:92
act of incorporation 1:29
by-laws 1:73
donations 1:79
library building 3:188
list of members 2:165
list of officers 1903 1:31
officers of the society, 1906-1907 3:188
report of librarian 3:187
New Jersey's indebtedness to New Hampshire 1:145
Newington Church, baptisms 3:57,105,154,-4:14,59,105,153, -5:73

marriages 2:167,-3:1
Newmarket births, marriages, & deaths 6:59,133,151,-7:37
North Church baptisms 4:51,97
North Church records Portsmouth, N.H., admissions, 1693-1697 3:51
baptisms 3:53,-5:38,-6:76
baptisms by Rev. Joseph Buckminster 6:94,-7:11
baptisms by Rev. Samuel Langdon, D.D. 5:86,129,183,- 6:41
list of members, 1671-1697 3:49
list of members, 1699 3:54, -4:49,97
marriages by Rev. Nathaniel Rogers 5:39
Note & clipping 6:94
Notes and queries 1:32,80,110,180
Notice 1:109,-6:8
Origin of the name Pinkham 7:46
Parish Register Society of Dublin 3:76
PIKE, Rev. John journal 1678-1709 3:77,97,145
Piscataqua Pioneers 3:45
Portsmouth, genealogical records 1
gravestone inscriptions in Point of Graves Cemetery 1:13,-2:17
landgrants & surveys 2:22,59
selectmen 2:98,157
subscription list 1671 1:11
subscription lists 1658 & 1666 1:9
town clerks 2:97
Queries 2:39,92,143,189,-3:46, 92,142,186,-4:45,92,141,188, -5:45,92,142,191,-6:47,94,142, 190,-7:47
Residence of the Canney family 5:102
Rev. Hugh Adams & family 6:1
Reward offered 4:82
Richard Hussey & his descendants 6:97,-7:1
Rye births, marriages, & deaths 1:33,81,129,-2:135,-3:191
Sarah Burnham, daughter of Robert, of Oyster River 5:190
SAWYER, Hon. Charles Henry

memoriam 5:81

Some errors in Howard's genealogy of the Cutts family 5:95

Stratham births, marriages, &
deaths 1:183,-2:9,49,113,151,
-3:11,121,161,-4:20,71,113,
-5:35

Strawberry Bank landgrants &
deeds 1:1

Thomas Downes of Dover, N.H.,
& his descendants 6:145

THOMPSON, David indenture 2:1

TIBBETTS, Hon. Noah memoriam
6:129

Traill and Spence families of
Portsmouth, N.H. 4:1

Wants 3:137,189,-7:10

WENTWORTH, William Trickey
memoriam 4:81

Wille Hill of Durham, N.H. 5:97

www.ingramcontent.com/pod-product-compliance
Lightning Source LLC
Chambersburg PA
CBHW070400270326
41926CB00014B/2632